Venture Capitalists at Work

How VCs Identify and Build Billion-Dollar Successes

Tarang Shah
Sheetal Shah

GW00566752

Apress®

Venture Capitalists at Work

ISBN-13 (pbk): 978-1-4302-3837-9

ISBN-13 (electronic): 978-1-4302-3838-6

President and Publisher: Paul Manning
Lead Editor: Jeff Olson
Editorial Board: Steve Anglin, Mark Beckner, Ewan Buckingham, Gary Cornell, Morgan Ertel, Jonathan Gennick, Jonathan Hassell, Robert Hutchinson, Michelle Lowman, James Markham, Matthew Moodie, Jeff Olson, Jeffrey Pepper, Douglas Pundick, Ben Renow-Clarke, Dominic Shakeshaft, Gwenan Spearing, Matt Wade, Tom Welsh
Coordinating Editor: Jessica Belanger
Editorial Assistant: Rita Fernando
Copy Editor: Kimberly Burton
Compositor: Mary Sudul
Indexer: SPi Global
Cover Designer: Anna Ishschenko

Distributed to the book trade worldwide by Springer-Verlag New York, Inc., 233 Spring Street, 6th Floor, New York, NY 10013. Phone 1-800-SPRINGER, fax 201-348-4505, e-mail orders-ny@springer-sbm.com, or visit http://www.springeronline.com.

For information on translations, please contact us by e-mail at info@apress.com, or visit http://www.apress.com.

Apress and friends of ED books may be purchased in bulk for academic, corporate, or promotional use. eBook versions and licenses are also available for most titles. For more information, reference our Special Bulk Sales–eBook Licensing web page at http://www.apress.com/bulk-sales.

For our son Raj, our parents, and Gurudev

Contents

vi

Foreword

There have been a number of books written on venture capital, but very few capture its heart and soul. Ostensibly, venture capital is about predicting the future. Venture capitalists predict a distinct type of future: one where a newcomer unexpectedly seizes a discontinuity, and transforms the way societies and businesses behave. The fastest-growing transformations at first appear innovative yet dubious. But they quickly mature into something that feels familiar and perhaps obvious. Such were the cases for companies like You-Tube, Facebook, Groupon, LinkedIn, and Twitter, all mentioned in this book. In this sea of potential, what a venture capitalist does is assess the future of the start-ups that he or she meets.

But what's often underappreciated is that at its core, venture capital is intensely personal. It is an unnerving task. What is obvious is often less valuable. What is dubious might become the next big winner. To manage the ambiguity, a VC will use his or her history, expertise, and outlook as guideposts in decision making. He or she will draw upon his or her partnership for input and insight. However, in a world where a start-up's uniqueness often wins big—and conventionality might not win at all—there's a premium for original thinking. At the end of the day, it's a deeply personal process that a venture capitalist goes through to render a decision.

Equally personal is what happens after funding a start-up. After funding, a venture capitalist then focuses on doing whatever he or she can to help improve the start-up's ability to thrive. Sometimes that means doing nothing at all. At other times, it means bringing institutional and personal resources to bear in ways that are handcrafted for that company. Start-ups are as deeply personal as the VCs and their firms. Imagine Facebook without Mark Zuckerberg: Might it look like Apple without Steve Jobs? What a good venture capitalist does is personalize the resources to reflect the people, culture, and situation at the start-up at that moment.

Given the deeply personal nature of venture capital and entrepreneurship, it's no surprise that I would highly recommend Tarang Shah's book, *Venture Capitalists at Work*. This book captures the personalities and approaches of a number of leading VC practitioners as they discuss their work. It displays the heart and soul of the venture capital process, by offering an exclusive window into the voice of the practitioners. What you'll find is that each VC has a unique point of view. Yet when you step back from this collage of discussions, you'll sense some core fundamentals important to all successful start-ups. Fundamentals such as:

- Creating customer delight efficiently;
- Building passion into the team's culture;
- Scaling the company beyond $100 million in revenue; and
- Daring to be authentic so that you can dare to be great.

Each of the interviewees may prioritize these fundamentals differently, but all of the VCs have approaches on how to accomplish them. The variety of approaches simply reflects the personal uniqueness of investors and teams.

I find the depth and candidness of the interviews remarkable, but I guess not surprising. The rich material reflects the respect that we in the industry have for Tarang Shah. His reach within the tight venture capital industry is quite unusual but reflective of his character. As a side benefit from reading this book, I believe there's a personal lesson in here on how to lead with integrity, sincerity, and goodwill, as my good friend Tarang does.

While aspiring venture capitalists should find this book as the go-to reference guide for developing one's own venture style, *Venture Capitalists at Work* should appeal more broadly to all entrepreneurs, as well as to followers of technology and technology investing. Entrepreneurs should benefit from having access to robust discussions on how to build fundamentally sound start-ups. Given that common start-up problems are discussed by several VCs, entrepreneurs facing those problems can extract from the interviews the nuances of approaches and tailor a solution that personally suits them. Further, there is a trove of real-life examples of successful decisions (and some less successful) that contributed to a start-up's success. If an entrepreneur can learn and benefit from one of these examples, they can save valuable time and resources.

By reading this book, technology enthusiasts and investors will develop a deep sense for how entrepreneurs, technology, and discontinuities manifest themselves into much larger, life-changing trends. Technology disruptions are happening at an accelerating pace. This book will help you see these trends as they emerge, and ride the waves more gracefully. You'll get answers to questions like, "Why was Twitter funded? What contributed to its success?" For investors, perhaps you'll see answers to the question, "What's the next Twitter?" For this last question, I believe the answers are in here.

—Gus Tai
Trinity Ventures

Foreword

For years, I have been asked to contribute to various works on venture capital. And for the first time, I found the spirit and focus of Tarang Shah's interest in the topic to be exactly like mine. That spirit and focus is really about how to help entrepreneurs build great companies and drive real contributions to their customers and, ultimately, the world.

Venture capital is the business that provides capital, advice, networks, and support to these entrepreneurs. And it has existed in various forms for centuries, or longer. Tarang's approach has been to de-mystify the venture capital process for the benefit of entrepreneurs. And that's why I wanted to contribute to his work.

Since 1995, I have had the privilege to be in the venture business and back great entrepreneurs. It's incredibly rewarding. Yes, the financial returns can be fantastic. Even more gratifying is the great personal pleasure in seeing great people you believe in create great new businesses and products for the world. And that's why I am in this business and why I love it.

As an entrepreneur and venture capitalist, I have personally noticed that entrepreneurs really want to understand how venture capitalists make decisions. Decisions on which founders to meet. Decisions on which founders to invest in and support. This incredibly gritty, real-life decision making is at the heart of the day-to-day operations of a venture capitalist. When I go through some of what makes venture firms work and how a venture capitalist makes decisions, entrepreneurs always remark how much it helped them to understand the venture business.

I've seen entrepreneurs get frustrated and waste a lot of valuable time and resources because they don't understand the role of the venture capitalist, before and after they get funded. Frequently, it takes repeat start-ups for founders to learn more of the context and content of the venture business and how venture capitalists can help them succeed.

Tarang Shah's book *Venture Capitalists at Work* is a foundational pillar in an entrepreneur's understanding and resources. I am thrilled that Tarang has pulled together the viewpoints of varied, successful venture capitalists and shown how they work. This is a first in terms of the level of detail, quality of discussion, and value to the entrepreneur.

What is particularly useful for the founder are these conversations. The content is riveting and unrivaled in terms of its open, honest, and vulnerable exposure. It's very clear to me that this content will help entrepreneurs find a venture capitalist that is a good match for them, and get funded. And it will help them efficiently and effectively work with that person and improve their chances of success.

Entrepreneurs will clearly benefit from this book whether they are first-time or repeat entrepreneurs. And importantly, this will move entrepreneurship a huge leap forward. This is what humanity needs for economic progression, job creation, and the great products and services that serve the world.

—George Zachary
Charles River Ventures

About the Authors

Tarang Shah is a venture capital professional. At SoftBank Capital, a venture capital fund, he assisted with $50 million worth of investments in mobile, digital media, and enterprise software start-ups. He has reviewed well over 1,000 start-up companies and has served as a board member and CEO advisor for more than a dozen of them.

Tarang is the developer of a venture model, the Start-up Analysis Model (SAM), which assesses the success potential of start-ups. He is currently a technology innovation executive and mobile payment/commerce expert for one of the largest financial institutions in the United States, where he has built and now leads a start-up risk assessment practice based on his venture model.

Tarang was a co-founder of Ariants, a VC consulting firm; the lead product manager for Ericsson's first 3G product line, which invested $300 million in R&D; the business leader responsible for Ericsson's CDMA450 product line; and a marketing manager for Qualcomm's CDMA technology.

Tarang has an MBA from the Thunderbird School of Global Management and an MBA and BSEE from Gujarat University in India. He passed CFA Level II in 2005.

Sheetal Shah is a contributing author. She is an expert at analyzing Wall Street–listed public companies and translating that analysis methodology into a start-up analysis framework.

Sheetal was a co-founder of Ariants, a VC consulting firm, and is the co-developer of the Start-up Analysis Model. Sheetal has a BS in bioscience from the University of California, Irvine. She passed CFA Level II in 2005.

Acknowledgments

Whether it is a great product, start-up, or a book, anything meaningful that touches many comes together when a remarkable team strokes together in great harmony with a common mission. I am proud of the fact that this book was made possible by the combined effort of more than 100 individuals, including interviewees, researchers, reviewers, a publishing team, and industry experts. We all were motivated by one common mission—to help entrepreneurs with knowledge gathered from some of the best investors and practitioners in the venture capital industry. These are people who have helped create over 70 game-changing success stories like YouTube, Groupon, Facebook, PayPal, Twitter, Bloom Energy, Zappos, LinkedIn, and many more. We all wanted to improve entrepreneurs' chances of success by sharing what we have learned about how to and how not to build great companies. Nothing will be more satisfying than seeing this book positively influence the outcome of many start-ups and the hardworking, dedicated, persistent risk-takers behind them.

I would like to thank Sheetal Shah, my wife and contributing author, for making this project a reality. She has relentlessly kept this project together and lifted it to new heights by helping me dream big, driving the project forward, and assisting with everything from content to format, selecting interviewees, the design and review of interview questions and interview chapters, and other innumerable aspects key to publishing a book. Most importantly, her belief in me through ups and downs, her incredible patience with my crazy ideas and schedules, and her guidance and motivation as a true friend and co-founder played a pivotal role in the success of this project.

Our son Raj Shah's arrival in this world was a true inspiration for this book. He brought with him a divine spark that motivated us to reach for our dreams. We are very appreciative of Raj for teaching us to do what's joyful and seek joy in everything we do. We also owe thanks to Mukundray G Shah, Sheetal's dad and my father-in-law, whose belief, encouragement, and ideas greatly inspired us as well.

I feel grateful to the incredible group of interviewees who participated in this book. They genuinely believed in this project aimed at helping entrepreneurs.

They joyfully dedicated their time and energy to review interview questions, participated in the interviews, went through various drafts of the chapters with incredible diligence, and made sure the lessons garnered from their years of successful venture building and investing are communicated to entrepreneurs. They were very patient and supportive of my ideas, questions, and how best to present their thoughts and experiences in this book. Their true love for entrepreneurship was evident in every step of this journey. It's natural to have some of their magic dust sprinkle over you as you read this book.

For this book project and also for Idea to Billion (our research project focused on analyzing and testing the success criteria of 100 leading start-ups), we were fortunate to have research support from several MBA as well as management students from the leading graduate business schools, including Harvard, UC Berkeley, UCLA, Pepperdine University, the University of Southern California, and the University of California, Irvine. They conducted more than 100 research assignments, helping us look into every imaginable aspect of what creates successful start-ups. The four rock stars that I am especially thankful to are Sunil Dhuri of Harvard (no assignment is beyond his reach and capability), Ana Gonzalez of Harvard (for unbelievable depth and attention to detail), Holly Sixiao of Pepperdine (for amazing analysis of start-ups), and Jonathan Kroopf of Berkeley (for unmatched business acumen and speed). This fantastic four's dedication and contribution has played a key role in the success of this project. I would also like to thank the following individuals for their research contributions: Shaw Saw (Harvard), Matt Needel (Boston University), Monika Prasad (UCI), and Abhishek Thakur (UCLA).

I am not sure if this project would have been possible without genuine motivation, guidance, and encouragement from my dear friends, including Avikk Ghose, who was the first to see why this could be a great idea; Gus Tai (Trinity Ventures) who made himself available for every question I had and to fill in critical gaps in the project; George Zachary (Charles River Ventures) for recognizing the value of this project's potential in helping entrepreneurs—and for leveraging his network to promote the project; and Randy Komisar (Kleiner Perkins), a venture capitalist and author, for always lending his helping hand and words of encouragement. I am also very thankful to Gus Tai and George Zachary for doing the honor of writing the forewords for this book. I am thankful to the legendary angel investor Ron Conway for endorsing this project. Ron, Gus, and George's burning love for entrepreneurship has been very inspiring to me.

I would like to thank the following individuals for their help with the review of the content and providing invaluable critique and guidance to make this book very relevant and useful to entrepreneurs: Tom Taulli (Taulli.com) for his incredible critical review and guidance as a business writer; Avikk Ghose for staying up many nights and weekends to make sure he got to review every word and sentence, and provide a start-up founder and corporate executive's perspective; and Jonathan Kroopf for his critical review and summary from a college entrepreneur and student's perspective. I would also like to thank the following individuals for their help with editing and review: Amy Grady, Toby Prosky, TM Ravi, Kelly Dillon, Rachel Moore Weller, Jennifer Acree, Jeff Titterton, Trish Striglos, and Jane Barrett. My special thanks to Mark Dempster for his extraordinary help with editing and review.

I would also like to thank following individuals for their support and for making key introductions for this project: Tom Burgess, Ted Alexander, George Zachary, Gus Tai, Avikk Ghose, Woosung Ahn, David Young, Prashant Shah, Rich Wong, Ron Bouganim, Jim Scheinman, Kevin Hartz, Joe Medved, Jonathan Katzman, Saeed Amidi, Amir Amidi, Kevin Baroumand, Patricia Nakache, Terry Moore, Toby Prosky, David Zilberman, Vish Mishra, Dan Murillo, Viney Sawhney, and Marc Averitt.

Sheetal and I would like to convey our sincere thanks to our publishing team at Apress. Jeff Olson has been an incredible believer in this project from the moment he saw my book proposal. His diligent editing, focus on quality, and presentation style to help readers get maximum value out of the content of this book is second to none. Jessica Belanger has been tremendous force in running this project and taking care of every little detail to ensure its success. Jeff, Jessica, Kim Burton, Rita Fernando, and the production team have been extremely agile and supportive to accommodate the requirements of interviewees and authors while maintaining the successful conversational style of the At Work series.

My special thanks go to my mentors and teachers who helped me in my journey in the venture capital industry and gave me foundation for attempting this book. I would like to thank Tom Siegel and Peter Fisher (Shepherd Ventures), who encouraged me to consider a career in venture capital and helped me every step of the way. I would like to thank the SoftBank Capital team, including Ron Fisher, Eric Hippeau, Mike Perlis, Steve Murray, Jordan Levy, Craig Cooper, Ron Schreiber, Karin Klein, Cindy Sperling, Joe Medved, Dave Kimelberg, and Phil Shevin for teaching me venture investing and giving me tremendous exposure to the entire start-up investing process from deal sourcing to board participation and exit planning. I would like to convey my sincere thanks to all my VC colleagues who taught me a lot about the venture business. Most importantly, I feel deep gratitude towards the start-up founders and teams that I had opportunity to interact with and learn from. Their passion, creativity, and relentless drive to bring new products and services to the market despite many odds have inspired me beyond imagination.

Sheetal and I would like to thank our true teachers—our spiritual guru Pujyashri Gurudev Rakeshbhai Zhaveri and our parents—who taught us what's most important in life: selfless love for humanity and leveraging our gifts and resources for betterment of the mankind.

The purpose of souls is to assist each other.

Introduction

For years, this question has played in our minds: why do some start-ups defy all odds and become multibillion-dollar successes while many others fail? Is this purely a stroke of luck or is there a science behind the success? If so, what are the common characteristics among successful start-ups and entrepreneurs? To find answers to these questions, we went straight to the source and asked the venture capital investors who were part of some of the most notable successes of our time.

In this book, you will hear leading start-up investment practitioners discuss, in their own words, how they identify promising ideas, markets, products and entrepreneurs, and how they helped build game-changing companies. We explored with them the lessons learned from not only the successes, but also their failures, to identify the factors that separate the two groups and also to draw the common patterns. Finally, we asked them what advice they would give to entrepreneurs aspiring to build the next Google, Facebook, Groupon, or Twitter.

To provide you with a 360-degree view of how to build successful start-ups, we have included interviews with several phenomenal entrepreneurs and exceptional start-up operators. We explored with them the end-to-end journey from formation to exit and discussed the most common operating challenges along the way, and how they tackled them.

As you'll read in the pages to come, many interesting revelations and patterns emerged.

One of the most surprising revelations was that many successful companies arose out of non-consensus, unconventional, and in fact contrarian ideas. Most people didn't think those ideas would succeed at all, let alone become multibillion-dollar companies. In each of these cases, the entrepreneurs had a very strong intuition and access to asymmetric information based on their predisposition toward, and early exposure to, a potentially huge untapped or emerging market opportunity. Groupon, Twitter, and Facebook are great examples of that. Given the general market disbelief, these companies enjoyed very little competition until they broke off the chart. On the other hand, the riskiest start-up ideas tend to be those most people can see are great ideas. Hence, there is so much competition that it negatively impacts everything from gross margin to valuation.

Surprisingly, most successful start-ups were not started with a goal to build a billion-dollar company. They rather started with a desire to solve a meaningful "pain point"—a VC term for a problem that causes people a lot of frustration. This is usually something that affects the entrepreneur personally and directly. Then the entrepreneur does a wonderful job of solving the problem for a small group of customers. Eventually the entrepreneur, with the help of venture investors, finds a way to expand the solution to a very large group of customers. This doesn't necessarily put management before market, but rather it emphasizes the fact that the best companies are created when great teams intersect with large market opportunities.

Whereas entrepreneurs focus on identifying and solving these burning pain points, venture investors try to find those extraordinary entrepreneurs who are trying to solve potentially huge problems in a meaningful way. Venture investors tap into their tremendous network of contacts and "pattern recognition"—the art of leveraging lessons drawn from past successes and failures to identify a combination of factors and behaviors that may point to promising markets, entrepreneurs, products, business models, and so forth. Together, these build a "prepared mind" or "gut feel" about the emerging market opportunities created by the tectonic shifts in customer behavior and the enabling technologies that can be successfully applied to those shifts. Entrepreneurs are true visionaries, and venture investors are great pattern recognizers with an experienced toolkit of how to build companies—and how not to build them. Successful start-ups are created when a trusted relationship and line of communication is established between the visionary (entrepreneur) and the pattern recognizer (investor) for two-way knowledge transfer.

In discussing the characteristics of the successful founders, the words repeated most often are extraordinary passion, intelligence, authenticity, intellectual honesty, dogged persistence, risk-taking, and integrity. Many of these entrepreneurs were scarred by past failures, were hungry to win big, or came from humble backgrounds. They also had this fact in common: they were hardly known to the world before starting companies that made them successful and famous. Most of these successful founders also paired with one or more co-founders rather than going solo. The co-founders they partnered with had not only complementary skills, but more importantly, a long history of working together. They had built a great chemistry with each other well before they became co-founders.

xviii

It's also clear from the interviews that most successful start-ups have an "A" team of 30 to 40 people stroking together in harmony towards a common mission. This gives them ten times the productivity advantage over their competitors. These teams come together when the passion, intelligence, and charisma of the founders serve as a talent-magnet to attract some of the best people in the industry to solve the toughest and most challenging problems for their customers. The first 10 to 12 hires in the start-up team are extremely important, as they determine the DNA and culture of the company and, in turn, its success trajectory.

It's quite interesting to notice that successful start-ups are extremely adept at "rapid iteration and fast fail." This technique of quickly trying things out is one of the most important characteristics of the "A" team and it becomes a core part of the start-up DNA. Successful start-ups use it to figure out a product/market fit and optimize everything from product features to pricing.

Successful start-ups also end up making drastic changes to their original plans in what's called a "pivot." Only a small percentage of such pivots—one in ten—are successful, though. The successful pivot is a function of the "authenticity" and "intellectual honesty" of the entrepreneurs, where a deep knowledge of the market space and its fine nuances, combined with their ability to quickly adapt to new market realities, plays a key role in determining the effective degree and direction of the pivot. The journey to a successful pivot has a logical progression without any leaps from one strategy to the next, and the domain knowledge of the founders remains relevant in the new plan.

The interviews also reveal how important market timing is in determining start-up success. It's probably the most overlooked concept by the entrepreneurs, and they usually end up being too early or too late to the market. Many companies fail not because they are too early or too late, but because they don't recognize or admit that, and change their plans and cash burn accordingly.

Equally revealing is the fact that the so-called "first mover" advantage is not that important for start-up success, unless you can turn that early position into a sustainable competitive lead. An example might be a consumer internet company that would leverage the network effect to build a massive and sticky user base—like Groupon. But usually a successful start-up might be coming to the party late, yet with a better solution and better execution of its strategy. Remember, Google was the 99th search engine to launch and Facebook launched a couple years after Friendster and LinkedIn.

These findings are just the tip of the "knowledge iceberg" hidden in this book. We are confident that quite a lot of actionable insights will be revealed to you as you read through various chapters. We have spent enough years in the venture industry to know some of the most pressing challenges faced by the budding entrepreneurs. We also know that there is an ocean of untapped knowledge hidden within the leading practitioners in this industry. This is our humble attempt to bring a few buckets of that knowledge to much-deserving entrepreneurs who can learn and apply these findings to their specific situations and improve their chances of building successful companies. Nothing will be more satisfying than seeing this book positively influence and lift the success trajectory of the entrepreneurs whose relentless passion, dedication, and dogged pursuit brings great products and services to us against all odds. They are a true blessing to the world economy and mankind.

For the love of entrepreneurship!

Roelof Botha

Sequoia Capital: YouTube, Xoom, Green Dot, Dropbox, AdMob

Roelof Botha is a partner at Sequoia Capital, where he works with financial services, cloud computing, bioinformatics, consumer internet, and consumer mobile companies. Before joining Sequoia in 2003, he served as PayPal's CFO and as a consultant for McKinsey & Company.

In discussing Sequoia Capital's partnerships with YouTube, AdMob, Green Dot, and Dropbox, Roelof offers insight into the characteristics of special entrepreneurs and their start-ups. I love how Roelof translates successful operating and venture experience into identifying promising ideas.

Tarang Shah: What are the key ingredients in building a billion-dollar start-up?

Roelof Botha: To achieve a big success, many things have to come together. In some cases, what looked like smooth sailing from the outside was more like a near-death experience; a few small changes, and the outcome could have been dramatically different. There is always a healthy mixture of skill and luck involved.

The key to start-up success is purity of motivation. The most successful entrepreneurs tend to start with a desire to solve an interesting problem— one that's often driven by a personal frustration. The best companies are started by people who are motivated beyond money. They're not initially trying to build a billion-dollar company.

If you think about the sort of sacrifice and endurance an entrepreneur needs to succeed, I just do not see how money is a sufficient motivator. If I were an entrepreneur, I wouldn't do it just for money. I would do it because I really care about something.

Omar Hamoui, who started AdMob—which Google acquired and where my partner Jim Goetz sat on the board—is a great example. Omar was a mobile application developer who was frustrated because he couldn't sell advertising to support his business. So he tried to solve the problem by building a mobile ad exchange, starting with emerging mobile developers. When we first partnered with AdMob, it was just him, running the company while finishing his degree at Wharton. He did this not because he thought he could sell the company for $1 billion—he was just trying to solve a problem for himself.

Now, to build a successful business, he had to recruit the right people early on. The first ten to fifteen people you recruit have a huge impact on the DNA of your business.

Another example is Dropbox, which my partner Bryan Schreier works with. The spark that led to its formation came from personal frustration. The founders, Drew Houston and Arash Ferdowsi, were CS students at MIT. They got tired of having to walk from their dorm rooms to the computer labs, carrying flash drives back and forth. Sometimes copied files would be inconsistent or they'd forget a flash drive, keeping them from accessing a document they needed. That led them to ask, in a world where more and more people have multiple devices, why isn't there a common file system so you don't have to think, "What documents are on *this* machine?" I don't think they had any idea that the company would reach tens of millions of consumers and grow to the scale it has. Now they're focused on making it a successful big business.

Shah: What attracts you to start-ups and individuals to back?

Botha: We listen intently to founders who can clearly articulate an ailment and artfully describe an elegant solution to relieve that pain. If they can weave a believable story with a compelling value proposition, they'll have us hooked.

We then focus on the size of the market opportunity. This isn't an easy exercise. Part of it is having a prepared mind. We go to great lengths to be very tuned in to market trends. Say someone came to us and said, "We've just met the guys who started EC2, and they're building a cloud infrastructure company that's providing private clouds to enterprises. Do you want to join us in funding it?" If I'd said I didn't know anything about the subject and needed to take the next three months to learn about it, we wouldn't be in business with Chris and Willem.[1] We'd have been too late.

That's why we spend much of our energy speaking to people in the industry, understanding the currents, and identifying interesting opportunities. If you don't understand the problem firsthand, you don't have insight into creating a solution. And that is why entrepreneurs are special—they have the insight. We spend a lot of time making sure we're prepared for those companies when they arrive, so we can help them succeed.

Shah: What attracted you to Xoom?

Botha: People continue to emigrate throughout the world and send money back home. Traditional money-transfer agencies are a $15 billion a year market. Seven years ago, when we met with Xoom founder Kevin Hartz, he had the innovative notion that the problem could be addressed with an online model. We had to ask ourselves whether this approach could sufficiently capture a segment of that market. What's the value proposition? Is it cheaper, faster, and more convenient for people to transfer these funds online? By asking these and other essential questions, we got very comfortable with Kevin's idea.

Shah: Can you share your thinking on how you identified YouTube as a great opportunity?

Botha: Let's be clear—it was the founders, Chad Hurley, Steve Chen, and Jawed Karim, who identified online video as a great opportunity. Timing is very important in any business decision. Think of Apple's Newton, which was sort of a precursor to the iPhone or the Palm. Those products succeeded more than a decade after the Newton failed. Often it's a question of timing rather than of an idea's merit.

With YouTube, video had come and gone—for example, with RealPlayer—but never became a huge hit. So what changed that made YouTube possible? At Sequoia, we'd investigated related ideas back in 2004 and 2005. We were keeping an eye on broadband penetration in the US—where was the tipping point at which a large enough percentage of US consumers had decent home internet connections? And what new services would that unlock?

We looked at markets in Japan and Korea for examples of how shopping sites changed. They went from having three small pictures of a product to having fifteen large pictures—pages could be that heavy given the quality of the connection. We also kept tabs on the state of browser technology.

---

[1] Benguela founders Chris Pinkham and Willem van Biljon

Before YouTube, you couldn't play a video inside a browser; asking the user to download a plug-in was too much friction.

At the same time, we were keeping an eye on both technology and consumer trends. We were listening to semiconductor companies that made the components for handheld devices—devices that made it easy for consumers to capture pictures and videos. There was the emergence of blogging, photo-sharing services like Flickr, and review sites. People wanted to express themselves through text and pictures; the next natural step was video. Despite all this, I couldn't have predicted that YouTube would grow as big as it has, or as quickly.

Importantly, the value proposition and the product were both fabulous. When I first encountered the website, I uploaded a few videos. In just a few minutes I'd posted them and e-mailed out links. People were watching videos that had been sitting on my hard drive for years. Other video sites at the time had clients that you had to download. Even with the browser-based ones, their products just weren't as good.

With YouTube, I was lucky to know the cofounders from our days at PayPal. I knew how good they were. And they were fantastic talent magnets. When Google acquired YouTube, there were only fifty-five employees in the company—it's phenomenal how much they accomplished with so few people. That's because they did such a good job recruiting high-quality talent. None of the founders were widely known at that point, but they had seen some of the things we did right at PayPal, and learned from some of the mistakes.

Shah: What happens in start-ups like Xoom, Google, and YouTube that hit the nerve of the market and grow exponentially to become "flywheels"?

Botha: The answer lies in two essential variables: the size of the market and the strength of the value proposition. Any growth goes through an exponential curve, then flattens with saturation. If the ceiling on the market opportunity is $200 million, even if you get a flywheel, it will take you from twenty to sixty or seventy, then peter out because you saturated the available space. The bigger the market, though, the more runway you have—so if you hit that need in the curve, you can grow exponentially, and keep going for a long time. Doubling a business of material size for three to four years leads to a really large, important company. That's a key element of the flywheel idea.

Another factor is the strength of the value proposition vs. the need to sell. Products and services that need to be sold do not have a good enough value proposition. We're excited to partner with start-ups where consumers *want* to buy, where people are dying for a solution. Dropbox has millions of customers. They haven't spent a penny on customer acquisition. People find out about the product from friends and family, through sharing of folders and file distribution. Google did it through a couple of distribution deals. Once you discovered Google, you didn't want to be anywhere else; it was so good at addressing the problem.

There is something special about entrepreneurs who can identify and execute on this unique combination of market size and value proposition. The world did not know who Chad and Steve were before YouTube, or who Larry and Sergey[2] were before Google. Most of these companies are started by underdogs. They're hungry; they want to prove themselves. It's quite rare to find a phenomenally successful entrepreneur who does it again.

Successful entrepreneurs also have this ability to articulate a roadmap for the sort of things they want to build over time. We rarely do business with a company where there's a six-month roadmap and then it's all done.

Shah: How does the role of the founder evolve as a company goes from seed to early growth to later-stage scaling?

Botha: The role is different at different stages. Sometimes, founders want to step back, because the company has gotten to a certain scale and they're not sure they have a place in it anymore. The ability to create something where nothing existed is a rare skill. Sometimes people just love that. They would rather do it four or five times in a lifetime than pick one thing and build it for twenty years.

Of course, the founders of many successful businesses have grown with their companies. Steve and Chad took YouTube all the way; Sergey and Larry are still running Google. Omar took AdMob all the way, as did the PayPal team. However, as you build a billion-dollar company, you need to hire a large number of superb employees. Much of it has to do with charisma. "A" people do not want to work for "B" people. An "A" person who cannot communicate the value proposition of his or her innovation to ten to fifteen great "A" hires will struggle to build a business.

A great example of this principle at work is Green Dot; my partner Michael Moritz sits on their board. The company went public last year. Founder Steve Streit has grown so much over the last seven years, to become the sort of person who can lead a $2 billion company. He literally started the company at a card table in his bedroom. He came to it with creativity, charisma, intelligence, and the ability to recruit people. But those characteristics are not always consistent with the ability to run a huge, complex organization. Steve

---

[2] Larry Page and Sergey Brin

has built a strong team around him, some of whom take care of the operational details. At the same time, he himself has adapted in a way where he can pay attention to those operational details without sacrificing his creativity, his ability to come up with new business ideas or product innovations.

At Yahoo!, in contrast, cofounder David Filo still leads the technology side of the business. But he knows himself well enough to know that he did not want to be a business leader. He's involved in the details of building the underlying software. The money doesn't matter to him. I think at one point, long after he became worth an enormous amount of money, the board actually made him get a new car—they were worried that he was driving an old, dangerous car.

Shah: Does age really matter in entrepreneurship?

Botha: It's true that many large technology businesses have been built by young people. Part of why consumer companies are often started by very young people is because younger people tend not to have ingrained habits. If you're eighteen, you don't have twenty years of watching television in the living room holding a remote control. If you get pretty decent video through YouTube and Hulu, you're happy to watch TV on a laptop or tablet. Or you didn't grow up listening to music on LPs or CDs—you're comfortable with the new mode of behavior dictated by MP3s, and now smartphones.

Technology skills can be acquired almost independent of age, much like musical talent. That's certainly part of why it's possible for young people to build a wonderful, disruptive company. On the other hand, someone who is thirty-five or forty-five can easily be an entrepreneur. Many wonderful companies were started by people over 40. Netflix, Green Dot, Isilon weren't started by twentysomethings. More experienced individuals may start different businesses—not necessarily consumer-facing companies. VMWare, for example, was started by people in their late thirties, early forties, who were computer science professors and industry veterans. Building a company like that doesn't require thinking about the nuances of consumer taste.

Consumer companies are often embraced first by the younger crowd; Facebook's average age, for example, has crept up over time. The sort of person who can start a company that appeals to today's nineteen-year-old is probably closer to nineteen than forty-nine. YouTube, Twitter, and Facebook were started by people closer to the demographic, who understand the problems that demographic faces.

Shah: Great insight. Earlier, you mentioned that the first ten to fifteen people hired build the DNA of a company. What are you looking for in those employees?

Botha: The key characteristic is the desire to solve a problem for the customer. That is the driving passion, not "I think this is going to be a billion-dollar company and I want to hop in because I can get rich." We're looking for people whose ideas get floated around. People who fight over the chance to work on solving a problem rather than passing the buck.

You don't want someone whose gut reaction is, "No, we can't do that. We tried it before and it doesn't work." Think about the number of frustrations that people around the world have every day. Most of the time, when people are frustrated by something, they just shrug their shoulders because they're too lazy to do anything about it. They don't care. People with "great DNA" see problems—and they roll up their sleeves and try to solve them. It takes a very special person to do that.

Good entrepreneurs should also have passion and drive. One of the things that keeps me excited about venture capital is the opportunity to listen to someone who is passionate about their business idea. You can sense that passion. Clearly these people are smart, but they also have a drive to take on incredible odds, to change the world and make it a better place. It is such an invigorating and electrifying characteristic.

Shah: When do you know that a start-up is beyond recovery?

Botha: That's a very tough question. Some of it has to do with the original premise. Sometimes the premise moves. And sometimes a market dissolves. How the company responds in that case makes all the difference. Pure Digital, for example, was founded before phone cameras took off; Sequoia got into business with Jonathan Kaplan and the company in 2002. At that point, there was an enormous market for disposable cameras. You'd buy one, take your vacation pictures, bring the thing back, they give you your pictures. The premise of the company was to make that process digital. They would recycle the hardware. But then, two to three years later, camera phones took over the world—and shone a spotlight on the viability of the disposable camera market. The original premise no longer held.

Now, it would have been easy to throw in the towel at that point. But Jonathan saw what was happening with YouTube and noted that most consumers were frustrated with their camcorder experiences. He saw a market opportunity and decided to pivot to video. It was a tough call, but he was passionate and could articulate a new direction for the business. Pure Digital ended up selling more units per year than the high-end camcorder business as a whole.

Shah: What are the key considerations with such a pivot?

Botha: Led by the founders, we think very carefully as a team when a company wants to pivot. To be clear, most companies do pivot to some extent. There isn't a single company we've worked with that, twelve to twenty-four months later, was on the exact same path. A company might move ten degrees to the left or fifteen degrees to the right. There is always an element of iteration and evolution.

The question is, do you spawn a new species because the market is different? When mutation is that extreme, survival rates are low. Will some of the DNA accumulated in your prior existence be a liability? Those are very, very tough questions, with no simple answers. We try to be disciplined about the decision.

Much of our approach resides in clearly articulating the market opportunity, how much of what we have translates, and if the people have the right DNA for the opportunity. I've been in situations where business-oriented companies wanted to pivot to more of a consumer focus, but didn't have the right team to pull that off. Should they replace a significant portion of the team in order to go after the opportunity? That sounds more like a new company than something that evolved. Running a services company requires fundamentally different DNA than selling a product.

Many companies get to that point, do a bridge round, then try to close a small tack-on financing. They're not really willing to face the tough decisions. I think that's a huge mistake. If you have six months of runway left and you really do not have it figured out, you need to find a solution in three months.

Shah: And it takes a good six months with strong metrics to raise money.

Botha: I've been through this one other time. A company built a decent business, a couple million in revenue—but in my opinion, and in the founder's opinion, we didn't have enough to get a nice standalone financing. The company ended up being acquired three or four months before cash ran out. You can get a better exit if an acquirer sees that you have several months of cash left. If you wait until the eleventh hour, you may not get much. People underestimate the importance of knowing when to make those tough decisions.

Shah: When a company is doing well, acquisition offers are bound to come its way. What are the key considerations in deciding whether to sell or keep growing?

Botha: At Sequoia, we've been fortunate to work with founders who aren't just looking for the quick buck. They're out to put a dent in the universe, to borrow a phrase from Steve Jobs.

We have a predisposition toward the long view. If you were to hold onto the shares of every IPO company we invested in until today, you would have made significantly more money than if you were to invest with us at the venture stage alone. Of course, many situations do go south after an IPO. Even including those, you would do better on average because the long-run winners dominate. Yahoo! was huge; Google went way up. That doesn't mean we're not judicious. I think we generally have a bias to go along, though, because people overestimate the impact of technological shifts in the short run and underestimate them in the long run. But the long-run effects are just so spectacular.

Shah: Tons of examples in your portfolio prove that.

Botha: Think about private investing. It's very different from hedge-fund investing or public investing; you can take advantage of market psychology and short-term mismatches because you can exit. We don't have that luxury in venture capital. We can't bet that this trend will be fashionable for the next three years and then fade. By definition, we have to have a long-term stance.

When we decide to work with founders, it's a long journey. Maybe the company goes public or is acquired in three years, five years, ten years—who knows? With Green Dot, we've been their partner nearly ten years. It's a public company now and we're still on their board. If we saw it as a trendy thing, we'd have dealt with it differently and figured that, say, the peak value of the company was five years after investment. But we waited seven for the IPO. We like long runways.

Shah: What do you see happening in funding now?

Botha: Most companies started in this country are not venture- or angel-financed. What I like about the current trends around technology, whether for mobile or PC/web, is that the barriers to entry are so low. Today, you can run a very nice business at a relatively modest scale, launch a website, and market yourself through Google or Facebook or Apple. You can be a small developer, build mobile applications and sell them through the Android marketplace or the Apple App Store. Many companies of ten to fifteen people are making $2 to $3 million in revenue selling a couple of niche applications. They're wonderful businesses; they love what they're doing and the customers love their products. That doesn't mean that VCs should finance those particular companies.

Entrepreneurship is much more than what VCs participate in. People get to do what they care about and continue to solve problems. Much of this is due to technology. Twenty years ago, you needed a huge conglomerate.

Today, you can rely on partners and other relationships to pull your business together. The average size of a business is getting smaller and smaller because of technology, improved communication, and commerce. That, to me, is fantastic.

Mike Maples

FLOODGATE Fund: Twitter, Chegg, Digg, Demandforce, ngmoco:), SolarWinds, ModCloth

Mike Maples, Jr., is the managing partner of FLOODGATE. He was named as one of "8 Rising VC Stars" by Fortune magazine and number 17 on the Forbes "Midas List" for his investments in business and consumer technology companies. Before becoming a full-time investor, Mike was an entrepreneur and operating executive who worked in a variety of senior management roles in high-growth companies.

Mike is a rare breed when it comes to venture capital investors. His unconventional investment style is evident in his investments (Twitter, Chegg, Digg, and others) and when he invested in them—when other VCs wouldn't touch them. Unlike traditional VCs who flock after "hot" deals, Mike takes on non-consensus start-ups that won't pass the filter at most VC partnerships. He has a knack for boiling the venture investment down to its core essence, an exceptional founding team and a disruptive opportunity.

I had the good fortune of working with Mike on the board of a start-up. It's amazing to see him in action. He's an extremely thoughtful investor and an indispensible business coach.

Tarang Shah: What is your secret sauce for venture success?

Mike Maples: I invest in stubborn entrepreneurs who chase huge opportunities and hopefully several of them turn out to be right.

Shah: I will turn the question upside down and ask your opinion on why start-ups fail.

Maples: The most obvious answer is they run out of money! But I think it's a little deeper than that. I have a little bit of a different view on start-ups. I basically believe most start-ups are not meant to be successful and the high-tech business is a business of "exceptionalism" and winner-take-all. What happens is, there are very disruptive technology shifts that occur from time to time and a small number of companies ride the wave created by these shifts. And through a combination of luck and skill and timing, produce huge outcomes that were just meant to be.

I think in any given wave, a very small number of companies can truly monetize the underlying opportunity. Most of these businesses have profound fundamental network effects and monopoly businesses. If you took the value that is created by that small, exceptional base of companies, you could almost round it off to all the value that is created in the entire venture business.

You look at Google and Facebook over the last ten years, and I do not know what Facebook is going to be worth, probably $40 billion or more. I heard that Facebook this year will be greater than a billion in revenue. I do not know Google's worth. The last time I looked, $150 billion or something like that. Take a company as successful as YouTube. It seems like a great outcome, but next to the wealth created by Google, it is an irrelevant exit in the scheme of things. That is always the frame of reference.

When people ask me if the VC model is broken, I am never sure how to answer that because I expect most VCs to fail, and I expect most VC firms to fail. To me, it is like asking if start-ups are broken. Only a small number of them are meant to be successful. I think the entire business is finding those exceptional, awesome companies. If you find one of them every five years, nothing else matters. There is nothing else, and I think people forget that. There are a lot of good models out there. There are guys that invest at low prices and have an 80 percent chance of making four to five times their money and that kind of stuff, but that just does not play in my world. That is not what I am in it for.

Shah: That probably works at a quite later stage much better than at the early stage.

Maples: I think the tech business is just fundamentally characterized by—Darwin had a term for it in evolution, "punctuated equilibrium"—where the world is evolving a certain way and then bam, it changes completely and fundamentally. You can even see this in the fossil records. Where the fossils progress at a certain rate, and then bam, there is a whole new layer of sediment that looks fundamentally different. The theory is, maybe there was a flood that wiped everything out or some new organism adapted and survived and crowded the old organisms out. I think to make money as an investor in the tech business, you have to find those. If you cannot find any of those ever, I think it is hard to argue that you have a business.

Shah: If you draw the curve of the number of companies with close to a billion or more in exit valuation, there is a very sharp drop-off. Then there is just a long tail. The long tail does not really matter because you add their value up against the amount of money they raised and the ratio [of exit value to money raised] just does not work.

Maples: Yep. For example, CubeTree exited for $50 million. I am sure it affected the entrepreneur's life in a meaningful way and I have great respect for the founders. I look at that but then I look at Twitter, which just raised a round earlier this year on an $8-billion plus post-money valuation. So, as an investor, I have to get a CubeTree every year for 160 years for the same result.

Shah: That is a different business model and I do not think it is a venture model.

Maples: I look at Mint—$170 million exit. That is 10 percent of SolarWinds. I do not mean to cast aspersions on CubeTree or Mint or any of those. I am just saying that as a student of the economics of the tech business, to me, that is not where the action is. That is sort of a sideshow, where the main event is Facebook, Google, Twitter, Cisco, Microsoft. Let's give the "main event" some generous wiggle room. Let's say any company worth over a billion dollars is fundamentally interesting. You could even argue against that. You could argue that one Google is worth more than one hundred of those today. This is a fairly extreme point of view. I am willing to live with that. Some people will say, "Can't you get excited about the $150-million exit?" I can make money on those deals, but I cannot get excited about them.

Shah: Say you put your venture portfolio in three buckets: "hit out of the park"—10 times the return or more—"okay," or "lose most or everything." Now if you are only working with the second and third buckets, then you do not get the real venture returns.

Maples: We do not even think that much about our portfolio. Every company we look at, is there a chance it could be something *huge* if things go our way? To us, there is nothing else. There is no other question that matters. There is no other analysis that we care about. That is all there is.

Shah: Great phenomena are all extreme phenomena. I do believe that the universe doesn't work in an incremental way. What you are saying is nor does the tech business.

Maples: The huge upside and the real returns in venture are really in the fundamental changes. What I find interesting, the way our model works, most people think, okay, you guys are super angels.[1] You invest small amounts of money and you have a lot of flexible exit options and that is a good thing. Because you have a fund, it is easier to return the fund by skillfully exiting portfolio companies at various prices. But, that is not the real advantage. The real advantage is that, because we are investing small amounts of money, we can afford to do very controversial deals. The deals that end up creating a fundamental change are always controversial when you do them. Most of the best deals that we have done would not have survived the scrutiny of a partnership.

With Twitter, you tell people we are doing blogging with 140-characters or less. People are like, "Are you kidding me? That is a joke." People wondered how we could invest in something so frivolous as that. Prior to Twitter, the co-founder Evan Williams started a company called Blogger, and now there are a million people doing blogs. He told me, "I have this theory that if we let people do microblogs, a whole lot more people would do blogs, maybe tens of millions of people." I thought that is not totally crazy and if anybody can, he can. So I gave him some money to try that. If you had gone into a partnership and said this guy invented Blogger, he now wants to do 140-character blogging, I do not know how it is going to make money, but that guy is a stud and he is going to make me money. People would just look at you like, "But it is 140 characters or less! Huh?!?"

Shah: I was studying how you did the Twitter investment. What struck me was the two key aspects to that investment—one is the market, which as you said was "potentially huge." The second thing you said was, "the guy needs to be a stud." Here you are talking about authenticity of Evan Williams. When he talks about microblogging, he has an authenticity on both understanding what he is talking about from the customer's point of view as well as an exceptional capability to execute on it. I see here a pattern in Evan Williams, in Osman Rashid [the founder of Chegg] as well as few others that you backed.

Maples: Erin McKean of Worknik was an Oxford English lexicographer. Susan Koger at ModCloth has been thrifting for clothes since she was

---

[1] Early-stage investors who put small investment in companies with exponential growth potential.

thirteen. We do not look at serial entrepreneurship as a positive trait. We look at authenticity and unconventional, proprietary insight as the key difference.

Shah: Well, that is one of the hypotheses I am testing. Do serial entrepreneurs have a better chance of success than the first-timers?

Maples: It all goes back to how you define success. I define success as "I have to create a punctuated equilibrium or I was not truly successful."

Shah: A billion-dollar company is a success. An extremely high capital-multiplier[2] that really matters.

Maples: I would bet you that not many serial entrepreneurs have created those. When they have, it is usually in a bubble time. It is more a function of the time, than a function of the person. That is my theory.

Shah: What is happening there? What do you think is driving that?

Maples: My point of view is that the authentic entrepreneur is more likely to have the non-consensus, and the right, epiphany. So Rashid goes to the All Things Digital or D conference with this notebook prototype [an e-reader for textbooks]. Everybody says it is huge and way too big. He knows that textbooks are freaking big. Students, when they read a textbook, they want to see the whole page. They do not want to be scrolling around, pinching, and moving. They want the text in front of them. He did not make it big just to make it big. His non-consensus view of the form factor was informed by his knowledge of college students and how they consume textbooks. Maybe he is right, maybe he is wrong, but the fundamental issue is that if he is right, he is going to have a huge lead on people because people think it is too crazy-big to ever want to copy what he is doing.

I believe that the authentic entrepreneur possesses an implicit set of instincts about what will work in the markets they serve, what they know that the rest of the world does not know. When they pivot and make an adjustment, they are more likely to know when it is important to pivot or not. They are more likely to adjust in the proper direction. It is sort of like what made Sam Bradford, who won the Heisman Trophy [while at Oklahoma] in 2008, a great quarterback. What makes him great? Arm strength, height, all that stuff. But what really makes him a great quarterback is that he scores touchdowns whenever he is inside the twenty-yard line. When he is inside the twenty-yard line, everybody on his team knew they were going to score a touchdown and everybody on the other team knew that he was going to score a

---

[2] The ratio of exit valuation to money raised by the company.

touchdown. Is there a formula for the plays he is going to run? Maybe, but the fact of the matter is, he just has a feel for the game. He knows, as he is backing up into the pocket, which receiver just broke loose and he will hit the guy.

I think that when you are an authentic entrepreneur, you are more likely to just have a constant feel for the game you are in and your instincts are more likely to be right and your unconventional wisdom is more likely to pay off. I think the other reason they win is love conquers all in start-ups. Every start-up has a bunch of near-death experiences and if you do not love the idea with all of your passion, you will give up. The person who says, "I can't imagine doing anything in my life but this idea," just has an overwhelming advantage in terms of sticking to it. When you consider somebody who has the multiplicative advantages of being more likely to be on the scent because of their unconventional wisdom, coupled with a greater willingness to persevere, I just think that the multiplier effect is such a fundamental advantage that it is hard for me to justify investing in any other kind of person.

Shah: Then you go back and reverse engineer everyone from Bill Gates to Mark Zuckerberg. I have been watching their documentaries time and time again and see how they did it and what drove them. You see the same drive and craziness towards a singular idea they believed in.

Maples: In the face of everybody telling them they are wrong. Let's take Google. You see these stubborn entrepreneurs, even in the face of the guy who gave them the money saying, "Do it this way, you are wrong." And they say, "No, you are wrong, my vision is right, screw you." They end up making the most money.

Shah: There are examples of people not taking advice and they drive the company into the ground. That is why there is a fine separation. What do you think that separation is?

Maples: I think sometimes they are right and sometimes they are not. I think it is rare to be right. It is hard to be exceptional.

Shah: I think with the exceptional entrepreneurs, you try to force consensus on them, and they probably agree with a smile on their face, but they cannot go to sleep at night.

Maples: I think a lot of VCs, unfortunately, say, "This is a hot sector, we need to fund a company in that sector." So they do. The CEO behaves almost like he is an employee of the VC. The best founders I have seen, they do not care about any of that stuff. They are just pursuing their vision with a relentless abandon.

Shah: I think what they are saying is, the future is not a function of the exterior environment that I will be subjected to, but I will keep working on my future. That is what they are doing basically.

Maples: I find this myself. The entrepreneurs I end up liking the best are the ones where I am struggling to keep up with their insights about what is going on. All I am really there to do is to help provide acceleration. I do not even give myself enough credit to call myself a coach. I am sort of like, "Hey, are there any bottlenecks I can help you with?" Those are the ones that always make the money and build awesome companies.

Shah: On a day-to-day basis, you have five to ten companies pitching to you and you have to make a decision. In that process, there is a small window where you make that judgment call. What strikes you the most when you run into these exceptional guys?

Maples: The thing I have found most interesting is that the best deals we have done are the ones where we decided the quickest—which is counter-intuitive to me. I would have thought that the ones where we did the most diligence and the ones where we thought about it the most would be the most successful, but in fact, that is not the case. I do not know how this ModCloth deal is going to go, for example. It is one of our recent ones that seems to be doing well. My partner, Ann, basically tells me one day, there is this company called ModCloth. It is a fashion e-tailer. It is a husband-and-wife team in Pittsburgh. She said I needed to meet this company and I couldn't figure out why . . . until I met them. Ten minutes into the meeting, I put my hand up and I say, "Eric [Koger, ModCloth co-founder], I hope I will not offend here, but I need to stop you right now. I have decided I want to invest."

Shah: So what happened in those ten minutes?

Maples: I just thought that this is going to be an awesome market. It is moving really fast. This company has momentum, has traction, it has authentic entrepreneurs. Sometimes I will just see a company and I will think, *that is going to work.* I can just tell it is going to work. Sometimes we are right and sometimes we are wrong. I just thought it would work. I could just feel it.

Shah: Authenticity came through in those ten minutes?

Maples: When Susan Koger comes walking in, dressed to the nines in her ModCloth clothes, she says she has been "thrifting for clothes since I was thirteen with my grandma." [She told me,] "I started this thing in my dorm, selling vintage clothes. People started buying them. Now the community helps us name the dresses and pick the ones we are going to sell and that helps our supply chain." They did $700,000 in revenue in December last year. I really thought it would work. Maybe having been an entrepreneur myself, I will just see an idea and I can see if it is going to work.

Shah: It becomes intuitive.

Maples: Usually within fifteen minutes, I have found at least the best ones have been such that I get that feeling in my gut of *we better not let these people leave the building*. You just get that feeling. If we do not get that feeling, usually that means we are probably not going to ever do it. And then we spend our "diligence" coming up with reasons to talk ourselves out. It is not like we do not do any due diligence—if a person is an ax murderer, we will find out. If they have bad references, we will find out. If the business is not what they represent it to be, we will find out.

Shah: Whether it will work or not, in the context, it is a business.

Maples: Will they find a path to their profits?

Shah: Market opportunity as well. I bet you are a big student of the market that you invest in. It does not come to you as something new.

Maples: There is this book by Isaiah Berlin, *The Hedgehog and the Fox*.[3] The basic premise is the fox knows a lot of things and is really smart. The hedgehog only knows one big thing. Not to confuse politics in this, but people would say, Bill Clinton is a fox, and Ronald Reagan is a hedgehog, among politicians. I think I am more of a hedgehog. I cannot compete with the people on Sand Hill Road based on the analysis of a deal or being a student of business models, or any of that stuff. I think that one of the advantages I have is that I will just look at something and just say, "Yeah, that idea is being put together in a way that is going to work." It is not overly complicated; it is not a domino-rally business model.[4] It just makes sense. What I find is, sometimes it can be an advantage.

Let's say that you are in a room and there is another person in the room and they know the taxonomy of the top twenty-five business models. They are sitting there thinking, okay, is this is subscription business or is this a perpetual license business, or is it an ad business, or this or that? Whereas I tend to say, "It makes sense to me that students are going to like the idea of renting textbooks. I really think they will." I called a couple of college kids and asked what they thought about Netflix for textbooks. I asked them if

[3] Isaiah Berlin, *The Hedgehog and the Fox* (London: George Weidenfeld & Nicolson Ltd.) 1953.

[4] Business models that require a number of disparate events to happen in order to be successful.

they thought it would work. I did not know what the margins would be for sure, but it just felt very strong to me.

Shah: Then you see there is a fundamental pain and if the pain is big enough, you can always put a model on top of it.

Maples: Like with Twitter, let's say you buy Evan's premise that ten times more people will microblog than might blog. Well that would suggest a very strong motivation in people to self-express. If that many people do it and the motivation is that strong.

Shah: You already have the precedent of online blogging. It is easy to extrapolate.

Maples: This is why our approach would not work in a big partnership. In our stage of the market, we are trying to spot a mutation. We are mutation spotters. The problem with spotting a mutation is you cannot really explain all the consequences of when it mutates. You cannot package it in a form that people are going to feel comfortable with what is about to happen. Almost the opposite is true. The virtue of the idea is that nobody really knows all of the ways it could disrupt.

This is why I like the book, *Fooled by Randomness*[5] by Taleb. The basic premise is that the guy likes to make fun of people who are too certain in their knowledge of things. His theory is, there is a hidden role of chance in life and in markets. People underestimate that. That makes a lot of sense to me. Rather than have a false worldview about the role of randomness, I am going to try to make it my friend. I am going to try to make it one of the weapons that I use to compete. The only way I can is to relieve myself of the burden of knowing the short term. I never ask what unit of economics it is or any of that stuff. I just ask if it is going to work and tap into something really big. With Twitter, for example, there is no logical path to do that.

Shah: I was talking about this with one of my research teammates. She said it is really knowing that this guy is the guy. Maybe one idea failed, but this is the gold. I think you have probably run into people that lost money for you and you did not pursue them again, but there are exceptions that you picked up on. There are ones that you hang on to. There is something that you know about the authenticity of the person and what he will do.

Maples: And they are the type of people who could do something great in the right circumstances, if they collide with the right market and the right time.

---

[5]Nassim Nicholas Taleb, *Fooled by Randomness* (New York: Random House, 2004).

Shah: Have you seen a correlation between what I call a billion-dollar success to the age of the entrepreneur?

Maples: I think that being young is a big advantage, but to me, the real correlation is the amount of time you have available to focus on the idea. Have you read the book *Outliers?*[6] I think that some of Gladwell's books are so good. I do not really read business books as often as I read books like that. He gives all of these examples of how some people are born at just the exact, right time for what they care about [to] matter in the world. I think he gave the example Bill Gates being born at the right time to capitalize on microcomputers, etc. Apart from all the obvious stuff, I think that young guys have the advantage because they are willing to work 24/7, do not have a family, do not have any commitments. They can focus rather than hedge. I think the better reason is it is more likely that their unique body of skill and knowledge will be in the right place at the right time, and the world is just about to be ready for it.

Shah: YouTube. That was just the right communication mechanism. People in their fifties or forties would not have understood what was going on.

Maples: That is what goes back to the authentic entrepreneur. You are looking for that person who put in the ten-thousand hours at the perfect time in the universe for them to have done it. Evan Williams just walked right into microblogging. You just hope that right as they hit their ten-thousandth hour, the world is gathering this huge wave for them to surf to greatness. When that ten-thousandth-hour person collides into a great market opportunity, it is tailor-made for them. Then there is a spectacular, huge thing.

Shah: I look at companies that continue to struggle, then something happened, and one day they go from $200K a quarter to $50 million a quarter revenue in two years. The right timing can allow the successful pivot.

Maples: I think that Chegg was an example where someone was willing to pivot. To me, the thing that was great about Chegg, was that it is illustrative of a couple of things. Being non-consensus and right about textbook rental is one. The other thing is the idea of focusing and not hedging.

We had Chegg, a "Craigslist for colleges," and people were trading textbooks and were making some money on ads. We have a classified business here and we had textbook rentals on the backburner. Facebook gets into classified. If Facebook fails at classified, why would we succeed? And we sure

---

[6] Malcom Gladwell, *Outliers: The Story of Success* (New York: Little, Brown and Company, 2008).

would not raise any money. If Facebook succeeded at classifieds, it does not matter what we do, we are hosed. Osman basically says, the only idea that has a chance of winning is textbook rentals. It is not in our plan to do textbook rentals right now. We do not have enough money to do textbook rentals, but I am going to shut everything else down. Shut down everything. When people go to Chegg tomorrow, it is not going to be Craigslist for colleges, it is going to be for textbook rentals. That willingness to say, "If textbook rentals do not succeed, we are out of business. Therefore, we will do nothing else but textbook rentals." That is the thing. Everybody says that is obvious, but most entrepreneurs do not do that.

[Osman Rashid] had ninety days to prove that textbook rentals would work, or he was dead. Just that willingness to be focused like that is just really rare. It is golden. Understanding that it does not mean he has to do it perfectly, either. First of all, he said, "I [will] do nothing else but that," and second of all, "I just have to prove people will rent them." People went to rent a textbook from the Chegg site, and he would ship it from Amazon. By then, he was able to prove that people will rent textbooks. He said if he could get more money, he could rent more of them and have a warehouse. Books are piling up in the conference room. He had this ability to be very zero-based and said this is the first thing he had to prove, that and only that, and then this and only this. Nothing else mattered. People would look at it like it is sloppy, and crazy, and out of control. It was that willingness to be just so single-minded. And this idea if it is not going to contribute to achieving greatness in the core product market fit, then it is irrelevant. What is the minimal viable product, even now that it is narrowed down so far? He wanted to deliver just the minimal viable product within that scope. He was execution focused. And that made all the difference.

George Zachary

Charles River Ventures: Twitter, Yammer, Millennial Media, Jambool, Scribd, Metaplace

George Zachary *is a partner at Charles River Ventures (CRV). George led CRV's investments in Twitter, Yammer, Millennial Media, Metaplace, Jambool, CloudShare, Scribd, and Geni. At Mohr Davidow Ventures, his investments included Accrue Software, Critical Path, and Shutterfly. Previously, George led the Nintendo 64 development business at Silicon Graphics.*

The majority of George's investments are seed and early stage. In this interview, he provides amazing insights into what key factors determine start-up success and where they are visible early in the life of start-ups. As a co-founder of Shutterfly and an early investor in some of the best successes of our time, including Twitter, George leads us through a discussion on key success characteristics of founders, team chemistry, and why entrepreneurs should go after really bold ideas. George also provides invaluable advice to entrepreneurs on how to increase their chances of getting funded and building huge businesses in today's rapidly evolving social and digital economy.

Tarang Shah: What are some of the key reasons why start-ups fail?

George Zachary: I think that is a very good question. I would say if there is one main answer, it is the real failure on the part of the founders to find the right product-market fit. And there is usually missing a relentless, robust process to find it. It is as much a science as it is an art. You have to be relentless as an entrepreneur and have to have a very high IQ, which I think are the two underlying factors necessary for start-up success. While getting to product-market fit is really important, I think something that is more important from a personality perspective is that if you are not relentless as an entrepreneur, you are probably going to fail. You are exposing yourself way more to luck. The relentless drive of founders is what allows them to get opportunities and not just be subject to luck.

Shah: And we all know that the first business plan you prepare hardly ever makes it to a successful company. And the pivoting necessary to land the right product-market fit is not possible without the relentless iterations. It is that determination to find the fit and do it "scientifically" that are key to success here. George, can you shed more light on the science aspect of that process?

Zachary: The process is getting product-market fit. The science is having vision as to what will happen in the market and have clarity and focus on it. Visions without clarity and focus usually result in very weak products. It results in products that do not have a lot of engagement or love by the users or do not fit well into their processes. On the science side, there are so many things you can do, like getting feedback from customers, or doing continuous A/B testing of features. Those are some of them.

Shah: Is this process applicable only to consumer internet companies or is it applicable to software/enterprise companies as well?

Zachary: I think it does not matter. Certainly in the case where more data is known and there is more diligence, you can go around the customers to ask them exactly what they want. Like in more of an enterprise setting, it is easier to be a little bit deterministic about it. So that balance of art and science tends to tilt more towards the science side of things. You can see it in things like the iPhone. Why do people love it? Great design and a human-centric perspective on what the product should be as opposed to having the best screen, fastest processor, and most open APIs. Consumers do not necessarily react to that. They react to the experience they have when they have the phone.

I think the iPhone is a good case study that is part consumer, but also part infrastructure. One thing I think Apple did incredibly well is think from the consumer-centric perspective. This is something that Steve Jobs has been awesome at from the beginning. That is why I think they continue to win. You can argue Android is starting to gain more market share, but at the end of the day, it is more about profitability than market share.

Shah: I agree.

Zachary: If you were going to go develop a new network switch, you can ask people what the switch should do in terms of speeds and feeds. That is not as much art as it is science in new breakthroughs in technology, in physics technology, in processer design. That is not as subject to creativity, like Facebook. A lot of people could argue that Facebook was a linear extrapolation off of Friendster and Myspace. I certainly have used all these products. One of the things that I noticed right away when I used the Facebook product, I said that whoever designed this thing is a genius. He understands exactly the way that people in college think, and he coded all their behaviors and the way that they expressed their relationships in their micro-group of friends—not in their group of five hundred friends, but in their group of ten to fifteen—as a way of getting them online. It was a great product from the beginning and I think that is what drove the success of Facebook.

Shah: What goes behind that genius design? Is it someone who is engrossed in understanding what his customer requirements are? Or does it just come very naturally to some people?

Zachary: I think it is a founder who understands the problem well personally. The founder thinks about it and has insights about it, and a real internal passion for it. For example, you can tell someone you want them to come up with a social network that is better than Myspace and just have somebody design it. They did not have that insight and passion. And for whatever reason, [Mark] Zuckerberg did.

I am starting to see a rise of what I call the product czar. I think the prototypical product czar we have is Steve Jobs with Apple. Having design and product insights are more important as the leader of the company than understanding sales and marketing. That is one of the cool things about the internet—it shifts the balance back to the creativity side of things, away from people who can control the organization or run the organization because they are sales and marketing experts. The internet in a big way is a great leveler for allowing great product people to rise to the top of their organizations.

Shah: Distribution is not as big of a hurdle in the digital economy. If you do the product right, you do not have to have sales and marketing experts run the company by controlling distribution.

Zachary: It is almost as if you had some sort of military army. Historically, some of the generals who have run military armies are awesome at supply chains and knowing how to move troops to the front. The internet is a brand-new thing. Instead of having this complex supply chain of moving the product to the front, all of a sudden you can "teleport" them to the front of the battle. To me, that is the great leveler, and I think it brings the rise of this product czar. Steve Jobs, I think, is a prototypical product czar. Zuckerberg is definitely one. Larry Page and Sergey Brin are other examples. The last ten years has really seen the rise of this. I had a venture in the mid-1990s and product czar people never made it to CEO. They became CTO or chief product officers at best.

Shah: Because hardware was probably the biggest product and was sold through traditional sales channels. As software rose and especially with SaaS [software as a service], the distribution model changed dramatically.

Zachary: You can see it early on, when Jobs got fired from Apple and they hired a great sales and marketing guy, John Scully, to run Apple because they thought then the company would be better managed. It might have been better managed, but it did not actually have better product. And at the end of the day, people want better products.

Shah: The assumption there was that Apple had exhausted the creative potential of the product. The market had commoditized and now it was just about the distribution edge and pricing edge and operational efficiency.

Zachary: Jobs just turned the whole thing around and said, I can charge you double, but the creativity I built in this product is just beyond what you can imagine through the linear curve.

Let's talk about one of the most successful entrepreneurs of all times, Bill Gates. Bill was a superior sales and marketing guy who used borrowing and cloning of technology, which Jobs did early on too. But one of the things that Gates did, he took sales and marketing to an art form and that is what Microsoft was all about. It is interesting, now that Apple has surpassed Microsoft's market cap, something ten years ago most of us thought was nearly impossible. Now we have Apple with a bigger market cap than Microsoft and Steve Jobs recognized as a product czar. I think we are building into our culture now that superior product thinking should be rewarded and should be a key part of driving the company forward.

Shah: That is very insightful. If you translate that into how you evaluate the seed and early stage investments, does this represent a different lens for you now?

Zachary: I currently do two seed investments a month, and one to two traditional venture investments a year. When I am talking to a founder or co-founder, either the co-founder or founder has to really impress me that they have insight and passion about what they are doing. They can speak in depth about the product, but in a way that is very simple. That to me always shows that there is a great depth of thinking when someone can explain what they are doing in a few sentences. I look for founders at the seed stage and Series A stage who basically can quickly explain to me what it is that they are doing, why it is so important, and in a way that the passion comes from them authentically, not like somebody taught them how to make a presentation. It is their passion and enthusiasm about the specifics of what they are doing.

I met this team coach, John Bard. He has coached an Apple team on and off for the last twenty years. He has worked with a lot of high-performing teams. I met him through an Apple executive who is a friend of mine. We used him actually at CRV to help tune up our investing process. I asked him whether—after working with Jobs and the management team at Apple and lots of other awesome companies, and some not-so-good companies—he had any important takeaways that I should know. He said there was only one takeaway I should know. He said all the successful companies he has seen have this one following factor: they have a leader who gets the team excited by offering them focus and the clarity of what to do.

The leaders without the focus and clarity do not work. They cannot translate the desired result into action, and then you have different VPs translating it into different action and you do not get a great, focused result. He said that people who specify things with lots of clarity and focus, but without visionary leadership, cannot usually get people in the company excited. You have to have both. That reminded me that leadership is very different than management. I think one of the mistakes people make sometimes as board members is replacing CEOs because they think they are not good managers. A great manager is important, too, but you can hire somebody to be a great manager to help the CEO translate those things into specific actions.

Shah: That is the difference between CEO and COO. The biggest job for any CEO is to say what to do and most importantly what not to do among fifteen things the company can do. It's that razor-sharp focus on the next key milestones and getting teams excited about them. I have been on a number of boards and you can set apart a CEO from the COO.

Zachary: I saw it with the early days of Twitter. The person who had the product insight was Jack Dorsey and the flip-flopping between him and Evan Williams and Dick Costolo, who was the CEO, I think has negatively affected the company.

Shah: In fact I was just talking about it with my co-author, Sheetal. You see an interview with one founder in one magazine who says one thing and then another founder says something else in a newspaper. It comes across very strange and makes you wonder if/how much of Twitter's potential was squandered in such dissonance.

Zachary: That was my experience working with them early on.

Shah: You can read through those stories and can put the pieces together.

Zachary: The person who had the real product insight and depth was really Jack. I think there has been a bunch of articles recently in *Forbes* and *Fortune* about this issue. The loss of Jack was big. He lost his job at the peak of the downtime issues at Twitter. I am not on the board there, so I do not know the exact board dynamics, but I think that was a real loss for the company. Personally, I really like Evan, I have been friends with him for a long time, but I think Jack should have stayed the CEO from the beginning through recently. It turns out that Jack loves being a chief product officer, so I am not sure he would have wanted to continue as CEO. The real loss was Jack exiting the company.

Shah: He should have stayed as product visionary.

Zachary: I was shocked. Jack went on to found a start-up called Square, which is working remarkably well. Now he is also involved in Twitter as well, trying to help on a product-vision perspective.

Shah: Have you seen this dissonance at the founder level, probably too late for Twitter, but in early start-ups? Can it lead to failure?

Zachary: For sure. One of the things I noticed, when the company is early on and building product and has cash, you can hear it in disagreements between the founders, but it does not get amplified until either the company starts growing really quickly and people feel a lot of tension over what decisions to make, or the company is running out of cash quickly, which then the founders start freaking out about what to do. That is when the dissonance really comes in and people's relationships get negatively affected.

Shah: When you meet the team of founders for investment, does the chemistry come through or does it only come out when something negative or something great happens?

Zachary: It is always there. In meetings, I observe the founders' body language towards each other. Do both of them show up in the meeting when I show up? Do they sit close to each other in meetings? Do they sit close together in office settings? I try to take a lot of physical cues as to what is going on. When visiting their office, I can see what is going on.

I read a book years ago that basically implied that the architecture of a software product is actually connected to the architecture of the company that created it. There is a relationship between the two. I started thinking, maybe that is also related to the relationship of the founders and their body language. I try to get a sense if these guys are a team, united, and working together. A lot of that is just a gut-level reaction. I am not sure it is always correct. I try to get a sense if these are guys that will stick together, even if everything is going wrong.

I would say Twitter, out of all the investments I have ever made, was the most different, in the sense that at the beginning it came out of a previous company that I had invested in, called Odeo. Evan was not totally sure that it was a great idea. Jack thought it was a great idea. The whole formation of the company was pretty non-traditional. I would show up at two o'clock in the afternoon, and there would be one or two or no employees there. There was a different work ethic. It was not the obsessively maniacal nonstop focus of people like Zuckerberg or Larry and Sergey. It just was not that way. When you talked to them, it did not come across. It did not come across that these guys had relentless drive. That was the only time in my career that I have seen that and still things have worked out well.

At the same time, you can see that the fact that they did not have that relentless drive early on, maybe now they are paying some of the prices for it in terms of why there is not better monetization, not knowing what kind of company is Twitter going to become, where the product is going to go.

Shah: Scalability is still an issue. I cannot take my Google contact list—it's quite big but still—and add it to my Twitter account. The moment I try to do something big, they shut it down on me.

Zachary: The really big accomplishment of the company in the past three years is getting from 70 to 80 percent uptime to 99.9 percent uptime. The majority of Jack's frustration and objection to the product plan was due to this issue.

Shah: What was your investment thought process in picking promising start-ups like Odeo [now Twitter], Geni, and Yammer?

Zachary: There are three companies in my portfolio that I am really excited about: Twitter, Yammer, and Millennial Media. They have three very different styles. Yammer was started by David Sacks. I knew David because I met him through Elon Musk [co-founder of PayPal and founder of Tesla Motors] in 2001. I was really impressed with him and we became friends. That is how we ended up working together. David was the head of product at PayPal. He was the COO there and is the guy who figured out what the product should be. Two of the four founders of PayPal, excluding David, told me that David is the one who made the company happen, and without

David, they never would have gotten to that product and figured it out. David is a product genius. He is like Jack Dorsey, in terms of being a product-focused guy. David produced an award-winning movie called *Thank You for Smoking* [(2005)]. He was known in Hollywood that year as one of the top-ten new producers. It is unusual to see an internet entrepreneur who does that. He just has it and it goes across categories. He is deep in a couple of areas and has this product brilliance that goes across all areas. It is very surprising to me. I have not met too many people like that.

Shah: That's fascinating! As an investor, can you identify when you run into these product geniuses when they present their business plan, or does it take a little while to get to know and identify them?

Zachary: I think it takes a little while to get to know them. Just listen to the person talk about how they think about what a good product is and what should be in a product vs. what should not. That is the insight that will drive the product road map. All that stuff I think comes from a pretty deep understanding of human psychology: what makes people do things, what makes groups of people do things. There is a layer there of deeper philosophical and psychological understanding on a part of those founders, I believe, vs. just being a technical expert.

David Sacks was that way. David is just relentless—relentless and really smart. He loves winning. You have probably read about all the PayPal chess championships. He is a hyper-competitive guy. He has been in the World Series of Poker. He told me while he was in law school getting his law degree, he watched an average of two movies every day. He has encyclopedic knowledge of movies. He is a super-interesting guy.

One of the things he did was spin Yammer out of Geni in the same way that Twitter spun out of Odeo. On the Yammer side, I had been talking to David about Twitter, and he thought it was pretty cool. He said that the issue is that in organizations, people do not know who is working on what. Organizations are going to need a social network and the social dynamics in organizations are going to change. Yammer was built at Geni as a development tool to help the engineers build stuff faster. David spun it out of Geni and basically was the CEO of both companies, up until recently. We have a new CEO of Geni now. He is just relentless about building the company and the business. While he has the strong product insights that Jack does as a natural part of his personality, he is just maniacal in driving the company and the business. He is a very good leader.

Now another one in my portfolio that I really like is a company called Millennial Media. They are a mobile ad network on the East Coast. It is the third-biggest mobile ad network behind Apple and Google. Apple and Google are about 18 to 19 percent market share. Millennial is about 15 percent market share and gaining on Apple and Google. The company is in Baltimore. It is not here in the Bay Area. It has a different feel to it. There are not too many other tech start-ups in Baltimore. The core of the company was the company that built Ad.com, which was sold to AOL. They understood the advertising business.

The VP of sales came from Ad.com. He and the others started Millennial at the beginning, and they were more deterministic. They said mobile is going to be just like the ad network that we just built online. We know how to do this. They had very deep experience and they spent time in a deterministic process to talk to publishers and advertisers to figure out what would work. The founders and team that run it, they are execution machines. I have to say they are probably the best executing company I have ever backed.

Shah: How do you define that execution machine? What are a few things that really matter in start-up execution?

Zachary: I think since I invested in the fall of 2007, they have not missed a quarter. They have been over their projections every quarter and it has not been for sandbagging reasons either. They just focus on how to build the biggest, most important mobile ad network. They are very mechanistic about it. From a product perspective, they also tend to be mechanistic. They talk to publishers, they talk to advertisers and they figure out what they want and they build it into the product. It is not like they are creating an iPhone, or Twitter, or Yammer. They just continue to execute.

They have been hiring and buying some companies to add new, cool features on top of what they are doing as a differentiation. If they were smart product-insight guys from the beginning, but not good at execution, there is no way they would have been able to get to this point. Running an ad network is operationally intense. If you do not deliver with your first set of campaigns, you will lose the customers.

Shah: You have to prove yourself with every campaign.

Zachary: Those to me, in my portfolio, are three good successful examples that are also very different from one another.

Shah: Across the board it shows variety, but at the same time it shows some key characteristics that lead to their successes.

Zachary: Now the team at one of my other investments, Scribd, are more like the Twitter guys. They are young, they love what they do, they have product insight and product vision and they execute off that. They are not in the same class of business execution as Millennial. I think few companies are. They do not have the incredibly diverse experience as a David Sacks. But they have eighty-million users that come to the site every month.

Shah: You talked about a few key guys at PayPal, but we have seen, even the YouTube founders came from PayPal. Considering the so-called "PayPal mafia" and the whole culture of PayPal, why is it that so many great companies came out of the folks at PayPal? What is the secret sauce here?

Zachary: My take is that PayPal had a culture of only accepting smart people and having intense internal competition. In more of a positive atmosphere. I was not in the company, so I cannot tell you. I have talked to some others a bit. What I got from them is they just recruited the smartest people and everyone knew they had to recruit smart people. That was part of your job. I think that was a big part of PayPal. The other part was, they had a lot of self-esteem built up inside the company. They beat Yahoo! and eBay with payment mechanism. They beat eBay on their own platform. I think that added a lot of confidence—that you can take on a giant and win. I think everyone across PayPal learned that. I think the biggest mistake, after eBay bought them, was letting all the founders go.

Shah: Isn't that a story of acquisition by big players? They value things very differently than we investors do.

Zachary: I think it was a strategic mistake. I think none of the acquisitions that Meg Whitman [former eBay CEO] did have really worked out that well because of something they did. PayPal was a machine that was running from before eBay touched it. They have not really done anything to make it any better. Skype was a company that was mismanaged when it was acquired and got slightly better management at eBay, but not really.

Shah: I could put PayPal and eBay together. I cannot put Skype and eBay together.

Zachary: Here's the reason there are so many good companies that come out of PayPal: They had an intense, competitive environment internally and obtained really smart people. They managed to attract people who are smart and really competitive, which are makings of good entrepreneurs usually.

Shah: Putting these all together, when you review early-stage investments, what are your criteria?

Zachary: At the seed stage, I ask, can these founders create a big company out of their pure product thoughts? Are they product innovators? Are they people that other people will be attracted to and join the company? Are they the key "crystals" that you could build a company around? Do I believe in the vision and am I excited about the vision? Is the early prototype or product they create proof of their vision? How is it being accepted, how is it working? Is it easy to understand? It is a frequent mistake at the seed stage, especially as we approach tops or peaks in the venture business, that the ideas tend to get narrower for some reason and there are less really bold ideas as a percentage of the total mix. I am sure you saw that at SoftBank. When the sector gets "hot," all of a sudden you start seeing very narrow ideas—like a social network for people with dark hair who live in Menlo Park!

Shah: People just get too niche about the whole market opportunity because they cannot take a shot at the emerging leaders who have cornered the market. The only way they can do it is by further segmenting the market.

Zachary: I remember talking to Elon one night. He said, "Why do people spend all their energy working on these little problems?" "Little" is coming from a guy who built a car company. I think people are nervous to take big risks and they think this is a safer way to maybe make some money. It is kind of ridiculous. If you are an entrepreneur, you are going to work fourteen hours a day no matter if it is a big problem or a little problem you are solving. That is what your personality is.

Shah: Whether it's a ten-million or ten-billion-dollar market, most of the risks are the same.

Zachary: And you probably work the same amount.

Shah: Why is there such an aversion to big risk? The biggest wins happen on the far end of the risk-reward continuum.

Zachary: I do not know. What I think is, some people are nervous for the really bold stuff because the really bold stuff requires non-stop energy with lots of people telling you that you are doing something crazy. On more narrow ideas, you can probably find people who say that kind of makes sense. The biggest, boldest ideas do not come out of consensus. If they did, then there would not be so many of them.

Shah: And it would just be incremental like most business plans investors see.

Zachary: I also think there is something on the part of founders who want to do something bold. They have a strong need to show the rest of the world that they are doing something bold. Money is certainly part of it, but it is definitely not the whole thing. The whole thing is them feeling they are on a very important mission in life. Before Elon started the rocket company, SpaceX, he was talking to me about the fact that he thinks that someone is going to screw up the planet, that it only takes one person to do something horrific to screw up the planet, or how big accidents can happen and we have to learn to survive on other planets. He wanted to be the entrepreneur to lead humanity off this planet into the rest of the universe. Now that is pretty bold.

Shah: That is like a chapter out of a *Star Wars* movie.

Zachary: As we got together for coffee and he was telling me that he was thinking about sending a mouse to Mars, I asked why. He said it was kind of a test. He said, "Do you think people will think that is crazy?" I said probably people will think that is crazy. He centered on building his vision through first building a business around a satellite launch and to become the most innovative supplier of vehicles into outer space to help explore space.

Shah: So it really comes to having a really bold vision and not worrying about whether it's non-consensus. If most people tell you it's a great idea, you wonder why in world there aren't so many companies already solving such an obvious need.

Zachary: That is right. He does not care about consensus. It is internally driven in him that he has to do this. In the same way that you and I might say, "I have to drink some water," he says, "I have to go to outer space."

Shah: Do you think that passion and conviction ooze out of their skin when you meet with them?

Zachary: Yes.

Shah: That is a great test for someone at seed level.

Zachary: It is those people who tend to attract others through their passion, not just the chance to make a lot of money. I do think it is both. Those people do want to do something great, but they also want to make some money. It is probably in that order. To recruit awesome people to the company who have multiple opportunities to go to different companies, you have to get them excited about what you are doing and not the way an HR person can. I think a lot of people want to feel a sense of purpose in their lives, commitment to a mission. And when people feel that there is a mission that they can engage themselves in, something they believe in, they are happy to join a company like that.

Shah: This is really insightful. What needs to happen between the seed round and Series A for someone to even make it to Series A? Do you see a lot of fallout there? We talked about some of the reasons they fail, but is there a short formula to get to Series A or a sure way not to?

Zachary: There is a very sure way—which is the fastest way to get to Series A—show that there is product-market fit. Not necessarily revenue, but the potential for a revenue model to exist.

Shah: Where does that product-market fit show up in a short period of time?

Zachary: In consumer internet, it is user engagement. I remember the early days of Twitter. There were not a lot of users, but the users that were using it, used it a lot. There was never any kind of intermediate, medium responsive people about Twitter. They said they love it or thought it was really stupid. Nothing in between.

Shah: That is why you do not see a lot of investment interest in the early days of Twitter. Most people thought, why would you do that? A 140-character microblog doesn't make sense in the world of YouTube and video blogging.

Zachary: When I invested in Twitter, a senior Facebook executive asked what was I really investing in. He said, this is like a feature on our newsfeed. He said he could save me the money and people will not do it.

Shah: Facebook tried that feature, but it did not really take off.

Zachary: I thought that they never implanted it well. The Facebook Lite thing did not work well.

Shah: I think the combination of Twitter with LinkedIn status update is amazing.

Zachary: That was a very smart move by Jeff Weiner, the CEO of LinkedIn, to make that happen.

Shah: As an investor, what are some of the key things you wish entrepreneurs knew?

Zachary: One thing that I think a lot of entrepreneurs do not know exactly [is] how venture people think. For example, one of our major LPs[1] told me that roughly 8 out of 4,000 funded companies, angel as well as venture companies, drive 80 percent of all the gain in the business.

A lot of people ask why venture people are only looking for billion-dollar companies. The data shows that a few companies drive all the gain in the business. An entrepreneur with an idea is not competing necessarily on its own absolute basis. He/she is actually competing on a relative basis with all

---

[1] A limited partner who invests in venture capital fund.

these other investment possibilities. That is something that entrepreneurs should understand, which I think they do not. Next year, Facebook, assuming it goes public, will return I think $30 to $50 billion to investors, which my guess is, that will be like 90 percent of the gain for all of next year out of technology venture capital.

Shah: If you take a couple of those out, like Groupon, LinkedIn, Twitter, etc., then everything else is a rounding error.

Zachary: In some ways, a lot of people thought that the rise in the internet would lead to more successful big companies than successful movies coming out of Hollywood. The hits would have better distribution than concentration. What we are seeing is that the results are actually more concentrated. That is because there is a global audience that can use the product and there is momentum to the product. That is a frustration of mine. A lot of founders do not realize that a few hits generate all the gain and what venture people want to go after are the really bold ideas that could be one of those eight hits.

Shah: Isn't a network effect a big success factor in this whole "new world order?" In any big success, from Facebook to LinkedIn to Twitter, there is a built-in network effect. Do you think that defines the new wave of opportunities in the consumer internet and eventually mobile?

Zachary: I think that is true.

Shah: Everything else, as you said, is a feature in Facebook. But if there is a network effect on Twitter, you cannot just take it over by adding that feature, an even better feature than Twitter, on something as big as Facebook. That is why I think a lot of entrepreneurs are not getting it. It is not about coming out with a better mousetrap. You need a mousetrap with built-in network effect!

Zachary: The other thing about pursuing a big idea is that if you pursue a really big, bold idea and in your execution of it your product is off the target a bit, nobody says the company is busted and is not going to work. If it is a narrower company, if your idea is off, then everyone says the company is over, the product is not going to work. I think there is a lot of benefit to doing things that are bolder, but it just takes people's insight and relentless drive to do that.

Shah: Now you had said someone sent you a business plan that was based on creating value out of roadkill! That was a pretty bold idea.

Zachary: I remember it. Years ago somebody sent us a plan that said that.

Shah: But you are talking about really bold opportunities targeted at solving really big problems here. What are other key things as an investor you wish every entrepreneur knew?

Zachary: So, pursuing really bold ideas is number one. Number two is to approach VCs that know your space. People should not come to me for restaurants or hotel complexes. I do not know anything about that. A relevant investor is really important. Then approaching them in a way that is easy, but also comprehensive—find an introduction to me, e-mail me directly with a simple executive summary, etc. I frequently get business plans with really good ideas and they want to meet. I wish I could, but my schedule tends to book two to three weeks in advance. Every day I get about eight new referred companies. I cannot meet everyone. I wish I could. I average about twelve hours a day at work. The only way for me to do that is to see people's summaries up front for me to figure out whether I want to take a meeting.

Shah: That goes to your earlier point, having that focus and clarity in their presentation.

Zachary: I can see a lot from that presentation. A lot of times people say, it is different when we tell it to you. True, but if the base presentation is not any good, I do not think it is going to get that much better in person.

Shah: It is a reflection of your thinking process.

Zachary: Number three is, when you get invited to present to investors, bring your founding team. I want to meet not just the founder, I want to meet the other people in the company. That tells me a lot about the founder's ability to get other great co-founders involved.

Sean Dalton

Highland Capital Partners: Starent Networks, Altiga Networks, Telica, PA Semi

Sean Dalton is a general partner at Highland Capital Partners. He focuses on leveraging disruptive technologies in the mobile, enterprise, and media markets. He currently represents Highland on the boards of Calxeda, CENX, Movik Networks, QD Vision and Zoove. Sean's been part of some of the most notable investments in the communications sector, including Altiga Networks (acquired by Cisco), PA Semi (acquired by Apple), Ocular (acquired by Tellabs), Telica (acquired by Alcatel-Lucent) and Starent Networks.

By taking examples from his investment in Starent Networks (sold to Cisco for $2.9 billion) and a few others, Sean provides an in-depth account of the crucial role of the human element in start-up success; how he picks world-class entrepreneurs; and what needs to happen to build a billion-dollar start-up, including the product, the go-to-market strategy, and market timing.

What I love about Sean is his incredible knowledge across the entire spectrum of start-up building from an idea to founder to team to product, and from marketing to business model and finally to an exit, and how he applies that to a wide variety of market-leading start-ups he backs.

Tarang Shah: What are the key reasons why start-ups fail?

Sean Dalton: You have been a VC and you know that we venture investors accept failure as an integral part of the entrepreneurship and venture capital investing process. In my experience, there are two ways in which start-ups fail.

The first one is when the board, despite very clear evidence to the contrary, continues to fund a losing proposition. This is really a variant of the definition of insanity—doing the same thing over and over again, and expecting different results. It is my sense that often when a company fails, it really has already failed multiple times. What has happened is that the entrepreneur and the board together refused to give up, despite signs to the contrary.

There is a second, less common but I think more honorable way that a start-up company fails. That is when the VC and the CEO or management team sits down and basically says, "Look, we got into business to do X. It is not working. We have tried to make other things work and they too are just not working, so let's call a spade a spade and figure out how to gracefully exit from this. Then we can find the next great opportunity to work on together." I think when the investors are applying the investment model right, this is the more preferred way to fail. I wish it were 80/20 [in favor of success], but unfortunately I think it is the other way around.

Shah: So it really boils down to objectively assessing whether the original investment thesis is working or not. What are some of the signs one should look for to check whether the original hypothesis is still holding?

Dalton: I think when it becomes clear that the story is not really well put together or panic has seeped into the system; those are the yellow and red flags that require you as an investor and board member to say, "Stop this and let's take a deep breath. Let's go to the drawing board and let's start from the beginning and ask ourselves some fundamental questions: "Why are we in business, who are our customers, how do we make money?"

I am a firm believer that you let the entrepreneur/management team define their own plan. But when the entrepreneur or management team is consistently not hitting their own plan, it is time for a radical change. While this is easy to say, it's hard to do. We have all heard of the phoenix rising from the ashes and every successful company had that brush with death. Maybe I am just unlucky, but I tend to find a lot of my companies do go off track at some point. The question is, if all of a sudden you find yourself at that crossroad, how do you figure out which path you should take?

For me, the answer lies in how the board and the entrepreneur together embrace the situation. Are people panicking? Are there real issues that have led to this poor performance? Has the management team thoughtfully developed a path forward? Has it been measured or is it a story? I am therefore looking for a combination of conviction as well as thoughtfulness for how we are going to move forward. I am willing to believe a lot of things. But I am looking for that conviction and a measurable plan that we all buy into.

The only way I know how to do this is to really engage with the team. During this process, I'm trying to figure out whether they really believe it or are they grasping at straws? I believe the companies that do rise from the ashes are the ones that recognized where they were heading and made fairly noticeable, if not dramatic, changes rather than stick to a plan. They not only get back on track, but are even more successful than they had originally planned.

Shah: You are expecting the management team to come to the board meeting with the plan rather than just the problem.

Dalton: That is exactly right. Now I think the responsibility of the VC is to really engage and challenge the team. Was it a plan that was put together the evening before the board meeting or a serious effort has gone into figuring out the new direction for the company? It is not so much the questions you ask. It is how they are answered that really lets you know how solidly management is behind the plan.

Shah: What needs to happen for the creation of a billion-dollar start-up?

Dalton: I think it really comes down to a great market opportunity that intersects with a great team. As a VC, I am certainly in the people-first category. I choose to back people over market. I have also learned that ultimately it is the market that allows for an outstanding VC success. One of my more recent investments is a good example of that. The management was an A team from top to bottom and the founding entrepreneur had a very successful track record. He was just as hungry as when he started his first company. He had methodically put together a great team. He made very difficult decisions, letting some early people go who were stars, but were not cultural fits. Ultimately the company found itself late to the market, despite being recognized as a market leader. We redid the plan to reflect these new market realities. The result was a good company, but not one with great return prospects. We had alternatives, so we decided to sell the company. While that hurts because it's so hard to put together A+ teams, we were all quite rational in terms of what was a likely outcome given the market. That is why I think a billion-dollar opportunity requires a great team that then intersects with a great market.

Shah: Fantastic insight!

What are some of the key characteristics you look for in the entrepreneurs and founders you back?

Dalton: I look for a maniacal commitment to work hard and succeed. What underlies that is a real authenticity and real passion to succeed and create a great company. That goes back to how well I know the person I am investing in. That is where I go to her story, not just the résumé stuff. "Tell me about your parents. What moments changed your life? How does your personal history bring us to this moment?" What I am really trying to get is a deep understanding of her motivation. Does it all tie together?

Shah: How does the family background impact the entrepreneurial motivation?

Dalton: It is one of those open-ended questions where there is absolutely no single answer or right answer. One of my partners likes backing "PSD" entrepreneurs—grew up Poor, very Smart, and Driven. That's a solid framework in many ways, but what I am really trying to understand is, "What is the motivation here? What makes you, truly, so special? What does success mean to you? How do you know you are being successful?" You cannot teach someone to work hard. You either do or you do not. I am trying to understand those motivations that lead you to this approach of working hard.

Now the answer could be something like this: "I grew up as the son of the CEO of *Fortune* 100 company. All my life people have expected me to just enjoy the fruits of my father's work. Heck with that. I am going to create my own identity and success." There is never a right answer, but it is part of the story. I believe in the story because I believe in the person.

Frankly, the answer that I am not looking for is a response like, "Gee, that is an interesting question. What motivates me?" If you really have to think about what motivates you, do you really have true passion?

Shah: In the compelling entrepreneurs, passion oozes out of their skin, it's so contagious.

Dalton: Exactly. So in terms of how I pick companies and entrepreneurs, I bet on these passionate, committed, authentic and hardworking entrepreneurs and hope their hard work will intersect with a great market opportunity. I think it is very difficult, but that is what it comes down to.

Shah: Does it really matter if it is a single founder or multiple co-founders?

Dalton: If it is a single founder, [I tell him] no one person can build a great company. Then I am going to say, "Tell me about the team you would like to build." Now I am going to begin figuring out how this person thinks about hiring. I coach my founders and CEOs to hire the strongest team possible. I think ego, wrongly directed, will destroy the chances of building and retaining an A team. By definition you have to have a big ego to be a founder and to build a company, but if you take that to the extreme and you are not willing to bring on people to round you out, then you will build a mediocre team because if you are an A, and you hire Bs, then those Bs hire Cs, and it gets pretty bad.

Shah: What is a key to building great teams?

Dalton: I believe that recruiting is just something that you need to do relentlessly. And how well you balance your ego ultimately shows up with your approach towards recruiting. I am a believer in taking risks with hiring, adding additional DNA to a system. There is no perfect hire. I think that is a myth, but you generally know a really strong hire when you see her. But that's not the whole story. To me the Zen of hiring is firing. I've seen even the most talented founders really struggle with that. There's an old adage among VCs that you never fire too early. If you're really good at hiring, you're probably quite good at sensing when someone isn't working out, a sixth sense if you will. Don't ignore that voice, but seek to get conviction around the signal either way. Part of building a great team is just focusing on bringing in those very best individuals, adding to the DNA, and also making tough decisions on the other side, making those separations promptly when needed.

Shah: What is a key to attracting and retaining great talent to build an A team?

Dalton: It really boils down to appealing to the most basic human emotions. You want people to have pride in what they do and you want people to create some intrinsic value as a result. You really need to appeal to both of those. You can be a tough-ass, pounding on your VPs all day, but if you are creating a lot of intrinsic value, you can get away with that. On the other hand, you may be creating a lot of intrinsic value, but if you have not caught the hearts and souls of your team, they will leave for a better opportunity. They will likely overact to your first misstep and either turn on you or, worse, silently leave the company.

I do not envy start-up CEOs. I think it is the single, loneliest role in our entire ecosystem. That is why we get back to stage one, which is no matter what style of CEO you really are, if you really can develop an open and trusting relationship with your board, you will be better off for it. All else equal, VCs really do not want to change CEOs. It is the most disruptive thing you can ever do in a start-up.

Shah: When you meet with a start-up team compared to just founders, what really stands out in exceptional or A teams?

Dalton: For me, it starts with the CEO who I would say is abnormally talented in one or more dimensions—those dimensions being product insight, sales capabilities, or recruiting. Those, to me, are the fundamental roles of a CEO—developing a product, selling a product, and doing that simultaneously with recruiting a great team. An A team is really just the foremost reflection of an A CEO.

Now implicit in your question is what separates A teams from B and C teams. Again, this is like the famous definition of pornography by the Supreme Court Justice [who] said, "I cannot define it, but I know it when I see it." Well, yes, there are meetings where I walk in and pretty quickly I know what type of team it is. But with all due respect to "blink judgments," I think making good people decisions is not solely a function of experience, but also the amount of time spent with the team.

I remember one particularly poignant example. I vividly remember walking into a board meeting at Starent Networks in 2004 or 2005, as we were about to raise a Series C financing round. They had been working really hard to get a commitment from a major customer, which would have buttressed a really great round, but the CEO started the meeting with the dreaded news: the order did not happen. From there, he calmly and in a factually driven way walked through all the reasons why they did not get the order. He was brutally honest about where the faults lay inside the company. He was also brutally honest about what he felt was going to happen with this customer. On the surface, some of those arguments took faith. There were statements like, "They made this decision, but they are going to be proven wrong and here is why."

I remember walking out of that board meeting with another colleague, who was panicking. "Holy shit, they missed their window," and all that. My reaction was very different. I was convinced they were on the verge of a breakthrough. I felt this for two reasons. Number one, the CEO was being intellectually honest and adding his experience into what he felt was going to happen. Number two, he was also making changes that reflected reality of the business at that moment. Although he was projecting a recovery, he also recognized that we needed to make some changes so that in case that does not happen, we would not be betting the entire company on that outcome. So rather than panic, I sensed an opportunity and was excited to double down and own more of that company.

It is moments like these that tell me certain things about the CEO and the team. It told me that this CEO really knew more about what was going on than anybody else—about the company, customers, and the market. But that instinct wasn't a blink decision. Instead, its seeds were planted through many, many hours getting to know the CEO, and his approach and motivations, long before we were faced with such a crucial decision. Fortunately, just as he predicted, the customer came through and the rest was history. That is an example of an A CEO and A team for sure.

Shah: Earlier you mentioned that you look for great teams that intersect with great market opportunity. What are some of the signs that tell you that you are seeing a market on the verge of an inflection point?

Dalton: Ultimately it becomes a gut feeling, but I try never to solely trust my gut. What I try to figure out is whether the market is about ready to take off and whether you are positioned as perfectly as possible. To do so, I look to construct a rational and plausible story that takes us from the current situation to a winning context. I ask, "What are the big trends that are likely to happen—the known knowns. What needs to change for you to be successful? Do you control enough variables that can place you in a leadership position?" It may sound a bit subjective, but if you've been thoughtful and the story ties reasonably well, then a good piece of your gut becomes conviction—"Yes, this is likely to happen and this team really can uniquely capitalize on it!" Now, you've really developed a thesis and a direction, rather than a lottery ticket.

Now, a critical part of figuring out whether the plan is right is to develop direct relationships with people making decisions on your company's product, the ultimate customers of the product. Those discussions with the customers are incredibly illuminating. Generally, I've found that customers tend to give investors the super-honest version of where the company really is, especially if you have a pre-existing relationship. Customers often share information with investors that they may not necessarily share with the company. You will hear very interesting things from a customer, which, again, provides more data pointing to the market trend.

On the flip side, there is always the fear that you might be too early to a market or too late. There are signs for that as well. If the dog is not eating your dog food, and there are a bunch of fat dogs lying around, you are on a wrong side of the market timing. That is, you are probably too late because someone else is feeding those dogs. You are not winning your fair share, and now we are back to asking some very fundamental questions about the business.

Shah: Are there any signs that point to one being too early to market?

Dalton: I call it a legion of blank stares. The more you try to convince the customer that they are wrong and you are right, you can at that moment recognize that at a minimum you may be too early. But it's important to recognize that customers make mistakes all the time about their readiness for a product. So how can you tell the difference? For me, the initial investment in Starent proved to be a great case study.

I had known the founder for many, many years and really wanted to be in business with him. The problem was that on the surface Starent appeared to be the seventh or eighth company started to go after the mobile data market, and one could have easily concluded it to be too late to the market. However, the founder's strategy was quite unconventional relative to his competition—he was going to go after a smaller market segment than the others. I had to get better understanding of whether that strategy and approach had merits. Fortunately I had a great relationship with the CTO of one of his target customers. I flew out to meet him and delivered the company's sales pitch. I asked what he thought and I will never forget what he said. He said, "These were beautiful slides."

Shah: When you hear how beautiful your slides are, you are in real trouble!

Dalton: Then he just said, "Look, first of all, the amount of mobile data Starent is saying is going to happen, that is just never going to happen. And oh, by the way, if it does happen, and I do not think it will, but if it does happen, my existing vendors, US Robotics, 3Com, Cisco—they already told me they are going to get there."

So among my most unusual experiences as a VC was the following Monday explaining to my partners the feedback from the CTO of a top-three US wireless carrier. "It is all negative, but here is why he is wrong." I was able to present to my partners why this CTO was wrong. To be fair, he was partially right. We were a little bit early, so he was right on that first statement in the sense that significant mobile data traffic arrived later than most people expected. But he was way off on that second statement—that his existing vendors could provide the product to meet that demand. We knew mobile data was going to come to the US eventually because it was already there in Asia. We also knew that Starent's direct competition had a similar view on our market—small and uninteresting. So it was really a matter of waiting it out.

Recall the other story I shared with you—about that infamous board meeting where a customer wouldn't commit, but we knew we would eventually win that customer and we just had to be patient. You earn your keep in the VC business by making these decisions. Your guide is the quality of the arguments and capabilities of the team. If you have both and a thoughtful plan to move forward, you're in a great position to assess the risk and reward and make a good decision. If not, you can wind things up honorably as we discussed earlier or you can buy a lottery ticket.

Shah: What stands out when you run across a compelling product? Does the product tell you a story?

Dalton: It does. I am obsessed with products. While I bet on management and market timing, I need to believe that the product will sell itself. The initial product may only be a fraction of the final product that defines the company. But getting early market validation is not only critical for product development. Doing so also provides critical signals about the team and the market. A case in point, I recently participated in a forum by a major bank in which they shared their technology roadmap. The CIO of the bank started out by saying that if you have product, we have a problem you can solve with that product. I thought that was great because it really makes the point that there are a lot of problems to be solved, but the real question is, why will your product stand out? One way to measure that is when people get emotionally excited about product, you know you are on the right path.

Shah: Between a great product with mediocre go-to-market strategy and a mediocre product with great go-to-market strategy, which one has a higher probability of huge outcome?

Dalton: It's a great question and I've seen both approaches work and fail. As we discussed, founders tend to excel in product, sales or recruiting. So this addresses the question about how much relative weight one places on product development vs. sales. This is one of the questions that I'm trying to figure out pretty early when I am getting to know an entrepreneur. If she's a product whiz, I really want to explore how that great product will get into the customer's hand. If he's a sales whiz, I'm keenly interested in his views on why a product works and doesn't. A discussion around the ratio of engineering and sales heads or engineering and marketing heads is always revealing.

The ratio question is a great test to find out, especially if you are that product or technical founder, whether you really respect sales or not. That is going to be an important data point to know if you are going to have a great relationship with your sales team, because I know you could build the best product in the world, but still have a mediocre outcome without a solid go-to-market strategy. Whereas conversely, you could build a mediocre product but if you really nailed a go-to-market part of the strategy, you may really have an awesome outcome.

You really need a very strong technical team to be successful in today's market. You also gain a lot of leverage through having a great go-to-market team. I think this is a particularly painful point for someone that has spent a good amount of their time in Boston, where I think traditionally we have built really rock-solid products but we have rarely figured out how to effectively market them. Whereas in Silicon Valley, good to great products are built, but even with those good ones, the Valley companies really know how to market them well. Marketing is a really powerful thing. It sets expectations in customers' minds even before you walk through the door. But it also has an important impact on engineers, all of whom deep down will admit the thrill of seeing someone use a product that they helped build. So the truth is, engineers really do value sales and marketing. And companies can use this to their advantage.

Think about Cisco. For a long time, they were the most desirable company for engineers to work for. If you were in a start-up, you really wanted to be acquired by Cisco. Why? Yes, they paid well. But they also had the very best sales people in the business. Apple is another example of that. I know that because we've sold two companies to Apple—PA Semi and Quattro—and the founders of each truly looked forward to joining Apple. It's the same inside of start-ups. Engineers may not give marketing and sales people enough credit, but the reality is that a great sales team will keep a great engineering team very, very happy.

Shah: Does the first mover advantage really help in start-up success?

Dalton: I have seen success in both situations. So I am not sure if being first is really a major determinant of overall success. I think being the first mover is less relevant than how you are assessing the opportunity. The one wild card I would say is being first around a patent. That applies for any company. Patents are becoming critically important. You definitely want to be first on the patent side.

Shah: How important is culture in determining start-up success?

Dalton: Culture is always a very challenging subject. Like entrepreneurs, I think the culture needs to be really authentic. It needs to reinforce and bind a company toward its mission.

We have all heard of things like, "Our culture is work hard, play hard," or, "Customer first above everything." There is actually some usefulness to that, but is it differentiated? The next step up is to describe your culture in a way that makes it catchy and actionable. One of the companies we recently backed described the company culture as "awesomeness." The VP of engineering piped up and said, "When I am interviewing, I tell every recruit, right off the bat, that I am building the most awesome engineering team." The CEO then chimes in and says that when people ask him what he is building, he answers by saying, "We are creating a product that people will say is 'awesome.' " That to me is going from a lingo—work hard, play hard—to a philosophy.

The point is that the culture ends up being a balance between being able to describe with extreme pride what the company is doing and how you are doing it. That is infectious.

Shah: So where would the infectious culture show up? Like in case of Zappos, the culture is built around "Happiness in a Box." And the happiness does get delivered in the shoe box.

Dalton: How that stuff manifests itself is how you really get the flywheel spinning. As Zappos showed, it is very powerful when your company culture is recognized and shared by your customers. It's mutually reinforcing. Your employees feel great about what they are delivering—happiness in a box. Your customers share that happiness when they see that box. Again, we're appealing to simple human nature—wanting to belong and wanting to contribute. When you see people really excited about what their company is doing, that is when the magic happens.

Shah: So like at Zappos, everyone in the company, even the guy who is putting the shoes in the shipping box, sees how his contribution is bringing a smile on a customer's face when the customer opens that box. Every employee in his or her role can really see how to work that single-line mission statement or catchy phrase into a day-to-day work philosophy.

Dalton: Absolutely. The strength of the people you recruit into your company reinforces the direction of the company and hence the likelihood of a successful outcome. So culture really is an X-factor in recruiting. It is one thing to have a great pitch, but quite another when that pitch is authentic. When it is authentic, it is really powerful.

Shah: So not just hiring the best people for a job and throwing them in the mix, but having a deliberate culture, making sure every new hire fits into it, grows with it and helps grow and evolve it.

Dalton: Exactly. But let's not forget that culture is reinforced by not only what you do, but also by what you don't do. Take the example of the super-talented, but disruptive, employee. Trust me, the rest of the company has already recognized this and surely is forming an opinion on how you're dealing, or not dealing, with the situation. How this plays out puts your culture to the test. Allowing someone to be disruptive and to continue to behave that way creates the assumption that you are blessing them. Sometimes the best way to reinforce a culture is to make an example of what is not culturally acceptable. Some firings are very tough decisions. On paper, they may not make sense. But companies do not exist on paper. An important part of your culture is defined by how you manage the balance between talent and behavior.

Shah: Agreed. In what cases or scenarios do you feel you need to have a business model figured out now vs. developing one later once you grow the company to a certain point?

Dalton: This is tough to answer in the abstract. To get to the core of the question, we need to understand the distinction between creating value and monetization. They are linked, but they are different. Let's first talk about monetization. However you get there, at some point in a company's lifecycle you really need to demonstrate whether or not someone is going to buy the product. Then you need to ask whether that person is unique or whether there are four hundred thousand or millions of similar people. From there onwards, it's math. How much does it cost to acquire a customer? How profitable is each customer? And so forth. That is the basic calculus behind monetization. I am very excited about all the new ways to monetize. For example, the "freemium" models—companies that make money on customers that pay nothing.

We were investors in Vistaprint, whose whole value proposition started with offering free business cards. They created a multi-billion-dollar enterprise off that value proposition, as they learned to monetize a relatively small percentage of those customers, but in a substantial and profitable way.

Value creation is ultimately about increasing the enterprise value of the company. Value creation may or may not completely align with the monetization. Particularly in later-stage companies, it is completely in line with monetization—you have this much revenue, you apply this revenue multiple, and boom, there is your value.

Other times the valuation, as we have seen in numerous examples, is completely unrelated to the monetization. This is almost always the case in early-stage companies. But it can happen in later-stage companies too. A very modern example of that was Microsoft's acquisition of Skype. When you look at Skype's financials, it is an okay business. It [has] a lot of revenue, but not high enough gross margins. From a numbers standpoint, it's not a sexy or super profitable business, compared to say, oil and gas. However, if you ask about creating value, tremendous amounts of value were created for what on paper does not really look like great monetization.

Compare that with its acquirer, Microsoft. Microsoft is a company that has not created value in a decade or more. But from a monetization standpoint, it is one of the most beautiful business models in the world. So I think when you start separating value creation and monetization, you really get to the deeper discussion with companies: where are we really taking this business?

Zappos is another example of this distinction between value creation and monetization. I am not even sure the company was profitable when Amazon acquired them, but if they were, they were barely profitable. So from a monetization standpoint, it's not a great story. But from a value creation standpoint—it's happiness in a box for employees and investors. I even had that experience with Zappos. I did not think I could ever order shoes online, but I decided to give it a try. I think I ordered three or four pairs, and I had to send them all back. As promised, there was no hassle and I received replacements that fit. I was so thrilled with the experience that I actually wrote them an e-mail. It went something like, "I am a VC, and I begrudgingly give credit to companies that Highland is not an investor in, but I have to say that this was an unbelievable experience. You guys are doing a great job."

So, especially at the early stage, there are some really interesting discussions with management teams around value creation and monetization, and how each plays in the development of a strategy.

Shah: You really drew a great distinction here that a start-up's job is to create that distinct value, and if it is big enough, someone is going to pick it up one way or the other. Skype is currently valued at $8.5 billion or so, but undervalued in terms of the value it created. When YouTube was sold, I do not think it was anywhere close to being profitable, but it is still a tremendous value for its users. Twitter is on its way to figure out monetization but it has already created huge value.

Dalton: You must have a plan, certainly, for how to increase monetization over time. Amazon is a very good example of that. It seems like for years after its IPO, there were questions about whether it could ever be a profit engine. Despite the skeptics, Amazon has clearly shown it can be a great profit engine. But the company is far from its original concept of an on-line bookseller. It has successfully monetized its customer base across countless products. It has changed the economics for brick and mortar retail business. It has even leveraged its technology investment to run its own enterprise into one of the most formidable players in the cloud computing space— amazing! It's taken them around 15 years to do all of this, but they have done it. So whether you are a start-up or a twenty-year-old company, I do think you need to constantly look at how to build off of your customer base and leverage your other assets, yet the real art is bringing them together in an effective strategy.

Shah: Earlier we talked about when to shut down or stop funding the start-up. On a positive note, when the start-up is doing great, you are bound to get multiple acquisition offers along the way. What is your thought process in deciding whether to sell now or keep funding and growing?

Dalton: I am very front and center on this subject. Often from the very first meeting with an entrepreneur, I let them know that, ultimately, if the management wants to sell, then I will support that decision. That may potentially put me at odds with my own beliefs in the business prospects, or it may put me at odds with other board members. I have certainly been in that situation and it is not comfortable. But I believe in supporting the management.

Now, with that said, I believe a very important part of my role is to understand why management is making the recommendations they are making. For example, when it is time to sell the company, is it because of market reasons? Product reasons? These are what I would call things that are within the direct domain of the business. If it's a strong team, those observations tend to be valid, and management has probably reached the right decision.

On the other hand, there is the whole bucket of more personal reasons why management may want to sell. A founder may say, "I put all my eggs in this basket and I cannot let it go to zero. I have been doing this for four years and I cannot keep this pace up anymore." This can be addressed. I've just found that if you've built a strong relationship with management, you're in a better position to help influence an optimal outcome.

Shah: What are the three things you wish every entrepreneur knew?

Dalton: The first one is about developing a relationship with your investors: Carefully select your VCs and be brutally honest in your communications with them.

I literally just had a meeting with a young, first-time entrepreneur who is in the fortunate position of being showered with love from a lot of VCs. He only started raising funding a few days ago and by tomorrow he will have two term sheets. I told him that what you get from a VC is not just money, but a partner that, for better or worse, will be with you for a long time. While the value-add that comes with a VC is important in success of the start-up, what is more important is finding a VC that will be a great partner to you. That's generally not something you can discover in a few days while you are evaluating several term sheets.

As an investor in their company, the relationship with entrepreneur is very important for me. I am always very interested in understanding what motivates an entrepreneur, what his history is, what his parents did, etc. I am looking for a real story when making the initial investment so that when we are in a difficult situation, we are having a qualitative discussion alongside a quantitative one. All along I am thinking back to the first time we met as well as the many discussions in between. I am looking for whether this person is being brutally honest. Investors are not going to penalize you for being honest, even if we don't like the news. But if you are not honest, then we are removed from what is really going on and cannot be helpful. That is garbage in, garbage out. If you can't be objective about what's going on, you can't solve it or take advantage of that pivot along the way that can turn the company into a billion-dollar success. Hence that trusting, open, and honest relationship between the entrepreneur and investor is very crucial.

The second thing that I would say is this: Effective recruiting is the life blood of all these companies. I know a company is heading in the right direction when the team being built around the founder and CEO is just getting more awesome with every board meeting. This is particularly true in today's market, which is as competitive for talent as I have ever seen.

One of the early signs of things not going well is when I hear that you are having trouble recruiting, or even worse, you're losing employees. VCs have the advantage of being able to assess trends across the board. If you are far off that benchmark, or if you are having any trouble retaining people, then I know that the company is off-track.

The third thing is to be intellectually honest with the investor about your business. Whether you're pivoting or reiterating or whatever you call it, I've generally seen that most successful companies are regularly "zigging and zagging" their way toward the ultimate goal of being a valuable company.

We look at that initial product and plan for sure, but what we are really backing is the founding team. We go in with the eyes wide open. We expect markets to change. We expect technologies to change. The one thing we expect is change. It is very rare, among all these changes, that a venture-backed company does not also change. Just know that to win in this turmoil, you must be intellectually honest about where your business is at any given time. Our job as your partner is to be thoughtful about whether this requires change that is dramatic, if this is the type of change that should be embedded into the existing plan, or if it really just doesn't matter so let's stay focused.

Alex Mehr

Zoosk

Alex Mehr is the co-founder and co-CEO of Zoosk, the fastest-growing social dating site, with more than 50 million members. Before starting Zoosk, Alex worked as a scientist at NASA, where he worked on projects for both robotic and manned space missions.

Alex's PhD dissertation focused on the optimal design of complex engineering systems. He is the author of more than 25 peer-reviewed published articles on a variety of subjects, including theory of complex systems, risk management, design optimization, aerospace systems, genetic algorithms, decision theory, and numerical modeling. He is also an authority on the rapid iteration/fast-failing method for testing ideas to unearth latent customer demand, pick compelling features, and optimize the business model.

In this interview, Alex shares his journey in the creation of Zoosk and the rapid iteration/fast-failing method he and co-founder Shayan Zadeh followed. He also discusses how he leveraged social media to take on established players like eHarmony and Match.com to build and scale a leader in online social dating—at a fraction of the cost it took competitors.

Tarang Shah: How did you come up with the idea for Zoosk?

Alex Mehr: Random discovery. We actually started [the] company as a completely different company. We started a company called Pollection. It was a Flash widget that would be distributed through blogs and social networks and provide multimedia polling to users, and then we would slice and dice the data in the back end.

The idea was that we were going to provide the Flash widget for free, but people who were more serious pollers would pay for advanced data as a premium. We put in a lot of time to develop this widget so that you could upload videos and music or whatever through it, and then you could use it on different blogs and social networks and users could actually watch the videos. Let's say it's an *American Idol* contest. You could upload the performances from all three contenders and then users could click on option A and it would play the video. Click on option B and it will play a video, and then [users] would vote.

Shah: How did you arrive at Zoosk from there?

Mehr: From the very beginning, the reason we started Pollection was because we wanted to start something. We built the product and we even raised a seed round based on that business model. We had a working product, and subsequently we were making some money. At the same time, we had our eyes open for other opportunities that were happening in the market and [the] Facebook platform opened up at about the same time. We created a Facebook application that used the same technology for polling. It was called Polls. We were seeing what variation of this we could try. There were bigger markets and bigger opportunities out there in this new environment that we were just not seeing.

And then one weekend, Shayan Zadeh and I were brainstorming, and we came up with the idea of using our Flash widget to pull in Facebook's friends' photos and then have people rate them on how hot they are. It was a weekend project. It took off like crazy. It grew to about two hundred thousand users in two weeks.

We saw what the market wanted vs. what we wanted to push to the market, meaning our original idea. We decided that we should go where the market is telling us to go. And we should just switch because we see there is a market here in the sense that people want to look at photos and they want to flirt. We went to the board, right after we had raised the seed round, and we said we haven't really touched the money and this is a brand new space and we see a big opportunity for online dating—let's just switch here. We did a pivot, we launched Zoosk, and went into online dating.

Shah: Which year was it?

Mehr: That was 2007.

Shah: So, this happened when eHarmony and Match.com and few other players in the online dating space were already quite big and successful.

Mehr: Correct. The way I look at it is, in online dating, the size of the network is everything. So the bigger you are, the harder it is to displace you because there are more people using your service. Therefore, your service is more inherently valuable. You don't get a shot at a Match.com or an eHarmony that easily.

At that point, we saw what the market did without us spending any resources on it. Immediately there was an "aha!" moment there. There was a vacuum in this new market, which was the social-level application market. It was so huge for an online dating player that we did something over the weekend and it was taking off. You get this chance literally once every fifteen years, in my opinion.

We identified the window of opportunity. We had the test product out. The market was speaking back to us. So we said, you know what, we are going to laser-focus on this one thing, so let's push it through. We took our shot.

Shah: Take me back to your Flash widget idea. You must have looked at fifteen other ideas before you said let's do a Flash widget for polling. How did you pick that idea? What was the reason it didn't take off and what is the message for entrepreneurs here?

Mehr: You are correct. We went through many, many ideas. There are two pieces to this. The first is the brainstorming process and how we picked the Flash polling widget idea. That's the first piece. The second piece is that once you pick up an idea and enter a particular market, what do you do after that?

For the first piece, my co-founder and I knew we wanted to do something. We had certain skill sets, like there were things we knew that we could deliver given the team we had at that time, which was basically the two of us and two other friends who expressed willingness to come in. We knew our skill sets.

We brainstormed all sorts of ideas. [For example], we designed an internet-controlled remote cat feeder. I actually developed the models for it. It allowed you to play with your cat from work and feed it remotely. So that is the range of ideas that we are talking about.

Our logic at that point was that we wanted to do something cheaply and quickly but fail at it quickly enough so we could have a second chance at trying something new.

John, one of our co-founders, was good at Flash, so we decided to develop our first product in Flash. I had some marketing background and understood statistics. Shayan was a great software architect. Brad, another co-founder, is a great back-end guy, so we had the tools and skill set to implement the polling product in a very short amount of time. I'm talking about one month—on nothing.

We implemented a basic product and rolled it out. Some people started using it. Before I went out and started raising money for it, I wanted to find customers for it, again with no budget. I wanted to start getting customers. We worked it out and I made phone calls. We didn't even know what would be the best use-case scenario. We quickly found out that one of the use-case scenarios for it would be people who want to have focus groups. They want to do a very light interaction with a customer.

Let's say there is a new video game coming out. I want to do a focus group around it. I want to talk to gamers and I want to ask two to three qualifying questions before I actually tell them you can come join the focus group and we will give you $200. There is a qualifying question.

We immediately saw a need there and we sold that product to two or three major focus groups. They did pilot projects with us, and we distributed their questionnaires through blogs. Then we got the leads from them. We sold back the leads to the focus group company. I am talking about very small projects, $300 to $400, but that was enough proof that I could go out and pitch to VCs.

Shah: How do you quickly "test and fail" to recognize that this won't work so you can go to the next idea? I ask this because I was in companies that just didn't look at themselves in the mirror and say, "I am failing," when numbers told them so.

Mehr: I really tried to be very cautious about that. We have tried many, many things, and they have failed. Even now we always roll out features and test them. If it doesn't work, it doesn't matter how good we thought the idea was or how personally vested in the idea we feel, we will yank it.

Ideally we wanted to try it quickly with the prototype and first customers, so that I could go and raise enough seed money that we could have an office and feel like a company and try more things quickly.

Once we had the term sheet for seed funding, that was the point where we were thinking, "So let's just go at this with all we have." Facebook had opened up the platform. We had already launched our first Facebook app, which was a polling app. We were getting some users, five hundred or something like that.

People were creating polls. I can't remember the exact numbers, ten to fifteen maybe a day or something like that. It didn't look like it would scale quickly. But we said, "Let's try to see if we can sell it to customers."

Here is a potential use-case scenario—the customer creates a poll. These people are getting certain results for free. However, what happens if we allow a poll that is created for free to capture up to fifty votes. If you want your poll to get more than fifty votes, you should pay $5 to upgrade your poll.

Shah: So you did the "freemium" model, free to a point and then you have to pay to get more?

Mehr: Exactly. I was looking at the type of polls the viewers were creating. They were uploading photos of five clubs or restaurants and saying, "Where do you think my next birthday [party] should be?" Or they would upload a photo of the newborn baby and ask the public, "Should call my baby John, Jack, or Greg?"

I was trying to see what the market opportunity was. We had to implement a credit card charging infrastructure. That opened a whole new thing. I remember we were selling four a day at $4.95. We were talking $16 or $20 a day in revenue. I was looking at this and I said, well this looks good, but it is not growing. There were quiz apps that were going rapidly on Facebook. It felt like we could do better than this. That was when the idea of a trial period came up and we also started launching apps in different markets.

In the very earliest stage, you have the luxury of saying, you know I can continue to incrementally improve what I have or I can look at a drastic change. Right now [with Zoosk], I can't change my model. I can't go out of online dating anymore. But back in that day, I could totally change my business model.

We said, okay, let's try this. We will continue to incrementally work on it, but let's give ourselves two months and try ten different things as quickly as we can. We were literally putting things together to see what works, and one of them was the one that I just mentioned, that picture-hotness rating. And then after that I added a leader board [so people could] actually chat with each other. It became a very crude way of online dating—and it took off.

We said, this is it. We put something together in two days and we were able to generate literally one thousand times more users than what we had generated before.

We said, can we monetize the users here? What if we don't allow users to see who viewed their profile and then charge $3 to reveal that? All of a sudden we were generating $850 a day. It was a lot more in a shorter amount of time.

Once we decided to do a major shift, that's when I went to the board and said, "I'm changing the business model altogether."

As I said, the burn rate[1] at that point was low. I said to the board, "We have this other thing that has one thousand times more users and it is growing like crazy and it is generating ten, fifteen, twenty, thirty transactions a day and it is taking off. The market has spoken, so let's go in that direction."

Shah: You had a scientific way of stumbling upon something that the market wants. What's the message for the entrepreneurs here?

Mehr: I know it has become a cliché. But the way I look at it is that depending on where you are in terms of your resources, you get a limited number of shots that you can take. You have to be able to think of an idea and take your first shot. A lot of people won't even do that. A lot of people would continue with their job and if they had an idea, they would never take that shot.

Know that even though you invested a lot in your first shot, you still can take more shots. If you see that it is not working, then take your second shot. If it doesn't work, take your third shot. Continue until you feel like, "I am comfortable with where I am," and maybe continue to do some discovery around it, continuous experimentation. Even right now, we are always experimenting with new things. You have to hit it. And once you hit it, you know it.

Shah: You being an internet-based company, your measure of traction is how rapidly the dog is eating the dog food?

Mehr: Absolutely. People are attracted to the internet industry because it is a hot thing. But I think the internet industry is special because you can experiment fast and fail quickly, not because of any other reason. There are in fact a lot of arguments against entering the internet industry. One thing that works for the industry is experimenting quickly and cheaply. If you don't take advantage of that, you shouldn't be in the internet industry. You should be opening up a sandwich shop.

Shah: Tell me the process of building Zoosk in a market where challenging eHarmony and Match.com would have seemed like an impossible task.

Mehr: Even once we launched it, we went through massive, massive changes. We launched it. We knew we were going to get traction from our previous experience. We got a lot of traction and we were adding users. We were adding servers and all that, and then the nature of the game changed.

The question became, how can we grow faster? How can I retain users? How can I modify better? We knew from our previous experience that really you have so much dependence on what the market wants, but the

---

[1] The monthly cash spent.

best way to do it is to take your questions to the market and see how the market reacts to it.

We were growing very rapidly back then. I was not sure this was going to work. We started trying new things. One day Shayan and I decided that we were going to try a paid model and we went to the house of one of our board members, who was the seed fund investor. We were sitting on the porch talking about this and we said, "You know, we have not done a paid model, but we didn't want to do a drastic change. We are going to pick a country, and we don't want to pick the US or UK because they are our two biggest markets." We picked Australia.

One night we designed it. We didn't spend much time on it, just a simple subscription page. Everyone from Australia who is on at 5 p.m. today is going to hit it. At 5 p.m., we flipped the switch and everyone in Australia who was trying to communicate was presented with the subscription page. They started converting to subscription! There was some backlash because people were using it free. But backlash is really a one-time thing, so you should always see what the best model is going forward. You can deal with backlash by giving free subscriptions to existing members.

By that time, we were measuring things, like how many people were converting, etc. We measured and did a back-of-the-envelope calculation, and then we said, okay, this is the way it is. This was in March or April 2008. We decided that this was the way to go. We said, guys, this will kill our traffic a little bit. It is obvious that if you go from a fully free model to subscription, some people are going to leave the site, but I have a hard time not believing that what this site is doing is going to work.

The main principles of business always work. If you don't have revenue, it doesn't matter how much hype you have created around you. We didn't want to go out there and try to pump the company and sell it and go on to the next venture. We are not like that. We want to improve our product and actually make money from a lasting business.

So I think, that's the strategy and I think we should start making money. It has worked in Australia—let's put it out somewhere else. We turned it on in some other countries, and then turned it on the UK and then in the US. This is one example of what we have done all the time. Most of the major decisions we have made, we have tested in some form or fashion, and most of our test ideas have failed, but the ones that succeeded became part of our long-term products. Basically, we invented our business model by trying different things on actual people and seeing what works, and just doing more of what works.

Shah: Amazing!

Mehr: Really the best way to try out a new idea is to roll it out to real customers. If you ask a customer whether your idea for a new product appeals to them, they will tell you something totally different from how they would react to the actual product. What they say is not really what they do. This is why focus groups may not be the best way to go about finding real customer needs.

Come up with a hypothesis. Put it in front of a customer, and see how the customer actually behaves once put in that situation. Customers are great at giving you feedback by buying or not buying your product, but they suck at telling you what they want. That's really the only way to understand if something is working—have them pay for it.

Shah: If Steve Jobs had described the iPhone to users, they would not have understood what it can do and most would have shot it down. Not until it really got into people's hands did people realize what it can do.

How come someone like eHarmony or Match.com missed what you experimentally stumbled upon?

Mehr: I always say that the only advantage of having a small company is the fact you are nimble, meaning you can really change things quickly. Match.com and eHarmony are not like that, so they are set in their ways. Put yourself in the shoes of the executives of Match.com. They have revenue lines, top lines, bottom lines that they have to hit and they have plans for how much they are supposed to grow quarter over quarter.

With us, you are telling people to go and try this wacky new thing that may really not work and go off the familiar revenue stream that you have. That is really the advantage of small-company entrepreneurs. And that is why big companies have labs. They proactively say, this is my familiar revenue stream, but I am willing to spend money to look into other things, and if they work I'm going to take them and scale them. That is really the best model.

Most companies are unable to change. Therefore, they are easy targets to beat once there is a change in the market. They are unbelievably hard to beat in normal conditions because they are really good at what they do. Match.com has been doing it for fifteen years, but if there is a paradigm shift in the market, that is where a small company has to come from a different angle and has absolute advantage over it.

Shah: What was the paradigm shift in your case?

Mehr: The shift in our case was social apps. Ours is a network-effect game.[2] We had to beat Match.com in terms of the economics, like quick conversion to subscriber. You can't beat Match.com unless you have a considerable number of users to the point where your product is as effective in finding matches for people locally as Match.com. This is a very local phenomenon and for your product to work, you have to have a significant number of people of matching demographics in that particular local area. To reach that mass, you have to invest heavily.

Match.com has been investing in this for fifteen years. It is very hard to reach that critical mass, very expensive. What would actually trigger another player to invest so much money to get to that critical mass is two things. You could raise $40 million up front, and try to create a replica of Match.com. You will lose $40 million in marketing because at the beginning, you are not going to convert very well but you will keep pushing until you hit critical mass, and at that point you become a replica of Match.com. No one would have invested in me [to execute that model].

Even if they invested in me, I wouldn't have been able to deliver it because to reach that critical mass, I had to go through my own learning curve. That's what protects a company like eBay and Match.com from competitors. They have users. eBay has buyers and sellers. Match.com has gals and guys who are looking for right match.

The ecosystem of users really protects them against new entrants. What we were able to do was to get millions of users through new paradigms, which were social networks such as Facebook. We were able to get users super cheaply through this new partnership. We changed the game. Their customer acquisition cost was ten dollars a profile. Our customer cost on acquisition was twenty cents a profile. That allowed me to reach that critical mass at a fraction of the cost of Match.com.

Now that we have this network effect, it does two things: one, it protects us against the next guy, and two, it allows me to compete with Match.com in their existing channels.

Shah: Tell me more about the process of building the company to this scale and making key decisions along the way.

---

[2] A network effect game is where a user invites friends to join or use a service and such participation increases the value of the service for all users. This leads to viral adoption, as well as stickiness—where group benefit prevents users from leaving the service to go to a competing service.

Mehr: Rapid iteration is how we have built and scaled this company. We are always testing out new ideas by rolling them out to a small group of users. If it works, we roll it out to everybody, otherwise we yank it rapidly and move on to the next idea. Rinse and repeat.

Shah: Great point. And when you hire someone, you can tell them the philosophy by which you operate. But how do you make sure the candidate is not just nodding his head to get in the company, but that he really is the type of person who can live and breathe by your philosophy?

Mehr: As a matter of fact, we discuss our philosophy in the interview process. I think there is really no way of knowing for sure by asking the person in the interview process. What we have done is interview people who at least demonstrate that they are not set in their ways, and that they have the flexibility that you need in an environment like ours to be able to evolve with the company. It's something that most of the time you can see in their previous choices, where they worked, what they did, how they present themselves.

One of the things that you do, and I do this all the time, is throw a curve ball at them. I ask them an out-of-the-blue question, like it could be a brainteaser or it could be to estimate the size of something—something that has nothing to do with what they have been doing. If it is a marketing job, I would ask them how many ping-pong balls can fit in a Boeing 747—and see how they react to that. Do they get pissed off that they were asked something that had nothing to do with marketing? Are they the type of people who, when they see a puzzle, actually enjoy doing it? Are they mentally lazy?

All of these things we look at in an interview process. Sometimes you just can't tell. At the end of the day, some people can work in that culture, some people can't.

Shah: Earlier you made an interesting comment: "On the internet, it is very easy to make money and it is very difficult to make money." So landing the right business model is key to making money. How did you go about finding that model?

Mehr: On the internet, you can have a business that is horrible in terms of traffic or revenue. And then one day you change something somewhere, and all of the sudden it goes from a horrible business model to a great business model. That's the thing about internet companies. That's very difficult to do if you have a brick-and-mortar company. If you have an internet company, you can change things and immediately apply the changes across the product.

The difference between us and the bricks and mortar companies is that they want to try putting music next to the cashier. It takes a very long time to roll it out. For us, it is just turning on "whatever" at the shopping cart. Let's try this option for twenty-four hours and it rolls out to the users and you can measure things. That's why the experiment of trying different things should never go away. We look at this short term and long term. We do very specific types of A/B testing[3] that we found to be very effective. I don't mind sharing this with others.

The way we A/B test different revenue models is that we say, okay, we want to answer two questions. Consider making a particular change—it could be a drastic change like going from a free model to a subscription model, *or* it could be a minor change like changing the pricing point. If it is short term, is it going to generate more money? Is it going to continue to generate more money in the long term? So there are really two specific questions: short term/more money/engagement? Long term/more money/engagement?

If we don't have the feeling this is going to generate more money, then we try 10 percent and 90 percent—we put 10 percent of users in the new model. We look at it for twenty-four hours, sometimes six hours, sometimes two days, but never more than a week. We look at it and we ask, did the 10 percent monetized model look better? That is the first thing. Whether or not if it is monetizing better, it answers question number one: in [the] short term, does it provide more money? You can do a lot of things to make more money in the short term.

You have to see what the long-term impact is, though. If in one week we are comfortable with the finding that the 10 percent sample is monetizing better, we flip it. We say, let's roll it out to 90 percent of users, but leave 10 percent of the users in the old model. Then we look at it in a month, then two months, etc. I just put a note in my notebook that a month later, I will look at it. I end up looking at it every week out of curiosity, but the point is that you want to see the long-term impact even though it has proven to be better in the short term. We haven't had a case where we have had to do a complete reversal, but it may very well happen. You might find things that work better in the short term but will hurt your business in the long term.

Shah: How do you manage costs and revenues in the short term while still dreaming big? How do you know something is a long-term, sustainable money maker rather than a short-term squeeze?

---

[3] A method that businesses use for determining the best online promotional and marketing strategies.

Mehr: There are obviously two things here. One is your gut feeling, and the second one is quantifiable measures. Let's look at something very simple. Let's say you want to look at the optimal price point for your product. So let's say you want to increase the price point for your product, and you are setting it at $20 right now and you want to set it at $30.

At the shopping cart point, you separate out a small sample of your users, just a few percent, and show them a different price either as a discount or higher price point. You see whether or not the increase or decrease in demand improves your overall revenue from that small percentage, once you normalize the entire population who visit your shopping cart. If you see that the new price point is better, then you roll it out.

You say, okay, I did this short term. If I roll out the new price point to everyone, my revenue is going to go up. However, what you missed is that by increasing your price point, the number of people who actually buy at the shopping cart drops. But it doesn't drop as much as the price point increases, so your overall revenue goes up. You can do that and in the short term, your revenue goes up. It's a no-brainer. The problem with that type of thinking is that there's a caveat, and that is long term. The fewer people who actually buy from your store, the less likely they are to tell their friends or come back and purchase more. You may miss a long-term opportunity.

After a week, you decide it's a winning scenario. You decide you are going to roll it out, but there is something in the back of your mind that is nagging you. If I roll it out long term, you think, it may actually not be to the benefit of the company because [of] fewer recurring customers. It is very easy to test. All you have to do is keep 10 percent of your users at the previous price point, look at it over next two months, and see what happens to those users. Do they actually end up spending more at your shopping cart because they had recurring purchases? That is quantifiable.

Then there are strategic things like, what is the impact of this on the uptake of my product in a particular market? Those things are not very quantifiable. Those are gut feelings, and you can't A/B test them, but they are very case-specific. I am not saying that what I just mentioned will solve all problems. It solves certain problems, like testing a free model vs. a subscription model. Price points are easily A/B testable. Package sizes are easily testable. If you are selling virtual currency, what package size should you sell? How do you test that? It is very easy. Divide your population into three pieces and give them different point-package sizes. See how customers behave.

I'm not saying everything can be scientifically experimented with, but these are fundamental questions that you should be asking yourself. And for many of them you can actually measure the results.

Shah: I have seen companies either make it too pricey and alienate customers or leave money on the table by being too conservative.

Mehr: There is a way to think about that. The model that I have in mind is a graph where the X-axis is the price and the Y-axis is the revenue. At a price point of zero, you make zero money. A ridiculous price or a very high price point, again you make zero money because no one buys your product. This curve starts from zero and then goes up and then comes down. There is a peak, the revenue maximizing price point. Theoretically it is there whether you know it or not. It depends on your product and your demographics, etc., but if everything else is fixed, there is a revenue-maximizing price point. If you actually know the revenue-maximizing price point, you can do say, okay, that's the top of the peak.

However, I prefer to make 10 percent less money but have 20 percent more customers. You want to stay a little bit to the left side of the peak. It is around 90 percent of the revenue maximization point. The way I think about it is a little bit different. I don't look at it as a continuous thing.

I would try to pinpoint the revenue-maximizing price point and then find the nearest round number right before. If my revenue maximizing price point is somewhere between $20 and $30, I would shoot for $19.95. I can tell you that there is at least 20 to 30 percent additional profit you can get by optimizing your product packaging and your product pricing. If you can figure it out, you can go from a company that has no margin to a company with great margins. That is the difference. You have to be very careful with these things.

Shah: How do you take into account the cost of customer acquisition and the cost of delivering the service to make the model work?

Mehr: In reality these things aren't as black and white. The way we look at it is you have cost of acquisition. None of these are absolute numbers. They are actually a function. How much money you get from a customer increases over time and so you have an upward revenue curve. You have customer acquisition cost, which is a downward curve, meaning that if you spend a certain amount of money, you get some customers, but because of those customers, you get more customers. If you look at it that way, then you have a customer acquisition cost that is trending down and has a lifetime value of a customer that is trending up.

At some point the two curves cross and that is your break-even point. Then you want to make a margin on top of that. We look at it as basically how long it takes before we get our money back.

Shah: This is applicable to most internet-based businesses—from the day you acquire your customer, you look at how many months to break-even on that acquisition, and then can you keep the customer longer, much longer than that.

Mehr: In Zoosk's context it is very simple because it is far simpler than a lot of other companies. I actually don't know what the curve looks like for Amazon customers, but it is probably something that is a curve that doesn't plateau any time soon.

So you are looking at a curve that starts increasing. The amount of money they make from a customer increases over time, and it doesn't plateau any time soon. For those businesses, you have to first discount the revenue to present value and then compare it to customer acquisition cost. It is a different model.

Shah: This is fantastic. I am a big student of this model and have spent some time digging into Netflix and Vonage models. How much of what you can charge is a function of how compelling your product is to your customers.

Mehr: It is very dependent on that. And at what point you make the sale is also another thing. It is not for e-commerce, because e-commerce comes in a certain package. Amazon doesn't have this problem. This applies to social companies and companies like us with premium models. The trade-off you are trying to solve is at what point you are going to bring down the pay wall. How much value are you going to build before you ask the customer to pay for it?

The trade-off here is as follows: if you do it too early, you haven't built enough value, meaning you haven't engaged the customers quite enough to actually overcome the barrier for customers to take out their wallets and put the credit card number in. You are going to have a lot of bounce, meaning users come to this point on your web site and quit without paying.

However, if you do it too late, meaning you wait for the customer to engage with your game or your dating cycle or whatever for too long before you ask them for money, what happens is that the number of people who keep engaged with your product drops at every subsequent stage. So you end up with a narrow stream of really dedicated users at the end, and you show a pay wall to those users and they convert, but you have lost 90 percent of the volume.

Sometimes the answer is really one of the extremes: either go ask for money up front or ask for money at the end. Sometimes that is the correct answer, but most of the time it is somewhere in the middle. You basically have to structure the money somewhere in the middle and eventually you increase the pressure. That's the premium model, and a lot of web companies who actually market to consumers these days are doing this model.

Match.com doesn't have this problem, or maybe it is a problem but they don't do it. They ask for a subscription up front. They don't have a premium model.

Shah: Can you give me an example?

Mehr: Skype is a good example. Let's say I open up a Skype account for the first time as a user. Skype can do multiple things. It can, say, require you to pay $10 to buy these many minutes to be able to make international calls. It is up front. Or it can say your first hundred hours of calls are free.

In the first approach, they are going to have a very high volume of people who hit that page, but they bounce. In the second scenario, a lot of people would never hit the hundred hours of international calls. Either they turn over or they stop using it, or whatever. So there is a point in the middle. You tell the user, oh, you open the Skype account and we will deposit $2 to your account for free. So you put [up] the wall [but] not all the way at the end, you put it somewhere in the middle.

Shah: What are some of the key characteristics for success as an internet entrepreneur?

Mehr: Of the successful entrepreneurs in web companies that I have seen and respect, a lot of them can handle performing in paradoxical situations. The paradox is between being a leader and manager and the paradox between being an individual contributor and a team member.

Let me give you an example. Jeff Bezos,[4] one of the people that I really respect, goes and sometimes works as a shipping clerk. He says, "I want to understand this particular role—what is the best way to do it?" You have multiple ways to do it. Let's say you're the CEO of Amazon and you want to know if there are new ways to improve inventory management. You can get a bunch of consultants to go and talk to people and compose a 100-page PowerPoint for you. Or you can do what Jeff Bezos does and work as an inventory worker on the ground. Assume that role for a day, and that is a much faster, much better way of figuring out what is going on in the company. You hit different functions.

---

[4] Founder and CEO of Amazon.

That is one of the things I do. It is easy for me to bury myself in management issues. I reply to e-mails and deal with the board and all that. That is a good skill set to have. However, I think a successful entrepreneur that builds a great company not only does all the CEO-level stuff, but he becomes an individual entrepreneur, meaning he goes and actually does work in that area. He sees what is going on. That gives you a much better perspective the day after, when you go back and you are doing your management role—you know what is going on in that particular function. That is something I have seen others do, and I have done it myself, and I find it very effective tool.

Now we have forty-five people. There was a time when I knew everything that was going on in the company from marketing to engineering to management to legal to financial to everything. Right now, I can't. Now I focus two days a week on very specific issues. I just go to that aspect of the product or I go and sit down next to marketing people and work with them for a day. Or I go and sit in the customer support area and take on one of the e-mail queues. It is really easy to lose sight and forget and not know what is going on, on the detail side, if you just do what I call "busy work"—responding to e-mails, board meetings, and dealing with management issues.

Shah: What is a key to creating the sustainable competitive advantage beyond initial competitive lead?

Mehr: If you have the luxury of having a business that has a competitive edge built in—let's say you have a secret formula or a patent, or the network effect—you should try to go into those businesses to start with. They are easier businesses. Nothing is easy, but once you have built it, you can hold on to it for a while. This is the first category. In this category, you generally don't have to worry about your competitive edge unless there is a correction. The only thing you have to do, other than all the details of funding a business and optimizing it, is to look for paradigm shift.

The second category of companies is where the barrier to entry is low or there is nothing protecting you. In those companies, it usually comes down to quality of service or exceptional execution, as in retail stores or fast-food chains. That is a completely different category. I don't like those companies. I don't want to create one of those, but if you are in that business, you are in a completely different business. You have to be super-efficient and operationally everything has to work perfectly.

In general, if you open a sandwich shop and your next door neighbor opens another sandwich shop, you are in trouble. There is no network effect so to speak. If another sandwich shop serves a slightly more delicious sandwich than you, almost all your customers switch to it. You can still succeed in those businesses by focusing on brand, on customer support, customer experience, atmosphere, whatever. So you can succeed in that, but your customer is in a completely different ball game than what we were talking about in the first category. It is not about the trends or getting ahead of the curve, etc. It is more about execution and excellence in operation and customer support. It is a different game.

Shah: What are the big companies that come to mind who are doing this the right way?

Mehr: In the first category, I think Google is an amazing company. They have a product that has 90 percent of the market. It is very difficult to go against Google for a variety of reasons. They have a killer product, which is their cash cow.

And they have Google Labs. Eric Schmidt[5] has a very interesting philosophy. He believes in experimenting with many, many different things and taking what works and scaling it up. That's what Google Labs does. They have hundreds of projects that die and never make it out of Google Labs. They have one or two that succeed and they take it up. That's how you create the killer company and continue succeeding.

Shah: One thing many first-time entrepreneurs struggle with is raising money. What advice will you give to them?

Mehr: I learned a lot about it myself by going through the fundraising process. The first thing that I always say is that if you have the luxury of building a business that doesn't require venture capital or even a company getting to a point where you don't need more venture capital, shoot for that.

When we tried to raise money the first time, it was very hard. We didn't have much of a business, and it was really hard. Once we began to make a little bit of money, all of the sudden it became a lot easier because I could tell people I make $200 a day and I can pay my rent, so I don't need to raise the money. This has happened throughout our funding. We have always taken the company to cash-flow neutral right before fundraising.

Many people would give you advice that is the exact opposite of this. I have my own philosophy about this. When you present to a VC, your approach should be, "I am comfortable right now. I want your money to scale up." VCs love that. That is my experience. If you have the luxury to do that, that is the best thing. Not every business can do that, obviously, but many web companies can because really the cost of building an application is not much.

---

[5] Chairman of Google.

So it is a matter of whether you can figure out your monetization early on or not. You should be able to figure out your monetization. Otherwise, VC money wouldn't help you anyway.

The other thing I noticed is the more desperate you feel or that you come across for money, the worse off you are. Your attitude should be, "I am going to make it somehow, someway. This train is not going to stop. This train is going. You tell me 'No'—I don't care. I will either go find someone else to finance it, or I am going to put it on my personal credit card, or I am going to change my business model, or I am going to turn on the subscription model and increase the price. I am going to somehow figure this out. If you want to jump on the train and go along for the trip, I will be more than happy to have you. I am going to get to point B. I am on the way. You can hop aboard and help me out, or don't waste my time."

You give them that attitude, which should be your attitude regardless of whether you are presenting to a VC or not. I talk about attitude more than anything else when presenting to VCs because while everything else is specific to your business, attitude is common across all start-ups. I have seen actual VC presentations like that come across as, "I have a plan and my plan would work if you give me $10 million. I wouldn't be able to pull this off if I can't raise $10 million. If I can't get the $10 million, I can't execute on this plan."

To the contrary, I say, "I am going to dominate this market regardless of whether you invest or someone else invests. I don't care, so we are going to figure it out. Here are fifty different ways I am going to make it happen depending on whether or not I can raise capital. I am going to figure it out by trying one of these things and I am going to take it to point B. If we get capital, then these other doors will open up that make our job easier and make us go faster and grow bigger, faster."

Shah: You show Plan A and Plan B. Plan A is your default plan and Plan B is how plan A transforms if you add more capital to it.

Mehr: We can do this, or we can do that, or we can do that. If you give us this much money, we can do this. You can elaborate on two or three of them. The point is you should go in with the attitude that I am going to win anyway.

Shah: What advice would you give to fellow entrepreneurs, especially those who are running internet-based companies?

Mehr: A lot of times it is easy to be lazy and just assume certain things about your customers. But more often than not, you are wrong. More often than not you either overestimate or underestimate your customer's willingness to pay. You can experiment with it, and it is quantifiable. If you are not quantifying it, your competitor is.

You might be leaving out 20 to 30 percent of your revenue on the table. If you are leaving your potential revenue on the table—and you are in an internet business and you don't have strong barriers to entry—the competitor will catch up with you in the long term. You better start experimenting now.

Shah: Many start-ups think of an exit as an end-game or final milestone of success. What is the end-game for you and what role does that play in your day-to-day operations?

Mehr: I actually have a slightly different view on that. I think exit is the definition of success for a VC or for an investor, because they want to increase their portfolio size and show return on money, return on investment, and go and raise more funding. I am not saying that's a bad thing, but that is a VC thing.

I think a successful business person actually builds a business or has the mentality that I am going to build this business to dominate the market. This is a long-term thing, and I am not here for the short term. If you have that approach, short-term opportunities open for you because you build companies that have the momentum to keep going. A lot of short-term opportunities for exit do come along and then it becomes a personal decision. Do you want to keep the company public and continue running it, or do you want to sell it and still continue running it, or do you want to sell it and get out and do some other business?

Your attitude as the manager of the company is different from your attitude as the investor in the company. You should always remind yourself of that. You are not building a company to exit in two years. I am not building a dating site to sell it to a bigger dating site in a year. That has never been our attitude. Our attitude is we are going to build the biggest dating site, the most useful dating site. It's a "take over the market" approach, and that is still our attitude. That means I consider myself in this business forever.

However, in the process, during this journey, if there is an exit point, I might think about what is the best way to approach it. Investors see the business going up. They obviously don't want to exit yet, but at some point, they want to exit. There are solutions for that. There are always private equity firms who come and give investors the return on the investment that they want. You, as an entrepreneur, shouldn't be thinking about it. VCs should be thinking about it.

Howard Morgan

Idealab: Overture/GoTo, Citysearch, eToys, Snap
First Round Capital: Mint, myYearbook

Howard Morgan is a pioneer of venture investing in internet start-ups. His research on user interface technology and optimization of computer networks led to his bringing the ARPAnet, a precursor to today's internet, to Philadelphia in 1974. As a managing partner of First Round Capital and director of Idealab, Howard has been involved with many well-known start-up successes, like Overture/GoTo (sold to Yahoo! for $1.6 billion), Citysearch ($3.5 billion IPO), CarsDirect, myYearbook, and TweetUp. Howard currently serves on a number of public company boards, including Franklin Electronic Publishers and Internet Brands, as well as a number of private companies, including Energy Innovations, Evolution Robotics Retail, Snap, MagicWorks, and Math for America.

I have been a big fan of Howard's sharpness and clarity of thinking in analyzing internet trends and start-ups, and combing them with a unique methodology for testing start-up traction to make "fast fail" decisions. In this interview, Howard draws from his investments and his pioneering work on the internet to provide us rare insights into how he picks promising ideas and entrepreneurs, validates customer needs, picks "A" teams, and builds companies for successful exits.

Tarang Shah: Why do start-ups fail?

Howard Morgan: Well, [there are] two reasons why they fail ... people do not buy their product, that's number one. Number two is being undercapitalized. They do not have enough money to sell it after they have it built.

I think much more rarely they cannot build it. In today's world, that is less common, mainly because we usually do not see the product until they have built a pretty good prototype. Certainly in the software side of the world that is true. In the hardware side, it is a little tougher. Then of course, [there are] people issues.

Shah: Why don't some of the most promising products take off?

Morgan: The product may not be enough better than what is out there now, so you cannot get behavior change. People do not change behavior easily. There is huge inertia.

Shah: So not as revolutionary, but more incremental and people will not change for incremental benefits.

Morgan: VHS and Beta. Beta was better than VHS, but there were too many incremental network effects. We see a lot of better social networks than Facebook, but to try to get 500 million people to shift is not easy and not very likely. The mistake is you see something that could be a better product, but it is not so much better that it will force the inertial shift.

Shah: What is your ideal start-up?

Morgan: The ideal start-up is a start-up with an entrepreneur who has done it before, a serial entrepreneur. A start-up where people come first. A start-up attacking a very large, established market—and the way we say it is, "making a dollar by taking ten away from the leaders." [A start-up that is] shrinking markets.

Shah: "Making a dollar by taking ten." Tell me more about that.

Morgan: Think of the media industry. You take ten dollars away from television advertising and make one dollar in internet advertising and it can be just as effective, so it is shrinking markets.

Shah: And that is because you are making it more efficient?

Morgan: Making the markets more efficient, taking the middleman out of the markets, taking cost out of the markets, and doing it in a way that will make money for you where the existing market leaders cannot do the same or have not seen how they can do the same.

Shah: Like Netflix [did] to Blockbuster and Amazon to Circuit City.

Morgan: Those are ideal start-ups. We personally prefer start-ups that are pure intellectual property so you do not physically have goods. There are a lot of companies that need physical goods, and those can be great companies.

Shah: You have been a part of many successes. Any of those that you want to particularly mention?

Morgan: Overture was created by Idealab. It was a huge success except Google then did even better. The concept originated in the next office with Bill Gross.[1] It was paid search and people thought it was crazy. Then Google made really two major tweaks to the model we had. They ended up paying for the patents, which amounted to $600 million.

But the two major tweaks they made—one was to separate the paid and unpaid results. We had shown which was which, but they were in a single list. They separated the paid ones to the right. The second was to order the advertising not on the amount or bid, but by the expected value per click. This was something that we were in the process of looking to do as well, but they got to it first and that is what drove the revenue models so high. They used the expected clicks, and they got much higher expected value. We might have had a ten-dollar click at the top, and they might have had a one-dollar click at the top, but theirs was clicked through thirty times more than the ten-dollar click, so their expected value was three times what [we] were getting. So [Google] then went on to dominate the market in the advertising world.

Citysearch had been a great success that came out of Idealab. We did Citysearch back in 1996/1997 and then IAC acquired it. And then we did Insider Pagers in the early 2000s and sold that to IAC. The yellow pages were getting tens of dollars and we were taking a tenth of that with a much lower cost structure.

Shah: So how do you pick the markets you want to go after?

Morgan: Two ways. First of all, need. You see a problem and find a solution. The problem could be, in the case of Citysearch, trying to find a local merchant and seeing what the need is and how to solve it. Most recently it was "my tweets keep falling off the search" because it is last-in first-out. What if somebody wants to pay to keep their tweet up there for a longer period of time? We created a solution. So we pick the markets, first by need and secondly by size. If you want to make a billion-dollar company, you better go after a market that has a billion dollars in it. So need and size.

Then, we slightly prefer to disrupt existing markets—because they already have a lot of sales channels and a lot of awareness of problem—than creating completely new markets. But we will do both. You know the size already.

---

[1] The founder of Idealab, which Bill started in 1996 to create and operate pioneering technology companies.

When going after the automobile market, we know the size of that market. With solar energy, we do not know the size yet. It is a newer market. Or a robotics scenario where we have created a couple of companies and they are doing well and then the issue is we do not know what the size is because people did not know they needed these products. You are sitting here with an iPad, but nobody knew they needed an iPad or iPhone. The tablets and phones are not quite new markets, but they are really disruptive because they are providing a feature function that is so different.

Shah: Do you like to go after new markets or disrupt existing markets?

Morgan: We do both. It is easier to disrupt and we would rather disrupt an existing market because we know how to reach the customers in most existing markets.

Shah: How do you go about identifying such promising unmet needs?

Morgan: A lot of it is talking to potential users and getting a sense of whether there is a very quick reaction or nod [to], "Yes, I would use that," or, "No, I would not use that." Obviously, it is your own gut reaction after a while, particularly when it is consumer-related. So whether it is Bill Gross, or my partner Josh Kopelman at First Round Capital, we have a lot of experience in the consumer markets and we have a sense if something will work or not work. Not always perfect. Obviously, we started eToys here at Idealab and it worked for a while but ultimately didn't because the toy market was not a great one for being online at that time.

Another thing is timing. There were ideas that a lot of people came up with in the mid and late nineties that did not work. They are working now because of broadband everywhere and wide adoption of the internet as a marketplace. There is trust that you can use credit cards online. So with things that may look good, you may be too early. I have always said I invest in two stages, too early and way too early. Sometimes ideas have to be right for the time as well as for the market size.

Shah: Is the first mover advantage overrated?

Morgan: Absolutely. Google was not first, Facebook was not first. There is no question in the internet-related space [that] you do not have to be first, but you cannot be too late either. There is a time frame between the first mover and being way too late in the process. Fast followers can easily win. People seeing a trend and jumping on it a year late maybe can win, but if this huge network effect is involved, then it is harder. Foursquare has a million users now. Can you beat it? Yes. Twitter has several hundred million. Can you beat that? Hard. Not impossible, but hard. The first mover advantage is overrated. It depends on how big and how much is related to the network effect.

Shah: How do you differentiate between too early and way too early?

Morgan: One of the things is to see how long it is likely going to take to build the product or service. We tend to not want things that are going to take three to five years. Sometimes they take that long anyway, but at least going into it you want things that can get to market sooner. Because of the way that products are built, particularly internet products today, you can prototype much more quickly. We do a lot of work with what used to be focus groups, but today you just build a quick prototype, throw it up on the 'net, and see if people will use it. True test-marketing, if you will. Fast fail. We are huge believers in "fail fast and cheap."

Shah: Nowadays it's easy to develop a prototype over the weekend and send it to beta users Monday morning.

Morgan: Classic example: Mike Zisman, who was CEO of Lotus and with IBM, was a grad student of mine. He has created a company called GolfTrip-Genius.com to schedule complex programming for golf trips where you have eight people who want to play at different courses over the weekend. He built the company for $10,000 using outsourced web development in Bulgaria and elsewhere in Europe, and outsourced design firms. The whole thing came together really inexpensively and then he started to spend some more money to market it and so on.

So to get something built now can be done very inexpensively, to the point where you can then test it. So you have not lost $2 million, instead you have lost $50,000 or $100,000 and you can do twenty of those for one Series A investment of $2 to $4 million. Once it works, you put a lot of money behind it.

Shah: What do you look for to see if something is sticking or not?

Morgan: We do a number of things, depending on what kind of a company it is. We like companies where a customer comes back over and over again. I am not big fan of companies where you sell something to somebody once and then you have to get a new customer to sell the next thing to. We want repeat interactions. If that is the kind of company it is, then what you do is look very carefully at the first few months in what we call a cohort analysis.

So all the people who came on day one, how many are still coming on day ten? How many of those are still coming on day twenty? What level of sticki-ness, what level of retention? How many new customers or new looks do you have to get to replace a customer? Ten percent of the people become customers, and that is great, but the question is how long do they stay a customer? Then you have to get ten bodies in to get a new customer, but if that customer only stays there for a week, then you have to get a lot of people in. If that customer stays with you for six months or a year, better. A lot of cohort analysis is figuring out how to keep the customers.

Shah: Is there anything you look into when you say you are way too early in supporting infrastructure?

Morgan: We now look to see whether the rest of the infrastructure is there to support it. Today, with the services that somebody like Amazon offers, it is not just cloud-computing services, but their shipping services, payment services. If you are building an e-commerce company, there is so much more infrastructure available and you can do the logistics a lot better. We tend not to want things to compete solely on price. On the internet, there is a huge transparency on price. You have to provide value because price alone is hard to win on. People will cut margins.

Shah: How do you determine if the market is early vs. non-existent?

Morgan: That again is where we do the prototyping and a very rapid test to see whether or not you can force the market. We did that with Cars-Direct when we started selling cars on the internet. We were not sure that people would pay $20,000 to $50,000 for a product they would buy on the internet. We did a test where we got pricing information so we could put up a test to see whether or not people would buy a car. We put it up on a Thursday night, we drove traffic to it with Go To/Overture at the time, and the next morning we had sold five cars. We were selling the cars at invoice price, which was a cheap price. It turns out in California you cannot say invoice price, but we sold a few cars and we delivered them, which was relatively expensive to us. But the focus group said yes, people will buy a $20,000 car this way. It was not asking people if they would, it was seeing if they actually did. We made that work. That is what we try to do, to see if it is a non-existent market. You put up something and try to offer it for sale and see what the behavior is. Do people actually take the action?

Shah: Technology has come to the point where it is so easy in case of internet and mobile start-ups.

Morgan: Correct. But it's not true of our solar-energy projects where you need millions of dollars and you have to use test plants and so on to see if they will work. That is tougher, but because we know what the cost of energy is and what the trend is, and where green energy is, we have an idea of measuring what price we have to get to make it viable. We know that there is huge demand for green energy and it is only a question of if we can build it at a price that makes sense. There it is a little more complicated than the internet. There is the cost of silicon for photovoltaic. But we are also projecting learning curve cost, installation cost, labor rates, all sorts of things because you have a target to hit.

Shah: Can start-ups create trends or do they just ride them?

Morgan: Twitter certainly created a trend, if you will. They were very small. I do not think you are too small to create trends if you are creating something brand new. You can do it even if you are small. We are seeing that with foursquare. I think you can create some trends. You may not be the ultimate winner, very often the person who started the trend is not the ultimate winner.

Shah: For instance, Myspace vs. Facebook.

Morgan: Andrew Weinrich started it all with SixDegrees back in the late nineties, but again, there was no broadband or a lot of people on the 'net. So social networks really did not take off then, although all the concepts were there. Myspace really took off with a certain group. You can still slice that market. So we have, at First Round Capital, myYearbook, which is the third-largest one, but it is focused on the high-school demographic. You can slice it in other ways, but I think it created the trend in the high schools, which was not the same as what was happening with Myspace vs. Facebook.

I think the answer is you can create trends even if you are small. I think that once there is a huge player in there, then it is harder to get people away. The question is, what is that scale? Well, Facebook started in a controlled way. It went after a slightly different audience than Myspace. As that audience matured, it got them away from those who were on Myspace, moved away, and spent more of their time on Facebook. By starting these close communities at the high-end universities, they got a lot of strong usage patterns. Then expanding out of that is what got them to expand beyond Myspace.

Shah: You talked about the importance of market timing. A lot of times, we as investors find we are either at the top of the trend or just falling off the trend. One sign I see is too many competitors. Are there any other signs?

Morgan: I think prices are going way up on the venture side. Right now group buying is hot. Groupon has raised $100-plus million. We have seen thirty-five start-ups in that group-buying space. It is too late. There are ideas whose time has come. There is something about being a fast follower, but there is no room for thirty fast-followers. That usually means things are too late.

Shah: So when you see too many players, some very well-established and with strong brand names, you know you may be too late to the game.

Morgan: Yeah. You see one brand name and then you see a fast follower and then at the venture level we will see twelve business plans in a month. We know that the trend is too late.

I remember an experience back in the late nineties. We created a company called Pay My Bills, which meant that your bills got sent to them, they scanned them, then they e-mailed them to you and they would create a payment structure, even though there was no electronic billing yet. We went to AOL with it and AOL saw it and liked it. They were surprised they were not asked for an NDA [non-disclosure agreement]. Usually a company will come to us and close the blinds and shutters, and then they ask us to sign a tough NDA. Then they show what they have, and we tell them they are the fifth of those we have seen in the last month and a half. That happens very, very often when an idea is sort of right. It gets there in the air.

In that case, there were two companies that were started about the same time, PayTrust and Pay My Bills, and we actually merged them and then the company was bought. There is a notion that something is in the air and there are too many start-ups and it just does not pay to invest anymore. It is hard to pick the winner when there are so many. The probabilities are lower. So if you have a great entrepreneur, maybe we would back it, but if it is sort of the normal entrepreneur, we would back it if he or she had a new idea, but not a variation of an existing idea.

Shah: Google was the ninety-ninth to enter the search market?

Morgan: Yes, they were and they entered with some slight differences. AltaVista was arguably the best search of the time in terms of relevance, but Google, with the page rank algorithm, really did have better relevance in their results and slightly broader search at the time than anyone else. Kleiner had already backed Excite. And at GoTo we were already doing a lot of that. You would have thought, gee, another search engine. They really did have a better mousetrap and they focused really heavily on speed, response time. If you put a search term in and see how fast the response comes back, it still comes back fastest from Google.

Going back to the eighties with Lotus 1-2-3 vs. VisiCalc, user experience of speed and responsiveness does dominate and does allow you to unseat existing players. It was not just that their search was also better, it is that they loaded so fast. In fact, you can show that getting the results you wanted took longer with Google than some other search engines because with Google you get that list and you click, but the first one was not what you really wanted. Then you click and go back and forth. By the time you got to the place you wanted, you could have gotten there much faster with Bing to the right results, but the dominance is so great, it may be too late. Maybe not; Bing is making some headway. But still, that speed is a critical issue for Google. That is why the home page is still the white page with no frills.

Shah: How do entrepreneurs come up with start-up ideas—do they stumble upon huge problems or get exposure to problems in their domain areas? What have you seen?

Morgan: We have seen both. Bill Gross tends to be sensitive to his environment so when he sees a pain point for himself, he does not just let it pass by. He tries to make it better, as with the Twitter stuff or with the original Citysearch. A lot of people do not do that. A lot of people find it much harder to uncover those pain points or those needs. I do not know that there is a systematic way to do it. Maybe there is, but we have used brainstorming quite heavily at Idealab to try to uncover new ideas and new places to work on. When we were looking at building Snap.com,[2] we were trying to figure out what you could do with broadband to create a search engine. We did a lot of focus groups and so on.

Shah: On the product, we talked about the speed and usability. When you look at a highly differentiated, high-quality product, what just jumps out to your mind besides usability and speed?

Morgan: Design. Apple obviously is the master of this, using various design firms. The same thing is true of what the screens look like … physical goods where design is a huge differentiator. The design says a lot to the customer and implies a lot of quality. An aesthetically beautiful design that is also functional says "quality" to the customer.

Shah: But then I look at something like eBay, Amazon, or Craigslist and the design is so rudimentary … so 1.0.

Morgan: I do not think Craigslist is a high-quality product. I think it is a marketplace. With any marketplace, when you get enough people coming, it feeds on itself. eBay has never been a great product. Search has always been disastrously bad on eBay. If you want to search for items on eBay that are misspelled, you are in trouble. For example, "Wedgwood China," which is the incorrect spelling, gets you a huge set of listings that are more expensive than if you spell "Wedgewood" correctly. It does not autocorrect for you. Google does quite a lot of that. Those sites are not high quality in that

---

[2] A start-up focused on distributed media network on the internet.

sense, but they are marketplaces and when you have most of the market coming to you in a marketplace, then you can win anyway.

Design can be very key in differentiating a high-quality product. Then of course, if it is a software product, do good testing so it is really a high-quality product that will stand up to real stress tests. That has caused problems for all sorts of people. Scalability is important—with Twitter over the years, scalability has been a continuing problem. As it has become more and more successful, it has had a lot of scalability issues along the way. I think Twitter will succeed because they are the marketplace in this, and they have learned about scalability. They have brought in some good people now. I think there was probably a year in which Twitter was vulnerable to somebody else, but fortunately for them, nobody took them on in that period.

Shah: So it really is building the architecture from day one that you can see you want to scale to a billion people.

Morgan: If you are building something that really should get to a giant scale, then you should have the right architecture as early as possible. Otherwise, you will have to swap in and swap out. Google Buzz now is trying the same thing again, but it is still not working very well.

Shah: Going by the popular terms A players, B players, C players, what are A players to you?

Morgan: We certainly do agree with hiring A players. One of the things about an A player is that they will hire people smarter than themselves. They are actively searching for people with other knowledge that they do not have. Secondly, we look for passion about their ideas. The A players always have the passion and transmit that passion to the other people they are trying to hire. They are passionate and persistent. They are willing to suffer through the setbacks which will come, and not see them as the end of the world. Solving problems as problems arise.

Shah: Does that summarize your hiring philosophy?

Morgan: We look for integrity first and foremost.

Shah: Where does that show up?

Morgan: It shows up in people who are willing to tell you bad news quickly. The thing that puts us most at odds with an entrepreneur is when you have to dig the bad news out of them. The best entrepreneurs are always the ones who come to you quickly and tell you, "We thought X, but not X actually occurred and here is what we are going to do about it," and then give you a plan. As opposed to the ones that hide it from you for two to three months or even hide it from themselves. I think that is really one of the things we look for. That sort of integrity. Then, the passion and so on. That makes the person the leader.

Shah: You feel the passion when you meet with a promising entrepreneur.

Morgan: You feel the passion. We do a lot of reference checking. You cannot do anything else. With the amount of information available today, both on the web and our network of friends and so on, it is rare that we cannot do some checking on people. If we do not know them, there is probably someone we know who does and preferably someone that we know that is not in their reference list so we get some independent validation. It is important to build an A team. The other thing about A players in general is they will not settle. They will wait an extra three weeks to hire even though there is a job that has to get done and they will do it themselves or force everyone to work a little harder, but they do not want to settle for a mediocre person because getting rid of that person is really hard.

Shah: Are entrepreneurs in their twenties and thirties better at coming up with and building billion-dollar start-ups than the older entrepreneurs?

Morgan: Probably true, for a couple of reasons. One is, they are in touch with the newest trends more so than the older entrepreneurs. Secondly, because they are less encumbered in their personal lives and they are more willing to spend twenty-eight hours a day at it. If you are talking about the biotech industry, I am not so sure. Certainly in internet related start-ups, you have Yahoo!, Skype, YouTube, and so on.

Shah: Do serial entrepreneurs have a higher probability of success than first-time entrepreneurs?

Morgan: I have seen some data on that. I think part of the problem is that serial entrepreneurs have a lower probability of failure, but the outlier success is probably not higher. They know more ways to not fail and to exit gracefully, but I do not know that there is a huge difference in the giant success.

Shah: There is no billion-dollar idea, but just a billion-dollar execution. What is your definition of great execution?

Morgan: I like to quote Stephen Sondheim from one of his songs—"Having just the vision is no solution. Everything depends on execution." We see that over and over again. Again, the same vision, the same company idea comes to several people and the ones that execute the best are the ones who win. Executing best to me means speed, great design, and a real marketing plan. A real understanding of how to reach the customer base and get them in there.

A go-to-market strategy, in the technology world, is sort of the "influencer strategy." How do you reach the influencers very quickly?

With Tweet Up, we orchestrated a campaign which got us in twenty-one major publications on the first day. *New York Times*, the *Wall Street Journal*, *Forbes*, *Fortune*, TechCrunch. By the end of the day, everyone inside the industry knew about it and were telling all their readers and followers about it. So we reached thousands of key people really quickly with that strategy.

Of course, Steve Jobs is *the* master of all this by creating suspense and trying very hard to maintain the level of suspense prior to the actual product launch or announcement. He has great go-to-market strategy. Being ready to sell something when you actually announce it, it is very difficult. Sometimes you cannot do that. If you are selling through a retail channel, then the buyers have to see it so you have to get them excited and that may be months before the product is physically in the stores.

One of our companies, Evolution Robotics, is starting up with a new cleaning system called Mint. Mint uses a Swiffer pad, so it is really meant for hard-surface floors. It is not a vacuum, it is a cleaning tool. Because it is square, it actually gets into corners and because of the way its robotics systems work, it does not do random coverage, it actually does complete coverage. It knows where it has been, it maps the room. We started showing that at CES[3] and then at the housewares show[4] and now we have huge sets of partners in the retail chain who are going to take this when it actually gets into the delivery cycle later in the summer. But the go-to-market strategy was to make sure all the key buyers get to see it early so they can put it in their plans for the fall. That means that we have been on a number of the top TV shows that focus on housewives, etc. There is a lot of pent-up demand now for the product, before it is released. We have a lot of buzz going. It looks great. We have done videos and so on, so we are doing things to get that strategy there. You want to mine the social networks. People trust their friends more than they trust an ad. First they trust their friends, then they trust editorial coverage, finally they trust advertising.

Shah: Does a better go-to-market strategy win over better product?

Morgan: Yes, the better go-to-market strategy wins over the better product. If [the product] is 20 percent better, probably, but if it is 200 percent better, maybe not. If it is two companies with relatively similar products, one is a bit better, the better go-to-market strategy will win.

---

[3] An annual international tradeshow by the Consumer Electronics Association.

[4] The annual International Home + Housewares Show.

Shah: How important is it to nail the business model early on?

Morgan: I think it is business specific. It is not like 1998 where you could just get a lot of eyeballs and you could figure it out later. I think, first of all, we have figured out a number of such models. Secondly, there is a robust advertising infrastructure, so if you are something that is fundamentally a media property, you can figure out some of that model right away. There are 400 ad networks you can use to generate revenue. You can look at what CPMs [cost per impressions] you will get. If it is not a media-type property, then we do want to know something about the business model.

I was just looking at a deal where they will be selling to hospitals. I said to them, "The problem when you sell to hospitals is, who is paying? The insurance companies, hospitals, patients?" Understanding the business model in healthcare has become very critical, especially since nobody knows what the new regulations are and how the pieces are going to fit. That is a system that is partly broken because the incentives are in the wrong places. If you show that using this particular system will save lives and money, whose money is saved and can you get them to pay? The problem is that too often the money that gets saved is by somebody other than the person who you have to get to pay for it. That does not work for long-term things. We do want to understand the business models. As far as the scalability of the business model, yes, because we want to know how big this could get.

Shah: What do you look for early on?

Morgan: We have been looking lately if it is something that has predictable revenues. A service where the revenues get very predictable very quickly, while you keep adding customers. Enterprise sales. We have reviews on hundreds of the top *Fortune* 500 sites. Each time they add a customer, we look at the monthly recurring revenue and it just adds to the whole thing. It makes the revenue very predictable because you know at the beginning of the year you have at least one-year contracts with people and now the sales team's efforts are more devoted to getting new customers to add to that and a little bit devoted to maintaining and renewing and giving the quality service to recurring customers. Those types of models are the ones we love.

Shah: You build modular blocks and then you just multiply the blocks.

Morgan: And because the customer you sold on day one remains a customer for years and is paying you for years. You do not have to keep finding a new customer every day. Retention is very key. The other is sustainability. Competitive advantage is something we look for right away. If there is an existing market here, how is this better? We ask how easy will it be for the competitors to copy this. Sometimes sustainability comes from intellectual property, but in general, patents are mostly defense and it takes years to make money from patents. So the sustainability issue is how difficult is it? Is there a piece of know-how that the competitors do not have? How quickly can you grow features so that your advantage continues to grow over time?

Shah: Eventually, all emerging trends face tremendous pressure towards commoditization. That is where many start-ups falter and lose out to somebody else. What do you do to sustain competitiveness?

Morgan: One thing is, when there is a network effect, you can build it. Facebook is not threatened by the commoditization of social networks because they have a network-effect working for them. That beats commoditization for a while. Maybe with eBay, put something on mobile devices, location devices. The sustainability is trying to get a network effect and try to stay enough ahead by additional useful features and keep in touch with your customers.

Shah: And keep embedding yourself deeper into the customer workstream/lifestyle so it becomes hard to unseat you.

Morgan: One of the things we look for in a start-up is if it's trying to dislodge an existing player. How easy do you make it to switch? Can I suck down all of your Twitters, if I was going to compete with Twitter, so I can take all your existing data instantly? Things that help your customers shift to you from what they are using now can be really important tools.

Shah: You guys invest very early so your metrics are very different than Series B or C investors [later-stage investors].

Morgan: We do create milestones before we invest with the entrepreneur. They are typically sort of related to product release, estimated number of customers that they will have at different stages, some of these cohort numbers. If it is something that is supposed to go viral, we target the matrix of what that is. Those are critical to us. We are always looking at how they are doing against their budgets. Are they over- or under-expensed? Have they met their dates? In terms of release dates, etc. Those we track very carefully at the seed stage.

Shah: Is there one thing that really sticks out that is a great thing on the map?

Morgan: Customer acquisition. Mint was trying to get 5,000 customers and then announced at TechCrunch and they got 17,000 sign-ups that day. It was clear that they had struck a nerve. We look at things like that. More top line. Unless the costs are out of control, more top-line issues, which is what is telling us that there is a market there. Is there a market there, do people use it, and then do they stay? Then we do an analysis to see if they are still using it a week later or month later. People will try it and if none of them come back, then you do not have anything. Those are the metrics that are most critical.

Shah: When do you know that there is no Plan B? That is a tough decision for investors to make. What is your experience?

Morgan: Because of the way that we invest at the very early stage, we are actually pretty brutal about it. We try to set the proper expectation with the entrepreneurs that these are the milestones that we have agreed on. If you are not making them, we are not going to keep investing. We do have the money to do A rounds, B rounds, and so on, but what we are really focused on saying is, this is the contract. We would rather fail cheap.

First round of our model is to do twenty $500,000-investments a year and then to follow on heavily on the ones that met their milestones, but not to follow on the ones who have not. We can fail if we only lose $500,000, whereas if we succeed, we may have millions in the company, which is exactly what we want. We want the percentage of our capital in the successes to be very high. We are not as focused on the percentage of our successes. We are trying to be a little tougher on that than the classic A-stage venture capitalists are.

Shah: That's a good point. As investors, we know the maximum we can lose, but the upside is unlimited. How often do you pivot and what is key to successful pivot?

Morgan: I'd say about one-third of our companies make a major pivot somewhere along the way. Most recently Fab.com, which started out as a gay social network, has pivoted to being a daily deal for design and furniture. The key to success is making sure the domain knowledge of the founders remains relevant to the pivot, and to always be listening to the customers.

Shah: As an early stage investor, what is your investment philosophy—do your build for an exit or just build a great business and the exit will come?

Morgan: We really think we are building a great business. Exits will come. We say build a great business with great cash flow. It really is all about free cash flow in the end. Then we will figure out the exits later. What we do like is to make sure that the entrepreneurs know that they should not take too much money too early because that allows them to have earlier exits that are very healthy for them. It is fine to have a $150-million exit if you only have $5 million in. If you have $60 million in, that may not be close to what venture investors want.

Shah: In our research, we are focusing quite a bit on what I call "capital multiplier" (exit value as a multiple of money invested in the start-up). It's very interesting to see a number of $100 to $250 million exits with better capital multipliers than some well-known exits like PayPal.

Morgan: It is logical. We talk about it with entrepreneurs. We talk about the fact they can go from Philadelphia to New York and can get there in an hour with no stops along the way. If you take the regular Amtrak train, you stop in Trenton, Newark, etc. You can have a $30-million exit or $70-million exit or $150-million exit, but once you have taken that $50 million, you have to go for the billion-dollar exit. Those are hard and less common. Statistically, they are extremely uncommon.

Mint, which was acquired by Intuit for $170 million, was a great exit when you really did not put that much money in.[5] The capital return ratio is huge. That is really what our limited partners [investors who invest in the venture funds] are looking for, what is the multiplier. Cash-on-cash multiplier. What you want to know is if I put a dollar in your fund, how many dollars do I get back? It is nice if I get it back sooner. I would rather get $5 back now than get a dollar back in a year, and then wait the two or three years for the rest. The fact is, Google-type returns are so rare as to be something you do not plan for.

The fund that had Google in it returned $3.1 billion to investors out of a billion-dollar initial fund, $3.5 billion of which was Google. There was a lot of money put in different things that did not work. The one that worked, worked so well and it covered a lot of that. By the way, that is not a bad strategy. Because they see the best deals and they have great people, they are able to make that strategy work. A lot of other funds have not been able to make that strategy work.

Shah: What would be your advice to someone trying to build a high-capital multiplier or a billion-dollar company?

Morgan: Keep sensitive, in everything you do, to the pain points you feel. Where you feel that pain, see how you can solve it. That is the key.

---

[5] It had raised $32 million over three financing rounds, giving it a capital multiplier of 5.3×.

Tim Draper

DFJ: Baidu, Skype, Overture, Hotmail, Parametric Technologies, Focus Media, AdMob

Timothy C. Draper is the founder and a managing director of Draper Fisher Jurvetson (DFJ). It was his concept to use "viral marketing" in web-based e-mail that was instrumental in the successes of Hotmail and Yahoo! Mail and became a standard marketing strategy used by businesses worldwide.

Tim serves on the boards of DoAT, Glam, Meebo, Prosper, Socialtext, and DFJ Plug 'N Play companies. DFJ's previous successes include Skype, Overture.com, Baidu, Parametric Technology, Hotmail, PLX Technologies, Preview Travel, Digidesign, and others.

Tim is responsible for launching the DFJ Global Network, an international network of early-stage venture capital funds. He has been listed among the 100 most influential Harvard alumni and has ranked on the Forbes Midas List. He was named an AlwaysOn Top Dealmaker (for venture capital) in 2008 and he was awarded the Commonwealth Club's Distinguished Citizen Award for achievements in green and sustainable energy. Tim's blog is featured at www.theriskmaster.com.

Drawing from his investments in Skype, Baidu, Parametric, and Hotmail, Tim provides a great insight into what it takes to build a billion-dollar success story, including how he picks promising markets and entrepreneurs, how to build great teams, and how to avoid common mistakes in building start-ups. What I love about Tim is his knack for identifying promising entrepreneurs, trends, and companies—from the internet to enterprise software and from the United States to China—and turning them into billion-dollar successes.

Tarang Shah: Tim, what are your thoughts on why start-ups fail?

Tim Draper: Well there are a lot of reasons. The first one is that they run out of money and run out of energy. The great entrepreneurs, they go and go and go and run on fumes, and keep their company alive. So it really has to do with runway. The company has to be able to be in business long enough for people to start to notice them. So how you would fail, it would be that runway ends either sharply or too soon. The runway can end sharply like when a bank calls the loan, or an entrepreneur just gives up and quits, or a number of other ways. People don't get along and don't believe anymore. Those kinds of things can happen.

Now, there are a lot of red flags when people on the team don't get along. And it's okay if they are not personally happy with each other, but it is not okay if they are second-guessing each other and they don't have faith in each other's decision-making ability. So, that doesn't work. I also think that there is one real red flag if it's missing—the motivation of the founders should be pure. They should have the attitude, "We want to make this fundamental change in this fundamental market." If they are just after the money or just after notoriety, then they don't have the right motivation. They have to have the motivation to build and be a successful company in an industry where they feel that they are doing it the right way and other people are doing it the wrong way. So they can fail if their motivations are not pure.

They can just have bad luck. They could lose a big customer or have something just go wrong in their business and that can cause failure. Usually, it's people though. It's usually the people that lead to failure.

Shah: In the age-old debate about market vs. people in building billion-dollar successes, what is your take?

Draper: Well, I think it's just people that get the thing off the ground. If you are going after a big, happy market, that really helps you grow bigger and faster than if you are going after a small, difficult market. So it's the enthusiasm of the people that gets it off the ground from zero to somewhere. Those are the people that make it happen.

Shah: When you picked Hotmail as an investment, what was your investment thesis on the market and team?

Draper: There was a situation where there was some good luck, too, because when we funded it, we didn't really have a way of marketing the product. And then in the board meeting, I came up with viral marketing. That made it hot, and it spread very quickly to all its users. So, part of that was good luck and it was good work on the part of the team along the way, because that wasn't part of the original plan. But, the people there were very good, very confident, optimistic, and they were talented. I think that was very much a people opportunity and then once it took off, it was a market opportunity. It reached hundreds of millions of people over time.

Shah: When you made the original bet, did you see a huge, underlying, market need?

Draper: No, we really invested in just a couple of great people and we had good sense that e-mail was going to be very important.

Shah: Especially web-based e-mail.

Draper: Yes, web-based e-mail was getting to be even more important because it was getting through the isolated networks.

Shah: What attracted you to Skype?

Draper: There again, we ultimately identified a trend. There was a new technology out there, peer-to-peer [P2P] technology that was going after something different and I knew that it was taking off with music. We knew that there was a lot of difficulty with the music industry in making the peer-to-peer music-sharing business work. I knew there were going to be other applications with peer-to-peer technology. It was something I always wondered about. You know, how you could use all the computer power of the world and bring it all together. And that was something very exciting.

So when the [original] Kazaa[1] team left Kazaa, they had sold it or whatever, we thought it would be a fantastic opportunity to call them and find out what they were doing next, and so we called them. But if they weren't really extraordinary people, we never would have funded them. It turned out they were. Niklas Zennström and Janus Friis were both quite extraordinary people, and so we funded them. We knew we had an enormous market with Skype. I mean, think of all the telephone companies in the world—that had to be a huge market even if we were going to make the market lower cost for people. We knew we had a huge market, and so after a certain point that was a market call. It started out with a good change in technology that was going to create new opportunity, and then finding really good people that were going after that change and then the market itself.

Shah: And the company was great at combining P2P with VoIP [Voice over IP]. VoIP was still emerging as a trend or being talked about as something that had huge potential to disrupt the telephone industry. Did you particularly like that combination?

---

[1] A peer-to-peer music sharing company pioneered by the founders of Skype.

Draper: Actually, the thing that I got excited about was just the peer-to-peer technology and then going after some new market with it, because any new market with that technology was going to be very exciting. And so, the fact that we ended up in the voice, and ultimately in the voice and video world, was incidental. When I met the team at Skype it was a different idea. And I still was willing to fund them.

Shah: Because you knew these guys would figure it out?

Draper: Yeah.

Shah: You probably see twenty people a week with new business plans and you decide to fund a select few over the course of a month or quarter. What stands out to you in the entrepreneurs who build billion-dollar companies vs. ones who fail or don't produce great returns?

Draper: Well, it's interesting. The ones that build billion-dollar companies have all been very strong, confident, charismatic people. And, the ones who we fund have been people who were completely dedicated to what they did, who were so focused on what they did. It wasn't really about the money and it wasn't about the notoriety—it had to do with them saying this is a better way to do something. And once it's a better way, then they become at least good opportunities for funding. It takes at least one person who is singularly and completely dedicated to the mission, and maybe another person who is just strong and charismatic and a leader, and maybe that's the same person. But to get really big, those are the people characteristics.

Shah: What's the difference between someone trying to change the world vs. trying to build a big business?

Draper: I think the mission helps people do the extraordinary. Building a business is a skill. Changing the world is a mission. People are attracted to the missionary.

Shah: Have you seen usually a group of two or more able to pull it off better than just the single person as a founder?

Draper: Yes. Except one of our investments, Baidu, was really a single person with a good team behind him. Skype was really two people and Hotmail was really two people. You need that.

Shah: In our research, we are seeing a consistent pattern of multiple co-founders in the majority of billion-dollar successes.

Draper: Our company Parametric had two founders as well. The founder was a brilliant Russian technologist, and they hired a CEO, who was a young, very young man—Harvard MBA. And that was a good combination.

So, yeah, often two is a good number because they can bang things against each other and make decisions as a group. And if they have different skill sets, they can trust each other with the ability to do this or that.

Shah: Are there criteria you use to assess if the emerging trends have potential to create billion-dollar markets?

Draper: There are a lot of ways to look at that. One is to look at markets with relatively high P/E [price/earnings] ratios in the public market. Look at big public companies and where they have created those big companies. There are some enormous public companies in medicine, energy, technology, and automotive sectors. These are things that people really care about and they are willing to pay a lot for and they need it over and over. Also, there are big consumer companies. So, you look and you say, well look at these concepts and they are possibly badges for what this new company is doing, and you say, oh, it's going to become quite big. That's one way to look at it. Another way to look at it is, here's how many total customers there are and here's how much they will have to pay us every year. How big is that?

Shah: Is it better to disrupt existing markets than go after new ones?

Draper: Yes.

Shah: For Skype, you looked at the telephony market and players like AT&T. And you could see the market had sized itself and it was huge. The number of customers they had and money these players were making was just huge. Then it was just a matter of disrupting it with a great technology.

Draper: Precisely. We knew the overall market for long-distance telephony would shrink in dollars, but it would grow in people.

Shah: And then you were looking at the emerging trend of P2P, though its first application in music had challenges due to copyright issues. But you could see what P2P technology can do.

Draper: Yes. And it's really technology that makes our business hum. You get a new technology or a new concept for how people do something, whether that's a new way for people to send e-mail [Hotmail], a new way for people to talk over the phone [Skype], new ways to search in China [Baidu], or new ways to design and develop mechanical tools [Parametric]. Those all were new technologies coming into existing markets and changing the way people did things. You earlier mentioned there's an old war between people and market. It's also the technological change and how that applies to the market. That's where we have been able to identify good opportunities.

Shah: Almost every successful company had its predecessors that tried to do something with the technology but failed because the concept didn't have the mass market appeal yet, or because the technology wasn't commercially viable. Do you believe market timing is important in building start-ups, and if yes, is there a way to look at something being too early or too late?

Draper: I don't think market timing is important in building start-ups. Start-ups have their own natural timelines. But I think market timing is pretty important for venture capitalists because we have invested too early on many occasions and then too late on others. Too early when, say, it's the only company in the field, and it's trying to break new ground, and there's a lot of science involved, and a lot of trial and error, and the product doesn't get quite ready for market for a long time. Too late in that maybe there are three or other four players in the market already, and they are already bigger and growing faster than our company is. So, yeah, market timing for us venture capitalists is really important.

With entrepreneurs, I'm not sure if that's market timing or luck or whatever. They've got to get their job done. They've got a mission and it's to get their company's vision executed well. They have to figure out how that applies to the marketplace and how they can "product-ize" it as fast as possible so their customers can get them feedback.

Shah: Is the first-mover advantage overrated?

Draper: No, but it helps to be the first mover.

Shah: If we look at players like Skype, eBay, Google, and Facebook, they all enjoy disproportionate market share in their respective sectors. Is there a window of time when you can build a search engine like Google or an online auction place like eBay or a P2P calling-service like Skype? And once that window closes, are you too late to start a company in that sector?

Draper: Google was way late in the market and they still ended up winning the big market. Once the world is sort of in your pocket that way, then you can keep building a business. That doesn't mean that there are no new opportunities in search to capitalize on. We made several bets on new technologies in search. Facebook is so big, but that doesn't mean that it's the be-all and end-all of the social network. But I think you've got a lot of little companies that have opportunities to come in there and change that. In fact, there were five or six social networks before Facebook became dominant. There was Myspace and Friendster and a whole bunch of others.

I think timing is a little less important than execution. But if you start a new company today, you would have a huge disadvantage because all these other companies are in existence in that market sector. But you have a huge, huge advantage in that you are taking advantage of the most recent technology available and those incumbent companies are sort of set in their ways—and that creates an opportunity to disrupt.

Shah: What stands out when you meet promising entrepreneurs?

Draper: Some of them just are breaking out of their skin. They are so excited about what they are doing, and you can tell that that's all they care about. A lot of these things will come out at the meeting—what someone is like, what they will do for success, how honest they are, how charismatic they are.

Shah: Are entrepreneurs in their twenties and thirties better at building billion-dollar start-ups than more experienced/older entrepreneurs?

Draper: Yes.

Shah: Are serial entrepreneurs more likely to build billion-dollar start-ups than first-time entrepreneurs?

Draper: No.

Shah: Some founders make it all the way to IPO as CEO and others get replaced. What are the characteristics of the ones that make it all the way?

Draper: Results!

Shah: When you meet an "A" team, what stands out?

Draper: A coordinated effort, where the team has faith in the abilities of each member in his or her area of expertise.

Shah: Is there a formula for building successful teams beyond the team of core founders?

Draper: The leader in effect creates a means that all the people in the company follow to one degree or another. Everyone in the company has picked up a piece of what that means. And, if that is the case, you know that if you want your company to act in a certain way, you're the leader, you have to act in that way.

You know, it's remarkable how if the leader smokes cigarettes, the whole company smokes cigarettes. If the leader is a triathlete, the whole company is a triathlete. If the leader is a jokester, the whole company is a jokester. They follow that leader, they actually do. You know they would argue that they don't, but they take on a lot of the characteristics of the leader, and so if you want to build a very successful company, you have to think that the things that you do are going to be followed or copied. That goes all the way down to your brand and how you treat your customers, and how you treat your suppliers, how you treat your employees, how you treat your shareholders—all of that permeates the entire organization.

Shah: How do successful start-ups go about hiring talent?

Draper: We find the best guy for the job, but he will take on the characteristics of what we do in the company, in some way or another. Potentially there's something great about that, a little Darwinian, if the leader is sort of crooked and he hires people, they all become crooked, and the company dies. If the leader is an outstanding member of society, and he has a bunch of employees, they all become outstanding members of society and they grow a big business. And if the leader has characteristics of selling too hard, the company will sell too hard. If he's too much an engineer, he's going to bring in engineers. Unless he's got a good balance, he's going to bring the team down because all they will do is engineer.

Shah: What's your definition of authentic entrepreneur?

Draper: I just call authentic entrepreneur anyone who is creative enough to break into a new market and dynamic enough ... that people will follow him into that new market [and] be successful.

Shah: How did companies like Skype, Baidu, etc., go about building sustainable competitive advantage?

Draper: The best companies grow aggressively and take advantage of the network effects and the market dominance.

Shah: Is it important to nail the business model down early on?

Draper: Yes. Business model planning is as important as product planning.

Shah : Does one with better go-to-market strategy win over one with better product?

Draper: Yes.

Shah: What are the key considerations in deciding whether to shut down or fund more?

Draper: We usually only make the decision whether or not to invest. Shutting down the company is a different decision. But, the key considerations are cash position, burn rate, customer enthusiasm, team dynamic, availability of outside or inside capital, fund capacity with an eye to proper fund diversification, board passion, etc.

Shah: What are the key considerations in deciding whether to sell now or keep scaling?

Draper: Market size, cash flow expectations, long-term prospects, price being offered. I tend not to want to sell. Ever.

Shah: When do you know the off-track start-up is beyond recovery or Plan B? What criteria do you use in determining that?

Draper: They are spending too much money. They have lost their vision. They are hiring too many people. Customers are sitting on their hands.

Shah: How often do you see your start-ups pivot everything from product to business model?

Draper: Ideally, the entrepreneur doesn't pivot, but adjusts the vision to the desires of the customer. The best entrepreneurs are constantly innovating. A complete pivot happens about 10 percent of the time, and is successful about 10 percent of the time.

Shah: In what cases is one able to pivot successfully vs. others who take a wrong turn?

Draper: Usually the best pivots are when the entrepreneur is reacting to a fundamental change or new technology that enters the market. The worst ones are just changing to try to convince the investors to keep putting money in.

Osman Rashid

Chegg

As an entrepreneur extraordinaire, a bright idea is never far away for **Osman Rashid**, who was the founding CEO of Chegg and is now co-Founder and CEO of Kno, Inc. Osman has always been involved in start-ups or worked in smaller size companies. He is currently leading an effort at Kno to help bring education into the 21st century by changing the way students learn.

Since its launch in 2005, Chegg has grown astronomically. Osman was inspired, along with his co-founder Aayush Phumbhra, to launch Chegg's textbook rental service because he wanted college students to have convenient access to textbooks at a reasonable cost. Chegg's purpose is simple: students don't need to purchase textbooks; they need to be allowed to rent them.

As a serial entrepreneur and co-founder of Chegg, Osman gives incredible insights into how he develops start-up ideas, validates them, and goes about building a lasting culture. At Chegg, he faced the near demise of their original service, but by using insights from the failed concept and interacting with advisors he identified a latent need for college textbook rental and turned that into a potential billion-dollar start-up.

Tarang Shah: What drove you to become an entrepreneur?

Osman Rashid: I've always preferred to approach problems in a new way and not follow the trend. Entrepreneurs have an itch to do something different and dynamic, and I felt that I could only do that in the business world if I had the freedom to operate without bureaucratic chains. When entrepreneurs see an obvious problem that nobody is solving, immediately wheels start turning. I think there is a certain kind of a person who is going to be better at being a start-up person, somebody who is aggressive and not concerned about taking risks, somebody who is willing to give it all. This is something that is fundamental to building a start-up.

Start-ups are more likely to fail than succeed. You need to have the mentality that you are not going to be one of those people who fail, you will be the one that makes it and know the reason why. Your start-up idea should also be something you are personally connected to.

Unless you can really convince yourself that you have a great idea, no matter what you do, you cannot convince investors and your employees that this thing will work. You have to believe at a core level that this is a great idea, but at the same time be rational enough to challenge yourself about why it may not be, so you can solve problems and move forward. Once you believe in your great idea, you need to completely commit yourself to it. Trying to work part-time on a start-up just doesn't work. The commitment level and passion just aren't the same.

Shah: In other words, you are "willing to burn the boat to get to the other side." Willingness to take risk is key here. Is this the philosophy you tested when you were young or is this something you tried out first at Chegg?

Rashid: Burning the boat is exactly right. When we started Chegg, I left a high-paying job, had bought a second house, just had my second daughter—essentially things were going really well. My father-in-law thought that I had gone crazy!

Risk taking is ingrained in a person to some extent from the beginning, but your life experiences—whether you have positive or negative responses to your early risk taking—can shape your attitude to risk as you get older. My comfort level with higher risk could have been because my father was a diplomat and we lived in different countries and I had to adapt to different environments. I always had a positive perspective that I will go make new friends and things will work out, and they always did. So the positive feedback and experiences definitely shaped me. I was definitely the lucky one who was able to take risks early in my life and have things go my way, which makes me much more comfortable taking risks now. Somebody else who may also have taken risks early but not had things go their way would probably become more conservative in taking risks.

I had really good friends in college and some of them are still in the same job they had when they left college. I cannot even think of doing that.

Shah: You were working in a relatively small firm of three hundred people and you still felt things needed to be done faster. You wanted to be in direct touch with the customers and address their needs.

Rashid: I hate company politics. I dislike people who try to do things which meet their own agenda. Usually, the bigger the company gets, the more those kind of people show up. For me, the only approach to take is to figure out what problem we are trying to solve and have everyone get behind a solution and take care of it. Otherwise, we are wasting each other's time.

Being an entrepreneur in a start-up, you have the ability to go build a company with that mentality instead of a company that has a lot of politics. In a big company, you can see a customer or process or a product getting completely messed up because of politics. I always say I would have a hard time surviving in a big company because I would piss off too many people and I would crunch too many toes.

My philosophy in other companies has always been, well they can fire me, but this is the right thing to do at this point and this is how it needs to get done. It is a really crude thing, but the concept of "shit or get off the pot" applies. You are wasting everyone's time, so move on with your life. That is a philosophy that gets things done.

Shah: You are hitting on some of the core drivers that make people move from the cushy jobs into doing something adventurous and risky, and more importantly, something they dream about doing, like starting or joining a start-up. What is your process for coming up with start-up ideas?

Rashid: Great ideas are always around you and a person needs to be in an entrepreneurial mindset to see them. So many industries are waiting to be disrupted—you just need an open mind. Entrepreneurs who have to sit down and think of ideas—I don't know how many of them really succeed. An entrepreneur is always thinking of ideas. You are always thinking about what is going on. In the back of your head, you are always asking questions. One day you see something that makes you tip your head to one side, and say, hmm, interesting, what is that all about? Something just hits you.

I think it hits those people who have their radar on all the time. I really do not believe in sitting down at a white board and trying to make a start-up. That is too logical and it is not emotional enough, irrational enough. It may not be crazy enough for you to get passionate about it.

In a start-up, the fundamental ingredient has to be passion. So much that it can get you through the bad days. You have to fundamentally believe in what you are doing. I have a lot of friends who try to think of ideas and they get frustrated. And then this random guy shows up with a brilliant idea, and they think, wow, that makes a lot of sense. If you look around, the simplest of ideas have been the biggest of things.

Shah: This is probably why a lot of big corporations are not able to come up with ideas that really stick, because they start with the whiteboard.

Rashid: Exactly. They are trying to fit it into their own strategy or category and then they have already put a box around the idea. If you put people in the box and they aren't allowed to think outside it, then the vision and creativity are killed right there at that spot. I just find it fundamentally hard for a big company to go and do start-up stuff because it is a different mentality. Even a proven idea from a high-flying start-up would take probably six months to gain any traction internally in a big company.

Shah: What convinced you that serving the college community was the idea that you wanted to build a company on?

Rashid: The core experience of the web site you build has to be something that has importance to you in your life or something you really feel passionate about. I remember as a college student how difficult it used to be find and buy items on campus. I remember trying to buy a couch for my dorm room and I had to go all over campus to see if somebody had one. I could relate back to the experience of college.

Shah: So you set out to create a marketplace for students?

Rashid: Yes that was the original plan for Chegg, which was called Cheggpost, and we wanted to build on the small marketplace that was already running at Iowa State University, where Aayush went to college along with Josh, our other co-founder. Actually the final Chegg was Plan B, not Plan A.

Shah: And Plan A was classified ads for college students.

Rashid: Exactly, a Craigslist for colleges. It was Plan B that eventually worked for us. Plan A was a good idea, but it was not working and you could not build a big company around it. We wanted to make a few thousand hyperlocal markets and then connect them to each other.

Shah: Let's take this further. There was a very inefficient marketplace on the college campuses and you tried to solve that with the internet.

Rashid: Highly inefficient. Buying and selling items on campus was a long process that consisted mainly of posting flyers and waiting for responses. With Cheggpost, we wanted to make that whole process simple and fast. It was like an eBay or Craigslist just for your campus.

Shah: What happened to Plan A? What led to Plan B?

Rashid: The fundamental problem Plan A had was that the college was so hyperlocal. In order to launch and scale a new college campus, there had to be a certain amount of activity on it. Our number one challenge was that anytime we would open on a new campus, we would do marketing and newspaper articles, but more buyers than sellers would show up at the college Cheggpost.

In terms of customer experience, a customer will typically give you two shots before they say it is not worth it. At the start of a new semester, we would have a lot of buyers but not enough sellers, and it became pretty impossible to keep people happy. We knew on each campus that once it got running, Cheggpost would be the place for students to go. But getting it to that point at each new campus was extremely difficult.

Our big goal was to build a company which was hyperlocal and connected the universities together to one big system and make an entire e-commerce system for students. We felt that the business would not operate fast enough to satisfy our own personal desire to build a great company like that. We had a passion for building a real solution and a real company which would make an impact on students much sooner.

Shah: So in this campus marketplace, the sellers didn't have the same motivation to sell as buyers had motivation to buy?

Rashid: When students come to campus, they need things for their dorm room or apartments—so there are more buyers than sellers at the beginning of the semester. At the end of the semester, you have the opposite problem: there are more sellers than buyers. Each group had their motivation, but their timings were off. We knew that if we spent enough time on campus, we would be able to build up the content. But that would make us a different company than we wanted to be.

Shah: This is a marketplace where two equally motivated parties need to come together for the marketplace to exist and grow. Did Craigslist and eBay initially have the same problem attracting sellers?

Rashid: Cheggpost had a limited time during the start and end of the semester in which it had to generate enough transactions to justify the effort. eBay and Craigslist were different in that they didn't have to worry about small windows of time. Craigslist spent about five years in the city of San Francisco just making their web site grow before they branched out. You could not even post anything in Palo Alto. It was just San Francisco. They took their sweet time.

When we were opening up Cheggpost on campuses, Craigslist only had eighty to ninety cities in the US. It was a very slow process for them. At some point, you have a brand recognition where you can take something to another place and you can just leave it there and it will run on its own because you are very comfortable with it. But for us it was a different story.

I could see that I would have to go and raise more funding and I did not feel that I would be able to raise money on the current model. I believed that something had to be done as a CEO. We looked into our usage data to see what our customers were really getting excited about. We looked at a lot of different things and we talked about one interesting idea, renting textbooks. Interestingly enough, 80 percent of our traffic was in textbooks. Then it occurred to us, why don't we do Netflix for textbooks?

As time went by, we kept looking further into it and really believed something had to be done in this area. The pain for students was too much. The students were complaining about how little they were getting back when they sold their books back to campus bookstores. They were getting $10 back for a $100 book!

We started playing with this "Netflix for textbooks" model and we built a spreadsheet first to see if the model would hold up. Then we began to do alpha testing with the dorm students. We let them rent their textbooks from us—they paid a rental cost and then just sent the books back to us at the end of the semester. Just like Netflix.

We got an amazing response from students after that alpha test. It clearly struck a chord with them. We did more research on textbook pricing and usage and decided there was a real business model that could be supported by customer demand. We were able to make the switch to this new model because we were not afraid to look internally and see that things were not working in Plan A.

Shah: What were some of the key things you did in testing Plan B?

Rashid: We applied the philosophy that we did not want to store books in our warehouse before we knew which books were important and even what the demand for the service would be because we could not afford to. We believed we would figure out over time what the right books would be. We would use the power of the internet to take the order and run like hell to secure the order from a partner and get the book to the student.

One of the interesting things is we shipped books and did not know how they were going to come back. We did not even have a warehouse. We did not even know what we were going to do with the book coming back. First we would solve the problem of getting enough books so we can prove that customers would buy.

We focused on testing whether customers would rent textbooks. We did not worry about building an entire business. Once we knew the customers would rent the textbooks, we needed to prove that the customers would send the textbooks back. That was the big risk. People said students will cheat you and you will never get your textbooks back. But we chose to believe in the overwhelming majority of students. Sure there would be some who would cheat, but most would return the books.

We had to test and iterate on everything, from figuring out which books to rent, pricing them competitively, sourcing them, shipping and tracking them from different sources. Every part of the process was something that hadn't been done before and needed to get proven out. We made mistakes, but we corrected rapidly because demand was growing incredibly fast. At one point we had to shut down the service because we couldn't process incoming requests fast enough.

Shah: At that time you knew you really hit the nerve of the market.

Rashid: Absolutely. Aayush, our young team, and I knew we had a tiger by the tail. Our board said, wow, this could be huge. Our revenues went from only $500K in 2007 to a run rate of higher than $100 million in 2010. It was growing massively.

Shah: This is amazing. First, you had an entrepreneurial bent—you just knew you needed to do something different than work for a big company. Second, you focused on the market you were familiar with, the college campus. Third, you took on the problem you were familiar with and tried to solve it, your Plan A of Craigslist for college. And most importantly, you took some time to think about why your Plan A was not working and you tried to figure out, from the current experience and customer data, what might work—your Plan B of Netflix for textbooks. And then you tested this new concept piece by piece, very scientifically, and when you proved that students would rent textbooks, you quickly went on scaling it. Brilliant!

Rashid: Chegg had an amazing team—we had seven people doing the work of 35 people. We had so much passion for what we were doing. This team made the product real and delivered amazing service. We learned a lot from Zappos and how they treated their customers.

Shah: At what time did you go to raise more money?

Rashid: Our current investors, Rick Bolander from Gabriel Ventures and Mike Maples, really stepped up when they saw the model working. We had told them that by the time we prove that the books will return, they should be ready. I got a commitment from them in October that year that if I were to show them the model was working and the books were coming back and more orders going out, they would give us X million dollars. And that's what happened. Then we continued to build the model forward. We knew that we had to raise more money to get to the next level and then we raised a couple more rounds based on continued success.

Shah: What was key to scaling and growing your business?

Rashid: A bunch of things have to come together for a company to scale and deliver solutions like we did. For example, you could not have done what we did eight years ago because the technology to do it did not exist, like Amazon web services and co-location servers.

Things have gotten easier for the entrepreneur because a lot of things that would have stopped you fifteen years ago are things that don't stop you anymore.

Eight to nine years ago, you would have had to go bookstore by bookstore to convince them to do a model like this. We took the power of the internet and went directly to the consumer. We also did lots of innovative things. For example, the way we figured out what books to rent and not to rent, how to price them, how to buy them. Our system would place orders across the internet with any online bookstore, wherever we found the cheapest price.

We would screen online web sites and place an order to get a book out of circulation if they were the only one who had it. We built the world's largest inventory management system for textbooks. We built one of the most dynamic pricing systems in education. We could feel out what was the right price to rent a book in any given second, based on what was happening on twenty-eight different web sites.

We had unique challenges we had to deal with as well. We were purchasing tens of thousands of books within days. An online bookstore can only take a payment from a credit card online, even from another company. So we put all these purchases on American Express. AmEx called us and said, "What are you buying? You can't charge this much on the credit card." We told them we were opening a library. Every day we had to talk to them to let us continue to use our credit cards, even though we were paying them back very fast. We got to the point where my own bank debit card was being used in the system just so we could continue to process books. It was a complete expense report nightmare!

Shah: How did you eventually solve that problem at a scale?

Rashid: We talked to Visa and convinced them to give us humongous gift cards. They gave multi-million dollar gift cards that we used to rotate payments on.

Shah: Do you only buy new books or used ones as well?

Rashid: We bought them used and new. We had a scoring system to see what was the best book to buy at any given second.

Shah: This was a unique market you discovered. How did you create and maintain competitive barriers?

Rashid: I think it had a lot to do with execution and managing potential competitors before they became competitors. We put effort into convincing the competitors that what we were doing was a really bad idea, but that we were just stuck in this business model and too stupid to back out.

We had an advantage over competitors with a huge amount of usage data. With the usage data we could very accurately predict what books would be rented and re-rented. Being able to rent books more than once was critical in getting to profitability.

The usage data also helped us build a very accurate pricing system where both us and the customer would get a fair price. That was a key part of the business model. Eventually the accurate prediction of ROI on a book is what convinced the VCs that it was a viable business. There was a competitive advantage.

Shah: How did you market the service initially?

Rashid: Initially we were picked up by a lot of outlets, *Time* magazine, CNN, and more. But the biggest driver came from word of mouth—97 percent of customers told another customer. And 54 percent of those told five or more people. We spent a lot of effort on customer service. We made a decision that we would give customer service like nobody else in the textbook industry.

We went for the college customer online. We did not go for the customer on campus. We learned that if you have to do something on campus, in many cases the administration comes after you and begins to harass you after some time. You need permission to do anything on campus.

Shah: Amazon does a wonderful job with customer service. Netflix does a wonderful job. But this is a slightly different business. What were the key challenges in providing excellent customer service?

Rashid: Our biggest challenge was that as a new service, we had to use third-party partners to ship our products at times because we did not have the books. We had to depend on their delivery speed—it was out of our hands.

In the meantime, we still had to manage the customer—they were buying from us, not third-party partners, so ultimately, we had to be responsible if something went wrong on the partner's end. We sometimes had a UPS tracking number saying the book was delivered to the customer—but the customer said they never got the book. If they said they did not have it, we would ship them another book overnight without any questions asked. It was things like that which really impressed the students.

Out of millions of customers, we would have a few problems. In many cases, the book got received by the parent and the student didn't know that it was sitting on the dining room table.

Shah: Tell us more about your team and how you recruited them.

Rashid: Our team was small but completely passionate and just hardcore. We would not sleep; we'd work eighteen hours a day. The founders may have the idea, but it's the team that has to implement and deliver the end result. As I was saying earlier, people in start-ups need to have the mentality of pulling together and just making things work. And that's what our team had. There were no ego trips, no company politics. Just a team of passionate people who would move mountains to make the company successful.

The first thing I look for when looking for the start-up type of person is passion. An interview can start out being stiff and formal. But if by the middle of the interview you don't know what makes the candidate tick, you have a problem. I do not always go for the experience on the résumé, because you can never find the perfect candidate with the perfect skill set. What I really look for is the person's ability to learn and adapt. I look for people who try not to make the same mistake twice. Are they problem solvers? If it is a manager, a manager's job is to remove barriers for their own team. How have they done that? How do they communicate with their peers?

Attitude is extremely important. If you have one person that has a really bad attitude, and it somehow got through your hiring process, you have a problem because those "everything sucks" attitudes are infectious. It takes very strong people to say, "What can we do to make it work?" instead of just taking the easy way and spreading the bad attitude saying, "Yeah, every-thing sucks."

If you have passion, and if you are a problem-solver and you are the kind of person that doesn't make the same mistake twice, then you are going to go very, very far in any of my companies.

Shah: To what extent were you involved in making the decision about who gets hired or not, especially when the company grew big?

Rashid: To a certain point, I was involved in almost every hire. Once the company got to sixty or seventy people, it got a little bit difficult to do that. But by then I have hired people I trust to hire the right people. If I can't trust the people I've hired to do that, then I haven't hired the right people.

Shah: What are some of the signs during hiring that point to a potential problem?

Rashid: I look for things like, do people speak more than they listen? If I say something to them, how much did they retain of what I asked? I think one of the fundamental problems with most people is that they speak too much and they don't listen enough. Unless you are listening, you are not going to solve a problem.

Shah: Very good point. What are some of the key things that matter from the execution perspective?

Rashid: Identifying personnel related issues is key. Once I was walking around the office, and I saw that one of my project managers was sitting with a long face. I pulled her into a conference room and asked what was going on. She said she felt that she was not staying on top of the project, and wasn't sure if all the projects would come together.

I told her that you have to assume projects will keep on shifting. You have a long-term project plan. But do you know what the three things are that need to happen this week in order to keep this project on track? Focus on those things—focus on the near term.

Shah: What was your thinking process in deciding whether to continue as a founder CEO or bring someone else as CEO?

Rashid: I really prefer the earlier stage of the company where there are more questions than answers. I enjoy solving real world problems and figuring out all the details of the solution. There were so many intermediate problems to solve at Chegg to put the textbook rental solution in place, every day posed a new challenge. But then it came to a point where we had figured out the problem and we had figured out the model, and it was now an issue of just scaling it up.

Sure, the growth stage has its own set of problems, but the kind of person who enjoys that stage and has that experience should lead. I had always suggested to our board that we find someone new at this stage, because that would be best for the company. So it was never a big issue to move on for me or them.

I have lots of friends at Chegg and I have a lot of good investors banking on this company. They are counting on a great outcome. So making sure the company reaches its full potential and gives the payout to the employees that they deserve really was the deciding factor.

Shah: So you were very clear about two things: One, your personal motivation and capability, and two, what is great for the company's current stage of growth.

Rashid: And for me the company's success was really paramount. My friends worked their hearts out in the company and they want to someday be able to, for example, make a nice down payment on a house. I had a responsibility to my team to make sure they got the fruits of their labor. One of the things that pushes me to work harder is the knowledge that I can help make my employees into millionaires. If I can get a hundred people to that point, it was worth it for me personally. These people can start their own start-ups and then help a hundred more people. That's when you really start seeing an impact. So the right leadership has to absolutely be in place to get the team to a fantastic exit outcome.

Shah: This is fantastic! Now what happens when you end up with a wrong hire? How long does it take to find out, and what is your personal philosophy of dealing with this once you find out?

Rashid: My personal philosophy is that before you let someone go, they need to know that they are not performing. My first instinct is to check whether the person is being managed properly. Maybe the employee is not being set up for success. I assume that if we hire someone to do a project, they must be good at what they do. So I ask the manager what they have done to really help the employee be successful.

If it turns out that, for example, there are too many projects and the employee has to decide between quantity and quality, then that is the manager's fault. The manager may come back and say that they need to hire one more person and that was not approved. I would push back to the manager that it is his responsibility to come and tell me the three things that are going to get impacted if we don't hire one more person. Then we can decide on priority and resources.

You always have a conflict in an organization. Recently we had a meeting, where we had an argument between two points of view. I made both teams argue against their own arguments because I could see that they were not one team. They were two teams trying to get their own way without really thinking about what was good for the company. The moment they had to argue for the other side, the problem was solved—in seven minutes!

Shah: As a founder CEO, did you deliberately build the culture? Or did it came together on its own?

Rashid: I think the first twenty people really define your culture. The edge that every company has over time comes from the core people, not just from the founders.

Shah: So the real beginning of the culture starts when you hire the first ten to fifteen people?

Rashid: Yes, because that is the foundation. Because people you are hiring early on are more likely to be your future managers.

Shah: Culturally, what is one thing you have paid most attention to?

Rashid: We had a company meeting every Friday at five-thirty, where I got up and I talked about things which most companies and CEOs usually don't talk about. And, I did that to show transparency. I talked about the current state of affairs, future plans, projections, ideas we were thinking about. And I made it a point to let them know, "Look, most CEOs will not tell you these things, but I just want you to understand I am telling you because I trust you."

I also told them, "Guys, if a leak happens, you have to understand that I can't do this anymore." They knew that I trusted them. They valued that immensely. In the history of this company, there was never a credible leak from the company itself.

Harry Weller

NEA: Groupon, Opower

Harry Weller *focuses on early-stage consumer, enterprise, and energy technology investing. He is frequently recognized as one of America's top venture capitalists, with recent honors including the* Forbes *"Midas List,"* Washingtonian's *"Tech Titans," and* Business Insider's *"The 15 Most Powerful Venture Capitalists on the East Coast."*

Harry's past investments include Echo Global Logistics, Riverbed Technology (acquired by Aether Systems), Sourcefire, Vertica (acquired by Hewlett Packard), Vonage, and webMethods. Harry co-led NEA's seed investment in Groupon and served on the board.

Prior to joining NEA, Harry was a partner at FBR Technology Venture Partners, where he learned the costs and benefits of a bubble! Early in his career with various consulting firms, including the Boston Consulting Group, Harry managed technology initiatives in the energy, financial, and telecommunications industries.

Drawing from his successful track record of building multi-billion dollar start-ups like Groupon and Opower, Harry emphasizes the crucial role of human endeavor in start-up success and provides a rare window into the relationship between the entrepreneur and investor.

What I love about Harry is his deep understanding of the role of human endeavor in start-up success, his emphasis on establishing strong and trusted lines of communication between the investor and entrepreneur and how he combines that with his sharp business acumen to help build some of the best start-ups of our times.

Tarang Shah: What are the key reasons why start-ups fail?

Harry Weller: When a VC-backed company fails, it's due in part to any number of external factors, like competition or shifts in the marketplace. But in my experience, there is almost always a common thread: the entrepreneur is unable to translate a vision into execution, and the people with the most skin in the game—the entrepreneur and the investors—stop working as a team.

By nature, entrepreneurs are visionaries. They are immersed in the improbable. VCs, on the other hand—even those who have been entrepreneurs—are always calculating probability. They use domain expertise, pattern recognition, and gut instincts to assess how things are likely to play out.

The ultimate success (or failure) of a company is inextricably tied to this delicate tension between the probable and the improbable. And it can go south in a hurry if the lines of communication break down. As soon as one party seeks to "control" another—the board needing control, or the CEO or Founder needing control—the balance is lost and the company is at risk. When you're building a great company, there are so many chances to make adjustments, and many ways to realize the vision—but only if the key players are functioning as a team.

Shah: What are the early signs that tell you that communication breakdown is starting to take place?

Weller: In my experience, the process of building a strong leadership team can be met with a great deal of internal resistance, or viewed as an assault on the people who have guided the company's earliest development. Trouble often begins here. When people are threatened by bringing on new team members—and I mean executives to bolster the team, not replacement CEOs—that is, for me, almost always the earliest sign that we are going to have issues.

In order to make the improbable happen, you'd better have the best talent you can lure to your team. And that does not mean simply hiring the best CEO. It means that you bring on the best board members (if it is a great entrepreneur who can develop into a CEO, you bring in great mentor board members), and you bring in a great COO, a great VP of sales, and a great marketing executive. A team who doesn't want to be better, or doesn't recognize where it *could* be better, is simply not goal-aligned, and it's a big red flag.

Shah: Why does that resistance take place?

Weller: It's about control. If you are more worried about control than about reducing the barriers to success, then you can't appreciate how much the human element has an impact on a company's success. A great idea is only one-tenth of the story.

Shah: Tell us more about the role of the human element in reducing barriers to success.

Weller: I like to tell entrepreneurs that, at the end of the day, this is an absolutely human endeavor and nothing else. It is not a technical endeavor. It is a human endeavor. You have to remember that when building a company. Technology risks can be tackled. If the innovation does not work, we will at least know it.

Shah: And if you don't see it that way, you are going to overlook the most important success factor, the human element, and chase technology or product issues, but then fail not knowing what happened.

Weller: Exactly. To me, it comes down to this: part of a VC's job is to help mentor first-time entrepreneurs as they learn how successful companies are built. The VC's ability to help turn the entrepreneur's vision into a reality— whether by recruiting or technical acumen or market understanding—is actually more important than the capital. But the entrepreneur has to be receptive of the value that the VC really brings to the table—the knowledge and network and the been-there-done-that scenarios. And when the rubber meets the road, the entrepreneur and the VC have to establish and maintain trust and trust each other's motives. It is hard to do. I think some people misunderstand VCs and the value they can really bring to a growing company. What is the difference between a venture capitalist and a private equity firm? Well, a private equity firm deals with risk through arbitrage, through leveraging terms and valuations. They are financial engineers. That is how they manage risk.

The way a venture capitalist manages risk is through company building—not valuations, not deal terms. We cannot financially engineer away the risk. We deal with it by bringing our [knowledge of] company building to bear. They bring their financial engineering talent to bear. So the critical human element cannot be underestimated in VC.

Shah: That is the finest distinction I have ever heard.

Weller: At the end of the day, venture capital is, by definition, high-risk. How do we balance the risk we are taking? With our company-building expertise. But that only works if we can establish open lines of communication and build trust with the entrepreneur . . . otherwise, frankly, it's probably not worth the risk. VCs are minority shareholders 90 percent of the time. We do not own these companies, we own a part of these companies. Yet we can play a vital role in the company's ultimate success or failure.

Shah: It is like having access to someone on the island through a phone line and if that line is not accessible or broken, there is no way you can transfer the knowledge you wanted to the island.

Weller: That is exactly right. Quite frankly, the company becomes an island, just like you described. You can almost think of it like that. You are trying to build a civilization on that island. If you cut off all means of communication, you are dead.

We really view company-building as a partnership, and that is why I think your interviews are so important. The fact is, some people who call themselves VCs are really not. They are not really company builders, they are just rolling dice to capital. A real VC, a real VC firm, is structured as a service provider to the entrepreneur for the purpose of helping them build their business. There is nothing passive about it, and it is no surprise that private equity firms have had such a hard time going downstream to venture investing.

Shah: Most private equity funds also lack the operational expertise that a lot of VCs have. Now, is this communication breakdown the primary reason why companies fail? Let's say a communication channel is working perfectly fine and the company still fails. Does that happen as well?

Weller: It does happen, all the time. There are a lot of different reasons for that. Sometimes you build the company and the market just is not there. Sometimes you are wrong about the market. Sometimes the science does not work.

But if you do the best job you can, with the best people you can, and you are just plain wrong, that is okay. It's like a basketball game: One of the things you look for is a team creating a high-percentage shot. What I am trying to do as a venture capitalist is create a high-percentage shot by finding a great entrepreneur with a great idea. I am going to surround him or her with the best team I possibly can and make our best effort to figure out what the users want, the consumers want, or the enterprise wants.

We are going to do all these wonderful tried-and-true things to make sure we take the best shot we freaking can, as a team, as a unit, as a board, as a company, and build a great technical advisor group. We leave no stone unturned in terms of factors that we can possibly predict, and then we take that great three-point shot. If we miss the shot, we miss the shot as a team, but we all look at it and say, "That was a high percentage shot. We missed, but it was well executed, and that is okay."

But in most cases, I can look at even the best-executed failures and say that there was a communication breakdown between the team and the board. The common lament is, "If I had just done X sooner." Hired a different CEO, hired a VP of sales sooner, etc. You look back on it, and you are almost always thinking you could have done something to change the outcome. And it almost always comes down to communication.

Shah: The classic example here is when you as an investor just knew you had to cut the burn down significantly, but you could not get the entrepreneur to do it fast enough.

Weller: Yeah. Or you cannot make the entrepreneur understand why it's necessary. But it's important to say here that sometimes it is the entrepreneur who ultimately persuades the VC. The VCs are not always right. If you have a very good means of communication and a trusted relationship . . . what I call it is a coefficient of friction associated with communication. If you have a low coefficient of friction, you are just going to be more decisive and move faster. There may be the wrong decisions, but the feedback loops are tighter.

I bet if you ask anyone about their failures and what they would have done differently, they know exactly what the answer is. And I bet you if you ask them if they knew that answer at the time, probably 80 percent of the time they would say that they did know, but that they just could not get it done.

Why does this matter? Because it underscores the vital role of persuasion— either the ability to persuade or the willingness to be persuaded. Because above all, it is critical to be decisive. If a CEO and a VC lock heads about an issue and neither is able to persuade the other to act, then they are stuck in a holding pattern. The holding pattern is death for a start-up.

Shah: If we take this to the forefront of building the VC-entrepreneur relationship, when you meet with the entrepreneur for the first time, what are you evaluating to see if you can establish that low coefficient of friction communications with this entrepreneur?

Weller: A lot of people say you look for integrity. I am not one of those people who look purely for integrity. You know, sometimes the best entrepreneurs have a bit of an edge—they think outside the box, they are used to being crafty, and they are not afraid to manipulate a situation. And ultimately, that might be what sets them apart from the rest.

The qualities that matter most to me are transparency and consistency. For example, over-optimism can be a huge asset, even a necessary asset for an entrepreneur. But if I know that this particular entrepreneur is *consistently* over-optimistic, then I know that I can discount him by 20 percent every time and I will know where we are. And he will still have that crazy optimism you need to proceed in unchartered waters. I like optimists. But I need consistency and transparency.

Shah: So you can correctly assess what the situation is based on what you are hearing from the entrepreneur.

Weller: It does not mean I see things the same way, but it means that I understand their red is my pink. Ultimately, there is a transparency and consistency to it. It does not mean I necessarily agree.

The second part, absolutely, without a doubt, is they cannot be control-oriented. I think that gets in the way of everything. I want them to be vision-oriented, meaning that they understand that the best thing of all is achieving their vision. Not strangling their vision to death by controlling it.

The last thing is just an ability to hire. I think that is so important. A little bit of charisma never hurts—you want somebody who has a little bit of charisma behind their idea. If not, they [need to] have the ability to hire someone who has that charisma. There are some people who have all that it takes to be a visionary, a CEO, a company builder, but the truth is, it very rarely lies in one person.

But getting that foothold in the unknown—the sense of who and where they are—is critical. I have to understand the entrepreneur's personality and motivations, and he needs to understand how I work. You are attacking the unknown. If you are going to be dropped off in an uncharted land, do you want to be with somebody you do not understand?

Shah: And start-up building is five, seven, ten years of uncharted territory.

Weller: The whole idea is you are going into uncharted land, and I am the guy with the backpack with all these tools and things. The other guy is the one with the vision about what we are going to find. I will not be there with him unless the person is passionate. I will not be there unless I think the person is transparent.

A VC is, in a sense, taking his heart and dividing it into, say, eight pieces. At any one time you are giving each one of those pieces to an entrepreneur. They are risking your career with each of those pieces. That is how I like to describe it to my entrepreneurs. I am handing you a part of my career. I can only focus on eight things at a time, so you have one-eighth of my career in your hands. So I need to know you.

For an entrepreneur, they are giving an even bigger slice—maybe even their whole career. Do you really want to do that with someone you do not connect with, that you cannot see how they work and understand how they think? It should be both ways. Again, you are trying to get a foothold in the unknown.

Shah: Tell us the story of how you identified Groupon.

Weller: Groupon is a great example. In Groupon's case, there were three co-founders. Two of them, Brad Keywell and Eric Lefkofsky, had been entrepreneurs that I had worked with before at Echo Global Logistics and MediaBank. So we had invested in this team in the past. We had made money and really learned to trust them. Eric, Brad, and I literally could finish each other's sentences.

I know exactly how those guys think and they are a very unusual mix: highly focused on building true businesses, but at the same time highly tolerant of visionary ideas.

So they had this young guy who had worked in one of their companies, Andrew Mason [now the CEO of Groupon], who had this interesting idea called The Point, as in the tipping point, that aimed to get groups on the web to unite and create a social action.

It was not a new idea, but I liked the way he was implementing it. The creative side of me loved Andrew, loved this pie-in-the-sky idea of empowering groups because the web to date has only really drawn people inside of it. You go to Amazon online, you do your transactions in the clouds. You go to an online game and you play online. It drives you into the internet.

Andrew's idea was to use the internet to drive people into action outside the internet. I loved that idea, and I knew it had no business model, but on the flip side, the more logical side of me loved that Eric and Brad were the other two founders in that company. I knew, for a fact, that these guys would not tolerate for very long a business that did not generate revenue. I knew that together, the four of us would be highly focused on how to take this pie-in-the-sky concept and make it a real-world company.

And obviously the idea hit that maybe we should use this Groupon site for couponing—but really it is not a coupon, it is a voucher—and use a call center to recruit the merchants. People keep saying [that] using groups on the internet is not new. What was new was the call center. The idea that you could use a call center to call small vendors that sell hamburgers. That was the actual innovation.

The point being, I felt like I understood each part of the founders—the logical, business-oriented founders along with the creative founder, whose major was political science and music. Along with NEA's managing general partner, Peter Barris, we all worked together to create what we did. Groupon stayed true to its vision. It drives people outside the internet. It is such a great execution of that first vision.

I resigned from the board when they filed to go public, because I think I bring the most value to early-stage companies. Groupon has an incredible board now, too. I think it captures everything you and I are talking about, both in terms of communication and talent.

In the end, Peter and I were making a huge bet on this company, but it also was a group of people we knew really, really well and understood really well. And so I was comfortable taking a massive career risk on a company that started as a vision without a clear business model embedded in it. Everyone else who looked and passed on investing in The Point passed on it because they could not figure out what the business model was. Because I knew the entrepreneurs well, I knew that was actually an overestimated risk.

Shah: That information you had was an edge in making the investment decision on Groupon.

Weller: But it gets back to knowing who they were, knowing how they worked, knowing how they think. Having that communication line. Knowing that if it went too long burning cash, I would be able to communicate with them that we have to reduce this burn so we can search for the right business model. This company burned hardly any capital because of that. It was cash-flow positive in no time.

Shah: It is a great business model and incredible execution. What are the other characteristics that you look for in the entrepreneurs you invest in?

Weller: I think the other characteristics are that they are so marinated in their understanding of the business that they practically are the business. There is almost an irrational passion for it, which I described earlier.

That passion, that exuberance, can create a powerful emotional connection to a VC, to a prospective hire, or to a customer. I think it can be very telling if, when you hear the entrepreneur's vision, whether you agree with it or not, you cannot help but be sucked into the enthusiasm and passion for it. Even if you disagree with it and you think it will not work. You look for that connection. You almost find yourself believing the unbelievable.

Shah: Tell us more about Andrew Mason.

Weller: When Andrew was able to describe the action of groups extending beyond the internet, you realized through his eyes that it was very much inevitable in a way, that the internet would not be something that turns into the matrix, where you get drawn into a virtual world.

The internet in its optimal form will actually do quite the opposite. It will draw you outside the internet, back into the physical world. If the internet accomplishes that, you are really tapping into the largest market in the world—a $7 trillion local commerce market. Now, Andrew had even broader aspirations that it would also impact the way retailers operated. If a group of us did not like the way Walmart was operating, we could do things as a group to impact the way Walmart operated. It wound up being more directed around commerce.

When he talked about that vision of action—through, but outside the internet—it was very easy to be drawn into it, and you were almost in a state of suspended disbelief when you walked out of the meeting.

The scary part is, you are in that state of suspended disbelief, listening to them, but you do not know if they will listen to you. But we had the added benefit of knowing that Eric and Brad were good at that. It was a big deal for Peter and I to know that they would be our partners, and that we were going to work with them and figure this sucker out. And that's how we got there. All of the other top-tier VCs they talked to couldn't get there, because they didn't have the relationships that we did.

Shah: Twitter went through the same thing. It was hard to believe microblogging messages of 140 characters would appeal to masses.

Weller: Exactly the same thing.

Shah: What is the message here for entrepreneurs?

Weller: The most important thing, to me, is to come to it with an attitude and an expectation that you need to build a relationship. Not only will it be incredibly beneficial for the business, it will also be the fun part.

The other message here for entrepreneurs has to do with greatness, and how it is achieved. Being a great entrepreneur has very little to do with management. It is about realizing a vision, not about being the CEO. There are rare exceptions who excel at both, like a Bill Gates or Mark Zuckerberg—but I don't think Mark Zuckerberg's true goal has anything to do with being CEO. It has everything to do with bringing his vision to fruition.

Shah: This is the best position for him right now at Facebook.

Weller: In that case, yes, but there are other cases where it is not. [The goal is to] really answer the questions, "What is it that I want to be? What is it I am really trying to do? What is it I am trying to accomplish?" I think being honest with yourself, way up-front about that, about what it is you are actually trying to accomplish, and being transparent about that up-front. It is okay if you want to be CEO and that is the experience you want to have—you just need to say that up-front and understand that is what you want.

Shah: It should not come up two years into the deal.

Weller: It should not come up a week after the investment. That is when it really becomes clear. I will give you a wonderful example. We invested in an enterprise software company, and I thought I truly understood the vision and the team. I brought the founder three of the top executives in his space. The best marketing guy, the best sales guy—all had built multi-billion dollar companies in his sector. He shot all three down. I knew he had no understanding that he had just thrown away billions of dollars.

And none of those guys wanted to be the CEO; they just wanted to join his team. But he wanted to hire his friends. To think it does not matter who you have as team members, is like saying it doesn't matter who I put on a basketball court against an NBA team as long as I'm coach. When I introduce you to Michael Jordan to be your power forward, and you do not have the context to understand that it is Michael Jordan, that's a problem. If I introduce you to the Kobe Bryant of the enterprise software space, and you do not even have the wherewithal to know who that is and understand the impact that guy is going to have on your team, that's a problem. That is my nightmare.

Shah: There is no remedy for that.

Weller: As an entrepreneur, you must be honest with yourself about what you are really trying to accomplish and what your measure of success will be. It's not that founders don't or can't make good CEOs—often they are the best person for the job. I've helped plenty of them grow into that role.

Andrew Mason, CEO of Groupon; Hooman Radfar, CEO of Clearspring; Dan Yates, CEO of Opower—all of these guys are under 35 and none of them would say their greatest aspiration is to be a CEO. But they are the right people to execute on their vision at this stage. And if they weren't, they wouldn't hesitate to get the right team in place to make their vision a reality. And everyone is very open about how we evaluate and make those decisions.

My point is, it all starts with being really honest with yourself about what your measurement for success is. Start there, then talk to people, get their input, see if you change your opinion over time, but then before you take capital or talk seriously about taking capital, make sure you are very transparent about what those desires are. Do not just pay lip service to it.

Shah: It goes back to the very reason you are passionate about this business.

Weller: Yes. It's asking, beyond the passion you have for this great idea, what are you trying to achieve? It is not just one thing, it may be a couple things, but what are the top three or four things you are trying to achieve?

Shah: Do you want to change your lifestyle by making tons of money, do you want to be well known in the industry, do you want to run the company as CEO?

Weller: Exactly. You need to know this about yourself first. It's like they say about romantic relationships, that you can't be with someone else until you really know how to be with yourself? Well, that applies to VC-entrepreneur partnerships too.

Shah: Does that come through when you meet them?

Weller: That lack of self-awareness is the surest way to get shot down. A lot of VCs are fishing around for this. They think, this is a great idea, but is this somebody I can work with? Do they know what they really want?

When you are doing the due diligence, we are looking for clues. A lot of entrepreneurs think that VCs are always trying to replace management. The fact is, what they are really doing 90 percent of the time is trying to figure out if this is a person they can work with. Is he or she honest, what are his motivations, who is this person? Once I have that figured out, once I understand what they are really after, sometimes I try to nudge them in another direction if I think it's the best path for the company. But the most likely thing I am going to do is keep them as the CEO. If I understand them.

Shah: That is so true. I go back to my due diligence days. When there are reference discussions, you are really trying to get an idea of who this person is and what is he after, what motivates him.

Weller: Exactly. If I like the idea and I like the market, those things can be tested and I know how to do that. Most good VCs know how to do that. A lot of people talk about market. Of course it needs to be large. Of course it needs to be a breakthrough technology. The hard part about this is the human part. That is the part that is the least controllable for me, anyway. It is a human endeavor for me. And it's about reading and influencing people in a positive way, not in a manipulative way. It's about successfully bringing tools like domain expertise and pattern recognition to bear on their vision to achieve the improbable.

All of that boils down to being able to communicate well with them and knowing them well, and them knowing me well, and being able to work all the way through it. When it works and when you pull it off, it is just great. The beautiful thing about the model is, it rewards you highly when that happens. But it is not just about the money, it is about the fact you created something with this group of people and you have been through a journey together.

Shah: This is why, after making so much money, a lot of entrepreneurs go back to build new companies just to re-create and re-live those experiences.

Weller: That's right. It really is more about the journey at the end of the day. Even for me, I think it is the difference between PE [private equity] and venture capital. We are company builders.

Shah: Looking at successes like Clearspring, Groupon, and Opower, etc., in your portfolio, what are the key elements of execution that you focus on? What you have seen great entrepreneurs do when it comes to execution?

Weller: One of the measures I look at is who is teaching whom on the board. Situations where, as a board member, you find yourself learning more and more about the space during meetings.

The great companies are leaning forward. The personality of the company is naturally inquisitive and naturally aggressive. Some good companies are created because they have the timing right, and the tide lifts all boats. But with the great companies, you just feel that no matter where you look, you will run into this company's roots. They are just embedded in that market, and they are everywhere.

And when that occurs, there is an opportunity to create some serious momentum. For example, the best sales people start leaving from the companies around that sector. You create your own gravity. Your compounding success radiates naturally from your network of people, places, all the things you are doing. You start becoming the largest mass in the market space. The largest mass has the most gravity. You can practically hear the huge sucking sound as it consumes everything in its orbit.

To me, the key to being able to do that, is again, building a very rounded team, building the right advisors, and assembling the top thinkers in the space. For example, the best scientific people like to work with other great scientific people. You just build a culture of leaning forward into the wind on these things. You are constantly attacking the market, constantly trying to learn from the market.

The way you really know you are winning is that you are defining what success in the market is. For example, Opower is attacking the utility space. They are the first smart-grid software company that penetrated the market.

Their story is based on the well-known fact that energy consumption in the United States is going up in a major way. And our options are increasingly limited. So what is one way to address the need? Reduce consumption. Believe it or not, the utility companies' profitability is not tied to the amount of electricity they are selling. Profitability hinges on whether they are hitting their efficiency targets or not. Public utility commissions, which are government-regulated entities, will actually tell them what their profitability can be based on those efficiency budgets.

To make a long story short, Opower provides a great efficiency program. They send you an e-mail or report that shows you your energy consumption against one hundred [of your] nearest neighbors in the same size house and same income, and weather. Then it gives you some simple recommendations on how to reduce your consumption. In the areas where it is deployed, it reduces consumption about three percent across the whole region—that is a massive number.

Opower attacked the market and really embedded themselves with the public utility commissions and with the utility companies. Metrics that Opower uses are now defining the efficiency market. The jargon that is being used to describe the market is Opower language. The way utilities now buy efficiency is by the rules that Opower set.

In other words, when a market emerges, an innovative company can often set the criteria that are used to define the market. When Oracle first came out, one of the things they were doing phenomenally was explaining that the transaction processing speed was what mattered with databases, not the reliability. It completely changed the dialogue about what you measured a database against. It changed how you defined it.

To me, when I think about execution, the question is, "Do you have the opportunity to define how this market is going to be judged?" You are not waiting for the market. You are not a sailboat waiting for the breeze to kick in. You are single-handedly defining the things that will make one successful, and that really hurts the competition because you can tweak the market to your strengths.

Shah: In India, where I grew up, I was big on kite flying and I still am. I will spend three to four months every year flying kites in my spare time. Most people can fly kites when the winds are strong, which is usually mid-January in India, but I learned to fly the kite in no wind at all. That art really helps when there is wind because you know how to maneuver in a no-wind zone and most people who are only used to flying it in strong winds cannot maneuver that way.

What happens is, when you want to cut someone's kite, you really have to get under them. And to get under them, you have to go left-to-right or right-to-left and in that process, you will get out of the wind. If you are not experienced in managing in a no-wind zone, that is where you get cut the most. Your expertise in managing your kite with no or low wind helps you execute against your competition.

Weller: I like that. It is exactly right. Then, the great part is, when the wind does kick in, you have defined the perfect wind.

Shah: Groupon is clearly doing that.

Weller: And Opower is doing it. There are a lot of examples in NEA's portfolio. Fusion-io does that, and Data Domain did it in its space. You know you are starting to win when you are the one who is defining the market and defining how it is measured.

Shah: Earlier we talked about the early signs of the communication breakdown between the investor and the company. What are other early signs that tell you the company is getting off track?

Weller: A wholesale shift in strategy out of nowhere. It means people are losing faith in their original vision. And instead of telling you facts that might have led them to a new idea, or bringing to light some data that suggests a weakness in the current strategy, they are simply offering up other strategies before even addressing the weaknesses in the current strategy. It says a lot of things, and number one is that they are not being transparent.

Number two, which is worse: "We still believe in that strategy, but these are other good ideas." We call that the "check the box" presentation, as in "We could do this, this, or this." If the original idea is so good, why are you offering up other ones? Focus, focus, focus is the key to success for start-up.

Once I feel a company veering from its strategy without explaining why, trust is in jeopardy. They are not telling me something. First and foremost, tell me why.

I am an investor. I am not managing the company, and I do not want to manage the company. If you have a VC that is trying to manage your company, you have the wrong VC or you have the wrong CEO. Either the VC is not letting you run the company, or the company is not being well run. The point is, like anything else where you are working with a company, one of the things the VC is constantly doing is trying to dead reckon the path. The path is always relative to the last data point. Anytime where the strategy starts getting blurry or options of new strategies are provided without a reckoning back to the original path of the company, it's a huge early warning sign.

Shah: Especially when the new plan is presented with such glamour.

Weller: That is the worst. It may even be a great idea, but you still have the sinking feeling: Did someone just pull the chair out from under me? But this kind of sudden shift is not to be confused with making adjustments to the strategy, which has to happen.

Shah: Where does the difference show up when someone is really pointing to the need to pivot to a new strategy? What does that conversation look like?

Weller: A pivot in strategy that is an educated and informed change based on prior decisions and the feedback from those decisions isn't the problem. But if the feedback loops are not informing the new decision, and if it seems almost disconnected, then you start worrying.

The worst case is that "check the box of the strategy you like best" scenario I mentioned, when there is no connection between the new options and what we have been doing. That is when you know.

Shah: How did The Point evolve into Groupon?

Weller: It was a constant path. We had a premise, a theory, we tested it, and there would be a feedback loop. We would have another premise, test it, feedback loop. There was no, "Oh my god, where did that come from?" It was a winding but consistent path, with not a gap in it. We were all there the whole time.

Shah: So everyone in that group knew, including the investors, that you were in the hypothesis-testing stage?

Weller: The path we were going down was always clear. We were all on board, and we all understood it. Never did I come to a board meeting and all of a sudden there are four options put on the board.

Shah: When you know the start-up is off track, at what point do you know that there is no pivot or Plan B?

Weller: One key metric is whether the company has the resources to rebound from whatever brick wall we've hit and reposition. It's usually one of the major vectors—technology, market, management or product—that just hits a brick wall.

Occasionally the management and the market are so good that you still have the general resources to pivot. But when one of those breaks down and you do not have the resources to pivot, that is generally when we decide to pull the plug. Most of the time, and I would say greater than 80 percent of the time, the management team and I agree on that. Occasionally you'll find yourself in a situation where the technology and the market are in good shape, but management is broken and we cannot fix it.

Shah: It's when the party that you need to fix the situation itself needs fixing.

Weller: In that case you may not have the resources—ability—to communicate. You may have to shut it down for that reason.

Shah: I had that situation where the board could not get through to communicate the need for a new plan and its execution and there was nothing else we could do.

Weller: Then what you do is you just resign from the board and you do not dedicate any more financial resources. Of the three, that is the saddest one. That is the worst because you see the market opportunity, you see that it is great technology, you have used all your powers of persuasion, all your skills, you may have even used the leverage of force that you have, but you just cannot move the needle. That, by far, is the most frustrating of the three.

Shah: This is where it goes back to your original discussion on trust and a transparent communication channel.

Weller: Yes. Of these three scenarios of start-up flame out, this is the one you have the greatest power to mitigate at the front end. You'll be able to figure out the probability range for the technology or product to work. You will probably be able to figure out, if you are good, the likelihood of the market being there or not. But the factor that enables you to have the greatest effect on the company's ultimate success or failure is the communications channel between entrepreneurs and investors. As in physics, "complex adaptive systems," are highly affected by their initial conditions.

Shah: That is why, for kids, so much focus goes on building their mind right during the initial few years.

Weller: I would say the same is true of a company. The funny part is, I think most good VCs are roughly equal in their ability to assess technology, product, and market. Where they differ is their ability to assess management—this is what sets top-tier VCs apart from the rest.

That is the condition where you have the greatest influence at the outset, and how you manage it will stick with you—and the company—for a long time. Groupon is a great case in point here. We were in a better position to assess the opportunity because we had long-term relationships with two of the founders.

Shah: In the Groupon case, it was not just Eric and Brad, but also Andrew.

Weller: It was definitely Andrew. Luckily, we saw something in him, too. He was 60 percent the reason we did it and Eric and Brad were the other 40 percent.

Shah: And the ability to identify that it is really the game changer.

Weller: I think of the three things we talked about—technology/product, market, and the human entrepreneurial part—the human part is the most unpredictable, but it is also the one that up front you can get largely right or wrong. It is amazing how many companies you invest in that start off as one thing and end up as something else, like Twitter. If you did not have that ability to pivot with your partners, you would be screwed.

Shah: This is very insightful.

Weller: The responsibility for communication is huge, and getting it right up front is critical. A lot of people say it's management, management, management. But it is actually entrepreneur, entrepreneur, entrepreneur. What is the character of the entrepreneur? What is the character of that person?

You need to know each other. That connection is so huge, and if you have it and there is transparency and a line of communication, then the other two things, the technology and the market, I think you can both nail to the best of your ability.

As I said, those last two things, I think most VCs will get right. They all have access to the best and brightest in the world, we all do. But I think what makes that magical difference for a guy like Mike Moritz or John Doerr, what they are really good at, is they pick up something about the person and they build strong relationships with them. It seems like magic fairy dust. If you do the due diligence on those guys, you learn that they build really strong relationships with their entrepreneurs. It does not mean those relationships stay strong, but they absolutely begin that way. And they are not always friendships, by the way. It's about people being able to read each other.

Shah: Mutual understanding and respect between the one who has the toolkit and the one who has the vision and passion.

Weller: That's a good summary. Like the entrepreneur, the VC has a lot at stake, and is usually risking more than capital. We need to make sure we're aligned from day one.

David Cowan

Bessemer Venture Partners: LinkedIn, Smule, Zoosk

David Cowan *is a partner at Bessemer Venture Partners (BVP). His investment focus includes network technology, SaaS infrastructure, consumer internet, and cyber security. His current portfolio includes CrowdFlower, LifeLock, LinkedIn, Nominum, Reputation.com, Skybox Imaging, Smule, and Zoosk.*

More than twenty of David's start-up investments have gone on to IPO. His historical portfolio includes network-technology companies Ciena and P-Com; internet-infrastructure services such as PSINet, Keynote, FlyCast, and Netli (acquired by Akamai); and consumer web sites HotJobs, Blue Nile, and Playdom (acquired by Disney).

In 1995, David co-founded VeriSign as a Bessemer-funded spinout of RSA and served as VeriSign's initial chairman. His other cyber-security exits have included Counterpane (acquired by BT), Cyota (acquired by RSA), ON, Postini (acquired by Google), Tripwire (acquired by Thoma Bravo), Tumbleweed, ValiCert, and World Talk.

The first Forbes *"Midas List" ranked David among the world's top ten venture investors, and he has been featured on every Midas List since. Drawing from his immensely successful investment track record and taking examples from his key investments—such as LinkedIn, Smule, and Zoosk—David takes us into a deep discussion on what creates great entrepreneurs and a great dynamic between entrepreneurs and investors, and he highlights what separates great businesses from great products.*

What I love about David is his deep understanding of key aspects of start-up success criteria and how he conveys those in a razor-sharp way to help entrepreneurs avoid costly mistakes on the path to building billion-dollar successes.

Tarang Shah: What are some of the key reasons why start-ups fail?

David Cowan: I think that there was a period of time in which most technology investments by venture capital investors were made in companies that were commercializing technology for the enterprise market, and during that period, there was a common error. I would say there was a common reason for failure, and the common reason was a fallacy that a solution designed for two or three beta customers could be extended to the entire market. And typically what happened is that the solutions were each customized just enough for the beta customers that you didn't really have a product that could work for anybody. What you had was a professional services business.

Today that's obviously not the case. Today, most investments are going into more consumer-oriented technologies, or B2B technologies that are served, are delivered, from the cloud to a large number of users. So today I think the reasons for failure are much more varied. I think that a common concern, a concern that I have that's common to a lot of venturers out there, is that the entrepreneurs are not really thinking two or three moves ahead in the chess game. They're demonstrating traction with some service, some service on the web, without anticipating what competitors and new entrants will do later to either leap frog or steal their share.

You know, if somebody comes up with one more fun way for teenagers to talk to each other and socialize, and share snippets of music or comments or something, let's just say it's subject to being a fad. People only have so many hours a day. And you know people who are using the web for recreational purposes are going to change what they do from time to time. Now, of course, sometimes there are phenomena that emerge, like YouTube or Facebook, that are enduring.

Shah: Is there a way to separate them out? What's happening in cases where it's a fad or some temporary phenomenon that shows a spike in usage for now, but eventually it fades away? On the other hand, to your point about YouTube, the early traction was just phenomenal with an exponential takeoff, and then it sustained the momentum. Is there something you can look at and say, yes, this could be a fad vs. this could be a new lifestyle?

Cowan: Well there isn't one thing. There's a combination, a recipe of things needed for companies like this to be successful, and if you're missing any one of those ingredients, then they're going to lose ground to a competitor.

So one of them is, as you pointed out, some application that just pushes the right buttons in lots of users. Obviously, you start there and you say, okay, we've got something interesting. There are hundreds and thousands and tens of thousands and hundreds of thousands and millions of people coming onto this site, and we haven't done anything other than just make it available. So that's certainly the key ingredient.

And then there are other ingredients. There needs to be a lot of attention paid to the community to make sure that the way that the service evolves is viewed in a positive way and actually encourages people to not only participate but become leaders. And there has to be a lot of attention paid toward the sensitivities and the feelings of the people in the community and how they want the community to evolve.

Another ingredient is, I believe, having some viral component to it. And the viral component doesn't have to be that users are going to tell their friends they have to join this new social network or content site. The viral component could be that the user creates some content that then actually gets indexed by search engines and performs well in searches, such that by virtue of people using some service, the service itself becomes more valuable and the content that people generate will, through search engines, attract other users.

There's sort of an indirect virality that can be just as powerful, and that's what we found for example at Yelp. Yelp is not a directly viral company, but it's indirectly viral because people use it to create reviews that do really well in search.

Shah: That's a great point. At TripAdvisor or Amazon, more reviews do drive more usage and more transactions eventually.

Cowan: And another ingredient I think is that companies that are successful are the ones where the founders are able to make that transition from a founding team to a professionally run company. And there are some pretty clear signs of when that happens and how that happens. For start-up companies, there's a time naturally when they should be run by the founders or the founding team, and that's it.

Then there's a time where you say, okay, now this company has demonstrated enough value that it's time to make the transition. And if the company doesn't make the transition, then I think they may be a company like Friendster or Craigslist, or something that could become successful for users, but not really a successful business.

Think of properties like Napster and others along the way where the people may have enjoyed the service, but in the end it wasn't a good business because it just wasn't run so well. There are blogging companies with great products and that are run by terrific, talented individuals. But some of the leading players in that space never built a real company. So that's the missing ingredient in those examples.

Shah: Yep, some great products like WordPress, etc., but I can't think of them as venture-return businesses, unfortunately.

Cowan: So this is a time when a company needs to make a transition. There are certain things that you want to see in a founding team. And then there are different things you want to see in the professional team. And so, companies need to make that jump.

The other key ingredient is the company needs a culture of intense metrics and analytics with rapid iteration. I've seen companies that have some brilliant application that people love, but they don't really have a culture of constantly trying to make it better, doing A/B testing, always iterating. How do we improve the workflow? How do we improve the funnel? How do we improve the registration screens? If they don't have that, then it's just going to be a limiter on their growth.

I'm having lunch with a guy today. He's got a company with this product that had phenomenal growth, and he's got nobody in the company who actually understands anything about how people use it, where they click or anything. And it's ridiculous. He should have much better analytics and he should know how people are using it, and he should make it better and better. But he's not doing it. So I think there's an opportunity there to make the company much better. That's just another ingredient to that data-driven culture.

Shah: So the underlying thinking process here is that it's really the rapid iteration and course correction that leads you to something a lot bigger and the real business opportunity. You need to scour through the behavior you are seeing in your users, understand where your users are resonating, and make sure that discovered product-market fit is baked into what you do going forward.

You are looking for things like, what are the things people may pay for? What are the things they may want for free? How much will they pay for it? Will it be subscription or one-time purchase, etc. Right?

Cowan: Well, there's two sides to it. There's the "how can we create better value for the user?" side. I mean, I can tell you that at LinkedIn, for example, there's an intense focus on "How can we engage the user more, what can we do to make people use LinkedIn more, how are they using it, what are they clicking on, what do they like?" It's "Try this, they like this, they like that," etc. The LinkedIn team is very good at that.

Some things that LinkedIn used to not be good at, but now they're getting better at it, is the other side—focusing on the business. How do we create value for the users? How do we create workflows that maximize the lifetime value and minimize the cost per acquisition?

For any internet business, those are the two key numbers that matter. Nothing else matters. Cost per acquisition and lifetime value. Everything falls into those two numbers. I can look at any internet business and see that the lifetime value comes from a combination of revenue sources—it could be ads, it could be subscription, it could be virtual currency, it could be transactions. How you're getting your revenue doesn't matter. The point is that for any user there's some combination of those things.

And there's some cost of getting them, either through ads or Google. Or maybe the cost sometimes is zero if it's through PR or through virality. And then you have the depth of channel, which is, given how you acquire users, how many can you acquire?

Those three numbers for me represent the financial value of any business I'm looking at. So when a team is really focused on those numbers and how everything feeds into those numbers, then every month those numbers get better and better. A company called Zoosk in my portfolio is like that.

Shah: That's great. I have interviewed Zoosk's founder and CEO Alex Mehr and his interview is in this book.

Cowan: Zoosk guys are the masters of this approach. Alex is just so focused on exactly how everything feeds into lifetime value, that everything the company does, lifetime value is just constantly improving in that company.

Those are all the ingredients that I can see and then you have to put those together, right? And if you're missing any of them, then, you know, you're not going to win. I think that's relevant for the world today. Like I said, it was different when enterprise technology was the key. It may be different ten years from now. But those are the ingredients that I think are necessary.

Shah: Some founders remain CEOs while others are replaced with external CEOs. What triggers such a transition?

Cowan: I think there's a fallacy that negatively impacts founders and their companies—that if they are not the CEO, then somehow they failed. Anyone who's actually been CEO in a significant business knows that it's hard work and it's not very much fun. It's pretty stressful. And actually being a founder and being in charge of strategy, vision, and that kind of thing, is really fun. Any founder who thinks that he or she has failed if the company has brought in a CEO is sort of a victim of status mentality.

I've seen founders hold onto their CEO titles to the point that they got run out of town. And then I've seen founders who say, "Wow, my vision is for this company to change the world profoundly. When I have the opportunity, not before, but when I have the opportunity, I will bring in a great CEO, someone who is going to change the trajectory of this business. And those people, by yielding control of that day-to-day job to somebody else, actually retain control, because they have the credibility as the person who's thinking about what's good for the company.

Shah: I agree with you. There is some kind of media attention created where it gives an impression that the founder was booted out as a CEO, and really feeds into that negative cycle of thinking or perception.

Cowan: Yeah. I think it's common and it's a mistake. And founders who are really focused on being the CEO are just hurting themselves. It doesn't mean there isn't room for the founders. The founders are actually the soul of the business, and the best dynamic that I've seen is where you have a founding team. These are people who trust each other, they know each other already, and they worked together before. Their qualifications are that they have an incredible passion about a particular market, they see something that's wrong—usually because they're customers of it—and they see a better way of doing it.

So this entrepreneur has a vision of changing something, and the entrepreneur brings together people with whom the entrepreneur has worked before, and they work very well together. That's a really good founding team. Those people build and build. Everybody does everything. Until they get to a point where they've demonstrated enough value that now they can go out and recruit the very, very best people to do each functional job, one by one.

At some point they're going to hire a VP of Engineering. That's usually the first one. Okay, now we've got all these engineers, we should really hire a VP of Engineering. And then at some point they're going to hire somebody in marketing who understands about lifetime value and doing all that. And they're going to hire a business development/sales person to bring partners in. And then somebody who knows how to close deals, not just run around and talk about the business, but somebody who knows how to find the decision makers, identify the budget, and who has actually carried lots of quota before.

And then somewhere next might be either a CFO or might be a CEO. When the company is doing really well, you can get a great CEO, somebody who has experience running bigger companies, somebody who has done very well and is willing to take the job. You are not going to get a good CEO early on until you've demonstrated value. When you've demonstrated enough value that you can get somebody great, of course you should get somebody great.

Shah: Sometimes you make a mistake and have to find a new CEO. You lose time that in some cases this could be lethal for the company.

Cowan: I think what Google did is the model, the way the founders there brought in a CEO and brought in professional managers like Jonathan Rosenberg and people like that, so at the core you still have Sergey Brin and Larry Page and Susan Wojcicki, but they've brought in this professional team. And that works great.

Shah: That's a fantastic point. It's not the status thing at all. It's really who can help you execute your vision to the next orbit. And that means success for you as founder. What is the right dynamic between the entrepreneur and the investor?

Cowan: I would say the right dynamic is very valuable for a business and it's not really common. And it's not common because of mistakes that the entrepreneur makes and mistakes that venture investors make.

Let me first describe the dynamic that doesn't work. The dynamic that doesn't work begins with an expectation, an understanding among everyone, that the team is there to execute, and if the team doesn't execute, then the investors will fire the team and get a team that executes. And it seems like a natural thing, right? I just said that and it seems like, well, what's wrong with that? You give them a job, they execute, they say we're going to do this, they do it. If they don't, investors get a new team. And then somebody else does it. I will tell you that when that is the understanding of the relationship between management and their investors, it leads to a lot of dysfunction.

The reason it leads to dysfunction is that in any interesting growth business, it never, ever goes according to plan. There will always be variances to the plan. We typically make plans for a year at a time. And during that year, things change all the time. Does that mean we should plan every quarter? Well of course not, because we don't want to spend our days planning. We want to spend our days doing. So we've got to have some planning, but we also want a lot of doing. So the plans are useful tools, but they shouldn't be the basis by which a team gets fired.

Shah: Is it more like a co-ownership structure between investors and the founders, rather than, say, an employee/employer relationship?

Cowan: Yes. So what works much better is where there's an understanding that things are going to change.

What I tell the people that I fund is that your job of course is to execute the plan, but if there are variances to the plan, it doesn't mean I want to fire you. However, if there's no transparency and you don't tell me what's going on, if I don't feel like we're partners in this, then I'm going to fire you. So a successful dynamic is where management is transparent about the issues. They're not afraid to tell investors about the variances, thinking that they're going to get fired.

I don't mean to put all this on the entrepreneurs and say, well, entrepreneurs are lying crooks. That's not the case. Entrepreneurs are sometimes liars because they know that they've got investors who buy into this understanding of how things are supposed to work. I don't know where they learned this. And so the entrepreneurs feel like they have to sugarcoat things and not tell investors about what's really happening, until it gets to the point where investors find out, and then hell breaks loose.

If a venture investor wants an entrepreneur to treat him or her like a partner, then the venture investor must acknowledge that variances happen, and they must treat them as interesting challenges, not deficiencies on the part of the founders or the team.

Shah: It's challenging when surprises are brought up at the board meetings rather than discussing things before hand.

Cowan: I don't even want to wait for the board meeting. I want the entrepreneurs to call me and say, "Listen, we've got a problem. I'm not asking you to solve it, I'm just telling you we've got this problem. If you can solve it, great. If you've got any ideas, great."

You should know there's a problem. I can tell you the people that I back are not afraid to tell me about problems, because I never turn around and point at them and say, that's your fault. I will fire somebody when they don't tell me about a problem. That's just something I can't work with. If they're not going to tell me things, then who knows what the hell is going on. I have no idea.

Shah: Start-up building is a very dynamic environment, so you've got to know in real time what's going on so you can really improvise and course correct.

Cowan: Also, if somebody's not telling me what's going on, it's just dumb. Because maybe we know somebody who can help. Maybe we actually have some ideas. We've got other portfolio companies who maybe have been through what they're going through. Why not use every resource?

Entrepreneurs who look at their board and look at their investors as resources are going to get something out of them. Sometimes in board meetings I've got entrepreneurs who put up worksheets and they hand out assignments to their investors to open up certain doors or introduce them to other investors or introduce them to a bank or bring in candidates for a search shop. They'll actually put up a worksheet, and say here's what Bessemer did, and here's what the guys at Morgenthaler did, and here's what the guys at Trinity did, and they'll actually put it up and say, "Hey Trinity, what's with you guys? Look what Bessemer did. How come you haven't done that?" Or say "Hey Bessemer, how come you haven't kept up?"

I love that. I love it. You know, this is what entrepreneurship is about. It's marshaling an unbelievably small pool of resources to achieve great things. That's the crux of entrepreneurship. So to completely squander the value of your investors is just poor business, bad business.

It is really important to me that I cultivate this relationship with my entrepreneurs. That they understand that I'm never going to blame them for the bad news. I'm only going to blame them if they don't tell me the bad news. That creates a really good working relationship. Tell me everything, and when things don't work, your job is to tell me, and then tell me what your plan is for fixing it. And if you don't have a plan for fixing it, okay then maybe we should go hire somebody. But that will be obvious. If you don't have a plan for fixing it, you don't know why it's happening, and you don't know how we're going to fix it, then it's obvious to both of us that we should go hire somebody.

Shah: Do these characteristics show up in your first or follow-up meetings with the entrepreneurs?

Cowan: When I meet an entrepreneur, what I am always looking for is whether this person is going to be able to participate in that kind of a dynamic. And the fundamental characteristic that I'm looking for in an entrepreneur—not just because I want to have a good working relationship, but because I think it's key to success—is intellectual honesty. This is the key characteristic that I'm looking for in entrepreneurs when I meet them.

So how do I look for intellectual honesty? I'm pushing on what they have to say about their plans or whatever, and there should be times when the answer is, "Yes, well that was actually disappointing to us." Or, "That's a challenge for us." Or, "We don't know yet how we're going to answer that. I'm going to hire the best person in the world who knows how to answer that question, but so far we don't know the answer yet." That's actually a good answer.

Here's something else. I ask them about the companies that they were with in the past. And every company has had challenges and problems, and I ask them about the problems in those companies. Maybe they worked at Palm, or maybe they worked at HP or Microsoft. Any company that they've been at went through some crisis at some point. And if this person was an executive in that company, I ask them about that. I say, hey, tell me about how this company got into this mess.

And there are two different reactions that I get. Sometimes people say, "Well, I'll tell you how they got into the mess. They got into the mess because they did this and they did that. And you know, I could tell at the time that this was going to happen, but you know, they did it anyway."

And then the other person says, "Well, I'll tell you how we got into the mess. We got into the mess because we thought this and that, but here was the screw up, and we learned." Obviously I want the second guy.

Shah: Yes, absolutely.

Cowan: The first guy is just pointing fingers at everyone else, and saying I told them not to do it. Well obviously you weren't very convincing. Obviously you weren't very influential in that company. Whatever it is that you thought the company should be doing, obviously they went in a different direction, and you obviously have no feeling or sense of accountability for what the company did. So that is not a sign of intellectual honesty.

Again, I look for somebody who in the meeting is actually looking to get something out of the meeting from me, other than my check. It's good to get a check. I understand that's what they're trying to get. But I like it when they come in there and they're actually hoping that I'm going to tell them something interesting. I'm going to ask them some challenging questions. I'm going to do something that changes how they think about things.

And when I push on a plan, there are two different reactions. One is that they get kind of annoyed that I'm pushing on them, because what the hell do I know about what they're doing, and they've been working on this for two years, and who the hell do I think I am to question it. And the other reaction is kind of excitement that somebody is pushing, and that they get a chance to test all their theories against somebody who's really poking at it.

And they'll ask me, "Well, how do your companies solve this? What do you see?" And when they're asking me, or if they say to me, "Hey, you know, I saw that in your portfolio you're an investor in Nominum, and you're an investor in Reputation. I really want to meet those guys because I have an idea that I think we can work with each other." People who are, again, coming in trying to squeeze all the value they can, I love that of them. To me it's intellectual honesty. They acknowledge that they don't know everything and they need help, and they're going to go find it, they're going to get it.

Shah: David, you are well-tuned into the entrepreneurial psychology and key success characteristics. In the cases where it turned out that your original assessment of the founding team was wrong, what were some of the things you as an investor missed? What happened in those cases where they did pass through your due diligence filter without raising any flags that it should have?

Cowan: I've made a lot of investments, but twice I've invested in entrepreneurs who were just psychopathic liars. They were very good liars, and I didn't discover it until six to nine months into the investment, and then suddenly everything just started unraveling. Suddenly I realized, this [person] is a psychopathic liar.

All these things they told us about customers turn out to be wrong, and when you ask them about it, they just spin new stories, which at first I believed. And then one of them unravels and suddenly I realize, oh, he made that up, and then everything he's ever said, I realize, could have been made up. That's happened twice.

Shah: And that's what investors really have to watch out for. It's rare but it does happen.

Cowan: You know, even references don't necessarily help. The former boss of one of the guys, a well-known CEO that was on the board of this company I invested in, didn't know the guy was a psychopathic liar. He didn't realize it until later. In fact, we even went to the board and said, "Oh my god, we've got a problem, this guy's a liar."

And that guy's former boss said, "You're crazy. I know this guy. He's good. You're the problem. You're a VC. You just want to fire the founder."

"Look here," I said, "he said this, and it was a lie, and he said this, and it was a lie."

The former boss said, "He just needs some coaching."

"What? Coaching? You can't coach honesty. It's not a coaching thing."

He said, "No, you VCs, you're just all the same."

So I said, "Wow, I've got a lot to do. Life is short. I've got no time for a company that's being run by a psychopathic liar and a board who doesn't care. So I'm resigning."

Which I'd never done before. I said I don't have time for this. I'm going to go do something else. Then a month later the board member and former boss of the founder came back and said, "Oh, you were right—he was a liar. Please come back to the board."

Shah: Again, that's not something you can plan for. You just have to deal with it if it happens.

Cowan: But that's an extraordinary case. I'm embarrassed that twice I've done it. But that's out of sixty investments.

Shah: That's not a bad track record at all!

Cowan: There was another company where the guy was a liar too, but he was more of a crook, not a psychopathic liar. But you're asking not for those extreme cases where somebody's a criminal, you're asking for the cases where somebody just seems like he's going to be a strong founder, but then for some reason, really disappoints.

Shah: Yes, exactly. That's more usual.

Cowan: I could think of lots of examples. You know there's one example where the founders turned out to be a little bit more interested in having fun than in building a great business. Having a little bit too much fun, and it was really impacting morale within the company. And it also was impacting the quality of the product. They just didn't have their heart in making sure that the product was really great. So that was one problem. I expect there's actually a lot of that going on today.

Look, half the investments are bad investments. That's the nature of venture capital. So half the companies, something goes wrong with them.

Here's a very common problem. It comes back to this intellectual honesty thing. Sometimes founders will ignore data. They'll say we're going to go do this test. This year we think we're going to be able to do this, and they try it, and it turns out the users don't like it, the customers don't like it. The partners don't buy it. And the reaction is, "Oh, maybe we were mistaken."

It may be the whole business is flawed, or maybe that strategy was flawed. But they don't view it that way. They say, "Oh, well we just had the wrong guy selling it," or, "They are going to buy it, it's just taking longer," or, "It was just because the button was red instead of green. If we fix it, they're going to buy it." They just don't want to believe what the market and customers are telling them. They want to believe that it's still going to work, so they refuse to listen to the data. That's actually probably the most common mistake I see founders doing.

Shah: So what you're saying is you should be really zeroing in on whether you're hitting the right pain point of the customer or not. If you are, then maybe you can tweak the product, and the distribution. But if you are pushing for something customers don't want, you should be actively looking out for those signals.

Cowan: Yup. Another pattern is having very strong technologists. And I can think of a couple of companies I've invested in where the founders developed something that was really technologically profound, but they were unable to translate that into a value proposition the customer could really understand.

So it's a problem if they really want everyone to understand the genius of the innovation itself, as opposed to just thinking about what customer needs were. That's something like, "I really just want to solve this problem I have. You've got this great security thing, but I don't really want to know about security. I just want to be able to send my messages without my IT department stopping me. And how you do it is lovely, but I don't understand all that."

So I've seen that happen sometimes. Great companies are able to take what they've done and deliver an elevator pitch to customers that grabs them without having to necessarily glorify the inventors.

Shah: That's fantastic. Earlier you talked about some of the key metrics that you follow to track the progress of your start-ups. What are some of the early signs that you track that tell you the start-up is off track?

Cowan: It's okay to start off a board meeting with a quick nod to highlights since the last meeting. But it's a bad sign if the entrepreneurs dwell on those highlights, especially if the highlights are simply mushy validations of their vision. For example, they may celebrate a great meeting they had, a complimentary article, or a fun off-site event that the employees are happy about. But these don't reflect real progress for the company, based on our business goals. The highlight for the quarter is we beat the plan. That's the highlight. That's the only highlight I want to see.

So when they're talking about other things besides beating their team metrics, that's a sign that not only is it off track, but there's a culture problem.

This is a company that thinks that they're going to spend their money until they run out, then they're going to raise another round somehow, by talking about all these great meetings they're having.

Shah: And they don't feel the sense of urgency, or keeping focus on the key business metrics. When do you know that something is not only off track but is just beyond recovery and there is no Plan B?

Cowan: If a team is performing well constantly, is very data driven, and intellectually honest, they jump on things. They're honest about the challenges. And if a team like that gets excited about a pivot or Plan B, I'm very inclined to support them. I generally do. So for me it comes down to the team and is that dynamic there where I have confidence that they're really on it.

Shah: Great! What is your thought process in the exit decision? How do you decide whether to keep funding them, keep growing towards an IPO, or sell it now?

Cowan: Sometimes it's just obvious that we should just stop. Those are actually good cases. I like those cases. I know what to do and I get to move on. And you're right that the hardest ones are the ones that are in the middle. And generally if I really like the team and I think they're intellectually honest and they're data driven, then I feel teams like that deserve a second chance.

And what I mean by second chance is, if they run out of money, they're not going to get it from outside investors. They need it from the inside, current investors. Are we going to give it to them? Those teams, I feel, get one more chance. If they're good. So if I like the team, then they get one mulligan. And then if they need another one, it's time to sell the company.

Shah: That's perfect.

Shah: If there were three things you as an investor wish every entrepreneur knew, what would those three be?

Cowan: A great team makes a great leader. If you're not making mistakes, there's something wrong. And there's no excuse today for not running business off very deep analytics.

Shah: This is wonderful. Those three cut to the heart of entrepreneurship.

Cowan: For very young entrepreneurs who haven't yet proven that their idea really has merit, one of the things that I would tell them, which is probably blasphemous, is this: failure *is* an option. You have a long life. Don't waste eight years of it through some idea that's not working.

Shah: And if you have the culture of rapid iteration and deep analytics, you just will know what's not working right away.

Cowan: Yes. Listen to the data.

Shah: How does the market, or size of the market, or timing of the market come into the way you look at investments and how you grow them? Do you look at it and say hey, this is a huge market and this is the right team? Or is this the right team based on everything I've seen—intellectual honesty, etc.—and are they going to figure out what the right market is?

Cowan: There are three things. There is how big is the market? There is how good is the team? And there is how interesting is their solution? How defensible, how unique, how innovative? How profound is their solution? And you're asking me which one of those I need to see.

It depends. I need at least two of the three. I need two of those three. I can think of examples where it was these two, those two, or the other two when we went in. There are cases where we had a good team and a good solution. We weren't sure if the market was really very big. I can think of cases where we had great market with an incredible solution with kind of a funky team, thinking we'll fix it later. And then sometimes we had a great market and a great team, but we didn't really know how they were going after it.

Shah: The great teams will eventually figure out a great product in a great market, but it's tough if either the big market or the right team is missing.

Cowan: Yes. I'll give you an example of that. Smule is an example of that. Amazing, amazing founders, just incredible pedigree and genius, going after huge potential opportunity in this amazing growth space. And when we funded them, we had no idea what they were going to build. They didn't know what they were going to build. All kinds of crazy ideas. They still don't know what they're going to be when they grow up. They're still just experimenting and learning and doing creative things.

Michael Birch

Bebo, Birthday Alarm

Michael Birch is the co-founder of Ringo, Bebo, and Birthday Alarm. In 2008, he and his wife sold Bebo to AOL for $850 million. One of the earlier pioneers of social networking companies, Michael launched Ringo, one of the very first social networks, within a few weeks of Friendster.

Having worked in a number of what he calls "boring computer-related jobs for insurance companies," Michael relished the chance to set up an internet-based family business with his wife and brother, Paul. Their first web site idea, Birthday Alarm, came from Michael's own embarrassment from constantly forgetting the birthdays of his friends and family members.

Michael is also an investor in about 30 companies, including Eventbrite and Pinterest.

As a one of the early pioneers of social networking and viral marketing, Michael provides invaluable insights into how he learned from his past failures, identified unaddressed market segments in social networks, and built Bebo—one of the very few successful social networking sites—on a shoe-string budget to eventually sell it to AOL for close to a billion dollars.

As an entrepreneur who beat Myspace and faced fierce competition from Facebook, Michael gives a detailed account of why only a few social networking companies survive, what makes Facebook so unique, what's next for social networking, and why Facebook is not the last billion-dollar name in this space.

Tarang Shah: How did your entrepreneurial journey begin?

Michael Birch: This was back in the UK. I started out working for other people. I did the normal university thing, graduated, and went to work. I did not become an entrepreneur until I was twenty-nine. I had a degree in physics. I really did not want to do physics. I ended up getting a job with an insurance company doing computer programming because it was what my brother was doing. My brother thought I would love it, but I thought it sounded incredibly boring. I did the job out of pure desperation because there was not anything else to do. I realized insurance is incredibly boring and computers are not that boring at all—they are quite fun. I enjoyed the programming side of it.

I always wanted to do my own thing, but I did not know what I wanted to do. I wanted to do my own thing for two reasons. One, my father was always very much of an entrepreneur. He was self-employed pretty much all of my life. He was a self-employed agriculture consultant. He was a botanist by training.

He was trying to invest in products, technical things like dental floss, that sort of thing. I was always sort of inspired by him. I would hear him on the phone. His home office was next to my bedroom so I would always hear him trying to convince people to start buying this new dental floss off of him and so on. I was always inspired by that, but I did not have the self-confidence when I was young to do that sort of thing. I looked up to him doing it, thinking I could not do it, really just due to a lack of self-confidence as a young person. So I was partially inspired by my father, but I also did not want to work for other people. I did not find that particularly fun.

I was working in companies that were very peer-crowded. I did not feel that I could be rewarded proportionally to the contribution I was making. At the same time, I really did not know what I was going to do. It is really hard to be an insurance entrepreneur.

In 1991, the internet was barely being talked about in the UK. The internet came along and I was quite late noticing it. Then came 1999 and we just had our first child, so it was the worst possible time to start a business. Then I realized that the internet was the thing I could do. I knew about computers, but I did not know about the internet. I left my job and said I would give myself three months to work at home, to try to build a web site and make a business out of it.

In those three months, I did successfully get a web site live. I certainly did not make a business out of it. I did not achieve it in three months, but I got addicted to the process, really enjoyed doing it. I enjoyed far more making no money for myself than making quite a lot of money from someone else. I thought this was it. I knew nothing about the internet when I started, and three months later I felt like I knew everything. In hindsight, I still knew nothing.

I thought I would carry on doing this. I convinced my wife it was a really good idea. She was also a freelance IT consultant. We had another child two years later. She would go back to consulting in between children. We moved twice, took equity out of the property, and continued making no money for those three years. We continued [with] just the two of us working from our bedroom at home.

During that period in 2002, we moved to America and although we were not really making any meaningful money, we had a start-up that was beginning to gain fairly meaningful traction, Birthday Alarm. I think at the time we moved we had about a million members, which by today's standards seems very little, but think back to 2002—hitting the magical million-mark was actually huge.

Shah: I remember when reviewing consumer internet start-ups for investment in 2005 and acquiring two hundred and fifty thousand users was a big deal.

Birch: In 2002, we were pretty happy with our million members. We still were not making any money. At the time, we moved to America we were making about $10,000 a month. From that, we had to pay living expenses for a family of four, and business expenses, which were pretty nominal. So we were not spending a great deal on that, probably a couple thousand dollars a month running the business. We were basically living month to month on the money that we could generate. We carried on doing that. In 2003, we launched our second web site. Prior to that, we had done three other web sites, but they did not work out. They didn't make money or get any meaningful traction.

Shah: Help us understand the process of coming up with the ideas for those ventures. Was there anything in particular you looked at to say "this is something I want to go after," or did the idea just come to you?

Birch: It was a general theme—something I was interested in. I never tried to get funding. I never got funding at all until Bebo, which was the first time I ever tried to get funding. During that whole period, nobody would give me funding because I had no evidence of success and no track record. I knew I was under-funded. If I didn't have any funding, I knew I could not spend money. My time is sort of free, but I can't spend money building a business. I cannot pay for marketing.

If you look at the three biggest costs for start-ups, it is usually advertising or marketing, content, and programming. I figured if I didn't need to pay for the first two and the third one was done by me, then I would not be spending any money developing it and I could just spend $10,000 on a bunch of servers and I am good to go. So that was that. If I did not have a go-to-market[1] budget, I knew I had to create my own web site. We were very close to the tipping point, but we did not make it. We doubled our money, but it was not much. The thing we really wanted to do was social networking.

My brother was also involved in the business. It was myself, my wife, and my brother early on. My brother is very similar to me in many respects. We both love talking about ideas and brainstorming. The three of us, we just continued to talk about things and tried to come up with ideas that we thought were good.

Birthday Alarm came about because reminders are very useful. It is kind of nice to be reminded of birthdays. That worked. People would register. So if you did not know a friend's birthday, you send an e-mail and they can submit their birthday for you, which a lot of people did. A lot of people entered their birthday without registering. The next stage was going to remind you of your friend's birthday—a lot of people said yes to that, creating an infinite loop. You lose people at every stage. We kept focusing on that loop and analyzing it and tracking it.

There were a lot of trials on inviting people and how many people we could get to invite, etc. In 2000, we did the "import your address book" from Hotmail. That was a big one at the time. We also did a Yahoo! import your address book.

I thought it was a fascinating idea, so I tried it on Birthday Alarm. It took me ten hours to code it. I went live that same night. Then the following day we went from ten thousand members in a day to one hundred thousand the following day. It just blew up. We were close to two hundred thousand members a day and we sustained that for over a year and I kept thinking Hotmail would cut us off and they did not, so we grew at least one hundred thousand members a day for a year.

We grew up to three million in a year and we started charging a small fee during that period. That was a financial turning point. We went from $10,000 a month to making $300,000 a month and still spent only $10,000.

---

[1] Marketing and customer acquisition.

Then we launched the social networking site Ringo in 2003. We already owned a domain name called Ringo.com. We started developing it and we went live two weeks later. Three months after the launch, we had about four hundred thousand members. It took a long time to build and scale the web site, though. It was kind of a rollercoaster ride. We ended up selling it prematurely. We had a long struggle from 1999 to 2003 financially and then in 2003 things changed when we sold Ringo.

Shah: Fascinating! When did you launch Bebo? How did it come about?

Birch: We did Bebo in 2005. It started out as a self-updating address book, which was the very first idea we had. I knew that it really did not work because you end up with an address book with 10 percent of your friends in it, which is pointless. We launched it really just so we could get members. We got a million members in nine days!

The ninth day it blew up and out of those million people, only about three people came back. We knew the original idea was not a very good idea. So in its first iteration, Bebo was a self-updating address book that nobody was using. Then we added photo sharing and people started coming back and engaging. Then we evolved it into a social network. We relaunched it as a social network. It was a huge success. The day after we launched the social network, we had six million page views a day. It stayed like that for about a month or two and then the user profiles started to fill out.

Originally all these members had no information on their profiles. Then as they started filling it in, it suddenly helped with new user acquisition and engagement and we were growing 10 to 20 percent a week for many months. We peaked at about three hundred million pages a day. This was the first time we attained funding. On average, we were doing about one hundred million pages a day at the time and we were only seven employees! I was still the only programmer. We had five people doing customer service, finance, and sales. Then we continued to grow and we ended up with about thirty employees by the time we sold the company.

We were late in the game. When we launched Bebo, Myspace was the biggest social networking site in the US. Facebook was about a year ahead of us and they were growing great. At the time we launched the social network, they were just breaking outside of universities. We were late in the game with a very undersized technology team. But for whatever reason we took off in the UK. Myspace was in the UK, but only about 10 percent of people were using it. It was a bit of a virgin market. Ninety percent of people were not using a social network when we launched ours. We just grew like crazy in the UK. Then Facebook launched soon after in a couple of colleges there.

Then as they started launching more widely, we were not able to compete with Facebook. We saw the writing on the wall and could see Facebook dominating the scene.

Shah: Fascinating story. You mentioned that it was you, your brother, and your wife. The three of you were brainstorming together and coming up with ideas and building the businesses together. Michael, is there a power of two or three here that you would advise entrepreneurs to focus on rather than just going solo?

Birch: We are kind of an interesting team because we were co-founders, but we were also immediate family. I found that quite easy to do. With my wife, everything is shared fifty-fifty anyway so there was never any kind of equity issues around that. We divided the work very well. It worked out quite nicely.

I am not sure whether I would personally want to found a business with people other than my immediate family. I get along very well with my brother and I found that enjoyable as well. If you can find that right person to work with, go for it. Some people seem to swear that you should not found a business on your own. I would say the vast majority of successful businesses have multiple founders, but there are always cases where solo founders are doing well. Facebook is an interesting case. Zuckerberg had co-founders, but they played a much more minor role. Zuckerberg has always been the main leader.

Shah: That is true. Michael, you were one of the very few individuals who thought of virality that early on. It is now a buzz word and people just take it for granted. What drove you to experiment with virality—did you follow some other successes in the market at that time or were you just restricted on the resources so you had to come up with low-cost customer acquisition?

Birch: I did it because I was fascinated by the challenge of it and I could build a system on my own. Virality is very exciting when it does work. Getting millions of people to join your web site for nothing is just an incredible way of building wealth in a way and creating a valuable business out of nothing. The idea of me going around spending money on buying traffic was the dullest thing I could spend my time doing. I absolutely did not want to do that. It just felt like a waste of money when I could get it for free. I was fascinated by that.

At the time, people knew what viral marketing was. It seemed that a few people were doing it, but it was kind of a secret thing. If you knew about it, you were not really meant to tell anyone. I would meet a few other people and they would say it was great what you have done and they would want to talk to me about it, but they would say for me not to tell anyone what you do or how you do it.

We started doing viral marketing using address books. I did not notice anyone else doing it for about a year and in that time we added thirty million members. There was no point in shouting it out. We sort of did it on our own. People were not really talking about it. We were doing all sorts of measurements and trials to try to tweak it and how it should work.

We still did not see a lot of other people doing that. And then I remember the time when suddenly everyone started doing it. Myspace did it and I saw them go live with it and then I watched their traffic shoot straight up. Facebook did it. It was just amazing, but it took a long time for people to come up with it.

Shah: So you definitely were one of the pioneers and did it in a scientific fashion.

Birch: There were other people. There were people from a science background experimenting with these things. But it was surprising how few people were doing it and how many people were still spending boatloads of money advertising.

Shah: It was probably the byproduct of the dot-com era, where people were spending so much money to do Super Bowl ads to promote their web sites.

Birch: The funny thing is, when you are growing a community, advertising can build a business, but it does not make sense and feel right. If I see a banner ad to join a social network, it is a very weird experience. But if a friend invites me to join a social network and I sign up and now I am friends with that person on that network, it feels much more natural and organic.

It is very hard to build a social community through ads. If you look at all the successful social networks, and there have been many, I think all were independent start-up companies. Even with their resources and reach, Microsoft and Google could not grow something by just turning up the fire hose. Communities just do not grow in that way, by mass promotion. Facebook, hi5, Bebo—all of them are new, independent-company start-ups that have dominated social networking. None of them spent money advertising.

Shah: Fascinating! Michael, let's go back to Ringo. It grew to a scale where you thought you had only two options, either to sell it or raise money to scale it. You decided to sell it. I have studied Friendster and why it failed, then Myspace made it big, but then lost to Facebook. Help us understand the scaling aspects of social networks. As you said earlier, these sites can grow a million users in matter of days. Your scaling challenge is enormous, especially as you add more rich media like photos and videos to it. What is the key to successful scaling here?

Birch: We did a bad job with Ringo and we did a reasonably good job with Bebo. With Ringo, we did not have any real money at the time. I needed to spend a lot of money and I could not afford to hire anyone. I needed to buy a lot of servers. I just could not afford to do the business. We could have raised money and I could have, in hindsight, quite easily raised money at that point. I was just feeling a little overwhelmed at that time so I decided to sell it and get a bit of money after having worked for four years without any money.

I learned a lot about what I did wrong. I never hit a big scale. I learned the hard way about scaling. So if I built a site again, these were all the things that went wrong with Ringo and this is how I would do it right next time. I came up with a game plan for Bebo and it scaled really well—not that we did not have daily hiccups along the way. We were always able to overcome those.

I think Friendster just went through that same thing, where they were inexperienced about scaling. They launched the web site. They thought degrees of separation were really important, sharing people within three or four degrees. It is an incredibly hard problem to solve. They spent all their time trying to solve a problem that they thought was critical, which in reality is completely irrelevant because Facebook does not even do it.

Shah: Facebook gets you to your friends' friends at the most and that's two degrees.

Birch: Friends' friends is not that hard to scale, but friends' friends' friends are. Facebook just lists your friends. But they do the inspection of two people's friends to show who the mutual friends are. Friendster and Ringo kind of got hooked up on doing something too complicated and irrelevant. We were trying to do the friends' friends' friends and thought that was important to our users and we got a bit stuck on that. I was using the database to work a lot of that stuff out, which was also really dumb. I think it is just a lack of experience for Ringo and a lack of experience for Friendster. Myspace actually did surprisingly well on scaling. They did not have a great technical team, but they did a very good job on scaling.

Shah: Michael, there were probably more than one hundred social networking sites that came, and then most disappeared into thin air. I remember doing a review of the social networking landscape in 2004 to 2005 for my first trend newsletter and had interviewed the co-founder of LinkedIn. They were just launching their experiments with monetization at that time. A couple of the ones I really liked then were LinkedIn and Tribe. Facebook,

Bebo, etc., hadn't even launched back then. Each of these was working with the same concept, connecting friends.

What was so unique about LinkedIn, Facebook, Bebo, Myspace, hi5, etc.? Why did they take off and grow while others either didn't take off at all or failed to keep growing and scaling?

Birch: I think it was a combination of things. Facebook was kind of unique. They did the college thing and they focused on motility[2], which nobody else was doing. The college thing was kind of interesting. I always felt they did not grow as quickly as they could have.

Bebo started out being more similar to Facebook, and then we moved away from that. We added the skin and self-expression, which we probably should not have done. We were always playing catch up with Facebook anyways.

Myspace succeeded mostly because Friendster didn't. Friendster shot themselves in the foot by just failing to scale for a year or two. It was so slow that people were looking for alternatives. Ringo was one of those alternatives at the time. We had four hundred thousand users and we were the second biggest, and then Myspace was coming up behind.

We sold Ringo and in doing so killed it because the acquiring company merged it into a social network that was not working. That really killed it. Myspace managed to scale with traffic and it was kind of a fun, free environment where people could be themselves and it did really well for a while. But I think it was a bit of a novelty and then people got frustrated with it and ended up moving over to Facebook.

Then hi5 came to the market in a big way and they did really well and understood viral marketing. A lot of these networks grew in certain markets and really failed in others. All networks were geographically located at first. hi5 did very, very well internationally in the foreign language market where Myspace and Facebook were not present. So they were the best game in town and they did really well.

A lot of them were terrible products, just not intuitive at all. The ones that did well had a combination of good product design and an understanding of marketing. They managed to cope with the traffic when it came. If you did not get all of those three things right—product design, marketing, and scaling with traffic—you were not going to be one of the social networks that made it.

---

[2] A biological term that refers to the ability to move spontaneously and actively.

Shah: One of them will kill you.

Birch: Any of them can kill you. You need all three for it to work. Marketing, interestingly—if you do build an amazingly good product—your customer base will grow virally by word of mouth. If you can accelerate it, you are much more likely to lead, and there is a network effect. You needed to build your network before others did. Once someone owned a network in a country, it was quite hard to compete with them. When Bebo launched, I would argue that Bebo was a better product than Myspace, but we could not compete with them in the US, because although it was a better product, it was not enough to disrupt the well-established network effect of Myspace.

Shah: It was not ten times better than Myspace to have people want to leave Myspace and move their entire network to Bebo.

Birch: When we competed in a virgin market here in the UK with Myspace, we won. They we were much bigger than Myspace. Here we were a better network. In UK, people would go in Myspace, look at it, and they would say it was not very good, and none of their friends were there and then they would immediately go away. Facebook came along with a better product in the US and they were able to beat Myspace because of it.

Shah: Turning to Facebook, how would you characterize their success and key ingredients that led to their success?

Birch: I think the whole university thing helped them grow. Had they just launched as an open social network, I think it would have been different. I think the reason they succeeded, one thing they did, which is different than most social networks, was they were very closed. Not closed in terms of colleges. When you signed in, the only people you could see in Facebook were your friends.

The problem we had and many other social networks had, was that we started fairly open. If you were not young and you signed in, you felt like you were in the wrong place. It was like walking into a bar in England. Now that I am forty and if the bar is full of eighteen-year-olds, I just turn around and walk out and go to the pub next door with people in their thirties and forties because I feel more comfortable. That was a big problem on Myspace. There were a lot of people that did not feel they fit in. They did not relate to a lot of the people who were on it who were posting silly comments.

If you were an educated thirty-year-old, Myspace was just not for you. If you logged into Facebook, you would find that it was full of thirty-year-olds, Stanford graduates working in Silicon Valley. If a fifteen-year-old logged into Facebook, they would find out it was full of fifteen-year-olds who they knew.

It was highly compartmentalized and I think that enabled them to keep on growing.

Shah: So by way of design, it turned out to be the way the social fabric is in real life rather than trying to merge the two layers of social fabric—for example, people in their teens and people in thirties and forties—that naturally did not get comfortable with each other's presence.

Birch: Exactly. They also did a few other things. They insisted on real names. They did not let you change your name. There was real identity. They were the first ones to do that. They were very insistent on it. Because they did it from the beginning, it was always that way. People expected that. Ultimately, it was incredibly useful way to find someone by their name.

Shah: Jonathan Abrams, the founder of Friendster, was also very keen on people keeping their original identity, unlike Myspace.

Birch: He was right-on with that idea. Facebook also adopted that idea. Facebook coped with growth, so they did not let scaling stand in the way. They built a fairly good, simple, clean product, which worked. That was all they really needed to do. In a way, they did not do anything that amazing early on. They did check all the boxes and get everything right. That was ultimately what people wanted.

When they matured, they became much slicker. If you remember the early days of Facebook, it really was not pretty. It was fairly ugly. Now they have become a very, very slick product with photo sharing and so on. They have become very, very refined and then continue to grow very, very well. We were growing at the time in the UK much faster than Facebook and we were an open network. They ended up beating us when they opened up. I think if they had opened up in the beginning, we never would have gotten a foothold.

Shah: How did you handle scaling at Bebo when you were offering very storage-intensive features like unlimited photos?

Birch: We never had a cap on photos. I tried to keep it as simple as possible. In hindsight, I would do it differently, but it seemed to work for the time. We did not do any complicated storage thing. We just had a lot of big servers. We just remembered from the database which drive we stored a photo on. It was very, very simple. You always have to try to come up with things that scale so they can still work.

The database is always the hardest thing. Databases, by design, do not scale. That is one thing I would do differently. At the time, we used Oracle and they are just not well-suited for these kind of applications. The way I decided to do it was dividing the tables across many databases. We ended up with about three hundred servers. I sort of felt we were always using too many databases and we should have done that differently.

Shah: You competed with Myspace in the UK, and you could beat them hands down because your product was better than theirs. You were an open network when initially Facebook was in several universities as a closed network. And then they decided to open it up so they competed head to head with Bebo and eventually got ahead of Bebo. What were they doing that you could not do to beat them or kill their momentum in UK?

Birch: The big, big problem with Bebo was it became young as a community. It alienated anyone over twenty-five. Even if they were twenty-one, the other members were too young. We ended up being this teen network, which was never by design. I designed it for myself. The demographics that used the site, they just dominated it.

Again, this was part of the benefit of having a closed network for Facebook. Not just the closed college network, but the fact that you cannot see everyone else, you can only see your friends. I feel if I would have done that one thing, we may have done much, much better than we did do.

We basically left the field wide open for Facebook to dominate anything other than the teen market. We stayed relatively strong in teens for a long time, but then Facebook continued to evolve. After we sold it, Bebo did not evolve. AOL did not pay attention to it. Facebook became a preferred product over Bebo. In the media, Facebook was constantly talked about. Then even a lot of the young teenage demographic ended up going to Facebook as well.

Shah: Great insights indeed. Every time we thought that social networking has been exhausted and it is at its full potential, someone comes along and surprises us. Facebook is the most recent example. You look at that as a network effect and you say someone is so big—too big to fail or have someone else to take over—but every time there is a shift and then something else happens or something bigger happens. Friendster to Myspace to Facebook. What are your thoughts on what's next for social networking and major opportunities on the horizon?

Birch: I think we are still in the early days. It is easy to think it's all done when you are in the thick of it. I think you will look back to this time and say, that was just the beginning.

As far as monetization, I think we have only scratched the surface as that has not been the focus for anyone in social networking. And yet, there are so many ways in which you can monetize. I think monetization is in its very early days. Most people are on a social network now. I think social networks will always continue to evolve, but I cannot picture what they would look like. Facebook is the dominant US-based social network. I do not see a day in the future where Facebook is going to be replaced with someone else.

What is interesting though, everyone thought Facebook was dominating and along came Twitter and Twitter has become a social network and an incredibly big force in social media. You hear about Twitter as much as you do Facebook in terms of media. It is interesting how these niches occur. People can create multibillion-dollar businesses out of them. I also mentioned earlier, once someone is entrenched in a network, it is difficult to beat them unless you are way better. Even if someone created a network that is a little better than Facebook, it is probably not going to win.

Shah: The dominant one has to really falter so people start looking for something else.

Birch: Or someone has to create something that is much better. I think it is quite hard to create something that is that much better than Facebook. Part of the reason I did do Bebo because I was looking at Myspace thinking you could definitely create something much better than Myspace. It was not a very good product. That is why I did it. I was told I was mad since Myspace was the biggest. I thought we could create something better than that.

Facebook was off to do the same thing. We ended up beating Myspace in the UK market, but not in the US. Someone did come along and completely beat them in the US, it just did not happen to be us. I think in my hypothesis, I did not execute well enough to be that one. There was that window of opportunity to be that one and Facebook was the one that did it. The only way to beat Facebook now is to create a multibillion-dollar business that could do something that they do not do, which is what Twitter kind of did. They positioned themselves differently. Carved out a market in doing so.

You look at Tumblr, which is kind of an interesting case where they are creating what could be a multibillion-dollar business. They are doing something in social media that is different to what Facebook is doing. I think that is the jewel. There are certain things Facebook will not be and cannot be without destroying what they already have. That is where the opportunity is for other people to come along. They can say Facebook will never do this, so we will do it, and we will do it very, very well. We can create a real business out of it.

Shah: Every start-up is a one-trick pony. They are so unique with that one narrow thing they do, but at the same time they leave a wide-open field around them for others to come in and take everything else. When you execute so well on one thing, which you have to do to survive and grow as a start-up, then that also means you are looking at X-1, where you are 1 and X is the whole market opportunity. The rest of X is open for someone to come in, because you are only good at one thing, which is 1.

Birch: Agreed. It is fascinating how broad Facebook and social networks can be, in that they actually come with a lot of stuff. They are not just photo sharing, not just playing games, not just staying in contact with friends. There are actually quite a lot of different things, but they still cannot be everything. I am not sure they could ever compete with Amazon, for example. I think it would be weird to go to Facebook to go shopping. There are certain markets that go against the brand.

Shah: When companies mature, I think these are those that lend themselves to the next big player or set of players to come in and take everything else.

Birch: You just have to spot the opportunity that is left open.

Shah: Michael, you were very good at segmenting the market and figuring out what existing players were not doing and really focusing on solving that. Bebo was a great example of that. I wish more entrepreneurs would come in with those kinds of market and competitive assessments to show what's left open and why they can execute very, very well in those white spaces.

What is your thinking process on exits? You have sold multiple companies. You sold Ringo and Bebo. You had a huge opportunity in front of you in both cases. At the same time, you had to make a call as to what is the best time to exit. How did you decide?

Birch: With Bebo, I just felt we had an impossible job ahead of us to continue growing it. We had not grown for a number of months prior to selling. We had not been going down in traffic, but we basically sat still. I thought we were doing too little, too late. We were in an interesting position because we were the largest social network that people could afford to buy as a start-up.

Myspace was already owned by Fox. Facebook really was not an option because they were clearly not willing to sell. They were going alone. Bebo was good. There were other sites like hi5, which was a little bigger, but very high on the price. If someone wanted to be in social networking, we were the best opportunity for them to buy their way into it. We thought we could spare some value. Our revenue was about $20 million a year. Had I believed early there was a good chance that we could continue to grow it and be much better, then I would not have sold. Not that it was impossible, but I thought it would be very difficult for us, alone and without help, to take it to another level.

Maybe we could grow it twice as big, but there was an opportunity to sell it at a pretty high valuation. Again, I never had a big exit prior to this. We sold Ringo for a couple of millions. I did not really need the money, but this sale was of a bigger order than anything else I had done before. It was a life-changing amount of money and an opportunity to sell.

Shah: You owned the majority of the company as well.

Birch: We owned about 70 percent, which was nice as well. It just felt like there wasn't a good reason not to sell it. Early on we decided that we did not want to sell when we were going strongly enough. I was looking forward—about how depressing it would be if I did not sell and it went downhill instead of up. This is what happened to a lot of competitors.

Shah: So it was an excellent judgment call on your part. Now in the case of Ringo, you just understood what your limitations were and couldn't afford to keep it going.

Birch: With Ringo, I probably should not have sold. I did not get much for it. It was early on and I should have probably waited. It did not go so well for Friendster, but maybe it could have gone well for us. In hindsight, the whole world economy crashed a couple months after we sold Bebo. That was not judgment, that was just luck with timing.

Shah: You have had successes and failures, and you are now entrepreneur turned investor. What is your thinking around why start-ups fail?

Birch: It generally always comes down to execution. Most companies are not executing the business or product. I think the hardest thing to do is build great products. If you build great products, you generally do quite well.

Shah: Now you are an investor in several start-ups. What do you look for in the entrepreneurs and companies you back?

Birch: When I do investments, I do not invest in anybody I do not like. I look for sort of a childish energy and excitability. If someone cannot get excited about what they are doing, they can't build great companies. You also have to be very smart. You find all sorts of people. You find very loud, outgoing people. You find very introverted, shy people, but they can still have that excitement and passion about what they are doing. They can still be very, very smart. I think the personalities can be quite different, but they still have to have those attributes.

Shah: So being excited and passionate about the problem they are solving and also being extremely smart about solving the problem in a meaningful way.

Birch: Yes, but they cannot be delusional. If you watch *American Idol*, you get people who think they can sing and they really cannot. You have to find someone where you do not have a one-way conversation. If they are just telling you about who they are and not listening to you, it's a bad sign. You want someone who can actually listen and reflect on things and change their mind.

Often people are the worst judge of their own ideas. You always think that your own ideas are quite good. If they are not willing to bounce ideas off other people and validate, that can be an issue.

Mitchell Kertzman

Hummer Winblad Venture Partners

Mitchell Kertzman is a managing director at Hummer Winblad Venture Partners. He has more than 30 years of experience as a CEO of public and private software companies. Most recently, Mitchell was chairman and CEO of Liberate Technologies. Before joining Liberate, he was chairman of the board and CEO of Sybase. Mitchell was founder and CEO of Powersoft, which merged with Sybase in February 1995.

A former programmer, Mitchell founded Powersoft in 1974. Hummer Winblad invested in the company in 1991, and Powersoft became the leading provider of client-server development tools with its flagship product, PowerBuilder. The company's merger with Sybase in 1995 was, at the time, the most valuable in the history of the software industry.

In this interview, Mitchell brings together his tremendous experience as a successful entrepreneur, the CEO of large companies, and a venture investor. He highlights the key characteristics of successful markets, market timing, entrepreneurs, team building, and product, which all play a crucial role in building market-leading products and companies.

What I love about Mitchell is the clarity of his thoughts on identifying promising markets and entrepreneurs, and converting them into billion-dollar successes.

Tarang Shah: How do you pick markets for investment?

Mitchell Kertzman: The company I founded, Powersoft, entered into a market that was already established. But we entered the market with a new solution, new technology, and something disruptive. Existing markets are relatively easy markets, because they have essentially sized themselves. You can analyze the openness of the market to replacements, disruptions, dissatisfaction with current solutions, competitive position of existing players, etc. So you can size and analyze whether your entry expands the market. For example, when we introduced Powersoft's development tools, we had a thesis that it was possible to expand the market with people who can develop using tools that were more graphical and easy to use. The harder part is the markets that haven't sized and identified themselves.

We are in the process of making an investment currently in the big-data market. This is a market that is unknown in size. We can't size the market. What we can do instead is use our knowledge of the broader market in which it competes—including data management, analytics, etc.—coupled with other factors like quality of the team. So this is a riskier investment and affects our investment thesis, valuation, etc.

It doesn't keep us from investing. It's in the market we are pretty familiar with—the enterprise software market. So the market size is essentially unknown. It will still be a great investment, because it's a great team and a great product, and we think the technology can be potentially important.

Shah: So when the market size is unknown, as it is the case for new markets, how do you determine the attractiveness of those markets?

Kertzman: We won't go into the market with the thesis that it's going to be a small market. However, when the markets cannot be sized, we go by intuition rather than analytics. I myself am not an analytical guy, but I always surrounded myself with people who are analytical. I am looking for *big* markets, but I don't really quantify that and there is no minimum quantifiable size. I am looking for large opportunities. No one in venture really says this, but I am not looking for niches. Having 100 percent of a niche market is not nearly as good as having 15 percent of the really big market.

Shah: You mentioned that you like the existing markets in which you can expand or steal market share from existing guys using disruptive solutions. Can you tell me more about this approach?

Kertzman: I like existing markets that you can disrupt. They are hard because they have existing players. If you can find real disruptions, real innovations, real discontinuous innovations—particularly if you find innovations that existing players are unlikely or unable to adopt given their commitment to existing technologies and offerings—then I like those kinds of opportunities.

Shah: This requires a very deep understanding of the existing landscape.

Kertzman: For sure. That's one of the reasons we are so focused here at Hummer Winblad on enterprise software. That's why we are not doing enterprise software one day and electric cars or medical equipment the other day. Those can be great investment opportunities, but that's not what we do. We are completely focused on this domain.

Shah: Are new markets really innovative or new flavors of existing markets?

Kertzman: I think there are a lot of successes that are new flavors of the existing markets. Even the entire personal computer industry was built on disruption, a disruption of host computing. The iPhone was disruptive. In a way it is brand new, but not a new market. I think what you find probably is that a lot of things people think are new markets are genuinely disruptive of the existing markets.

[Consider] real pioneers, like AOL when it came into the market. You had CompuServe, but those companies were really creating a new market, this online thing. You could say whether you give credit to Myspace, Facebook, or whatever, these social networks were new markets and new ways for people to connect and network.

If you define the market broadly enough, like web sites, then you could say it was an existing market, but in many ways it was pretty innovative. There are truly innovative ideas, but I think most ideas are essentially doing something in a manner that is more disruptive and yet playing in the existing market.

Shah: How do you get yourself comfortable about the new trend as an investment?

Kertzman: The issue of market sizing depends on how precise you want to be. I think the comment I made was I do not think I require a huge amount of precision on market size. We are always seeing entrepreneurs coming in with presentations that have Gartner or Forrester or IDC research, or something else that claims to show market sizing. I mostly ignore those because I do not know that they are any smarter about that than anybody else.

I think it is really important to have domain expertise, which is what we have in the enterprise software space. That is the importance of the focus. That is all we do. We only do enterprise software. If we have to go to IDC to determine whether we think a market is big enough for investment, then I think that may answer the question in itself.

Shah: How important is market timing?

Kertzman: It's pretty important. The question is whether you would rather be a little too early than too late. If you are a little too early, you can adjust the strategy. For example, you can fly a little lower to the ground, spend less money, and you are in a current position with the market as it develops.

It's easy to adjust when you are little early. It's really hard to adjust when you are late. I don't believe you have to be the first to market. So it is possible to enter the market with competitors when you have the superior solution, superior team, and superior execution. So I am not afraid to enter the market where there are competitors. But for the start-ups, you do want to know if some of these competitors have the momentum and the mindshare, such that the only real way to overcome them is by outspending them. I never want to invest in the market where the only way you can win is by spending more money than the other guy.

Shah: That's buying market share!

Kertzman: That was the strategy in the internet bubble. You spent more money to get more eyeballs and companies were valued on multiples of spend rather than multiple of revenue. The theory was that only the company who spent more than others would gain the market share. That's a foolish game. As a venture investor, you can't make money with that strategy.

Shah: What's the difference between being a little early vs. too early?

Kertzman: The ultimate question is, does the market ever develop and can you tell the difference between early and non-existent? Many entrepreneurs like to think they are just a little early. There is no way to prove that. All you can do is make sure you don't spend yourself off the cliff. That is no guarantee that a market ever develops.

It's very difficult for start-ups to spend enough money to create a market demand that doesn't exist. If there is no demand, if people have no idea that this is anything of interest, that's a challenging market to go into. You might say that there is big opportunity and innovation in those markets. That may be true, but that's the risk profile we probably don't want to pursue.

Shah: Are there any indicators you use to determine if the market is early, emerging, or non-existent?

Kertzman: I don't think there is anything specific. We tend to do diligence with potential buyers in the market, usually IT organizations. We need to be able to say to them, "Do you have this problem, do you even perceive you have a problem? Where is it on your pain-point spectrum? If somebody could offer this solution would you be interested in it, would you be likely to evaluate it?"

I have had cases where I loved the start-up and went out to the market and asked the customers these questions. And customers didn't give me any impression that this was important or an issue for them.

Shah: If the customer doesn't think this is a pain point, the start-up is not going anywhere, at least in near future.

Kertzman: That may mean today as opposed to four or five years from now. As venture investors, if we see something we like and the customers tell us that it's not the pain point, it's not that we write it off our minds forever. We wait until we are getting some indications from the market that there is a need out there.

Shah: What are the key characteristics of successful entrepreneurs?

Kertzman: I tend to like entrepreneurs who don't say, "I [would] like to start a company. Let me look around to see what interesting ideas there are to pick from." I am looking for entrepreneurs who are like Richard Dreyfuss in the movie *Close Encounters of the Third Kind*, who felt compelled to build a uniquely shaped mountain.

I like entrepreneurs who are building businesses because they have to. They have so much passion, so much belief in what they are doing that they almost don't have a choice but to build it. They have to do it—they have that kind of passion and commitment. I much prefer that approach to finding a business and market than the approach of "I want to be an entrepreneur and let me find and analyze various market opportunities."

Shah: Both as an entrepreneur and VC, what's your strategy and thought process when it comes to building market-leading and differentiated products?

Kertzman: When I first started developing software in the 1960s, I was a student and practitioner of ergonomics and usability. So I tend to put a high premium on usability, whether that's a user interface, instability, etc. If the market is big enough, then the market should be able to tolerate some amount of imperfection in the first releases of the software product.

The product can be good enough and doesn't need to be perfect initially because "good enough" is better than whatever else they are using, and hence able to accommodate some amount of imperfection to get access to this new solution.

Sometimes the company I invest in or I am on the board of doesn't want to release the software until it's perfect. I am not fan of that. That doesn't mean I want them to release a bad or low-quality product, but in software there is no such thing as a perfect product. The value of market feedback and customer feedback is so high in refining your understanding of the product need that you need to get the product to the market, though it's not perfect.

Shah: What role does the value proposition play in building market-leading products?

Kertzman: I am a fan of hard value propositions vs. soft value propositions like increase in productivity, etc. I like to be able to quantify value proposition. Beyond that, value proposition ideally shouldn't need to be that complex for customers to understand. If there is a market need, the value proposition should be self-evident. If the value proposition is complex and arcane, then you will never get time to explain that. Ultimately you will have two choices with the value proposition—more revenue or less cost. I think most CEOs will prefer more revenue as they figured they can control their cost.

Shah: What are the key traits of entrepreneurs you like to invest in?

Kertzman: It's an interesting combination of patience and impatience. You cannot give up easily, as it's hard to build the companies. You cannot simply relax and think it may come, but rather you must push, push, and push. I always say that an interesting characteristic is "not to panic." If you have seen the book *The Hitchhiker's Guide to the Galaxy,*[1] its cover reads "don't panic." I always think that there should be an "Entrepreneur's Guide to Billion-Dollar Exit" with the words "don't panic" written on the cover.

There are so many other characteristics that entrepreneurs need to succeed. They need to have tremendous domain knowledge. If you have an entrepreneur who is evaluating an enterprise software business and buying a fast-food franchise, those things don't go together. It's super-important that entrepreneurs have strong customer and market knowledge.

Other characteristics include high integrity and openness. Lots of entrepreneurs view venture investors with suspicion. I will never invest with an entrepreneur who has that attitude. I should be able to trust the entrepreneur and I need the entrepreneur to always tell me what's going on and be open to input. I don't want an entrepreneur to ask me, "What should I do?" Or, "What do you want me to do?" Ultimately, the entrepreneur or CEO has to take my input as input rather than do everything I say.

Shah: Are the entrepreneurs in their twenties and thirties better at coming up with and building billion-dollar start-ups than the relatively older entrepreneurs?

---

[1] Douglas Adams, *The Hitchhiker's Guide to the Galaxy* (New York: Harmony Books, 1979).

Kertzman: The ones in my area were started by people relatively young. When I started the company that became Powersoft, I was twenty-five. If you look at the really big, successful companies, they were usually started by entrepreneurs relatively early in their careers and in age. If you look at somebody like Google, they brought in Eric Schmidt. Although they were young when they started it, they brought in adult supervision.

I would say there seems to be a pattern that would say that if you are going to select for billion-dollar companies, then yes there seems to be a characteristic there of starting at a relatively younger age.

Shah: What do you think is the main reason for that?

Kertzman: I do not have any specific data on it, but I would say it is more likely that people early in their careers are more willing to take risks. You probably do not have a family and those kinds of responsibilities that perhaps make you more conservative later in life. When I started my company, I was actually going to start it with a co-founder, who had been my boss. He was in his forties and had five kids. Ultimately, he decided not to do that with me because he had kids that were going to be going to college and he felt he could not take the risk. So he went and found another management job at a large company.

It is not just a willingness to start a business, but maybe the willingness to take big chances and risk in the business that you might not be willing to take if you have kids, a family, and all that. You also may not know the things you are not supposed to do. That is not the guarantee of success. My guess would be that for every entrepreneur that started a billion-dollar business we know of, there may be one thousand young entrepreneurs that start and fail. It is not a guarantee.

Shah: Do you think serial entrepreneurs have the same probability of success as first-time entrepreneurs, or is it higher?

Kertzman: I think it is lower. I think it is a bit like the disclaimer they give in financial services, which is that past performance is no guarantee of future success. I think that there may be people who have great personal characteristics, but they do not necessarily have multiple billion-dollar ideas. There are not that many billion-dollar ideas. The likelihood that a single person would come up with one of them is quite low.

You have guys like Bill Poduska in Boston. He was the founder of both Prime Computer and Apollo Computer. He had a couple of really big wins, which is very unusual. But then his next company was Stellar Computer, which was not a successful company. Getting two was pretty amazing, but it is not a guarantee.

On the other hand, you are filtering by billion-dollar companies and I think there are a lot of companies that are extremely successful for their entrepreneurs and their investors. Look at Powersoft. It got to be about $150 million in revenue and had a public market cap of $500 or $600 million. We were acquired for nearly $1 billion, but we didn't get to be $1 billion in revenue or market cap. Yet it was a phenomenally successful company for all involved.

I think if you lower the bar from a billion to other numbers, which can still be big successes, then I think that you will start to find a serial entrepreneur capable of doing more than one. Or it is possible for somebody even in his or her forties to start a successful company. There are a bunch of advantages there. They have teams of people that they know from the past that they can bring in. They know investors. They have some advantages, although they may not have the characteristics that we talked about in young people.

Shah: How do successful entrepreneurs recruit their teams?

Kertzman: I like entrepreneurs who hire people who are smarter and better than they are at that job. When I started Powersoft, I was a one-man business and did every job myself. When I hired people, I hired people who were better than I was at that job, whether it was selling, programming, or accounting.

One of the great failings I see is entrepreneurs who are afraid to hire people who are better than they are. They are afraid that they will hire people that may make them look bad or make them feel insecure. That's deadly. In terms of hiring, the single most important thing is that I want people to aim high when they hire and aim for people who are ultimately going to be better than the entrepreneurs themselves.

Shah: How about founders who are deeply in love with technology but lack business acumen?

Kertzman: I don't think founders necessarily have to have tremendous business acumen as long as they bring co-founders or other partners they bring in to help with that. The founder could be just the technologist, and that's fine as long as they can bring someone in to complement that.

Shah: How do you analyze viability and scalability of the business model?

Kertzman: Venture Capital is all about "pattern recognition." You analyze the model for internal consistency to see if there are assumptions in the model that are untested or far out. Does it have flaws, like maybe it has a two-year sales cycle? It would be hard to make money with a two-year sales cycle. Then you look for external proof points and apply your knowledge of market to it.

I look at the business model and financial plan as a thesis. I never expect that to be predictive, as the final model frequently turns out differently from the original model. It's not like in three years I am going to say you missed this metric. But when you are evaluating an investment, you've got to test if the thesis is credible and consistent, and that various components of the model are achievable.

You should also test if it can ultimately scale in terms of market size, in terms of how many people you need to hire as it grows, and in terms of profitability. There are examples of models that tell you that you lose money on every sale, but you make up in volume. That just doesn't work.

Shah: YouTube is a great example of that. With every additional customer, you incur bandwidth.

Kertzman: Only Google or Microsoft can afford to keep it running like that.

Shah: What other factors are important in creating billion-dollar start-up successes?

Kertzman: There are a random set of economic conditions that you just can't plan for. So luck plays a role in building major successes. One can argue that great markets combined with great people create their own luck. There may be some truth to that. But if any successful entrepreneurs don't mention luck as one of the forces that played a role in their success, they are giving themselves too much credit.

Shah: I like what Steve Jobs says about hiring "A" players. You should hire A players, otherwise B players will hire C players, and C players will hire Ds, and before you know it you will have Z players walking around in your organization. What is your definition of A players?

Kertzman: I think it is self-defining. "A" players are the best there is at their jobs in their domains. I think it is not just knowledge, but there are all the cultural factors of fit, work ethic, and integrity. I am a big believer in the importance of cultural fit. In other words, it is not just about performance, but it is how you work with the team and how you move a consistent positive culture of the company forward.

I probably put as much weight on personal characteristics as I do on pure performance. If you are a sales person, look at your numbers. If you are an engineer, what is your productivity and output and skill set. I think all those things are fine, but I also think it is really important to have people that fit with the culture and fit with the team.

Shah: When you are looking to invest or help build the team in your existing investment, and you are looking for "A" players, these are the characteristics that you look for. But sometimes it is hard to tell during an interview or meeting with them that they are really what they say they are vs. what we like to hear. What is your way of separating this?

Kertzman: When I was running companies, it was important to what I did. If it is a CEO, then the board is doing the hire and you have all the members of the board do the interview. What is important is to have more than one input. Having a person interviewed by a number of different people gives you some triangulation and some other opinions. I think one of the ways you do that is to have a person talk to other members of the existing team.

I am a big believer in not just doing one interview, but in having many people interview them and then get everybody's feedback. That does not mean any one individual has a veto power, but it does mean that you get the benefit of a lot of different points of view, particularly around the issues of attitude style and cultural fit.

I think it is very helpful to have a lot of people give feedback on that and get a sense of the person, particularly if you are hiring sales people. Sales people by definition are pretty skilled at presenting things in a way they want you to see them. So you cannot guarantee that what you see is what you get.

Reference checking is good. A guy that was on my board early in my career, who had become a CEO of a large company working his way up through sales and sales management, told me that he once went to a seminar by some expert in how to recognize and recruit great sales people. He went through this seminar and at the end, the guy that was leading it said, "I have given you all the characteristics and traits of great sales people, but before you go out and follow this blindly, I want to tell you something. This is the exact same list of traits and characteristics of great con artists, and you will not know which one you have until after you hire them." To some extent, separating can never be perfect and you have to be prepared to recognize if you made a mistake and act on it.

Shah: Between the two competitors, who has better probability of success—the one with better go-to-market strategy or one with the better product?

Kertzman: Broadly, I always think that A-level execution with a "B" product will beat B-level execution with an "A" product. I think that a great product is insufficient without great execution.

Shah: What are the key components of execution besides go-to-market strategy?

Kertzman: I think everything in a business model is execution. It is team, pricing, and channel strategy. I think a lot of it is wrapped up in what you might consider go-to-market. It is everything about running a business. One of the things we had at Powersoft was a great HR department that helped us build a great team. That does not sound like go-to-market, but it was a super-important part of execution for us.

Shah: Do you need to be first mover to win?

Kertzman: Nope. Look at Myspace and Facebook. Myspace was first, but Facebook is the winner. I think first mover is overrated. You might say that there might be a slight benefit if the execution is there, but execution will beat the first mover. The first mover runs the risk of showing people that there is market, but it could be an inferior product or an inferior team. Look at Microsoft. They were not the first in the market. Digital Research was first in the market, but Microsoft beat them. They out-executed them. There are a lot of stories of people that came to the market that were not first, but ended up the big winners.

Shah: Because the first couple of guys are really educating the market vs. other guys coming in and saying the market is educated enough, let's just ride this through great execution.

Kertzman: Yes. And let's out-execute or let's bring a better product to the market. I think there are a lot of examples of that. Although not every first mover gets beaten, enough first movers get beaten to, I think, make me come down on the side that the first mover is overrated.

Scott Sandell

NEA: Salesforce, WebEx, Bloom Energy

Scott Sandell is general partner at New Enterprise Associates (NEA). He was named on the Forbes 2011 "Midas List," placing fifth among the top 100 venture capitalists. He focuses on investments in information technology and alternative energy, and he is responsible for NEA's activities in China.

Scott's board memberships include Bloom Energy, CloudFlare, Fisker Automotive, DreamFactory, Fusion-io, HelioVolt, SolFocus, Spreadtrum Communications, SugarCRM, Tableau Software, and Workday. He has sponsored investments in 3ware (acquired by Applied Micro Circuits Corporation), Amplitude Software (acquired by Critical Path), Data Domain (acquired by EMC), FineGround Networks (acquired by Cisco), Neoteris (acquired by Juniper Networks), NetIQ, Playdom (acquired by Disney), WebEx, and Salesforce.com.

Scott has been part of many billion-dollar start-ups across various emerging sectors and geographies, from the internet sector in the late 1990s to clean energy and China more recently. Leveraging his fifteen years of successful venture experience, Scott provides invaluable insights into what it takes to build billion-dollar start-ups, including key characteristics of founders, promising new markets, great products, and sustainable competitive advantages.

Tarang Shah: What are some of the key reasons why start-ups fail or fail to achieve their original potential?

Scott Sandell: I think one of the biggest ones is that the entrepreneurs assume things are going to happen in the way they want them to happen, and that the business is going to develop at the speed they plan for it to develop. They spend money accordingly. What happens is the revenue does not materialize, but the costs do. They fail to make adjustments to their costs because it is always hard to scale back.

On the other hand, the most successful entrepreneurs are very circumspect about when revenues will develop, when customers will show traction with a service or a product. Irrespective of whatever plan they presented to the VC in the beginning, they are just incredibly miserly with money. They never get themselves into the awkward spot of needing to raise money without having a compelling plan and compelling results.

The farther on you go in a business, the more your ability to raise money is a function of results as opposed to hope and potential. Those businesses that spend on plan end up raising money on increasingly unattractive terms or none at all if things take longer than anticipated. Whereas the business that spends it much more slowly than the original plan has a much longer runway to figure out the business they are actually in.

They still may fail, but they have a lot longer to figure it out. In that period of time, they often will raise more money long before they need it. I can think of two companies I am involved in, one of which will remain nameless, but these companies are similar—they are both doing hard, revolutionary technical things in different fields. Really big ideas, capital-intensive kind of things.

One of them is Bloom Energy. The other one I am not going to name. Obviously, Bloom is the successful one. Bloom has overcome more extraordinary technical and business challenges than any company I have been a part of. I have been on the board since 2003.

Shah: I believe Bloom was started by K. R. Sridhar from NASA, right?

Sandell: Yes. He came out a year before and John Doerr [of Kleiner Perkins] funded him in Series A, and I did Series B a year later. Relative to the original business plan, Bloom is way behind schedule. But Bloom is going to be a spectacular company. And it is going to be a spectacular company in no small measure because K. R. always raised money way before he needed it. Relative to the resources at his disposal, he always spends money in a way that means his runway is extremely long. He raises more money because people are always wanting to get into Bloom, so he has been able to raise money on attractive terms.

The other company did not think that way and arguably had a similar opportunity to Bloom, but it spent the money according to plan and slipped behind milestones and waited until the money was out before going out to raise more money, which made it hard to raise money. There are other factors at work, for sure, but it is a tale of two cities.

Shah: If you compare them and the CEOs leading those two, what are the daily, weekly, monthly metrics that they are looking at? What metrics indicate that the original hypothesis is not materializing and I need to be working on a different plan?

Sandell: I think the key factor here is how remarkable K. R. Shridhar is. He is not only the technical visionary but he is the rock star CEO, too. He knows the whole company from the technology through to the business and customers, which gives him an enormous advantage. If you can do both of those things, it gives you enormous advantage over the person who is one or the other.

Of course, there are companies who have great partnerships between the technical visionary and the business leader, but I think if you have it in the same person it is very powerful. In the case of Bloom, every time the original game plan did not appear to be working, K. R. himself would lead a very intense effort to figure out how to get around the problem that presented itself. He never waited for the board to tell him. More often than not, he would come to the board and say, "Last quarter we encountered this problem and it occurred to us that if we could not solve the problem, the game was probably over. So, we decided to start an effort, which involved the whole company. We worked 24/7 and we have been doing that for six weeks and just last Sunday at four o'clock in the afternoon, we figured out a solution to this problem." That happened at least once a year and sometimes twice in one year.

For K. R. and others, when something is not right, they go after it with a vengeance and they re-examine all their assumptions. It is not business as usual—it is life threatening. They reprioritize and change the way they are thinking about it as necessary to reach some new plan, which has the same or greater potential as the original. I think it is this ability to rapidly innovate and adjust that is crucial. We call it "open-field running." The really great athletes are the ones who do not need a play.

And when you look at the great plays, they often involve "open field running," which is running beyond what was planned. And the great players are masters of open-field running. They have the ability to make very rapid adjustments, assess situations as they present themselves, make good decisions, and go at it with the kind of energy and determination that you would expect to see in the Super Bowl.

Shah: Now this is very different than your personal favorite sport, rowing?

Sandell: Rowing is not that kind of a sport. I played football in high school. I much prefer rowing, possibly because I was not a great football player. The challenges of rowing also have something in common with achieving success in business. It is a sport that requires incredible determination and self-sacrifice and the ability to withstand a huge amount of pain. It is a sport where a lot of people try, and not very many people make it. Of all the sports I have done, rowing will separate the men from the boys the fastest. And it is the ultimate team sport, which is true of all businesses that scale.

Shah: Fascinating!

Sandell: Let me tell you about another guy that is coming into my office in two hours. His name is Sam Sheng. Sam is a guy that I had the pleasure to first meet because a famous professor at UC Berkeley, Bob Brodersen, called one of my partners, Forest Baskett, about six years ago and said, "Sam Sheng is starting a company, and Sam is one of the most outstanding students I have had at Berkeley and one of the best semiconductor designers I have ever seen." That is enough to get a meeting.

Sam came along with his partner, another PhD from Berkley, Weijie Yun. They invented something nobody thought was possible at the time, which is a chip that could put an analog TV signal on your cell phone. It would consume a ridiculously small amount of power and therefore not be a drain on the battery of the user, and it would work anywhere in the world. They could do everything in the standard CMOS process[1].

Right on plan and on schedule, they shipped that chip about two and a half years later, and that chip produced somewhere between $300 to $400 million of revenue in the next two and a half years. Over $100 million of retained earnings. That made Telegent Systems, at that time, the fastest-growing semiconductor company in history.

The second chapter is a harder chapter because it got commoditized when other people were able to copy it. The business today is a shadow of its former self. But Sam is one of those extraordinary entrepreneurs. He is not just an extraordinary technologist. What I enjoy most is to find people who are extraordinary technologists who can make these incredible breakthrough innovations, but who also have enough entrepreneurial sensibility and business judgment that they can become very effective partners with the business people around them, including people like me.

---

[1] CMOS is technology used in microprocessors.

What does Sam have that might not be so common? He has a lot of common sense. Ben Franklin pointed out to us a long time ago that common sense is not so common. [Sam] has a lot of common sense. He has a clarity of thinking which I think is essential to making the kinds of open-field running decisions that everyone faces.

It is not only the ability to think clearly about any given problem but also to be able to explain the rationale or the decision or the concept to people in everyday English, to communicate with anyone. That turns out to be an enormously valuable skill. A lot of people who are very technically astute do not have that skill. In fact, they come from some belief system that says the more complicated the words you use to explain something and the greater precision you use to explain what your concept is, the more intelligent you look and the better that works out, when in fact the opposite is generally true. If you cannot explain it simply, you do not get very far. That starts with clarity of thinking.

As it turns out, [Sam] is coming into my office later today because he is in the process of spinning out another technology and he wants to see if we want to fund it. It has nothing to do with what Telegent is doing today. Chances are, we will fund them. The reason is Sam. I would fund Sam if he came to me with a better popcorn machine. He is just one of those people. He will figure out something great.

Shah: If you combine these key traits you mentioned about K. R. and Sam, does it summarize the pool of characteristics that create great entrepreneurs?

Sandell: There are a couple other ones. Integrity is gigantically important. You just want people who do the right thing. Who do what they say they are going to do. Who treat you as a partner and not as an adversary. Who act with honor and decency in everything they do. Sam and K. R. are absolutely like that.

That is really important because people like that attract other people like that and they build cultures like that. Those cultures deliver extraordinary results. Cultures of people that are not trustworthy are generally dysfunctional. Certainly it is the relationship with the VC partner that gives you a sense of whether they have integrity or not.

In my experience, you learn most everything you need to know about somebody by negotiating a term sheet with them. That is the most important part of the due-diligence process. Term sheets contain terms that matter a lot. Valuation, the amount of the company the entrepreneur is going to retain at the end of the day, who has control over what kind of decisions, who has control over the company, who gets to change the CEO, etc. These are the things that are most near and dear to the entrepreneur and the VC.

This is hopefully one of the few times that the VC and the entrepreneur will be on opposite sides of the table. You get to pit people against each other to see how they will act as adversaries, and one of the things you look for is whether they are smart enough to realize that their behavior in that nego- tiation is a strong indicator of how they will treat you after the negotiation is over and how they will treat other people.

Shah: Because that is the same style of negotiation that they will do with everyone else—new hires, strategic partners, customers. I have negotiated many term sheets and have seen a range of behaviors. We had a saying that you are seeing the best of them now and if you don't like it, imagine what's coming.

Sandell: The best deals are often highly, highly competitive. Very often, dur- ing the process of negotiating, at one time or another each party will have an advantage over the other. There will be a question of how they take advan- tage of it or not. Will they go back on their word because something just presented itself that was not evident before that gives them an advantage over the other party?

For example, say you are an entrepreneur and you sign a term sheet and turn off all your other offers. Will the VC re-trade your deal? And especially, was it their strategy to re-trade the deal after they got rid of the competi- tion?

That is the way some people operate. They fully expect that they are going to win the deal and take it off the table, out of a competitive process, and then they are going to change the terms and valuation between the term sheet signing and the actual closing. That negotiating strategy is just wrong, in my opinion.

Shah: Yep, I have heard stories like that and it's just unfair and immoral, though legal!

Sandell: The opposite thing happens with the entrepreneur. They may have an opportunity. Let's say [you're with] the entrepreneur, you verbally agree on something, and then the next day they get a term sheet from somebody else at a 25 percent higher price. You have no signed term sheet—you just agreed on what you were going to do. See how they behave.

I happened to have been at a board meeting this morning where the entre- preneur faced this very situation. I had been introduced to this company, which is called CloudFlare, by Ray Rothrock. Ray told me that the deal was moving very, very fast.

So I called the founders, Matthew Prince and Michelle Zatlyn, right away and I dropped all my plans and agreed to meet them the next morning for breakfast, early, then I brought them over to present to my partners the same day. We worked out a deal that we agreed to verbally but without a term sheet.

The following Monday, I sent them a term sheet as I said I would, and they agreed not to shop it. But they also said that they had some other conversations that had to play out because they had committed to have certain meetings. Importantly, they said that they would not disclose to anybody that we gave them a term sheet. They said that it would not be to our disadvantage that we got to the table first.

Sure enough, they withstood an unusual amount of pressure, but they kept their word. This is one of these situations that does not always happen. The valuations offered by other firms were significantly higher than the one we had offered. The pressures that were exerted on these entrepreneurs were as extraordinary as I have ever seen, and they did not blink. I do not know how long the process went on for, but in the end, all these other offers came in, the board considered them all, and they said, "No, this is the one we want, and we agreed with him that we were not going to shop the deal." They said it was not the best offer, but they would stick to the original deal.

By the way, the company is going to the moon. Somebody will write a book about this company. Matthew and Michelle have so much integrity. People want to work there. It is really something. Integrity matters a lot to me. No integrity, no deal.

Shah: Take us to China. How do your investment criteria differ between the US and China? What are some of the key cultural differences that show up in how you pick entrepreneurs and build companies halfway across the world?

Sandell: It is a different culture, for sure. In the Silicon Valley, we have people from all over the world. We have a lot of different cultures here. But people behave differently here than they would at home, including people from China. If you go play ball in their court, their rules are somewhat different. That to me is a challenge and it can be fun to figure out a new culture and how to operate in the right way.

I think from a business standpoint the characteristics are very similar in terms of what it takes to create really successful companies, here, there or anywhere. I think the similarities are much greater than the differences.

One of your questions was about building billion-dollar companies. This is actually why I went to China, and why I got involved in clean tech when I did. I thought, at the time, which was after the last tech bubble burst, there was not much of interest happening in the Silicon Valley.

I was fortunate to invest in Salesforce.com and helped to create Data Domain at that time. There were some good things that happened, but they were few and far between. I was looking a little more expansively and I was also reflecting on what it was that made Silicon Valley so successful at creating these huge companies. It was clearly the case that the United States was the most fertile place in the world for new start-ups, for all kinds of reasons that were written about.

One central reason that is not always discussed: we had in the last century the creation of a large middle class, which has never really existed before in the history of the world. A large middle class that developed very rapidly. It had created a need and demand for products and services that did not exist before. That meant that there were opportunities for new companies to become very large serving those new middle class consumers.

Think about it—before you have a large middle class, you have poor people who have no disposable income and can only afford the basics of life, and you have rich people, who may be able to afford everything, but there are not very many of them. There is no need for huge companies to serve a small number of rich people. The middle class is the unique component of our society that demands things at scale.

If you combine that with all the technical innovation we have here and the size of the market, you can easily see the opportunity for companies to get fairly large before they even had to go overseas. In 2001, 2002, I was sitting around thinking about the US economy and I was not quite so confident. We were seeing the emergence of other places where the next billion middle-class consumers were being born.

Of course, we looked to India and China. In our partnership, people went different ways. I happen to be more interested in China. We started poking around in China and we decided to get educated the way we normally get educated about something new—jump into the deep end of the pool and make an investment. We have now made twenty-plus investments in China. We have had five IPOs. We have another four or five coming in the next twelve to eighteen months. The focus is entirely on companies that service the next billion middle-class consumers.

Shah: So, it's really going after huge markets and then applying similar investment criteria as the US, but of course with local flavors and nuances.

Sandell: Yep.

Shah: Let's talk about these investment criteria. When someone walks into your office with a business plan, what really stands out in the companies you fund—market potential, team itself, product, business model? What separates wheat from chaff?

Sandell: The first filter for me is the people. Are they extraordinary people? Are they people you can live with through thick and thin? Because there will always be thin. Are they people who really want to build a big company? Are they not in it to flip it and get rich? That motivation is not strong enough to cause people to withstand all the things they will have to withstand to build a big company. Furthermore, it tends to be the case that if they are primarily motivated by the money, they will take the first big check that comes along, and that may be a check that is good for them, but a small fraction of the potential if they were willing to hold on for the long haul.

I look for people who are not so motivated by the money, but are really driven to build a big company. The more years I am in this business, the more I look for that.

Shah: That is a wonderful insight. This takes us to exit strategy. This is another time where the adversity of the two sides plays out if the interests are not aligned. You look for extraordinary people and someone who really wants to build big companies.

Sandell: If you have those things and they get along with each other and have similar ways of looking at things, then the question is, can it really be big fast? The most exciting companies to me are the ones that grow really, really fast, that can get to be $100 million in revenue in three years. It does not mean there are not some great companies that get built more slowly than that. And I have been very patient in cases like that, if I believe that growing too fast would be destructive to long term success.

I have one really extraordinary company in the making which fits this description: Tableau Software. Early on, one of the founders, Christian Chabot, was very worried that I was going to pressure him to build the company really quickly. He is actually the poster child for why not spending money is a really good idea. He has built a very sizeable business on a total of $3 million of capital. He would have consumed a lot more capital if he submitted to the idea that he was going to grow it faster. I am not sure he would have been able to grow it any faster. Some businesses naturally cannot get too big, too quickly.

Shah: What do you look for to determine if the company has the potential to be a big player—trend, technology, pain point?

Sandell: You need to have all the things you mentioned, but I think the single most important question is: how strong is the value proposition? Is this something that is a must-have item? Is it something that could change your life or business, the way you work, the way you play? Is this a game changer?

Unnatural advantages accrue to those kinds of companies. If it is a consumer product and it is so fantastic and it changes your life, then you are probably going to recommend it to a friend. It could develop viral appeal and develop very quickly because of that. If it has a very strong value proposition, usually the cost of acquiring customers is not as high because it is obviously a great product you have to have.

Shah: Because it makes such an impact, you cannot wait to tell your friends and family.

Sandell: I happened to bump into Andy Brown, CTO of UBS recently. He was one of the first major adopters of Salesforce.com. One of the things that strikes me about Andy and other people like him is if they really like something, they talk about it to other CTOs, or they will be happy to be helpful to the company they like. They will say, it is working well for me, but there are three things you need to do better. I am just doing it to help you out because I really want to see you succeed.

Shah: Either it is consumer play or enterprise play. If value proposition is that deep and compelling, it is going to spread by itself. Given the short window you get to evaluate that, are there some metrics you look at to see what the value proposition is and how compelling it is?

Sandell: In terms of the product and technology, I look at the strength of the value proposition, I look at how hard was this thing to do and how hard will it be for the next guy to do? Is it defensible? I look for a rich vein of potential innovation, which is what it takes to stay ahead. You think of a vein or a mine, where the silver or gold goes down into the mountain and you just keep digging more out of it.

The same is true for technological innovation, which is that there is an obvious roadmap of features that the customer will value. If you have that, as long as you keep delivering on those new features, you stay ahead. You do not have to stay ahead by a lot. If you stay ahead by six months, and your product is six months more mature, and you have six months' worth of extra features. As long as those features are highly valued by the customer, they will pay a lot more money for your product than the next guy's product.

Shah: It does not need a couple of years of advantage, just six months.

Sandell: I think six months is enough. You would like to have eighteen months, but the reason I chose six months is because most people in our business think you have to have Fort Knox around your intellectual property in order to be comfortable. I think the problem with that mentality is it may lead you down the wrong path going to market. It may cause you to wait until your product is really mature and robust and has lots and lots of features before you even sell the first version of it.

I would rather get in the market with an imperfect product and have the customer tell me what the prioritization should be for the next features I develop. Ship it and see what happens. Learn from it and make it better. As long as you have that rich vein of things where you can keep making it better, better, and better, you can stay ahead.

Shah: Isn't it easier and much faster to innovate and iterate with consumer companies than technology/enterprise software companies? In a consumer-facing Internet business, you can put a feature out over the weekend, but you cannot do that easily for high-tech companies.

Sandell: That is true, but I actually think the really great consumer innovations are not really built overnight, either. Just the concept of simplicity is so important to users and so hard to do. Great design is really hard to do. It does not mean it is not done over a weekend. Maybe it is, but there are attributes of products in the consumer space.

A recent example is Dropbox. How many people have tried to create online storage before? The landscape is littered with dead bodies. What do they do? They made it really simple and elegant. Their market timing is perfect because now everybody has multiple devices and they want to share files with themselves, let alone other people. Their product is really well done.

Shah: I tried five other products for my book research team, and Dropbox is the only product that is working like a charm. Also, Apple is a great example of an elegant design. My two-year-old has his own iPad now and has more apps on it than my wife has on hers. To get to that simplistic design probably took years and years.

Sandell: Apple has proven the value of design more than any company in human history. Apple is a great example of creating a product which changes people's lives, about which they can be passionate. Look at the devotion Apple customers have. I have been an Apple customer since 1980. I am not changing my mind about Apple anytime soon. During all those years, Apple has not always produced great stuff or been a great company.

No surprise to me that Apple is the most valuable technology company in the world today. The amazing thing [is that] they are doing it in a business which is otherwise considered to be a commodity business.

Shah: That's a great lead into next question. Most new trends face strong pressure of commoditization. You mentioned Telegent earlier. Is there something one can do differently to stay differentiated? Are some businesses just not naturally protectable as others are?

Sandell: In case of Telegent, they could have done a better job than they did to create lower cost products that would have potentially kept other people out of the marketplace longer, but I think ultimately it was going to be commoditized and be hard to protect.

Shah: So some businesses are that way.

Sandell: Yep. But also the great entrepreneurs are constantly focused on creating either features of their product or aspects of their business model which make them naturally defensible. There are many different sources of defensibility, as you know, but the great entrepreneurs are thinking strategically about that question and they are paranoid and worried about how they will maintain an edge and keep their margins at an attractive model.

Shah: You do have to be just paranoid and constantly thinking, "What is the next thing I can deliver that has more value for my customer while creating that differentiation?"

Sandell: You have to be able to recognize where there is value and where there is leverage in your product or service. As we have seen in recent years, sometimes the leverage comes from giving your product away free. Create something compelling, give it away free, and the fact that you have millions or hundreds of millions of users may in fact be the differentiation.

With open-source software, we have seen it with all manner of consumer Internet companies. If you think about it, what an advantage it is to have all these users using your product for free if the other guy is actually trying to extract money for the exact same thing.

Shah: Dropbox is a great example. A small percentage of users using more than 2 GB have to pay annually.

Sandell: I have not paid Dropbox a nickel and it is great.

Shah: The same thing for LinkedIn or Skype, but a small percentage of the user base ends up more than paying for the free users.

Sandell: As long as the small percentage makes for a great business and the cost of serving the free users is not too high, you can turn that into quite an attractive business model.

Shah: Now it is happening with a lot of iPad and iPhone apps. A lot of apps did start out free, but we end up buying the $5.99 version because it is so good. Back to market discussion. Besides China, you also identified the clean energy market early on. What was your hypothesis there?

Sandell: That is a combination of things. One was a long-held belief that we were going to have to move away from fossil fuels as a society and a sense, before I had knowledge, that the technologies were maturing and the costs were coming down in such a way that alternative, cleaner sources of power generation would soon be attractive on a relative economic basis to the cost of either fossil fuels or electricity. I think and believe that much more today than I did back then, but I could see that it was an opportunity of enormous size.

The energy business is much, much bigger than the IT business, more than the media business. If you think about it, the entire US record industry at its peak was about a $9 billion business. The IT business, $250 to $300 billion. The energy business is measured in trillions of dollars in this country alone and it is a global business much more so than the other two.

You do not have to focus your mind too much before you realize the opportunities to build something really big are clear. Then the question is, which innovations are going to be the most disruptive and sustainable, and achieve the cost necessary and all the other things we know about?

Shah: Time for the exit question. Probably the toughest challenge facing an investor is to decide whether to shut down, keep funding, or to exit the start-up. What is your thought process in deciding on an exit path?

Sandell: I am probably not that good at this on a relative basis. I tend to stick with things a long time and give them more chances to succeed than they probably deserve a lot of the time. At least with hindsight, that seems clear. It always boils down to not whether they achieved on their original business plan, but whether there is a clear path forward to still creating something good and are the people committed and interested in doing that.

I take a lot of clues from the entrepreneurs. We have frank discussions about it. Truly exceptional people do not need a job. They are making a bigger investment than I am every day they go to work. That means a lot to me because then I can trust their judgment if it is worth their time. First thing I look at is there a clear path forward and are the people really excited about it?

Shah: That is the biggest test.

Sandell: It is one of the hardest things in the business. Certainly I have shut down my fair share of companies, and it stinks. Sometimes it ends in a really ugly way. I have been a part of a couple of them in which I wish I could have skipped the last chapter.

Gus Tai

Trinity Ventures: Blue Nile, Photobucket, Modulus, zulily, Trion Worlds

Gus Tai is a general partner at Trinity Ventures. He specializes in early-stage investing and, in particular, enjoys helping entrepreneurs at the time of company formation. A Forbes "Midas List" recipient, Gus has established himself as a mentor by working with founders to help build teams and refine business models.

Gus began his operational career in engineering management at Digital Equipment Corporation. He also worked at Bain & Company, consulting to technology firms on new product development and business strategy. More recently, Gus acts as the director of the MIT Club of Northern California.

At Trinity Ventures, Gus focuses on consumer services and consumer-enabling technologies. Representative companies that Gus has funded include Blue Nile, Esurance, mSpot, Photobucket, PlayFirst, Trion Worlds, Wetpaint, zulily, Badgeville, KIVA Software, MaxPoint Interactive, Modulus Video, and Speedera Networks.

When I first met Gus, I was extremely impressed by his thoughtfulness in analyzing start-ups. He has unmatched depth when it comes to looking at the human, team, and business aspects of start-up formation and building. This allows him to do one of the toughest things in the venture business—identify a single founder quite early on and help him crystallize the business concept and build the core team around that.

Gus and I have a lot in common in terms of how we see the world, which is in a very scientific, intellectually curious, and passionately disinterested way. He has been a tremendous supporter of this book project. He has assisted me with filling in critical gaps, generously shared his insights and contacts, and helped me think through some of the toughest areas of the start-up building process.

In this interview, Gus leverages his fifteen-plus years of successful start-up formation and investing experience with companies like Blue Nile, zulily, Trion Worlds, Esurance, and Photobucket. He provides incredible insight into how he goes about identifying promising markets, how to cherish customers and how to build the right team from the start, as well as the importance of personal characteristics like integrity, passion, intellectual honesty, and bias for action.

Gus also takes readers through the Start-up Analysis Model (SAM) that Sheetal and I developed, and applies key aspects of the model in the context of a start-up's journey from formation to initial proof to scaling and growth.

Tarang Shah: What are some of the key reasons start-ups fail?

Gus Tai: I believe the number-one reason start-ups fail is that the management team doesn't take enough time to truly understand the customer. I will put this under "cherishing the customer." Tarang, I know you understand this point. You are personally different in a distinctively good way in that you pause to listen to others. You are present to what the other person is saying, take the time to understand what that person's premises are, and cherish that person's perspective. I hope that I'm as open-minded as you are at receiving another person's point of view as it is, rather than trying to force my point of view on them.

A start-up needs to do what you do. It needs to be present with its customer. The company needs to listen closely and understand the customer's needs and mindset. It has to approach the situation with empathy and compassion. In short, the start-up has to meet the customer where the customer is at. It shouldn't force the customer to meet the company where the company is at.

When experts talk about listening to the customer, it's more than listening to the customer. It's even more than understanding the customer. It's actually about cherishing the customer. My personal belief is that you want to cherish your customer as you would cherish an infant. You don't order the baby to tell you what its needs are. Rather, you accept the infant as is. You do your best to discern what you can do to provide more comfort and ease, and meet the needs of the child.

Customers aren't infants, but it's equally important for a company to cherish its customers. I believe many start-ups fail because they try to legislate to the customer what he or she should want. These start-ups aren't offering something that is grounded in an understanding of the customer's environment and what the customer might reasonably and ultimately want. What a start-up needs to do is understand the needs of the customer, whether the needs are latent or known, and meet those needs in a delightful way.

Some companies are better than others at identifying latent customer needs, articulating them, and then meeting those needs. The best examples for me are Steve Jobs and Apple. Steve Jobs and Apple are just brilliant at cherishing the customer, deeply understanding what the consumer wants—whether or not he or she knows it—and then educating the customer quickly through product benefits and capabilities.

Shah: So true. Smartphones have been around. I had struggled with the phone interface for a long time, as a mobile product manager, as a user, and as an investor. I have helped with start-up investments in the voice navigation space to get around the issue, but nothing really worked that intuitively until Apple came out with the iPhone. It's an incredible example of understanding the latent need and meeting it beyond the customer's wildest expectations. Unlike most consumer internet companies, with something as hardware and software intensive as the smartphone, you don't get to test and iterate, and you have to get it right the first time.

Tai: A truly delightful experience. Apple very much understood the core desires of consumers for smartphones. They deconstructed the existing consumer experience and set out to define a new, better way. Every aspect of the consumer experience was examined. People rave about the device, but Apple even set out to improve the purchasing and provisioning process.

It's clear that consumers don't like to wait to have their phone set up in the store. So when the first iPhone came out, it was designed to be booted up at home and provisioned very quickly over the air. The whole iPhone experience was designed with speed and delight in mind.

Shah: I recently bought a netbook just before the iPad came out. I returned the netbook in favor of iPad and haven't looked back. It was just way too slow for the living room. Amazing thing is, my son Raj started playing with the iPad at nine months of age and he now has hundreds of educational apps on it. He uses it more than the books. He didn't need any training at all.

Tai: Yes, and that's why I think the iPad is going to displace a large number of laptops. Tarang, we've been talking about cherishing the customer and being open minded to anything the customer may want. That said, I think there are general guidelines of what consumers typically want. One truism for what consumers want is "no latency." When entrepreneurs ask me,

"What's the number-one error that start-ups make on product design?" I'll say it's highly likely the company is under-weighing the impact of latency.[1]

Shah: I agree. Take Friendster for example. It probably had the perfect opportunity to be what Facebook is today. It was the lack of understanding of what customers truly wanted that drove them to calculate six degrees of connections every time a user added a friend. Database technology wasn't mature enough to handle that level of scale, but the real issue was the users didn't really care about friend of a friend of a friend and their friends. They completely overlooked the latency in the process. It took minutes for the page to load and users ran away to Myspace.

Tai: The key was to render the page in one hundred milliseconds. One of the key reasons for Google's success is how they handle latency and deliver search results in the fraction of a second.

Shah: So back to the original question, what are some of the other reasons start-ups fail?

Tai: The number-two reason they fail is that they don't put together the right team to do the right things. I will put this under "creating the right team to tackle the right problems."

Successful start-ups are always under-resourced. The reason they are always under-resourced is that they are attacking a market opportunity that is much larger than their ability to serve it. The way that you hurt productivity and efficiency at a start-up is to try to do even more than what you're already doing, because you're already under-resourced.

What this means for human capital is that start-ups need to have the right experience in their people on Day One, because their employees don't have time to learn on the job. Companies need to maintain their discipline at hiring the appropriately skilled people to do the job "now."

As you know, I specialize in company formation. I find it fascinating how companies get formed. Regarding formation, one point that is easily overlooked is that companies aren't made by a single person. Those are consulting firms. Companies are made by teams. So it's important to ask, what does the second person, the third person and fourth and fifth look like as you add to the team? How does each one change the cultural norms of the company? What is this team optimal at accomplishing? What are their biases, and how will those biases help or limit them?

---

[1] Latency is the time it takes to receive a customer request to the rendering of service. For example, in the case of Google, latency is the time it takes to get back search results.

Companies that are formed properly have each person focus on that person's strengths and avoiding his or her weaknesses. It's not trying to have each person be a complete player or work on improving on weaknesses. The goal is to aggregate these strengths and establish a rhythm for team chemistry that matches the aspiration of the team. My philosophy in working with these companies is to help the team reach its full potential, but not try to be something that it's not.

I actually find team-building much simpler starting with one person. The old carpenter's adage is so true: measure twice, cut once. It's easier to get a team functioning well if it's designed properly up front. It's much harder to take a dysfunctional team and make it work!

When I start with one person, what I try to do is work collaboratively with the entrepreneur to find out what he or she is extremely passionate about. Then we work to ensure that the opportunity takes advantage of his or her unique strengths. Entrepreneurs can sense when they find the right opportunity for them. It's neat when you witness it. They develop this calmness and focus. They know that it's deeply authentic. The opportunity speaks to them in a unique way, and they can see how they will put their own stamp onto the situation.

Shah: So let's say you get approached by fifteen passionate people in the same area of your investment focus or expertise. What are the one or two or three things you look at to say, "Hey, this guy, I believe, is truly passionate and capable of making things happen."

Tai: Tarang, that's a great question—one that I keep asking myself. For context, over the last ten years, I've funded or have been part of funding around two dozen companies. The median size of them is four people. Most of them were pre-wire frame[2] at time of funding, and many started with just one person. While each of these individuals and small teams are different—just as each of your friends is different from the other—I do think they all have a number of characteristics in common.

I believe the most important characteristic of a successful company founder is that he or she has very deep integrity. Not only do founders need to have it, but they also need to radiate it. Here, I mean integrity in two ways: the traditional moral sense, but also in the personal sense. They need to communicate their conviction in how they're deeply aligned in who they are.

---

[2] Before the outline of the web site is created.

The reason this form of integrity is so important is that when a founder is trying to get someone else to join, any new hire needs to know what he or she is joining. What can the new person count on?

Remember, a start-up starts with nothing. It has no foundation. If the founder seems ambivalent or ephemeral, then there isn't something grounded upon which to join. What new hires are looking for are consistency and depth. What integrity actually means is being internally consistent and whole. It suggests depth.

A person develops deep integrity by reflecting upon his or her situations and experiences and abstracting out the things that really matter. Those facets that matter are woven into this consistent approach on how to engage in the world.

What a founder does is paint this worldview, just as J. K. Rowling paints the world of Harry Potter. Potential team members then can know what is it that they're joining. What are they standing on? What is it that they're betting on?

Strong founders stand for something. They know that they will not appeal to everyone, but their clarity about who they are and what they want to do will make it easier for co-founders to find them. Building up a start-up from nothing, you have to start with an asset. The founder's integrity and vision is the core building block around which to aggregate other assets.

Shah: Wonderful insight into what integrity means for founders!

Tai: After integrity, the next thing I look for is an orientation towards getting things done.

Shah: The bias for action?

Tai: Yes, the bias for action! You have to get the book done. You can't talk about doing the book, you have to actually do the book. You have to do the interviews, you can't talk about doing the interviews. What successful entrepreneurs and companies do is they mobilize action. Entrepreneurism is about bias for action.

Shah: Entrepreneurs have a tremendous bias for action and kind of self-created sense of urgency. No one is telling them you have to do this right away.

Tai: And passion really helps with that. Passion is the internal battery that provides the energy for the bias for action. Now, what is needed to harness this energy is the right direction and the right technique. You need to know where you want to go and how to best get there.

That's a good segue into the topic of leadership and management. There's an artificial segmentation between the notion of leadership and management. It's a helpful taxonomy for academic research, but in reality for a start-up, leadership and management are combined. You can't have people who lead who don't do management. You can't have people who do tactics, but don't lead. You have to have the two concepts be integrated because the company is too small.

So, what leadership really is about is creating a shared vision that people are willingly to follow. A leader orchestrates the shaping of the vision such that all of the participants feel that they own it as their own. The leader then ensures there's enough clarity on what to do and motivation for taking action such that the team members willingly follow.

This is where passion helps. If you have a shared vision and you have people being passionate around you, then they will feel compelled to do everything they can to accomplish that vision. If the vision is clear, the coordinated actions by the team will become a competitive advantage. You'll just accomplish a lot more than other companies out there.

Now, it's not easy for a start-up to have a clear, shared vision. Everyone is busy taking action, working on their specific tasks. That's why I tell CEOs I fund to "rinse and repeat" their message. Never worry about being too repetitive. If you think about it, employees at a company may be making hundreds of micro-decisions every day. Passionate employees will make even more!

They won't be asking for direct input from their boss or from the CEO. How do you make sure that each decision is maximally aligned with the goals of the company? The answer is to keep the objectives of the shared vision simple and keep repeating the primary objectives until they become ingrained into the culture.

I would imagine in the early days of Google it could have been around algorithmic efficiency, scalability and low latency. I wasn't on the board of Starbucks, but we were the first institutional investors there. I would suspect early on that Howard Schultz might have stressed the importance of a delightful in-store experience, one that would feel like a reprieve from a hectic world, and serve as a safe, personalized oasis.

Tarang, going back to what I look for in a founder, I mentioned his or her personal integrity and I talked about bias for action. I should broaden that second notion to be a bias and capacity for effective action. Moving on, the third thing I look for is intellectual honesty.

A major challenge for a newly formed company is that almost everything is uncertain. The market opportunity might be nascent. The product isn't yet built. The formula isn't yet proven. In this type of environment, it's important that the founder/leader keeps an open mind to respond to what he or she learns. It's a tricky balancing act. The founder has to believe wholeheartedly enough in a different vision from what exists, but be nimble enough to change it when presented with new information.

You have to be very intellectually curious and also want to know the fundamentals and how the fundamentals lead to the truth. You have to be driven by this deep curiosity of that is what's right. We need to know. I call it "passionate disinterest." You're passionate about knowing the truth, but disinterested meaning you don't want to force the truth to be what you believe. You want truth about the market, customer preferences, etc., be objectively revealed to you through the unfolding of the process. You don't want to force an answer, you actually want to assess answers.

In order to be really good at it and do it all the time, you become trained and expert at relieving and releasing biases and you just look and observe what is going on. It's a different process than ideation. Ideation is sort of begging an answer. This objectivity allows you to really listen to what the market is telling you and then quickly adjust your course accordingly.

Shah: Gus, tell us more about how entrepreneurs should evaluate their business and key success elements at various stages of the start-up building process. I am going to have the Start-up Analysis Model template reproduced in the book[3] so readers will be able to follow along.

Tai: First, this is a helpful template for any entrepreneur. Any entrepreneur that wants to start a business will go through all of the stages, if he or she is successful. For many entrepreneurs joining start-ups, they will want to be able to discern the current stage of the company and optimize for key things in each given stage.

I will start sharing some thoughts on Stage 0 to 1. What is great about your model is, with that framework, you can apply that to different sectors. Each sector has a different characteristic. Consumer internet investing, for instance, is quite different from semiconductor investing.

One of the interesting aspects about consumer internet investing, particularly in recent times, is that moving from one stage to the next can happen in a very short period and require very little capital. Take Twitter, for example. Twitter was a project developed by a couple of people within Odeo,

---

[3] You'll find the SAM model at the end of the chapter.

a company started and funded by Evan Williams. Formation within a start-up is typically unusual, but the company had a lot of entrepreneurial talent.

Using your model, I would describe Stage 0 for Twitter as being incubated and project-financed within Odeo. They required very little money. The team defined certain use cases for the product and released it. From there, they quickly entered Stage 1. Fred Wilson at Union Square and Charles River Ventures funded Twitter in July 2007 as a Stage 1 company. In about two years, Twitter was able to explode well past enviable scale, where they were able to finance their growth at a billion-dollar valuation.

In contrast, semiconductor investing typically involves start-ups taking many years to move from Stage 0 to 1 to 2. During these years, there are different types of risks and different financing requirements. Usually, valuations remain low for years. It's at Stage 2 when these companies begin to finally rise in valuation.

Using your methodology, an investor or entrepreneur could more easily identify what he or she needs to optimize in that given stage. He or she could say, if I move from Stage x to y, my cost of capital drops materially to reflect the reduction in risk. These are the typical ways to reduce risk that the entrepreneurial and investment community readily accept.

Shah: What do you look for in start-ups you back at various stages?

Tai: For background, I've been practicing venture capital for fifteen years, so I've invested in all stages of companies—0, 1 and 2. My particular expertise is starting at Stage 0. That is my practice. Clearly I have experience with later-stage companies.

As my companies grow from pre-product to half a billion-dollar outcomes or public companies, I'm serving on the board and providing governance and perspective in those later stages. But unlike most other venture capitalists, the majority of my initial investments are in Stage 0.

What you look for in a Stage 0 company is very different from what you look for in the other stages. A Stage 0 company does not have any obvious assets that it can merchandise. It might not even have a definable market. The key challenge at this stage is aggregating the resources you need to get to Stage 1. If you can't aggregate resources, you can't pass go.

The way you marshal resources is by crafting something of value that you can market and merchandise to attract resources to come work with you. The primary resources you are seeking to attract are human capital and financial capital, but it also could be other things, such as business partnerships, that give you some advantage.

The more effective companies at this stage clearly know what are the few things that make their company special. They home in on how they are different. These start-ups don't have answers for everything, but they make sure to differentiate themselves desirably in the focused, couple of ways. Faster at product, better at UI, more customer insight, past working relationships, reputation, and so on. Whatever those features may be, the team then markets and merchandises those aspects aggressively to attract the resources they need to move to Stage 1.

Shah: At this stage you do not have any tangible assets to give to anyone.

Tai: Yes. A good exercise that is customer-centric—if you frame the resources you're aggregating as your customer—is to sit peacefully and reflectively, and ask: "Why should anyone help me?" People have a lot of choices for whom to help. Why will they choose you?

When I evaluate a Stage 0 company, I am looking at two things. One area I examine is assessing the potential value the company may realize, strategically or fundamentally. What is the range of possible outcomes and value of this company, way in the future, recognizing I am going to be wrong, but there is some sort of probabilistic distribution, based upon similar situations. How big and large can that be? What might be its full potential?

The other area, which I find more interesting, important, and nuanced, is understanding the founders and the idea. Given the people involved, what resources and execution is needed to succeed and thrive? I look at the idea/approach and the people. What strength comes from each, and what strength comes from the combination? I ask myself if I fund this, can we together be able to efficiently marshal the resources we need to get to Stage 1?

For that reason, many times I center my attention on the question of whether the founder can be effective at recruiting the first couple of strong team members. That is the litmus test. Is this idea/approach big enough that when you combine the idea and the founder, they can attract great people?

There are some who can attract and close people regardless of what they are doing. Tom Seibel and Dave Duffield are examples of people who recently started companies and can recruit anyone they want. There are certain founders who are magnets for resources because of their charisma, track record, personal virtue or some combination.

But most people are not like that. At a minimum, most founders don't have the track record. What I look for is personal charisma and the person's ability to lead and recruit against the concept at hand. I pay particular attention as to whether the vision they are painting matches their skill set and who they are, so they are more likely to recruit the right people to be able to accomplish what they want.

When I meet super-talented entrepreneurs, I will work with them on their concepts for long periods of time, if that's what it takes. I am particularly sensitive to what fits them and will share with them what my perspective is about the people and resources that they need. Once their idea firmly crystallizes, they usually can identify and quickly hire two or three talented people. Strong people usually have go-to people they have worked with in the past.

Shah: Yeah, they have worked together before and probably this individual has socialized the concept with them for a long time with a notion that one day these guys may become a part of his core founding team.

Tai: Exactly. You will have a core founding team of two to three people. More than that number makes it a little bit tricky to split up equity if the company is venture-backed. In any case, one to three is the right number of founders. You add a couple of early employees and soon you have a team. Then you are off to the races, trying to get to Stage 1.

Having your team in place, what you want to make sure to do is conduct fast, hypothesis-driven testing. Learn from each experiment and overweigh any type of traction. I like to use a sailboat analogy. Find momentum first, and then tack in the direction you want to sail. For start-ups, what momentum represents is customer feedback. The customer is engaging with you and offering to share his or her perspective. This type of feedback offers you a great chance to learn and better tune your understanding of the customer. So overweigh momentum, and cherish surprises.

Shah: PayPal did not initially target eBay users, but it just happened that way that eBay users found PayPal.

Tai: Exactly. PayPal is an example of being open toward hearing what the customer wants, and winning big. That said, there is a risk that following early momentum distracts a company from a larger opportunity. Start-ups have to watch out for this risk. At the same time, continually testing in areas that yield only negative results makes it very hard to learn. Momentum provides you a gradient towards something. As you dig in further, you can move faster and learn more.

Another reason momentum is really valuable is that it helps cement a culture of performance and effective action. Start-up teams have an initial amount of bonding energy. That bonding energy dissipates every time there is a disappointment. You have a limited amount of time to hold together a team to accomplish something. Every time you have a micro-success, it contributes bonding energy.

Momentum holds teams together. If you do not get any customer momentum, structure the organization in a way to measure some other form of momentum. The team needs to feel that it is progressing, that it can accomplish goals. Most human beings like to accomplish goals that suggest progress rather than confirm the status quo. It is very hard to hold together people if all of the tests turn up negative.

Shah: Gus, what are some of the key considerations as the start-ups move from Stage 1 to 2 and prepares for scaling and growth?

Tai: As companies grow, they do face decisions as to what type of momentum best serves them, and when. Do they want momentum in profits, revenue, number of paying customers or users? Chasing after profit dollars is nice, but sometimes that is not the right goal at the time.

If Facebook focused early on profit dollars instead of building its network, I suspect it would not have been as successful as it is today.

Shah: Agreed. In some of these ecosystem plays where network effect drives the critical scale, you need to have a momentum of a certain scale for you to even say you have an ecosystem in place to build a business on.

Tai: Given that you have these strategic choices, I believe it's important for founders to have boards or advisors who can help with judgment and decision making. No one has all of the answers in an emerging market. Having a robust set of advisors should do at least two things: bring in outside perspective and make sure there is robust discussion.

In the end, though, it might be that many things for start-ups are unknowable at the time. In 2007, did anyone know for certain that Twitter and Facebook could command billions of dollars of revenue on their platform?

I recommend to start-ups that they should identify early on what are the key, big premises that may make or break their company. Premises such as consumers will purchase virtual goods, billions of ad dollars will move to a messaging platform. For the premises that the start-up can't easily influence, surrender to not knowing what will happen.

Start-ups have a big opportunity against others often times because they bet on a premise that incumbents and indirect competitors are not willing to make. In our portfolio, I would cite Blue Nile. We funded Blue Nile and Esurance and other companies in the nineties that had high transaction prices. Conventional wisdom was that consumers would not pull out the credit card and buy something for $10,000 online. We said they would. If that premise was wrong, we would fail. You could worry and say, "What if it fails?" Then you could build a business for low average purchase prices, but then what would the company be authentically tuned for? Which customer would it really be cherishing? At the end of the day, if the premise works and the company executes well, then it wins big. Sometimes there is only one way to find out.

Shah: Looking back, in the case of Blue Nile, you concluded there is a market for big-ticket items on the internet, but at that time it was an experiment or hypothesis to be proven right or wrong.

Tai: My initial hypothesis at the time was that people wanted to primarily purchase low price-point items—books, etc. That hypothesis actually is true and continues to hold. However, when I was examining it from a business model standpoint, it became clear that a $10 average transaction with high shipping and handling costs will not provide you enough gross margin dollars to cover the cost of customer acquisition.

Shah: Agreed. The volume required for you to have scalable profit with low-price, low-margin transactions is unbelievably high.

Tai: Customer acquisition cost in the early days was really high. Gross margin dollars from an initial sale would typically not cover that cost. If you had a retention-based revenue model, it could work, but it would be hard. Startups tried pet food because people buy pet food continually. Unfortunately, the gross margin of pet food less shipping and handling was too negative at the time.

The other angle would be to say, "Let's target a higher average transaction price." How do you have a high gross-margin-per-transaction basis so you can pay for the cost of customer acquisition on the first product?

Shah: You have to have a broad portfolio like grocery stores do or Diaper.com does. You try to expand horizontally in products such that the typical consumer basket lifts gross margin as it will have high-ticket items.

Tai: Amazon was able to increase their average shopping-cart size. But they enjoyed atypical success. This was also back in the nineties. Back in the nineties companies could not figure out a way to drive down the cost of customer acquisition. It was high. You either have the person buy many, many times over many years or you have them buy at a higher price. We said, "Let's sell things that have a higher price." Why not?

Shah: Then you do not have to worry about retention or high cost of acquisition because the gross margin will be large enough for you to make a profit on a single transaction.

Tai: Another bet you could have said is that we have a way to cause cost and customer acquisition to drop by 90 percent. Framing this discussion using your model, I would say that at Stage 0 of a company, you want to define up-front the premises you are assuming and the bets you are making. Stage 1 is proving out the bets and premises.

Shah: I like that summary. So what are some of the other bets that you are making that can lead to billion-dollar companies?

Tai: I should probably comment on two of my portfolio companies that I believe have that type of market potential in front of them: zulily and Trion Worlds.

Shah: What I have read about zulily sounds quite impressive. They raised a large financing round at a very high valuation recently and are expecting to have revenue of $150 million in only their second year as a company. That revenue level would be around ten times larger than Amazon's revenue in year two. Or bigger than year-two revenue for Zynga or Groupon, or probably any retailer in U.S. history. What was it that you saw in zulily that made you see the billion-dollar opportunity?

Tai: First off, the size of the market opportunity zulily is addressing is just huge. Zulily is an online store offering daily sales events on top-quality apparel, gear, and other goodies for moms, babies, and kids. That market is incredibly large.

Second and most importantly, I had worked with Mark Vadon and Darrell Cavens before at Blue Nile. I led the first institutional round at Blue Nile. I actually interviewed and helped to recruit Darrell to the Blue Nile team. As a fun anecdote, Darrell jokingly asked for a desk made out of Legos as part of his hiring offer. The team actually had one made for him!

Based on their successful track record, they could have chosen whomever they wanted as their investment partner. They decided to work with us on zulily and I am grateful for that opportunity they gave to me. I am very fortunate to be the only venture capitalist, and Trinity is the only firm, to have backed Darrell and Mark multiple times.

Given my familiarity and friendship with Darrell and Mark, I knew that any business that they started would become successful. They're that good at execution. And they know themselves well enough that they would only embark upon something that they could do well. The question I had when Mark first told me about zulily was how large the market opportunity was.

Shah: How did you go about assessing the market size for zulily?

Tai: In thinking about zulily, I focused on two areas: the mechanic for customer acquisition, and the mindset of the consumer and how that would relate to his or her lifetime value.

On the former, what Groupon and its competitors had proven was that consumers would respond quite efficiently to email offers. Companies had always made email offers. In fact, the email list of existing customers is typically the most productive marketing program for retailers. But what was different was that the email campaigns of Groupon and the others were running many times higher in open rates and conversion to purchase. My best guess is that email campaigns in late 2008 might have been 10 times more effective than a similar campaign run only four years earlier. Anytime you come across a 10x improvement, you want to pay attention!

As for retaining a consumer at zulily, I felt that if the company could create a relationship with the consumer where the customer would respect and enjoy the voice of the company, she would stick around a long time. Some of the early email merchandising companies, like Daily Candy, had very strong, loyal audiences of shoppers. Similarly, zulily would have the potential to build out such an audience, and with Darrell and Mark's great operational prowess, these customers would have a delightful purchasing and fulfillment experience.

Shah: What attracted you to Trion Worlds?

Tai: That's another company I'm grateful to be part of. Trion Worlds is revolutionizing the hard core gaming market by operating itself as a dynamic, gaming-as-a-service platform. The company develops and publishes AAA-quality games that are dynamically updated in real time. They develop content on a fast release schedule, thereby making their titles fresh and relevant to its players.

As an example, Trion's first title, RIFT, has had content updates roughly every six weeks. The customers very much appreciate the freshness of the content and report back that the other titles that they play feel increasingly stale. It's not that other companies cannot publish with that release schedule. It is more that they are not designed to have a dynamic game. They design games more with a shrink wrap mindset.

Dynamic, nimble programming matters. Take the example of Salesforce.com versus Siebel. Salesforce.com could react quickly to new customer requirements. They had one centrally managed service, which they could update anytime they would like. Their programming teams had a biweekly or monthly release schedule. So if a customer had a new requirement, Salesforce.com could release the product, and iterate quickly using customer feedback as input. Their "Chatter" product is a great example of rapid improvement in functionality.

On the other hand, a company structured with an eighteen-month release schedule simply would not add functionality that quickly. And they would not have the cycles to iterate on it to improve it. Culture and mindset can hold you back.

Shah: And so Trion has an advantage due to its fast iterations.

Tai: I certainly think so. I think everyone would agree that having more iterations of customer feedback helps improve a product. Compare the first iPod versus the most recent products. The first one was amazing at the time, but the most recent releases are so much better.

In the case of RIFT, the initial release was reviewed quite strongly. The company announced one million customers of RIFT after four months, making it one of the fastest growing MMORPGs[4] in history. That said, I personally feel the product experience is materially stronger today because of the aggressive update schedule. One of the major game magazines re-reviewed RIFT recently and increased its rating. Re-reviewing is highly unusual, and I think is third-party validation of the strength of Trion's strategy and execution.

Shah: You have made successful, early stage bets in multiple market segments including retail, gaming, etc. What's the key to identifying these opportunities early on?

Tai: Tarang, I don't know if I see the opportunities well, but I think what I see well is the potential for big things to happen. For example, I don't know what new, billion-dollar businesses will come out of tablet computing, but I do know that there will be major shifts in consumer behavior, and that there will be many successful new companies. Then I look at the teams that are best at executing in those areas and the premises that they are basing their ideas on.

For the tablet, two premises I'm currently investigating are: a) in what ways the "lean back"[5] experience for the tablet will be different from that of television; and b) how the tablet as a social device will enable different types of applications and services. Consumers share their iPad with others whereas they really don't with their iPhone or Mac.

---

[4] Massively Multiplayer Online Role-Playing Games.

[5] The ability you have to take the tablet anywhere and "lean back" with it—in bed, on a couch, on a train, at the breakfast table, etc.

At the end of the day, you cannot force a market. But you can be very clear about what premises you are making and what bets you are making. Do everything you can to execute against those bets. But sometimes at the end of the day, it is a premise, and there is nothing you can do about it. I've been doing this long enough though to know that great teams almost always figure out something. It's a heck of a journey worth taking!

THE START-UP ANALYSIS MODEL (SAM)

The origin of SAM goes back to 2001, when Sheetal and I first considered ways to analyze start-ups by applying methods similar to Wall Street's rigorous analysis of public companies. How could we identify the science behind the start-up success and capture that in a quantitative model?

It was a very basic model at that time and it eventually evolved to a robust model as we put more than 1,000 start-ups through it and tested various elements, like market size and timing, key characteristics of founders and the core team, business models, value propositions, and competitive aspects.

SAM looks into start-ups from a stage perspective, as different elements come into play at different stages of the start-up building process and their influence on success is dependent on the stage.

For example, when the company is nothing but a couple of co-founders, there is nothing to evaluate—no product, business model, competitiveness aspects, or even a market for the most part. It really boils down to the quality of the founding team. As you move from idea to product to proof of customer traction to scaling and growth, market size and timing become very important—the team quality becomes more important than that of just founders—and later the viability and scalability of business model become key determinant of success.

SAM looks at key success criteria across various stages of start-up building to determine success probability at each stage. SAM is also used for determining the survivability risk of start-ups from the enterprise perspective, where start-ups are selling their products and services to medium and large enterprises.

The following are the four main stages of start-ups analyzed in SAM:

Stage 0: Formation Stage (an idea attracts the core team, who builds prototype)

Stage 1: Build & Prove Stage (initial proof of product and traction)

Stage 2: Scale & Grow Stage (initial proof is scaled into big business)

Stage M: Mature Growth Stage (start-up becomes a mature private/public firm)

Steven Dietz

GRP Partners: DealerTrack, TrueCar, Bill Me Later, Koral, UGO Entertainment

Steven Dietz *is part of the founding team at GRP Partners,[1] a leading venture capital fund in Southern California. Steven has served on the boards of more than fifteen companies in the financial services, consumer retail, and alternative energy industries. These companies include CTSpace (acquired by Sword Group), Bill Me Later (acquired by eBay), DealerTrack Holdings, Koral (acquired by Salesforce.com), and UGO Entertainment (acquired by Hearst Corporation and more recently by IGN Entertainment).*

GRP has funded fifteen start-up companies that resulted in $1 billion exits. GRP takes a team approach and Steven was involved in many of these successes. His straight-from-the-gut discussion about what it takes to build a billion-dollar business, along with challenges faced by start-ups and investors and how GRP navigates around them, are extremely striking.

Tarang Shah: What are some of the key reasons why start-ups fail?

Steven Dietz: Start-ups fail for the same reason. They run out of money. Then the question becomes, "Why do they run out of money?" There are a

---

[1] I have had the opportunity to work closely with the partners at GRP and I am very impressed by how GRP approaches venture investments. Entrepreneurs may find GRP partner Mark Suster's blog, *Both Sides of the Table* (www.bothsidesofthetable.com), to be very informative.

few common reasons. Ultimately, they run out of money because the revenues exceed expenses and they cannot find investors to support the business further.

There are two core concepts here for an entrepreneur to focus on. First, get the business moving at the top line while managing operating expenses. It's common sense but many entrepreneurs think too hard about what they want to build and too little about how it will fund itself. Second, understand what your investors need to see in order to provide additional financing. Make sure you can deliver on the required results with plenty of time to raise your next round.

Revenues are the clearest evidence an entrepreneur can show to investors that the business is on track. As an investor, I am keenly interested in the traction a product or service has with its customers. Failure to grow the top line can result from a market that isn't materializing or from a poor solution.

But the problem that is most difficult to wrestle with as an investor is poor execution. Few management teams recognize this shortcoming in themselves and they point to external factors such as market size, too early to market, competition—any number of reasons that more time and more money will put things on track. As a general matter, my feeling is that investors should put more money into a company when it is achieving expected results or when there is a clear plan to change direction. Continuing to fund a business where neither of these factors is expected is investing in hope. I've generally found hope to be a poor investment thesis.

Shah: Does competition drive a start-up out of business?

Dietz: Never… well, almost never. Failure to respond to competitors' offering with a better message and a better solution is what weaker management calls failure due to competition. What competition does impact is the ultimate value of a business by influencing operating margins and the ability to attract the best talent at a reasonable price. Competition limits the size of exits much more than it impacts the viability of the business especially when the team is strong.

Shah: Can the economy play a role in start-up failure?

Certainly. But only for businesses selling a large-ticket solution where big buyers delay purchase decisions based on the prevailing economic environment. For most start-ups, the economy is a minor headwind or tailwind, and it is the market size and team quality that influence outcomes.

Shah: Very insightful. It really puts to rest some of the wrong excuses you hear in the market for why start-ups fail.

Shah: For Series A opportunities, what are your investment criteria? Is it a market that is potentially going to be big, co-founders who are so good that you know they are going to figure something out eventually, or the way the solution is put together?

Dietz: Let's start with the solution. It is rare that a solution is so damn good that I know with certainty that it is going to work. We have had fifteen companies where we exited at a value of over a billion dollars. Only one of those fifteen got to that point without significant business challenges. The solution is rarely spot-on out of the gate. It requires a great team that can refine the business and adapt to the market learnings.

We like having a strong team pursuing a large opportunity. Their first approach will need to be tweaked and changed, but a strong team can live up to this challenge. I'm interested in how a team has thought through their initial solution, and it helps when they have experience in the market they are addressing. Over the years I've learned that the business must evolve rapidly to succeed.

Shah: Consider market and management: Is one more important in the early phase of the company?

Dietz: They both have to be there. If either is missing, there is no point in looking. I want to know it is a big opportunity and I want to know it is a team that has the ability to adapt. Take for example the search engine market of the late nineties. We had an investment in a start-up called GoTo, which eventually became Overture. Google used our monetization strategy and combined it with their better search algorithm and a different distribution strategy to create a much bigger company. Fortunately, the market was huge and so it allowed Overture to be still a billion-dollar company.

Shah: How do you deal with being too late and too early?

Dietz: Too late is not generally an issue going into an investment. It becomes an issue if the team executes slowly and another stronger team pulls ahead.

Too early? It is really easy to be too early. The challenge is distinguishing between a market that is not ready yet and a market that will never be ready. We've faced this challenge a few times. When we truly believe the market will evolve and we have a strong team, the answer is to reduce cash burn rate dramatically to maintain the option to play later.

These are tough decisions and, made incorrectly, they can be costly.

We had a company called UGO Entertainment that successfully executed this strategy. They had a large audience for their content but the online advertising market was immature in 2001. We cut the burn[2] dramatically and were able to limp through 2000 and 2001 and 2002. We ended up selling the business for a lot of money to Hearst.

Shah: What are the signs that tell you that you have gotten into something that is too early or too late?

Dietz: We have one in the portfolio right now where we have concluded that we are in the right business, but we are too early. We sell a solution to physicians for revenue collection. We know from a regulatory perspective that doctors are going to get less and less reimbursement. We know the payments are being shifted more towards the patient, direct pay, and this solution helps doctors collect that money from the patients. We are signing doctors up. The ones that are signing up pay us, and none of them are dropping us. We are clearly, for the ones signing up, addressing a need. If we were not, they would be abandoning the solution. But doctors are not signing up in droves. They are just not seeing collections as a big-enough problem yet. We are certain the pain is there and needs to be solved. So we cut the burn, we cut the expense structure dramatically, and we made the decision that we have enough customers that we could cut back on the marketing, cut back on product development, and wait it out. It might take two years. It might take four or five years. We still believe the market will be there.

Shah: Like in the case of UGO, you know with high level of certainty that the need is there and eventually sizeable market will form around that need.

Dietz: In this case it is even easier than UGO because the company, having cut all those costs, is basically a break-even business. So with $6 million that has gone into it to date from us and another investor, we know that this business can just wait it out three or four years without needing additional funding.

Shah: As an investor, what are you doing with the company during this wait-it-out period?

Dietz: In this case, very little. We have made our decision. Getting to that point required making sure we were comfortable that the market would come together. It also meant understanding why physicians were not signing up, why those who signing up continued to stick with the product, etc. We were also looking at utilization. All those things led us to believe that we need to keep doing what we are doing and wait for the market to come around.

---

[2] The amount of cash the business was spending.

If that is the conclusion, the next question is why would we put any more time into it? There are other things to do with our time. We cannot make the market come together faster, and we do not face a decision on funding at this point in time. If this company were burning $400,000 a month, we would also have an easy decision to let it go. Fortunately, it's operating at break-even and no funding decision is imminent. Now I do not know if the market is going to arrive in a year or five years, but until it comes, we have the right structure in place to wait it out.

Shah: What are the steps you take for the companies that are too late to the game?

Dietz: As an investor, there are two ways you can be late to the game. Either investing in a business that was already too late when you invested, or you invested when the company was okay initially but competitive and market forces left it behind. Fortunately I haven't invested in a business that was too late. The conclusion you are too late in this case basically means that you have failed in your diligence in understanding what the competitive environment was and how well the company you just invested in was differentiated.

If I reach the conclusion that the competitive environment is meaningfully different than I had expected originally and the solution we have is not differentiated, and the CEO has not already figured it out since he is living in that business, then my decision is relatively easy. Why would I back the guy any further?

In the case that there are lots of other people doing the same thing and we do not have a differentiated solution, why would I put more money into a me-too company? In that case, my options are to either sell the business, which may be difficult or to shut it down. As we discussed earlier, the businesses fail because either they are not getting the sales or they are not executing well. That is clearly a failure on the CEO's part. He failed to correctly assess the competitive dynamics and position the product accordingly so he can sell the solution into the market. So to me, start-ups don't fail because they are too late to the market, but they end up being too late because they don't execute correctly. It is the poor execution that leads to being late and left behind and then eventual failure.

Let me give you an example. GRP funded a company called DealerTrack. I remember this story very clearly. We put money in on a Monday or Tuesday, and on the Thursday after we closed, a new competitor was announced.

DealerTrack connected automobile dealers with lenders to help vehicles get financed. The new competitor was a joint venture between Ford,

DaimlerChrysler, General Motors, and Toyota. They were going to create a joint venture called RouteOne and do exactly what DealerTrack was doing, but backed by the four leaders in automotive industry who had strong balance sheets at the time. They had lot of money and resources, including the key relationships with the auto dealers.

We had a very good management team. We got together ten days after the announcement. The company was in New York. They came out here to Los Angeles. Five of us sat down in a room for a full day and walked through what this competitor's entry into the market meant. What are the risks that entry presented to us, and how can we address them and significantly change?

Literally two weeks after we funded the business, we decided we needed a different approach. We had one other competitor before RouteOne entered the market. To effectively compete with RouteOne and build a successful business, we realized we had to integrate our systems with the banks. At that time, we were integrated with thirty-five banks. We had a competitor who was integrated with twenty-eight. We both knew how to do it. We also realized in that discussion that if RouteOne buys our competitor, we are in trouble because now they can marginalize our competitive advantage by integrating with banks. And given their resources, relationships and brand name, if they get a head start on bank integration, they will win the game.

The other company faced the same challenge that we did. There was a prisoner's dilemma here. If RouteOne approached either of us, you have to sell because if you do not sell and they buy your competitor, you are put out of business. So the solution was "let's merge the two businesses" and we went to them and said "here is our logic," and they agreed.

We merged the two companies and it worked exactly as we thought. It was a team that understood the dynamics of their business and was able to adjust to dramatically changing circumstances, accepted the new facts on the ground for what they were, and built a strategy around it.

Shah: Fascinating! When you meet with promising entrepreneurs like these, what stands out in them compared to others you don't invest in?

Dietz: They are passionate. They are able to attract great people. They deliver what they say they are going to. It means they have a good understanding of what the drivers are of their business. And I am comforted if they actually know the industry they are addressing.

On the other hand, there are people that will come and say, "Hey, I bought a car and what a shitty experience. I am going to make a better car company."

If they have never sold cars, never made cars, but the only thing they know is that the current car-buying experience does not feel right and so they are going to do it better—to me that is someone who has so little knowledge of the industry they do not even know what they do not know. I see that a lot. People who had a bad consumer experience. They decide they could do it better, but they have no idea what goes into the delivery of that. Those are the ones that don't end up getting funding.

Shah: Does it really matter if it's a single founder or multiple co-founders?

Dietz: There is certainly a greater risk that they will not get along if there is more than one. In fact, today alone this subject has come up three times in the last four hours.

The challenge of multiple founders is the interpersonal relationship. When there are two co-founders who are very talented and understand each other's needs and capabilities well, and respect and complement each other, that is an interesting team and that's fine. On the other hand, two people who have done the same thing (engineering or marketing or product development), and have a lot of overlap in skill set, that usually ends up being a problem.

When it is two people whose personal relationship supersedes the business relationship—husband/wife team, brothers, father/son—our experience is it is a disaster. The loyalty of a husband and wife to each other appropriately exceeds the loyalty to the business, and certainly to the investors. We have killed two companies where everything else felt good, but we said we would not get close to it because of that personal dynamics.

The interpersonal dynamics created in the business are very challenging. It is very hard for somebody in the organization to go complain to the president about CEO decisions and seek help to fix a problem when the president is going to go to bed with the CEO that night.

The other tendency of those teams is two brothers running a company. The team meets, they hash through something, decide on a course of action, and then the two brothers go off into a room and talk further and make their own decision, and the team becomes alienated because they are not part of the family. We have unfortunately made a number of investments in teams that were family in some way or another, and we are seven-for-seven in bad experiences.

Shah: Great insight. So if there is more than one founder, you would look for the minimal overlap in skill set, complementary skills, mutual respect and successful history of working together but not the family members.

Dietz: Yes. They need to complement each other. There has to be a reason you are working with this other person.

Shah: Do you prefer to disrupt existing markets or go after new markets?

Dietz: I prefer going into an existing market. It is much easier to define market opportunity including how big the opportunity is. You know who your customers are going to be and it is easy to figure out the basis for the differentiation.

If you are doing something totally new like an online game or Twitter, and if you are successful, you make the most money. There are a lot of VCs who like placing those bets, but there does not seem to be a lot of consistency of success in those. Someone is going to win. Someone will land on it, but I do not see a whole lot of consistency on figuring out who lands on it.

Shah: Do you have a preference for young entrepreneurs over more experienced entrepreneurs? Does your preference for disrupting established markets by definition assume it has to be someone more experienced than young students coming out of college?

Dietz: The generalization is that the entrepreneurs must be young. I would be inclined to say that is an appropriate generalization. If I were to look at the teams we have backed, there are a lot of them in their forties. Age is not a factor in entrepreneurism, but energy and experience are.

Shah: Do serial entrepreneurs have a higher probability of success compared to first-time entrepreneurs?

Dietz: Yes, the success probability is higher for the serial entrepreneurs. There are a lot of first-time entrepreneurs, and most of them are not going to succeed. All other things equal, I would rather invest with someone who has been successful in the past.

With serial entrepreneurs, there is less risk. I know they can be successful. There are some people who are not able to be successful. Would you rather invest in somebody on the hope that they are a prodigy or with somebody who has already proven they know how to do whatever it is?

For every Mark Zuckerberg and Bill Gates, there are ten thousand people who had ideas they thought were great and did not produce anything. There are probably fifteen of those people over the last twenty-five years who have built companies of $10 billion or more. Of those fifteen, I would say thirteen of them, except Mark Benioff,[3] were creating whole new businesses

---

[3] Salesforce.com founder.

first of all. Larry Ellison[4] had never done it before. It is pretty hard to have experience in something that nobody has ever done before.

Let's take it further and look at number of people who have turned eighteen in the US since 1975, since Apple and Microsoft were doing well. How many of those people turned into one of the fifteen or eighteen people we are talking about? As an investor, do I really want to buy that lottery ticket? You might, and you might win, but I sure as hell would not say that the fact that you won once means that is the number you should always play.

Shah: Some founders make it all the way to being the CEO of a public company, and in other cases they either get replaced or choose to get replaced or bring in somebody else. What drives that decision?

Dietz: It's a function of personality, ability, and ego. It shows up in the execution challenge, whether it exceeds their management ability. It doesn't show up in the board reports as he wrote those reports.

You see it in the performance of the business, you see it in revenue, the quality of the people being hired, and delivery of results. Are we achieving objectives? If not, why and how that is explained tells a great deal about whether the guy is cut out to run the company or not.

Now many of the founders choose to be replaced by experienced outside CEOs. For some reason, they feel an emotional attachment to the business they started and they want to see it succeed.

Shah: What separates exceptional teams from the mediocre teams?

Dietz: Exceptional teams have people who complement each other well, have experience doing what you expect them to do, understand the dynamics of an early-stage business and the activities they are going to have to engage in, and are passionate about what they are doing and the solution they are delivering. It is not a job for them. They are doing it for some reason other than the paycheck.

Shah: What's the secret of great CEOs in building great teams?

Dietz: Great CEOs hire people who are probably better than they are at whatever the task the person is going to do. Whatever the CEO could otherwise do, he is hiring someone who is better than he to do it. CEOs who are not as good tend to hire people who do not attract great talent. They determine not to hire great talent for whatever their reasons and end up

---

[4] Co-founder and CEO of Oracle.

building teams that are not that strong. It's classic As hire Bs, and Bs hire Cs, and then you have a very mediocre team.

Shah: Have you seen the best CEOs in your portfolio paying specific attention to team culture or does the culture come together naturally?

Dietz: I have seen a couple who specifically focus on development of culture. Usually it turns out that their focus was wrong. I think it comes down to who the leaders are, and what their personalities are, and if they are willing to hire great people. A culture ends up evolving. I think it is a very difficult thing to influence.

Shah: In what cases do you need to nail the business model early on?

Dietz: It is pretty much impossible to back the creation of a new business concept and set as the condition a precedent expectation that there is a clear business model. It is hard to imagine somebody looking to disrupt an existing market and not having a clear business model for doing so.

On the other hand, you cannot create something that is going to capture a ton of audience and actually know how you are going to monetize it day one. You will have ideas.

Shah: How do you decide between shutting down, keep funding, or selling your start-up?

Dietz: It is probably one of the toughest decisions in this business: when do you kill something? If you have conviction that it cannot be saved, that is an easy decision. That happens occasionally. If you are certain it can be improved, you understand clearly why it has not achieved what you expected, that is an easy decision.

Unfortunately, those two are the head and tail of the bell curve. Most of the time there is more judgment involved. There is no formula. Now there is a significant period of time between when the company is cash-flow negative and when it is ready to go public. IPO companies that go public in this market are growing rapidly and have earnings. So I do not very often face a decision of fund it or take it public. My decision is fund it, sell it, or shut it down.

Shah: If the start-up is doing well, in what circumstances will you sell it?

Dietz: It comes down to whether or not the price is worthwhile. If they are paying what it is worth today, that is one decision. If they are paying me an amount that I do not think the business will grow into for another three years, that is a different decision.

Paul Scanlan

MobiTV

Paul Scanlan is co-founder and president of MobiTV, Inc. In this role, he has played a critical role in all aspects of the company's success, from the scrappy early beginnings all the way through to the current position today as the market leader in a fast-growing space. Paul's entrepreneurial vision is balanced with a proven track record having pioneered an entirely new industry, then proving its commercial success with the launch of the platform across all five of the nation's leading mobile networks. Paul started his career in telecommunications sales at Lucent Technologies and then ventured into helping a friend start up a boutique advertising agency. Prior to starting MobiTV, Paul was a Managing Partner at Enterprise IG (now called Brand Union) where he led the technology consulting practice.

As a hard-core mobility guy and venture professional, I couldn't help but notice the rise of MobiTV against all odds. I had helped a VC friend with due diligence on MobiTV's competitor, PacketVideo. Later I came to know the early investor in MobiTV, Terry Moore of Hamilton Tech Ventures in San Diego. I couldn't pass the opportunity to learn more about how MobiTV rose to the top when Packet-Video and Qualcomm's FLO TV struggled.

From being a successful company co-founder to building a great team, and from creating an early prototype to scaling for growth, Paul provides a great window into the journey of a start-up that went from an idea to an IPO candidate.

Tarang Shah: Take me back all the way to how you guys came up with the idea and started the company.

Paul Scanlan: Well, actually, the initial catalyst for this company was a pretty funny story that Jeff Annison and Phillip Alvelda and I, the three co-founders, all remember vividly. Phillip and I met playing ice hockey, and he was a PhD from MIT and was then working with a lot of entrepreneurs in tech-based consulting and starting companies. For a long time, we just talked about different companies and things that we would start. We had a couple of ideas that we were tossing around, and we were all very entrepreneurial and creative, so we had more ideas than we had anything else. We were all sitting around at Phillip's house one rainy day in the Oakland Hills. As you know, there are not a lot of lightning storms in the Bay Area, and we were having this conversation and we were debating a few of the ideas that we had.

It really boiled down to two ideas: one of which seemed very realistic, very interesting, and fun to do, but probably not a huge business idea. The other one was extremely ambitious, borderline far-fetched, and kind of a little bit out of our league. So, we were talking about this, and Phillip, completely just overflowing with ambition, was making a bunch of statements about how big this new idea could be, how incredible it would be and if we could pull it off, what an accomplishment it would be. Literally, right in the middle of his speech, lightning struck. This is a true story; it's amazing. Lightning struck, hit a tree outside his house. The tree fell and crushed his back deck, which was only a few feet away from where we were sitting. He had a hot tub out there. The whole thing just came tumbling down.

We were looking out these big plate glass windows at this happening and then, of course, the power went out. It was just the most interesting experience and we were all kind of looking at each other wondering, wow, was that a sign from God or what? But what's interesting about it is, as entrepreneurs, we saw it as a positive sign. Like, oh, we have to pursue this. Where you could easily see it as the bad sign—that it is definitely not the way to go. As optimistic entrepreneurs, we said, okay, let's go! We were leaning in that direction anyway, but the lightning did sort of consummate it. So that was the path that we took. Now that path ended up being [something different]. We had some vision for what we are doing today, but it wasn't what we ended up doing. It wasn't exactly what we were articulating at that time.

Shah: Take me one step back to what created the three of you as entrepreneurs. Was there a start-up in your past that you co-founded or you guys took on as a first venture together?

Scanlan: It's interesting because we probably aren't the kind of prototypical, co-founder team. All three of us had been somewhat entrepreneurial in the past. I had a company of my own in high school that I ran and had employees, and then later I helped a friend start an advertising agency in Chicago. When I was working for a high-end consulting company later on, one of the primary jobs was working with tech start-ups and entrepreneurs.

I have been around, and Phillip had already started a company in his lab at MIT and spun that out and moved to California with it. He was getting to a point where he was getting ready to leave that company. And then Jeff is just a super-creative guy that had worked with Phillip in the past. And we were all friends. We all shared an entrepreneurial spirit, and we would spend a fair amount of our time together brainstorming new companies and ideas and things.

As I mentioned, Phillip and I were playing ice hockey together, and we played together for three years before we actually started the company. We had a hundred different ideas that never made their way out of the locker room, so to speak. We would just talk about it at hockey or after hockey, or whatever. With this idea, the timing seemed right. Which was ironic because later it turned out that the timing was absolutely wrong. It was probably the single worst time in the history of man for us to do what we were doing, but we lived to tell about it. But it felt like the right time, so we wrote a lot of different versions of the business plan.

One was going to be a high-tech toy company, so we had literally created some prototypes for night-vision goggles for kids that we thought we could get to a price point of about $50. Real night vision, infrared night vision. [Another product was] remote-controlled cars with cameras in them and a display on the remote control so you could drive it and see where the car was going. Cool ideas and creative things like that. So that was very realistic. We knew we could do it. Jeff had come from the toy industry. We knew we could come up with good product ideas, design them, and then sell them into the toy industry for production and marketing. That's an existing model.

The problem is, it's not the type of model that investors get super-excited about. We knew that if we did it, we could probably be successful and have like a thirty- or forty-person company some day that made a couple of million dollars a year.

But the other idea was telecommunications infrastructure software, which obviously was much more ambitious. It was the early days of data on the phones, so this was around 1999 to 2000. Phones were just starting to be capable of receiving data. We looked at the technologies in place to do it and identified a bunch of weaknesses. I had a background working at Lucent in Chicago, and my sister worked there. Phillip had done some consulting work for Qualcomm. So we had a little bit of experience. Just enough to be dangerous, though not enough to really be credible. I think that was actually what helped us in the end—that we were not drinking the Kool-Aid that the wireless industry was drinking at the time. At the time, the industry had convinced themselves that 3G networks were going to be here and they would solve all the problems. We looked at it, and had a different perspective. We felt strongly that the industry would be stuck with 2.5G networks for some time and there were just so many opportunities for us to take advantage of. We felt like the systems that were being designed to create the data connection from the phone—at the time what was a 2.5G network—was designed by circuit switch engineers that didn't completely understand packet switch delivery.

We took a different approach—we are going to rewrite all this software for packet delivery, because that's what most of the content is. Remember, the first, early wireless data protocols were circuit-switched. It was like you created a modem connection and then you hub it. But that's very hard to do in wireless, with jitter and all the fluctuation in bandwidth, etc. So this was the angle we ended up pursuing. The idea was to create a much more efficient and optimized pipe for delivering data to phones. Once we had done that, we could build and expand into applications.

The business model was really about the infrastructure software. There were a few paragraphs about being able to deliver video and TV services later. What happened is we were just barely successful in getting that software into the wireless industry, and we had just a six-person company. We signed a deal with Siemens for global distribution of the product and to all their networks.

Shah: What was the company called at that time?

Scanlan: We were called Idetic. It was a phonetic spelling of the word "eidetic." It means having a photographic memory, perfect visual recall. So the approach at the time was that we were using a lot of protocol optimization, compression, and optimization techniques to create what looked like a 3G connection over a 2.5G network. So the reason the name Idetic stuck was that it was relevant to what we were doing. Our compression would still give you the same recall and visual experience, or a better visual experience. It was a great name if you were familiar with the definition of eidetic memory. But since most people are not, the name came off sounding harsh and toxic. It was a terrible name. Let me just admit that up front. But, it was the only URL we could get at the time.

We ended up pursuing this and we got a lot of initial installations. The challenge was that while carriers understood the technology and saw the value in it, we would only get initial purchases. And the carriers had all been burned by the first wave of WAP gateways at the time, so we were getting all the upgrades to those platforms, but the carriers were starting with very low capacity. At that time, people still weren't using their phones for data. Our thought was: look, when users have a better experience, data consumption will take off and people will start using the data connection more often. The problem was, still at that point in time, even though we could create what appeared to be a much faster connection with lower latency—and the performance was much better—there still weren't any applications that people really wanted to use because the market hadn't delivered any yet.

Shah: This raises a great question on market timing. What were the data points or the thought process in deciding that timing was right?

Scanlan: I guess the part of the industry talk that we were buying into was that data is going to take off, and that people are going to use their phones for more than just making phone calls. Our two pillars were that these things will happen and that 3G will take longer to deploy than most people were predicting. Therefore, the need in the marketplace was obvious, which was that we needed better software for managing the delivery. And, by the way, that software would still have the same impact on the 3G network, so it would still be relevant when 3G deployed

There were also significant savings for the carriers who were all, as you may recall, completely strapped after getting gouged in the 3G auctions. Many of them were facing potential bankruptcy, had no money to build out their 3G network, and were just trying to figure out how to pay these auction licenses. They were in bad shape, and they needed data to take off, but they were at a crossroads. For us, it was really about meeting their needs. The challenge was for the industry at large. We were actually people who really got it, and people who didn't get it thought we were just being pessimistic about 3G. So there were so many people in the industry, including some of the big infrastructure providers who were the guys behind the hype around 3G. You know, Ericsson and Nokia and these guys were the ones trying to get 3G deployed sooner. The problem was that, (a) the equipment wasn't ready, and (b) the carriers couldn't afford it.

Shah: In 1999 to 2000 I was marketing 3G at Ericsson.

Scanlan: Oh, you were? Yes, so you know exactly what I'm talking about.

Shah: And later in 2000, I became the lead product manager for Ericsson's CDMA2000 product line.

Scanlan: Great, so you would probably remember, because we were working with the Ericsson labs here in Berkeley, and we had come pretty close to doing a deal with Ericsson, but Siemens was much more aggressive. At that time, if I look back at our business plan, it is really pretty entertaining. In 1999 to 2000, we were saying that 3G wouldn't be broadly deployed until 2004 to 2005. Well, guess what? It turns out we were actually under-bidding. Turns out that 3G took even longer than we had expected it to. There was a lot of hype around 3G equipment, but even if it was ready, the carriers didn't have the money to buy it.

So what ended up happening is that we were getting all these initial deployments. Siemens had basically taken our software and white-labeled it as the Siemens' mobile smart proxy. We're a six-person company, and we were running that for them. We would get POs [purchase orders] from Siemens every once in a while for new installations, and we had two big provinces in China, but of course the Chinese pricing was so low that you needed volume to make any money, and the volume wasn't coming. Consumers still weren't using data broadly and it hadn't gotten beyond the early adopters, and if you walked into a Sprint store or an AT&T store, most of the people working there had no idea how to even talk about data.

We decided to leverage our software acceleration capability and started thinking about applications that we could do with that capability that would draw demand for the product. The application that we had always anticipated being kind of the high-data, high-usage, high-appeal application was TV. We were calling it the seventy-five-year-old killer app and now, ten years later, it's the eighty-five-year-old killer app. It's still as popular as ever and growing. It's just that the way people consume TV is changing but the viewing continues to be on the rise.

Shah: What year was it?

Scanlan: 2003. We expanded the platform to deliver video and TV, and then, like any good entrepreneurs, we took it around to all the carriers and tried to coach them into deploying services with it, but still under a software licensing model. Most of the carriers that we talked to were apprehensive to go and develop a service around it. A lot of them looked at it and said, "Yeah, it's interesting, but what would we do with it?" We were saying, "Well, you go license the content, you create a service, you go for it, and you drive revenue." And they said, "Oh well, you know, we're not really geared up to do that."

Depending on who you talk to, a lot of the carriers, frankly, as you can probably imagine, didn't see the light right away. They were saying, "I'm not sure people really want to watch TV on their cell phones." So we said all right, fine. We'll go produce and create the end product. If we do that, will you sell it? Will you sell it to your customers? Alas, we finally got Sprint to agree that they would. So then we had to go get all the content lined up, which was almost harder than getting the carriers lined up, to a certain degree.

Shah: At that time it was a novel idea.

Scanlan: Yeah, at that time. Most of the doors were just slammed straight in our face, like, "What are you talking about? That's a terrible idea." We continued to keep after it, and the thing that really helped us was that we finally convinced the guy that we were working with at Sprint to sign the deal with us so that we could go back to the content industry with a carrier deal in hand, because we were still a very small company, about twenty people at the time.

Shah: To get to this idea of TV as a killer app, what extent did you guys try to understand if this was the real need consumers will pay for?

Scanlan: Well, I will tell you how it came about. At the time, the phones were really not very advanced, so delivering live TV, full-motion video, wasn't possible. So we were doing some brainstorming at the company around different applications and things that we could deliver, and one of the things that we thought was really potentially cool, that we initially called Snap TV, was something that would just be a peek into what's happening on TV right now, but it would be slow frame rate like motion JPEG.

As we developed that concept, and then built a prototype, we realized how useful and interesting it was. We started showing it around to people, and we put it on some phones and sent it around. People were really, really interested. What we had done, which is probably really helpful, is that we had studied very closely what some of the early companies like PacketVideo had tried doing and were in the process of failing at, at the time. They are still around today, but in a very different kind of incarnation, and at the time they were, for a short time, the darling of the industry. But the avenues and the approach they had taken, we felt were flawed and that helped guide us toward the right solution by demonstrating what not to do.

Shah: And what was that, Paul?

Scanlan: Their primary model was that they were focused exclusively on 3G devices, and we had a much more pragmatic perspective on when 3G would deploy. So we took a much earlier approach to it. The other thing is they, and RealNetworks, and a lot of others that had done some video streaming in mobile, were really focused on clips. Just clips, not even VOD [video on demand], because remember—at the time—you couldn't go license a full-length episode for VOD. You couldn't get that anywhere. You couldn't get it on iTunes or anywhere. You had to watch the broadcast program to get it. TiVo had just started, so even the whole time shifting concept was just beginning. So the content that was available in the form of clips was really, really lame.

It was basically promotional clips and advertisements for shows and outtakes for shows. PacketVideo had tried to augment this by creating their own content, which we thought was a total waste of time. They had a studio and hired actors and cameramen, and crazy stuff, but partially just because they had the money, they could afford to do it, and we felt like they were just pursuing things in a direction that didn't make any sense to us. So we looked at the space, and all the examples of things that had failed, or were failing, which we could learn from. In the end, we felt strongly that going out and getting the live TV feed was really the way to do it.

We marketed real, live TV not VOD. In fact, in the early days we didn't do any VOD. Now we do because we are able to get full-length episodes and full movies and all kinds of stuff. Our balance between live and VOD now is pretty balanced. About half of our usage probably comes from full-length episodes. But, at the time, the content just wasn't there, so we focused on live TV. Well, now we've got MSN, NBC, CNBC, Discovery, Discovery Kids, TLC, etc. The hardest thing back then was we would go to NBC and describe what we were looking for, and they would say okay great, you gotta talk to our online group because they handle all new media. We'd say, no, that's not who we want to talk to. We want to talk to your affiliate group that licenses the channels to the cable companies and they'd say, yeah, but all new media needs to be funneled through the online group. To that we'd just respond, don't even bother making the introduction. We don't want to talk to them. We know they don't have access to the linear feed. We only want to talk to the affiliate guys.

Shah: So you were focused on place-shifting the live feed to mobile, not time shifting it as VOD.

Scanlan: Exactly. Yeah. We wanted the live feed.

Shah: As alternative channel of broadcast, but real-time—just like it's happening on other TV channels.

Scanlan: The test case was a user turning on our phone and our application, and holding it up to their TV at home, and they would get the same content.

Scanlan: Now we weren't able to do that across the board because, obviously, channels like ESPN and stuff like that crawled into this space slowly with different approaches. So we would create a linear channel out of their available content. We would go get SportsCenter and other content and put it all together.

Shah: And at that time, they wouldn't bother to do that themselves because they didn't see the market?

Scanlan: No, they weren't trying to do it. Most of them were pessimistic about it.

Shah: So this was more of an intuition followed by a prototype that you ran by customers that led you to believe that there is a market for it?

Scanlan: Exactly. We felt like we had an approach that was unique. It's interesting, actually, if you look at a lot of new ideas, they are often times not entirely new. They are sort of a derivative of something that was tried before but with a better approach and potentially better timing too, because I think we also timed the market better than some of the others did. And our approach, in fact there was a point in time where, when we were doing the Siemens business and just the infrastructure software, one of the guys at PacketVideo, who ultimately later joined our board, suggested to Packet-Video that they buy MobiTV because he felt that it was the sort of horse before the cart. If PacketVideo had MobiTV—or had Idetic at that time— they could precondition the network with that software, sell that into the carrier, get them conditioned on that, and then sell video into them.

What PacketVideo was doing was going straight to the video, and the carrier was saying okay, well, video the way you are doing it, we'll do that when we deploy 3G but that's not happening for a couple of years. They didn't adapt fast enough when it became clear that 3G was going to take longer to deploy.

Shah: I think that's a great case study on being there with a great idea but before the supporting infrastructure is in place. And you guys were smart enough to say what is here now that I can cater to while keeping your eyes on what that will evolve into in the future. And then adapting as you sell.

What was happening with your financing? Were you able to fund the company yourself or did you have to raise money?

Scanlan: In the early days we raised seed finance and this was one of the things that was probably a blessing in disguise. But at the time, it felt like we were cursed. We all had our day jobs, we all agreed that if we can raise money to go do this, we would all jump in. So we were actually very quickly able to raise our first $500,000, and we had a term sheet for much higher amount but it needed a lead VC [an investor who leads the investing round] and a few other things. But it was a very strong indicator to us that hey, this is going to work, we should pursue it full-time. So we did.

Then in the middle of us getting out and trying to raise the bigger amount of money, which we all assumed was going to be a slam dunk, the telecom and internet bubble burst. So what seemed like a great time quickly turned into probably the worst time, but it ended up being really good for our company because it forced us to focus on revenue, which was a lost art back then, as you may recall. And while we were maybe a little disadvantaged because our competitors, like PacketVideo and other big companies, had deep, deep pockets, they had also over-extended themselves. While everyone else was laying off and downsizing, we were growing, even modestly, but we were growing. And so, with very little money in the bank and telecom software space collapsing around us, we decided to just be super, super scrappy. We were so scrappy you wouldn't believe it. We barely had carpet in our office. But we had no problem with that. It turned out to be really good thing.

We used to joke that every day we'd stay alive, we would gain market share because our competitors were going out of business, and we would continue to be an interesting company. Our seed investors were very impressed with what we were able to do, the sacrifices that we were making. So they stayed very supportive and dedicated to the company. They weren't turning their backs on us. They weren't beating us up in board meetings. Most of their companies were just hemorrhaging and dying, and they felt like we were actually surviving in a very interesting way, and they acknowledged the sacrifices that we were making. And then later, we did get the Siemens deal, which we structured to give us an advance on revenue, so over $1 million in advance revenue for that deal. As a six-person company, that's actually a pretty good amount of runway.

So we had that, and our investors were very satisfied, and then as we continued to grow, the investors saw the opportunity to put some more money in so we could expand. The good thing about the Siemens deal is that we got all that money up front, with an agreement to credit it back in terms of product/service over four years. If we got a new PO, we would receive 75 percent of the revenue, and the other 25 percent would go toward the advance. So we were okay. We weren't going to go public or anything, but we were okay. Then we ended up doing the TV opportunity, and we almost needed to raise more money because we had to make some minimum guarantees. But we ultimately structured those early deals so that they would be due at the end of the year, at the end of the contract, whatever wasn't owed. And then as luck would have it, we ended up exceeding all the minimums just with subscriber growth.

When we launched MobiTV, it was a runaway success. Sprint was the first one to launch it. There's a great story actually about the launch night and what happened there. They put it up and launched on two phones, and it quickly became their number-one selling app for ten bucks a month. So everything else was priced below five dollars, and here comes MobiTV at $10 per month. Our first day of sales at Sprint, they told us we were way higher than anything else that they had put up on their deck, and we were ten bucks a month.

Shah: And you had a revenue share?

Scanlan: Yeah, it was a revenue share. The model actually hasn't changed that much since then, except now we work with all the carriers and we power their branded services. For example, Sprint now has Sprint TV, and we power that for them. We do all the premium channels. We do basically all the video for Sprint and they bundle it, and they put it in their "everything" plan and now it just keeps expanding.

Shah: What a success story, starting with software, going into the app, and leveraging the software. Going from selling to enterprise to really selling to their end customers.

Scanlan: Exactly, and it's still leveraging the carriers to do that so that we didn't have to come up with our own consumer marketing dollars. The carriers promote and market the products for us.

Shah: Were there any indications that someone like PacketVideo should have looked at to cut through the hype of 3G and say you know what, though everyone says 3G will be there next year, these are the indicators that tell me that it's not going to be there until 2004 to 2005. What were the factual data you guys used to get to that hypothesis about the 3G delay right?

Scanlan: Mostly just adding. To be honest, part of it was being in the lab at Ericsson and seeing the kind of reality of 2.5G and 3G. Then we had some advisors at the time that had helped us with the company and just talking to the carriers, and understanding the marketplace and their financial situation, and just knowing that it was going to take longer. Especially when the telecom meltdown occurred. That was just going to exacerbate things.

Shah: Were you guys surprised when Sprint customers loved MobiTV service or did you somehow have a feeling that you were on to something huge here?

Scanlan: We expected it to be successful. I think we were a little surprised at how successful it was. So, you know, the analogy we use—I don't know if you ever remember that FedEx commercial, where they show the start-up company and they're tracking their sales on a web site and they are all standing around watching the sales and then the sales just start going through the roof?—we had that tracking capability. We could see it on our system. We all had a web interface into it so we could track it on our phones. It would show us every two minutes how many new subscribers we signed up. It was interesting. We called it the ticker and literally everybody, all of our investors, all of our families—everyone we knew—was tracking that ticker. My father-in-law would track that ticker and send me an e-mail, "Wow, good day today."

On that first day we had this all set up, and we were monitoring it, and it was a little bit crazy. So two things happened. On the day we launched, the ticker was really strong. I mean we were signing up twenty-four hours a day, every two minutes, five to ten new subs. It was just click, click, click, click, click, click. We were shocked at how continuous and fast it was. And then the other thing that we were really blown away by was the day we launched we put a press release out. We were a very small company. It's not like we had a big PR organization or anything. In fact, we barely even had a PR agency. We had a PR consultant. We wrote a press release, and we reached out to a lot of media outlets, and the press was unbelievable. It was a big deal. It was the first live TV delivery to cell phones, and we got coverage everywhere, all the local news, CNN, MSNBC, and CNBC. What's interesting about it, we hadn't slept for like two nights, because we were busy getting ready for launch and to secure all the licenses and everything, working around the clock. So we were all dead tired but still had to do all the press interviews, some of which were on live television. The media coverage ended up also fueling the growth and surprising us a little bit. Like, wow, this was big news.

Shah: And what month, year was it?

Scanlan: This was November 2003. And then that next year, we won a Prime Time Emmy from the Television Academy and went to the Emmy Award show and accepted the award for technology achievement, which was another huge thing. As a twenty-person company, we just couldn't believe what was going on.

Shah: And there was no one even next to you to do something close to what you were doing?

Scanlan: Not really. There were a few other companies that were trying to do similar things, like what PacketVideo was doing, but no one was really taking the live-TV approach. Even today, if you look at it, iPhone is probably the best example. There is no one else on the iPhone that does premium live TV. We are the only company. Take World Cup Soccer as an example. The only way to watch World Cup Soccer on the iPhone would be through the MobiTV platform.

Shah: Yeah, I saw a teenager in Yosemite National Park watching World Cup Soccer on the Sprint 4G network. So that was MobiTV?

Scanlan: Yeah, that was us.

Shah: That is just unbelievable. Tell me more about your venture funding.

Scanlan: We ended up closing the Series A with like a few million bucks, but it was mostly the bridge money that we had used. So the Series A ended up being the seed round that we needed to close before we would raise a Series B. And then when we raised a Series B, ironically it was at a point where we were profitable and generating cash. This was after we had launched MobiTV and subscriber growth was great. And with that, we raised about $20 to $25 million. There was about a total of $25 million into the company at that time. A little over $20 million, and we brought in Redpoint, Menlo,[1] and the existing seed investors put more money in too. And that was really to grow internationally, expand, and double down on what we had created in the US and not let someone else come steal it from us. It was good.

We were able to knock off a few more carriers. We went from Sprint to AT&T to Cingular to Alltel, so we had all of them. We hadn't penetrated Verizon and we hadn't penetrated T-Mobile, but no one else really had. Those two carriers weren't really doing live TV and Verizon ended up doing the Qualcomm FLO service, but then hadn't really gotten behind it. Now Verizon and T-Mobile are both big customers for us. Now we work with all of them. We work with all the major carriers. We work with Telus in Canada. We did a little bit of international expansion, at least we tried to, but it was probably too early.

We had too much demand in the US, so we kind of pulled back from that because we were at risk of spreading ourselves too thin and our board gave us really clear direction. That was, "Own the US market, because you have a really good chance of doing that. Once you do that, then you will be able to expand internationally." And that's what we're doing. And then we raised $100 million about three years ago and international growth is a huge focus for us now.

---

[1] Redpoint Ventures and Menlo Ventures.

Shah: When did my friend Terry Moore participate in the funding?

Scanlan: Oh, Terry was a seed investor. He was very early. He was back in the Idetic stage. In fact, he helped us raise some of that initial money.

Shah: When MobiTV took off, were the handsets capable of receiving streaming video?

Scanlan: Well, they weren't really capable. We could make it happen and that was one of the other advantages that we had. We had to, in the early days, create our own end-to-end video solution because the phones weren't shipping with video players or decoders on them. We had to use our own derivative of a motion JPEG or write our own MPEG-4 decoder in Java. So then later, obviously, the phones became more capable. But even now, we continue to be one step beyond what's on the phones. Right now we are pushing and doing fragmented MPEG-4 and most of the phones don't have support for fragmented MPEG-4. We'll get it in there eventually because we will be the ones that ask for it and drive it, but today we typically have to put our own decoder in there. So we also do RTSP [Real-Time Streaming Protocol], HLS and all the other progressive downloads, etc.

Shah: Do you believe it really helps to have more than one founder?

Scanlan: I do. I think it makes a difference because I think, in our case, we all brought something unique and our own unique sort of strength, and we all had clear acknowledgment of the others. I was really the marketing and business guy. Phillip was the technology and visionary guy, and Jeff was the engineering and product guy.

Shah: Did it help to have known each other when you started the company? But let's say you had come up with the idea yourself and then you had gone out to look for co-founders to build a team. What would have been the key difference between the two approaches?

Scanlan: It's a good question. You know I haven't had experience with the latter, but I think, let's put it this way, because we are really—and I think, especially in the early days of the company, we were—obsessed with chemistry. The chemistry across the team, even beyond the three of us is vital. Every new hire that we brought on needed to pass what we would call the "spidey sense."

Shah: Tell me more about it.

Scanlan: So the spidey sense is, did you ever watch *Spiderman*?

Shah: Yes. Love it.

Scanlan: You know how Spiderman would get what he calls his "spidey sense?" This was something that we really couldn't describe any better than a spidey sense, but if we were interviewing someone and we had even the slightest sense that their chemistry wouldn't mix with the rest of the team, we wouldn't hire them even if their skills and experience and everything were perfect.

Shah: Can you give some examples of how you used spidey sense in hiring talent?

Scanlan: Yeah, I mean you can kind of feel it out. What we were looking for and what we knew kind of gelled with our team was unfettered passion without an ego and a desire to learn and not feel hemmed in by what they already knew. We didn't want to hire people that were intimidated by things that they didn't yet know. But the biggest thing was always that we didn't want people that were obsessed with titles. So, if we had a candidate that we really liked and they were really, really kind of keyed in on title or something, that may trip us up. I would say, you know what, too much attention on title, willing to trade out money and responsibility and other things for title, probably not a good fit.

And you can weed that out, and we did especially in the early days where Phillip and I would insist that we interview everyone that we hired. Now, these days, it's much harder to do. I can't do that with this organization because of the scale. But in the early days it was just so important because you are literally working 24/7, and you are spending a huge amount of your time with these people, and because it's such a small company and there's so much going on, there's no time for distrust and politics. You have to have zero tolerance for it. In a big organization you can endure some of it, but as a smaller organization, it is just crippling.

Shah: Tell me about the DNA that gets set in the possibly first fifteen or twenty people you hire.

Scanlan: I would say up until literally the first one hundred people. We would have everyone, not just the people that worked at MobiTV but the people we did business with, the people that came in contact with us, would always, always, comment, "Wow, what a great, interesting team you have here." It was like it wasn't just something that the people that work here appreciated—it was obvious to other people. And it was an interesting phenomenon because then it attracts other great people. People want to work here. All of our customers wanted to work for us.

Shah: And what do you attribute that to, the ability to attract and build that kind of team?

Scanlan: Well, I think a big part of it was literally just our emphasis on chemistry over experience, and just staying true to that and not giving in to really tempting situations, like an individual who seems not to quite fit but has the skill set we need. We would much sooner go with the person that hadn't had the experience, but with the chemistry and the passion and the willingness to learn and challenge them to go learn it.

The other thing that we did early on [that] I think was interesting on a number of levels, was that we would do a challenge. We would have a challenge for the candidate, like a coding challenge or a marketing challenge or some kind of a problem-solving challenge. A lot of people would get kind of turned off by it, but that's okay. If they are turned off by it then they probably shouldn't work at our company, and we would, as part of the hiring process, explain it to this way: "Hey, look, what we are looking for here is creativity. We are looking for how you are going to solve this problem, how innovative you are going to be." And a lot of people, the people that could solve it creatively and innovatively, loved it. It helped us weed through the candidates. We didn't need just programmers and more bodies. We needed people that would break the mold and figure out how to get stuff done where most others would see a dead end.

Shah: Besides all these, I am sure people just filter through the cracks and you quickly learn that this is not the right person. Did it happen at all?

Scanlan: Yeah, we had a lot of that and we weren't perfect in our hiring. I think with hindsight there are probably some examples that we could have dealt with sooner. It's always hard to deal with those circumstances, but dealing with them is the important part, either addressing the situation or somehow figuring out some amicable way to part ways.

Shah: And what is the first sign you see that someone is just the wrong hire?

Scanlan: Productivity. If their team is more productive with them as a part of it or less productive. We had some people that we put in management teams or in management situations where productivity was better without them. And that's not a good situation. But, you know, those situations are thankfully few.

The other thing that I think we had and still have is a little bit of a contagious energy. Sometimes they have it even before they get to the company, it's just innate, and they are sort of looking for a company that they can apply it to. In other cases, it's people coming in and thinking, "Hey, this is going to be a good, comfy job and I'll work my regular hours." We'll ask them questions about work/life balance, lifestyle, etc. We support work/life balance. We think it's really important for people to continue to perform well.

I continue to play hockey, and it's a huge part of my life, and I need to do it to be effective at work. So we encourage that. But it's interesting that we don't force people to work long hours, but people do. And it's not because they feel like they are under some threat, so especially in the early days, it's because they can't get enough of it.

Shah: They are bought into the vision and have the passion to make it happen.

Scanlan: Exactly.

Ann Winblad

Hummer Winblad Venture Partners: Hyperion, The Knot, Dean & Deluca, Net Perceptions

Ann Winblad is the co-founder of and a managing director at Hummer Winblad Venture Partners. She is a well-known and respected software investment pioneer, software industry entrepreneur, and technology leader.

Ann is one of the first woman entrepreneurs to start a software firm. In 1976 she co-founded Open Systems, Inc., a top-selling accounting software company, with a $500 investment. She later sold it for more than $15 million.

Ann has served as the director of numerous start-up and public companies, including Hyperion (sold to Oracle for $3.3 billion), Dean & Deluca, Net Perceptions, The Knot, Ace Metrix, Karmasphere, MuleSoft, Sonatype, Star Analytics and Voltage Security. Ann co-authored[1] the book Object-Oriented Software (Addison-Wesley, 1990) and has written articles for numerous publications.

Drawing from her experience as a pioneering software entrepreneur and investor in companies like Hyperion, The Knot, Net Perceptions, Marketwire, Dean & Deluca, and Liquid Audio, Ann shares her insights on how she picks promising ideas and entrepreneurs, along with how she builds companies for successful exits.

---

[1] Also co-authored by David R. King and Samuel D. Edwards.

Tarang Shah: What are some of the most common blind spots of entrepreneurs?

Ann Winblad: Usually your strengths are your weaknesses. This is true of entrepreneurs as well. One of the strengths of an entrepreneur is a fresh lens on an opportunity. In many ways, it allows you to ignore many of the obstacles. It is a glass half-full approach. No one has looked at the market like this before, no one has looked at the technology pieces that could come together to provide a benefit to a customer or consumer of the product like this before.

Then the next step for an entrepreneur is really to build a company around that. The biggest blind spot of an entrepreneur is the harsh realities of operating a company around the opportunity—how do I keep my eye on the prize while having to meet milestones to deliver my solution to the customer? How do I now do two things at once, keep an eye on the prize and really have all the impediments around selling to the customer, supporting customers, and competing with competitors, I did not know about?

Second is, how do I also deal with psychodrama and a lot more people around me? Interpersonal skills versus the grand vision and great intellect come to play. You really have to know yourself well. Should I be the CEO and really be managing people? Am I an individual contributor? How do I coach when I am a young turk? There is always a lot of psychodrama around a start-up. Suddenly, it is like, oh gee, I did not realize I had to lead people.

The third thing is really knowing and breaking down vision into assumptions. Not a thousand of them, but maybe five or six. It is very much related to Michael Porter's value chain. What assumptions allow me to accomplish this vision? What are my technical assumptions? What are some of my broad market assumptions?

When I was a young entrepreneur and my company was acquired, this was a real surprise to me. When I was at my first board meeting as an acquired company CEO, I had my report all ready and the CEO of the parent company said, "I do not want to hear your report. I want to know your assumptions, the top ten assumptions about your customers, your competitors, your pricing, your technology, and are they still true? If any of them are not true, how will you change the way you operate?"

This is again back to how do you keep a strategy going while you are trying to roll up your sleeves and operate. That is really the conundrum that most entrepreneurs get into.

Shah: What needs to happen for creation of a billion-dollar start-up?

Winblad: The last start-up in our portfolio that we actually got the billion-dollar valuation for was Omniture. Here again, we funded a very young entrepreneur, Josh James. The average age of Josh and his team at Omniture was somewhere in the twenties. Realistically, they had a very big vision to be number one in the web analytics marketplace.

So number one, they were playing to win. They really, really wanted, from the beginning, to build a big company. They established a very big goal line. They always kept their eye on that big goal line [asking themselves]: "Are we winning? If not, why?" [Rather than], "Have we accomplished something?"

Secondly, Josh was willing to build his team around young, natural athletes with some accomplished expertise. We helped him recruit a top, accomplished lawyer, who was their in-house counsel. The combination of fresh and accomplished was also very, very key.

You can see that at Facebook right now with Sheryl Sandberg coming in as COO. Sheryl, just forty now, is this combination of fresh and accomplished. Sheryl has carefully made sure she did not eradicate and crush vision with veterans, but there is a good blend there.

When the veterans come in, they have to learn from the young turks and the young turks have to learn from the veterans. You really have to have a strategy and then be able to execute. You cannot just have a strategy and not execute. I think companies that have billion-dollar outcomes also execute and tune rapidly. They are in a hurry. They fail fast and succeed fast, simultaneously.

Shah: Why do start-ups fail or get off track?

Winblad: To me, most start-ups that get off track are usually due to leadership. You are looking at people with families and people that you may have worked with forever. You are saying to the CEO, "You are not it."

You have to be very strict to do this. Adherence to the strict success metrics is really one of the big reasons for success. You have to be very tough about following key metrics.

Shah: How do you know the start-up is off track?

Winblad: When a start-up is off track, right away you know that you do not have the right CEO.

Shah: I have been to a number of board meetings where it really shows up.

Winblad: It shows up when the board is doing all the talking. It shows up in a symptom that we will call over-reaching. We will all join hands and do the work of the CEO. We are not talking about forward-going strategies and we are sitting there defining pricing at the board meeting. The CEO, not the board, should be leading. This is especially a bad symptom for young venture capitalists because they think that is what they are supposed to do—help CEOs run their companies.

Shah: What is your ideal start-up?

Winblad: My ideal start-up is one where the founder can be the CEO. That is not always the case. Consider a special natural athlete like Josh James who founded Omniture, or Jim Dorian who founded Hyperion. They are basically natural athletes in all the things we talked about. We are not perfect, we are all human here, but if you get one of these start-ups where the founder can actually grow into the CEO, it is a beautiful thing.

In talking to Bill Gates over time, Bill said he has a lot of respect for other CEOs who are like this. Larry Ellison is one, Mark Zuckerberg could be one, Steve Jobs is one. They start their company by having this complete picture in their head: "Where am I going and how might I get there?" As the picture expands, the company gets bigger, the route to get there is much more multi-dimensional, and the vision of how it is all going to work from strategy to execution is in their head.

We have clearly seen this with Steve Jobs. These leaders tend to be tough bosses because they have a big picture and a small picture in their head at the same time—strategy and execution. They are highly critical bosses. They are very demanding, but the companies tend to win because there is this comprehensive leadership, not just the theoretical, big vision. They understand intuitively the execution model. It means that in their head they have this smaller assumption set that unifies everything. They are able to expand that over time.

The brilliant companies that we have had in this industry all had that type of leader—Bill Gates, Larry Ellison, Steve Jobs, Mark Benioff, and maybe Mark Zuckerberg. That is my perfect start-up; a founder that grows into a CEO. When the founder is really too micro or too macro and cannot use them together, we have to bring in CEOs who are really good at building large companies.

Shah: Can you identify them when you meet them?

Winblad: You get a sense of these people when you meet them. Certainly it gets tested really rapidly. You start hiring a few people. The micro gets bigger and the macro gets bigger and they scale really nicely with it. They have personalities, but not necessarily big, egotistical personalities. Mark Benioff is a great example. The guy is very confident, but he is not egotistical.

Shah: As an early-stage investor, how do you go about picking start-ups to invest in?

Winblad: There are a couple important things to remember about a first-round venture capitalist, which is very different than someone who is investing in a company fully formed. You do not get an opportunity to see the future. You must have a very opportunistic view of start-ups when they walk through your doors.

This is really one of the flaws in people who are not good venture capitalists. They think they can decide what companies they are going to fund and go out and fund them. That is great for follow along [later-stage investing], but does not work for early stage.

If I take Hyperion as an example, which we funded with Sequoia Capital, we were not looking to fund the next generation business intelligence company at all. In fact, we reviewed the EIS [Executive Information System] and decision support market, which is what it was called before it was renamed BI [business intelligence]. It was overpopulated and did not have many identifiable pain points for customers. It was a sector that was unappealing. Not fundamental to operating your business.

When two guys walked in, Jim and Bob, and they said, "Look, on the surface that is what it looks like, but underneath the surface there are a lot of pain points, and here they are. The reason it is a dead market is that there is an opportunity for a technology shift here, which could deliver extraordinary value to customers."

For example, we could look at one of the macro things—that in the early nineties we were moving to client-server computing, but we do not put a card to our head[2] and say that creates client-server computing opportunities.

The venture capitalists who think they are visionaries are not necessarily the best venture capitalists. Capitalists who have open minds to opportunities are good venture capitalists. Therefore, we do not know what the best company is going to be until it walks in, but once the opportunity comes into our view, then we do look at some requirements and those are pretty much the same.

First, what friction points would exist in the marketplace that would make the company, even if funded and a great product built, face obstacles on the route to the customer? What would cause it to be hard to even build the company?

---

[2] As done by Johnny Carson's "psychic" Carnac the Magnificent character on *The Tonight Show.*

Second, even if I do not have the future management team, do I have enough intellectual capital and talent to attract the rest of the team, including perhaps the leadership team itself?

Third, what is the step function that has been created in this market opportunity that gives this company a defined time period of unfair competitive advantage? Not long-term sustainability necessarily, but for a period of time an unfair competitive advantage. Then what risks do I have? Do I have technical risks in front of me? Do I have market risks in front of me? Do I have financial risks in front of me? And then you are back into being like a business school, which means anybody can do that part.

Shah: When two co-founders like Bob and Jim walk in to your office with a business plan, how do you know their point of view is more believable than other guys with similar points of views? What is the thing or two about these co-founders that stand out to you?

Winblad: One simple thing. They do not stand in front of us and talk like investors. They really have a broader vision that extends to a company view, meaning they can talk like the customer as well as talk like the technology.

Jim himself was the top sales guy in a leading company. He was at the customer's site selling this old stuff over and over. He saw a common problem that nobody's technology or product, his or the people he was competing with at the time, could solve. He, who was not even a real technologist, went in search on his own because he wanted to keep making more money as a sales guy and look for a solution. He found a breakthrough technology, which was effectively multidimensional analysis broken down to the technical problem, the ability to sort of handle sparse and dense data and perform analytics against them. A relational storage that you could access through a spreadsheet.

It was not like the guys from the university in the UK who had written that paper on how valuable such a product can be for businesses. In fact, when I finally did see that paper, it was one hundred twenty pages long. If that paper had shown up at my desk and if it was intellectually interesting, I would have read it, and I would have thrown it away. But Jim came with the paper and the problem and the pain point. He could define the market opportunity and he could assume the persona of the customer and he had found a developer who had never written commercial code, who is someone who he felt could finish the commercialization of this. He had done a lot, but most important, he could assume the persona of the customer.

All in all, we funded a two-person start-up. We syndicated the deal with Sequoia; total capital raised was $7 million before their IPO. They had the most successful IPO in 1995, which is the same year Netscape went public, and then Hyperion, that two-person start-up, was ultimately acquired by Oracle for $3.3 billion.

Shah: Reminds me of the Larry Ellison story, where he got exposed to a relational database paper and he was in the database field and he could see what the next generation of databases should be.

Winblad: Larry and Jim had a lot of things in common. I talked to a number of great CEOs about this. It's the thing that makes transitions really complicated for the likes of Larry Ellison, Steve Jobs, Bill Gates, etc. Larry and Steve and Bill are probably way better at this. As I mentioned, they have a holistic picture of a whole company in their mind. As the company expands, their holistic picture expands itself. This ability to holistically think out a company from the product to the customer to whatever. It does not mean they are great engineers or necessarily great sales guys or great financial guys, but they can holistically keep building a bigger and bigger picture of a whole company. For companies where you get a founder and CEO like that, it makes the succession plan very difficult because it is a very, very unique leadership skill.

Shah: You have spent some time with Bill Gates and you can draw the parallels here.

Winblad: I can remember years and years ago, before Microsoft went public, I went on a long walk with Bill. Microsoft's revenue was sub-$70 million. At that point in time, there was not any pure software company that had $100 million in revenue. A mainframe company was shortly going to achieve that, called Management Sciences of America. Bill was just stressed out. He seemed really worried. He said, "Ann, I can see a $500 million company."

He could see how all the pieces worked together. He could see the future of products, he could see how he gets to the customer, how to make money at that, but he could not quite wrap his mind greater than $500 million. Now that seems small today, but at that time, there was no company that was above $80 million in revenue that was a software company.

Shah: And a software company that can even claim a $500 million market cap.

Winblad: Let alone revenue. That is the perfect start-up for us. We see very few of them. It requires extraordinary leadership. A holistic view of the present, near future, and the larger vision. You think you know it when you see it. Certainly Jim had that.

Shah: If you look at Bill Gates, Larry Page, Sergey Brin, Mark Zuckerberg, and Steve Jobs, there is something so unique about these individuals. What is it and is it something identifiable when you meet with entrepreneurs with similar potential?

Winblad: It is. At different scales. There are just things about brilliant people that have this big picture. They are not necessarily the greatest managers. They are great at hiring because they are extremely inspirational. People want leadership and they can lead you into the future.

I will give you another good example. I am the co-chair of a non-profit called the Software Development Forum, which started about twenty years ago. The goal of the Software Development Forum was to provide access to venture capitalists for people who were not coming out of Harvard Business School or Stanford, but may be great entrepreneurs, venture capitalists, or co-founders. By the way, Jim and Bob had no pedigree. They were not from Stanford, Harvard, or Princeton.

What we did at the Software Development Forum was have these sort of open-casting days and we would come in and in the early days we would charge $25. We figured $25 to sit in a room with a venture capitalist for half an hour, it would cut out the riffraff. I was there with one of our associates at the time. He said I needed to meet this guy that had just pitched him. He was just a really great guy. I went in the room and here was this really young guy named Joe Gatto. He was clearly brilliant. He had this algorithmic approach to measuring the performance of equity analysts. He was ready to start a company on his own called StarMine. Today StarMine is owned by Thomson Reuters. It was purchased for over $100 million, and it was a single-person start-up.

We had never funded a single-person start-up other than Joe. Our first test with Joe, we found another really brilliant guy, David Lichtblau, who had been at one of our other companies and who was really picky about where he would be next. He immediately signed on to work with Joe. Just like Hyperion, StarMine did not wander around in the wilderness trying to figure out what business it was in. Jim had great guys that had brilliant marketing executions, so we did not waste dollars and the same was true with StarMine.

There was a big picture there. Here is our Trojan horse and how we get in. Every analyst today has a StarMine ranking. It is all quantifiable stuff about how the best analysts are rated. There is mathematics behind the thing. We helped them in the finer points of execution.

Shah: When you met Joe for the first time, what really caught your attention?

Winblad: He had a very focused, crystal-clear picture, which is not just to keep telling you product features for thirty minutes or competition for thirty minutes. It was a very holistic picture.

Shah: How do you know if the entrepreneur is authentic and credible? How do you assess that?

Winblad: When I was a young entrepreneur in Minneapolis, the only venture capitalist I knew was Don Valentine of Sequoia. Don had funded a bunch of hardware companies, which is how I met him. My start-up had some of the first network PC software that could run multiple users.

One of the companies that Don had funded was called Cado, in Torrance, California, which had a very successful IPO. That company resold our product. Don never once said, "Let me give you my vision." Don never asked me one thing about our product. Never. He just stared me down to find out if I knew what I was talking about. Holding the management team to a very high bar is important—really paying a lot of attention to the details of execution to assess very strong opportunities in their success.

We talk a lot about software because that is what we do. We live a lot in the software industry. We spend a lot of time in the software industry and we are also even advisors to some software companies versus having the software companies be advisors to us. But our job is to audition the visionaries and pattern match for success.

Shah: I am trying to put together a formula for identifying big market opportunities by adding pieces of market and technology trends. Do you look at the world that way?

Winblad: I think people are lying when they say they went out hunting for big markets. It is really not about us but entrepreneurs. What we do is pattern matching. When we see a number of companies starting to deliver pieces of analytics or other innovations and as a result of us being really great pattern matchers, we get more focused than watching a river go by.

When the client-server market was taking off, we started seeing a development tool company a day. We hired a senior associate right away. We actually sorted through the components quickly because we saw a fast-moving train and we funded a company called Powersoft, which also was the first company acquired for a billion dollars. We just funded an HTML tools company, same thing. All of our companies are saying we need a better tool here.

We have a war between Apple and Adobe. We have seen Microsoft say Silverlight is being eclipsed on the HTML side. We are seeing a bunch of little start-ups. All the Apple stuff is HTML. Once we said, who has seen this, this, and this, and we realized this team had left Apple and we funded them, just in the nick of time. When we proactively went to them, they were on the verge of getting term sheets. Because we were there first, and we thought they were the best one. It was pattern matching and talent assessment versus us as visionaries.

Shah: I believe pattern matching has lot to do with the domain expertise, network of industry contacts, and the start-ups one is already an investor in. It's interesting to notice how early exposure to the microprocessor industry and how its potential to fuel PC growth drove Sequoia's investment in Apple in 1977. Then PC growth led to growth of LANs and hence investment in 3Com and then the promise of a network of networks and hence investment in Cisco. And then how the growth of the network of networks could lead to the promise of internet and that followed investments in Yahoo! and Google. And very recently, exposure to the handheld camcorder market potential through investment in Pure Digital might have given good insights into the market potential of YouTube. The knowledge one gains from existing investments is unbelievable in anticipating upcoming growth areas.

Shah: Do you look at markets at all in terms of is this a promising market? If you do, what are some of the signs that point potentially to a billion-dollar market in making?

Winblad: It is a little hard as an A-round investor to do that. We have an investment in a company called Ace Metrix, which does overnight analytics on television ads. We were not sitting around saying, oh gee, there is $60 billion in television ads being run in the US alone, I wonder if there is a start-up around this space? We thought about how we could deliver value there.

So along comes Ace Metrix, which can automate the quantification of the quality of the ads. And they say, "Here is also how we deliver ROI to the customer in a market where there is a tremendous number of dollars being spent on consulting services, and it is under-automated." This again is a classic example of an entrepreneur saying I have a new lens on the market and technology has shifted enough that I can now automate this whole thing and deliver potentially a very large analytics company in this space.

If I am the later round investor, I can look back at that market and do more analysis of it and how this really works. However, we have to do quick analysis of who the players are, where the wallets are, is there someone who owns all the dollars here that we just have to try to displace or is it one where it is right for a software solution? Our test is—is it big, a lot of accessible dollars, and is it right for a new solution? The later stage investors can see a lot more proof points. We are swimming under the surface, mostly before these markets really open up. We do not get to do the market analysis and then go look for the trend. There are no trends when we invest.

Shah: How important is market timing and is there a way for you to know if you are too early or too late?

Winblad: I think market timing is everything. You know when you are too late. Too early is the hard thing. You have to get in these markets. You do not want to be the pioneer that takes all the arrows in the back, but there will be things you have to figure out. If you are too early, can you still sustain the momentum and opportunity and wait it out? That is really hard.

For A-round investors, the only thing that has changed fairly dramatically in the software space, in very recent history, is the whole capability of all of this open-source, cloud-compute capability that we rarely, rarely see as an idea on a napkin. The contemporary developer, who is a really big believer, arrives on our doorstep with an early-stage product versus just an idea. The very, very early adopters can have access to newer technologies without touching anything in the venture sphere, without needing much capital.

Ninety percent of the time, if you are doing a storage breakthrough or semiconductor breakthrough, we are going to have to take technical risks and we will have to not know for sure the timeline of deployment, and as a result we are going to take capital risk and market timing risk.

For a broad area of software, we get a peek at timing because they already built the stuff. If we have less technical risk, we can talk to real customers, even if they have not paid. We really can get a much better sense of market timing.

Shah: How do you think of the exit strategy of your start-ups in light of the overall fund?

Winblad: If your losses are not too large, if you can get double and triples from the ones that are good companies, but not great, you will have good venture returns. IPOs and bigger acquisitions make a great fund.

Shah: If you draw a bell curve of returns in the portfolio, you see lots of losses, ones and twos and very few home runs. Very typical. Which one was your recent home run?

Winblad: The most recent was Omniture and was acquired by Adobe for $1.8 billion.

Shah: How are these home run companies different than the rest in your portfolio?

Winblad: What you see in these very successful companies fairly early is a higher repeatable sales model. You also see them zooming into first place. You are never in one of these marketplaces alone, otherwise you are in an oddball niche.

There was an analytics company called Coremetrics. It was ultimately purchased for a few hundred million this year by IBM. Another competitor was Webtrends that went public and kind of blew up and now is owned by a private equity company. The other competitor, called WebSideStory, in San Diego went public as well, but had slower growth and was acquired by Omniture.

Shah: What are some of the key aspects of execution to get a billion-dollar outcome?

Winblad: Number one, you really, really have to deliver high value to your customer. It is also about the stage of the market. Years ago in the core software market, customers did not really know what software was. You could sell them software. So your sales skills were very key in the early nineties. That is why you see companies like Oracle having such a highly-tuned sales operation. Also, the cost of sales for these companies was very high. IBM made their mark on a highly-tuned sales organization.

Today, customers know what software is. Now what is more important to understand is what value you are delivering to your customer and also making the products highly consumable by the customer. In the case of the consumer internet space, the leading start-ups understand how to delight their customers, how to make it fun for the customers, and how to cause consumers to tell other consumers and make it social. You have to deliver something really special as a consumer company and you have to deliver something of a high value that is easy to consume as an enterprise company.

Shah: What are some of the common mistakes you have seen in execution?

Winblad: There are so many. It is really interesting. This is why we are called venture capitalists versus just capitalists. Companies have to make mistakes. We cannot tell them here are the mistakes you will always make, so do not make them. Although, I have seen a few common mistakes.

One mistake is not making a change quick enough when you hire a wrong person. If you get the wrong person in and you know it, make a change immediately. Secondly, we say if the dogs are not eating the dog food, face up to it. There is not enough traction in the product.

Go see your customers. Go early on. Have really tight engagement with your customers early on and listen to them. If they say this is interesting, but I want that instead, you have to move in that direction. It is really letting the market drive what you offer versus you coming up with great inventions for the customer.

The other thing is that pricing is really, really hard. It is something that the software industry does very poorly. It is changing rapidly because pricing is becoming more granular, but really looking at how you value your product, really paying attention to whether it should be free, when should you ask for dollars—basically how do you put a price on value, how do you interact with your marketplace to deliver value and get paid for it? It is the hardest thing and it is where companies can really screw up. To summarize it, how do you deliver value and how do you get compensated for it?

Shah: You do not have to follow just the old model of perpetual licensing plus maintenance.

Winblad: The good news is, you are not stuck with one model. There are a lot of nuances in how to deliver value and how to get paid for it. Performance-based pricing, premium pricing, land and expand, etc. How to deliver the value and price your product to value and when you get compensated for it is very hard and strategic.

I am sure in the case studies that will be written about Facebook, one can ask, should we charge a subscription for using Facebook or not? These are seminal decisions for companies. How do we monetize our business? The business model is tempered around pricing to the value you are delivering to customers. Facebook is monetizing through advertisers. The value there is reaching an extremely large audience for advertisers, even though the value in the beginning of the company was the social network for the consumer.

Shah: You can do what LinkedIn does—a small percentage of the user base paying a monthly subscription, and that is still big enough to cover all non-paying users and make a big business out of it.

Winblad: After they see me using it all the time, they say, gee, if you pay us just $25 per month, you can have these extra things. That is the classic enterprise premium model. You get this for free. If you want some of these other features, you pay a little bit more. Very different, but you are absolutely right. That is tricky and hard. That is a common failure point. It is not looked at as strategically as it should be by companies.

How will the wallet that I am actually going to get the money from ultimately quantify the benefit of what I am delivering? Where is that wallet? It is not that easy. In the case of Facebook, it was, "Let's get 50 million people on a social network and use the advertisers as the wallet, not the consumers."

For LinkedIn the question is, "What is the value of the professional social network?" If you read their S-1 filing for the IPO, there are a lot of components to their business model. I am using it for leads generation. I can be very specific about the types of leads I want to send e-mails to, etc. They also highly focus it to be a professional network. It has caused consumers of LinkedIn to be curators of their own network.

Shah: What are your thoughts on the ideal relationship between the entrepreneur and venture capitalist and what is key to building that relationship?

Winblad: We always say trust and truths are really important here. That requires maturity on the part of the entrepreneur and also maturity on the part of the investor. We all start these companies with the glass half full and we all want them to win. We realistically have to stand naked in front of the mirror together. Are we really making progress? Do we really understand the dynamics of our business? Are we really hiring the right person? How do we make sure we look at what the challenges are, in addition to how well we are declaring victory?

Shah: What triggers the exit decision?

Winblad: You know that you will have to sell it when you find that you have a really great product, and a reasonable number of customers are buying it, but it is not going to be a high-growth company.

Shah: So it is when you know it's not a venture return company, but just an average business.

Winblad: It is all about growth. If you do not have high growth in your early years, you are just an average business.

Shah: Let's talk about when your investment is doing well and you get an offer for acquisition and you have to decide whether to sell or keep building it. What is your thought process in making such a decision?

Winblad: First of all, companies are bought, not sold. We all have in our portfolio a certain number of companies that we know are not going to be big companies, so then we do have to find ways to sell them. That is hard.

It is easier if they already have strategic partners. We work with small boutique bankers and our partners in the industry and we work hard to find them good homes. We had two of our companies acquired recently that were not for sale, but offers came in saying we would like to buy them. Of course, if the entrepreneur wants to sell and they want to cash out, then we really cannot block that. We are not coding the stuff or selling the stuff or supporting the customers, so there is a trigger where the entrepreneurs say, look, I know we could go the distance and I know we have money in the bank, and I know we are growing, but we do want to take this offer. That happens frequently. Then the company is sold.

The tougher calls are if someone comes and makes an on-the-margin offer for your company. The company is growing and doing nicely, but all these companies have high risk at all times. So you say, okay, if we turn this down, it is unlikely that they will come back again. That is the surrender point. Should we take this? Should we go to the next inning? That is harder. You probably have investors in at different valuations so some investors might get better returns than others. So the on-the-margin calls where it is a good offer and the constituencies get different value out of the offer, that is harder.

Shah: An on-the-margin offer means if, say, current multiples are five times the revenue and the company is doing $30 million in revenue, someone says we will give you $150 to $175 million for it?

Winblad: For each company it's different. That might be a good example. So you say, "Gee, that may be a good offer for this company, should we look a gift horse in the mouth or not?" That is where also you want to carefully, if you can, choose your co-investors so everybody knows when they are taking a risk or not. Good companies do get offers like this along the way. They are hard calls. Once you say "no," you do not look back, you just forge ahead. If you say "yes," you do not look back, you take the offer.

Shah: What are a couple things you as an investor wish every entrepreneur knew?

I wish that every CEO was really perfect in telling their company story. If they do that, they can raise money, they can sell products, and they can build partnerships. Can they really tell the story of their company—who we are, why we are here, and why we are valuable. That sounds pretty easy. It is hard.

Shah: How about the operating plans?

Winblad: We require all of our CEOs to produce an operating plan and operating model. Numbers do not tell you what your strategy is, but they do tell you if you have one that might work. I just had drinks with the CEO of one of our companies that was recently acquired. She is a great CEO and one of the things I had to show her is how you build, maintain, and use the operating model.

If a company starts growing, you should know what the levers of the business are. And if it doesn't grow, what are the levers? Now the acquiring parent company is making her run models over and over as she is quite skilled at this.

Shah: Finally, what advice would you give entrepreneurs trying to build successful start-ups?

Winblad: Start-up building is hard. There is no manual for it. We really have to be willing to fail fast and correct quickly in all of these companies. There has to be this really high level of trust between the investors and entrepreneurs. We are all rowing the same oars together. We do not win if you do not win. We all want to win really big.

Jim Goetz

Sequoia Capital: AdMob

Jim Goetz's current areas of interest include cloud, mobile, consumer, and enter-prise companies. He has helped create and grow a number of technology compa-nies and product lines to market-leading positions both as an entrepreneur and as a partner to founders. He currently serves on the boards of Appirio, Barracuda, Jive, Metaswitch Networks, Nimble Storage, Palo Alto Networks, Pocket Gems, and Sencha. He was previously on the boards of AdMob (Google), Clearwell (Symantec), Dash (RIM), Entrisphere (Ericsson), PeakStream (Google), Peribit (Juniper), and Rhapsody (Brocade), and has been involved with Bluecoat, Timetra (Alcatel), and TopSpin (Cisco). Prior to joining Sequoia Capital, Jim served as a general partner at Accel Partners. In 1996, he cofounded VitalSigns Software (Lucent).

Leveraging his combined experience as the founder of a successful start-up and a general partner in a venture firm, along with the example of AdMob, which sold to Google for $750 million, Jim discusses key characteristics of winning entrepre-neurs in general, and the company founders he's been privileged to work with in particular.

Tarang Shah: What attracted you to AdMob?

Jim Goetz: AdMob was a one-person company when we met the founder, Omar Hamoui, then a first-year MBA student at Wharton. Before Wharton, he started a couple of mobile companies that he'd been unable to monetize. He attempted a handful of business models, but those early attempts failed.

It was clear to us that Omar had incredible insight into the needs of the mobile developer community. His vision painted an ad economy for the long tail of mobile developers. We thought he might be on to something.

Omar had an interesting combination of engineering and product-management skills. He not only did the business plan and go-to-market strategy, he also coded the original service. This is uncommon. Typically, you see people partner with others with complementary skills. Omar's location contributed to his solo status; Philadelphia doesn't have the deep start-up ecosystem of Silicon Valley.

Shah: When you teamed up with Omar the iPhone hadn't launched yet, and I don't think people knew that something like it was in the works—or that it would turn the mobile industry upside down by opening it up to a huge mobile developer community. With open OSs like Android and iOS, it's easy to make a case for such an opportunity now, but how did you get comfortable with it in the pre-iPhone era?

Goetz: At that time, there were a number of emerging mobile developers. Omar was one of them. He had tried to get a company called fotochatter off the ground by building a mobile business around Nokia and Motorola feature phones. Omar took the contrarian position that the market for mobile apps was on the verge of coming together. An open framework outside of the carrier deck[1] was an essential part of his vision, and he had a sense that it was on the horizon.

Omar left Philadelphia for Silicon Valley. For the first six months he worked out of our office, where we were available to him on a daily basis. Within the first couple of months, we had an inquiry from AT&T to meet with AdMob. I suggested that Omar meet with David Christopher, then VP of marketing for AT&T Wireless.

Normally an entrepreneur would jump at an opportunity like that, but Omar had no interest in meeting with AT&T. He wanted to build an independent offering that didn't rely on the carrier deck. He said, "I've dealt with the carrier deck when I was trying to get fotochatter off the ground. It wasn't easy working with carriers, and the company failed."

Because of his experience, his scar tissue, Omar was sensitive to the needs of the two-, three-, and four-person mobile developer companies. Today, with smartphones driving adoption, these very small companies are the

---

[1] A mobile carrier dictating the content and experience on the phones in its network.

heart of the developer community, which is millions strong. Omar's thesis was spot on.

Shah: And the scar tissue was the residue of failed start-ups?

Goetz: Yes. I was thrilled that he had the courage to try again. He had no money. He was in grad school, was up to his ears in debt, and had two very young children. We paid for his ticket to fly across the country to meet with us.

Shah: What entrepreneurial drive. What were some characteristics of great entrepreneurs that you saw in Omar?

Goetz: Deep-rooted ambition and intelligence, courage, and a willingness to take risks again and again.

Shah: In your presentations, you talk about how many businesses, including Yahoo!, Google, and Cisco, started as small feature or product concepts and eventually grew into multi-billion-dollar companies. The term you use is "humble beginnings." How can entrepreneurs identify a feature or concept that can become a billion-dollar start-up?

Goetz: We probably have a different perspective on this than most VCs. We try to dream with entrepreneurs. Steve Jobs and Steve Wozniak at Apple went after hobbyists with their first computer. Cisco targeted an enterprise niche. Our view is that, early on, if you're solving a meaningful problem, even if it's for a small group of people, there is an opportunity to expand beyond that over time.

Shah: And AdMob did start out small, addressing a pain point for a largely unknown community.

Goetz: True. And the customers Omar had in his sights weren't capable of writing big checks. Consider, too, that there were no brand-name advertisers, and Omar had no desire to work with carriers. It would have been easy to be dismissive.

In the two years before we partnered with AdMob, a number of mobile advertising start-ups came through our doors. Most talked about building relationships with the carriers and becoming part of the carrier deck. The developer community was viewed as the unwashed masses. Omar had a very different philosophy and perspective. But again, many successful start-ups hold contrarian views and focus on small niches.

Shah: When things really start taking off, like they did at AdMob, the founding team needs to expand and build. What's the key to building a market-leading team with a culture of success?

Goetz: Omar and the early team did an extraordinary job of keeping the bar high—they hired bright, high-energy people. Many, in their twenties, were given opportunities that they probably wouldn't have had in a larger company until their thirties or forties.

There was a great degree of empowerment, and the energy level in the engineering and product teams was high. They reached peak performance when the market started to lift, then gained momentum. They had engineers working till two or three in the morning. Not because they were told to, but because they were so excited about what they were working on.

We talk about "times ten" productivity. That's where you assemble a small group of elite engineers and get them amped up. Because they truly feel empowered, they advance into extreme levels of productivity, which is more likely with a small team. It happens because they're genuinely excited to their core.

Shah: What was the key to attracting that kind of talent when people hardly knew about AdMob? There was no iPhone developer community or any big advertisers interested in mobile advertising.

Goetz: Yes, that's what we were up against. Omar spent a big chunk of the first year recruiting early team members. Sequoia gave him the platform and credibility to recruit world-class talent.

Omar, then only twenty-six or twenty-seven, was intelligent, charming, mature, and deeply guided by his value system. I met his mother, who was the guest of honor at an event for the senior management team. Everybody thought it would be Omar, but we honored his mother. She did such a spectacular job of raising him.

The values and character that define his personality transcend culture. He is Muslim; his mother's devout. The way he's been wired from childhood played a big role in his success. Omar is a spectacular example of the good that can come from raising somebody in a positive environment.

As time went on, it got easier and easier for him to recruit world-class talent because of the people already in the company. But I also think that people were willing to take a risk based on his character.

Shah: Sequoia takes a long-term view and tries to uncover long-term potential. The majority of Sequoia IPOs keep building post-IPO. So when you've uncovered something as big as AdMob, and it's growing like wildfire, why sell? Why not grow it to IPO?

Goetz: We have a reasonable formula here. When things surprise us on the upside, as they did with AdMob, they normally continue to surprise. We describe it as "market pull." In the case of AdMob, we would have preferred to keep going, but the decision ultimately comes down to the founder.

We encouraged Omar to maintain an independent path. Given the importance of the mobile space and AdMob's early advantage, we saw a public company in the making-one worth billions of dollars. At the same time, competition was growing and Omar had his own life to consider. He felt it was a good time to exit.

Most companies we've worked with that go public have dozens of M&A offers while they're young. There are times that it makes sense to sell a private company.

Shah: The continued rise of the mobile sector was a strong tailwind for AdMob's exit potential.

Goetz: Absolutely, because it compounded the value proposition. At Sequoia, we're wired to look for long-term value. Investment firms look for short-term returns; they're worried about appeasing their limited partners.

Take YouTube, where my partner Roelof Botha worked with Chad and Steve.[2] It's still a phenomenon, not a fad. We wanted to keep going. But we also felt strongly that, in the end, it was up to the founders. We spent quite a bit of time talking with them, as we did with Omar, about our view of the tradeoffs.

---

[2] Founders Steve Chan and Chad Hurley. YouTube was sold to Google for $1.65 billion.

Roger Lee

Battery Ventures: Groupon, Angie's List, TrialPay

Roger Lee *is a general partner at Battery Ventures. His investment focus is software, consumer internet, and the digital media markets.*

Roger is a board member at Angie's List, FreeWheel, Gogobot, Groupon (Observer), Lotame, Narrative Science, PrimeRevenue, TrialPay, and World Golf Tour. He was on the board of Insitu (acquired by Boeing), and SafetyWeb (acquired by Experian), and he was a board observer at Neoteris prior to its acquisition by NetScreen.

Before joining Battery, Roger spent ten years as an entrepreneur. Most recently, he was a co-founder of Corio, a managed service provider that was acquired by IBM. Roger was also the co-founder and president of NetMarket, an online consumer internet service that was acquired by Cendant Corporation.

A serial entrepreneur turned investor, Roger draws from his experience on both sides of the table. By taking examples from his investments in Groupon, Angie's List, and TrialPay, Roger shares how he selects entrepreneurs, his thoughts on the importance of market size and timing, the key to a successful team and cultural dynamics, compelling aspects of product and business models, and his thoughts on when to exit.

What I love about Roger is his deep understanding of the consumer internet space and the key metrics that he follows to track progress. His three-axes framework (the team, market, and timing) and his ability to analyze start-ups through this framework impress me the most.

Tarang Shah: What are some of the key reasons why start-ups fail?

Roger Lee: There are three different axes against which you evaluate a start-up in the rear view mirror. One is the team, two is the market, and three is timing. You really need all three of those things to come together in order for a company to succeed. If one of those things is off, it is very hard for the company to be successful. If two or more of them are off, then you are more likely to fail. When we look at our companies that have not worked, it has typically been one or more of those variables that have been off.

Ideally, when you have the right team with the right product-market fit at the right time—right where the market is ready to adopt it—then your chances of success are much higher. They are certainly never guaranteed, but they are a lot higher. But if you are missing one of those three variables, the likelihood of a good outcome is just a lot lower.

Shah: Great framework for looking at start-ups! Are all three variables equally important?

Lee: You can navigate around them. If your timing is off, you could always just reduce the burn and be patient. You can ultimately survive. You just need to make sure that you do not die along the way. Companies may have the right team and the right market, but they are just early. They end up spending too much and burn out along the way. And then one, two, three years later—somebody new pops up and actually takes advantage of that opportunity and creates a successful business. So you can navigate around the timing as long as you have patience, but it's important to throttle your spending accordingly.

The most difficult variable to navigate around is finding the right people. Ultimately, you cannot hire passion. When you are backing an entrepreneur, you are backing someone with a particular vision that has a passion for a product-market fit. It is very hard to replace an entrepreneur with somebody else that has that same passion and that same vision.

I think about it in terms of those layers of control. Timing you can control, as long as you are patient and you preserve cash. With the wrong team, you have a chance of navigating around it, but it is risky because it is hard to find the right group to inherit that passion and inherit that product-market vision.

All that being said, if you do not have a market, there is almost no way of succeeding. The odds are really stacked against you at that point.

Shah: Terrific! What are some of the most common blindsides you have seen in the start-up building process?

Lee: A key to start-up success is the ability to be intellectually honest about the state of the company, the product-market fit, what is working, and what is not working. The entrepreneur who is honest about what is or isn't working can quickly step on the brakes, preserve cash, and either be patient and wait for the market to come or pivot the business to a market that makes more sense.

It is very rare where the business plan that we invest in on day one is the same one two or three years later. Much more frequently, the plan is tweaked in some regard, the market has shifted, and it is the teams that are agile, intellectually honest, and able to adapt to those changing markets who ultimately win. The entrepreneur, who blindly follows his or her vision, just takes a much higher risk. More often than not, you have to tweak the business ten degrees one way or another until you finally find the right product-market fit.

Shah: How do you assess intellectual honesty in the first couple meetings with the entrepreneurs?

Lee: Intellectual honesty is one of the key characteristics we look for in the founders we back. At the end of the day, an idea cannot stand on its own. We are investing in the people to bring that idea to life. So a fair amount of our diligence work is around the people.

You get a sense of intellectual honesty quickly when you talk to them about their past experiences, and when you talk to their past co-workers about how they handle adversity and ambiguous situations. Inevitably, those risks and questions will come up as they continue to build their new business. Those patterns tend to repeat themselves. Based on those discussions, we try to paint a picture of who they are, how they operate, and how they handle those types of circumstances.

Shah: What are some of the key characteristics you look for in entrepreneurs?

Lee: Number one is intellectual horsepower. Is this person smart, creative, and can he think clearly and decisively? They must have strong raw processing capability. That is important. The second thing I look for is their domain knowledge. Have the founders immersed themselves in this product market space over the past couple of years? Do they know exactly what the right user experience is, and then if they have built similar products before, do they know where the land mines are and where the potholes are so they do not repeat those mistakes? That type of deep domain knowledge is important.

The next thing is, are they passionate about it? Invariably there are going to be other entrepreneurs going after the same product-market space, and if the people that we back are not truly passionate about it and are not thinking about it twenty-four hours a day, someone else is. If they do not have that rabid passion, they aren't likely to win. Passion is likely to outperform the rest of the characteristics, at the end of the day.

Work ethic is also important. Are they willing to put everything else on hold to make this company a success? Again, if they are not willing to really commit themselves to making the company a success, someone else out there is. And that is just going to put them at a competitive disadvantage.

Equally important is their ability to attract talented people. At the end of the day, one person can only do so much and needs to surround himself with great people. We assess if the person can successfully attract and recruit talented colleagues to join him in his mission.

You never get straight As with anybody. We look at the total report card of all those different criteria. Does he score highly on all these criteria? If he does, that is someone we likely want to work with.

Shah: How much of start-up success is dependent on whether it's a single founder or multiple co-founders?

Lee: It's not that dependent on the sizing of the founding team. Multiple co-founders do add an element of risk if they have not worked together before. However, if they have worked together before, it diminishes the risk of the company succeeding. You have to look at it on that spectrum. The fact is, one person can only do so much. Eventually you are going to have to have multiple people come and work together to make the company successful. But if there are multiple co-founders, they are going to have an equal say or a lot of influence in the decision-making on a day-to-day basis.

If they have been in the trenches together in the past, building products, building companies, and know each other's style, strengths, and weaknesses, and if they know how to coexist, how to get the best out of one another, then that is a powerful combination. If it is one individual, arguably from a governance perspective, it is simpler because you have one person making a decision. You still do not know how he is going to coexist with the other people he brings onto the team, however.

So you have to look at each one on a case-by-case basis. I would say the riskiest situation is co-founders who have not worked together before and who come together in a rushed way to build a company. That is a high-risk situation because you are putting people together in a stressful situation. They do not really know one another, they do not know how they are going to react, how they are going to work together, how they can handle that stress, the strengths, weaknesses, tendencies, and styles of their other co-founders. All these factors can lead to a very challenging situation.

Shah: What unique dynamics do you see in the successful teams?

Lee: The only thing is how long they have worked together. I saw a study years ago that looked at the criteria that has the highest predictive rate of success [whether a company will fail or succeed] for a start-up. The single highest predictor was the tenure in which the founding team had worked together. Because so many start-ups fail due to personnel issues, you effectively remove that risk if it is a team that has worked together in the past. Our decisions do not hinge on it, but we feel a lot more comfortable if this team has been together through ups and downs in the past. It helps take that risk off the table.

Shah: How much role does a culture play in start-up's success and how do you assess it when you meet with the company?

Lee: Culture is a hard thing to diligence. You have to spend time with the people at the company and get a sense for it. Healthy companies operate at a certain cadence. There is a certain rhythm or cadence to their activities that tends to yield positive outcomes. They ship products every one or two days, their marketing campaigns are tested every three to four days with data, and they then A/B test them again. So there are very quick cycles of responding to data and subsequent iterating of the product. This cadence leads to high-performing organizations that drive incredible yield and output. I find this type of culture to be both healthy and agile, and I believe it is a model worth gearing companies toward.

You can try and assess culture during the diligence process, but you do not really know for sure, which makes the assessment a leap of faith, especially for early-stage companies. One way to get a feel for culture is through conversations you have with the founders about how they plan to operate moving forward, and how they operated their past companies.

In later-stage companies, it's more realistic to spend time at the company in order to get a sense for how they operate.

Shah: What are some of the early signs that point to a potentially great company or product hitting the big market?

Lee: I look at two things. One is just organic adoption. Are people using the product and are they talking to their friends about it? A very important variable is the equation of how people find out about it, how they talk about it, and what the awareness and viral, organic uptake of the product is. The second one is retention or engagement. If you look out one, two, or three months later, how many of them are still using it? How do they use it, how frequently do they use it, and do they still talk to their friends about it?

Those two variables, I think, have a huge impact in guiding you as to whether it is a big market or not. If you do not get a lot of organic adoption up front, there is a real question about whether or not the market is there. If you do not get long-term engagement or retention, there is a real question about how valuable the product actually is. Facebook, Groupon, Zynga, LinkedIn, etc., are very organic, viral services that people constantly talk about, and devote their energy and time to. Fast forward three, six, twelve months later and people are still actively using them. The engagement is very high. They continue to tell their friends about it. Those two factors are early signs to look for and can indicate whether or not you have, potentially, a really exciting company on your hands.

Shah: It's key to have the virality built into the product itself.

Lee: To the contrary, it is most compelling when the viral channels are not built into the product, where it is actually so good that people are talking about it independent of those channels. It certainly helps if you have all the right viral features built in, but it is particularly interesting when the product itself is not very good or is not very viral … and people are still talking about it.

Shah: That is an excellent point. I see Groupon and Angie's List in your portfolio having that kind of viral effect.

Lee: If you think about how the offer deals are structured in Groupon, there needs to be a certain number of buyers in order for a deal to tip. Because of that, in the early days it acted as an efficient viral channel. I would go online and it would say I could get $50 worth of dinner for $25, but only if one hundred people signed up for the deal. So I would e-mail a bunch of my buddies and tell them about that. That acted as the viral hook. I am not sure it is as important now because they have so much critical mass, and so many people are using it, but it acted as a very, very powerful viral hook for them in the early days that allowed them to grow the business quickly. The best, well-thought-out products have virality built in and around them.

If you think about Facebook as an example, one of their killer features is photos. Facebook is now the largest repository of photos in the world. Now what they did was integrate photo-sharing with e-mail. So whenever a photo goes up, and let's say I am tagged on the photo, I get an e-mail notifying me. Immediately, I want to see what photo I am in, and nine times out of ten, I will click on the e-mail and go into Facebook. So it provides a really great feature for the user. I can upload and share all of my photos with my friends. But more importantly, it has a viral hook built into it because it notifies the people who are in the photos to go check it out and then brings them back into Facebook, they engage with the photo, tell their friends about the photo, etc. Facebook has successfully built those types of viral paths into their product in a thoughtful way that drives user engagement, drives utility, and ultimately adds value to their product.

Shah: Take us back to the time you first encountered Groupon. How did you find it and what attracted you to the opportunity?

Lee: First of all, I had been investing in the local space for a while. I had already invested in Angie's List. I had this belief that people's online activity was going to drive offline behavior. In the case of Angie's List, I was going to find plumbers, roofers, doctors, and handymen through an online service. Traditionally, how people do such a search is by looking into the yellow pages or calling their friends. But this approach is inefficient and fraught with errors. Angie's List allows users to execute that process much more efficiently and effectively. So then I asked myself, what are the other local activities where online disruptions can facilitate offline behavior? And one of those was local commerce.

The web historically has done a great job at capturing certain types of transactions. It captures the book that I buy from Amazon, the plane ticket for my flight to JFK. It even captures my hotel reservation at the Hilton. But, it does a terrible job of capturing my dinner tonight at a restaurant with my wife or the manicure or haircut that my wife may have gotten earlier today. The web does a terrible job at those things.

What's interesting is that when you segment the world of commerce, 80 percent of the average person's disposable income is spent within ten miles of their home. Virtually none of that is captured online. So we always thought eventually that it was going to have to move online. It does not mean I am going to get my haircut online, but the process of me finding the barber would be facilitated by online services. The process of me finding the handyman would be facilitated by online services.

That was really the premise behind the investment in Angie's List. We thought there were a lot of different ways to skin this cat. There are other guys that would go after that same local commerce market. That is what led us to Groupon. When I saw the use case of leveraging the internet to drive local commerce, it immediately resonated with me. I am always looking for a new restaurant to go to. My wife is always looking for new spas to go to. We are always looking for stuff to do with each other and our kids, and this provides a tool to discover interesting and new activities for us, near our home, at great discounts.

So for the consumer it is very valuable. For the merchant it is an effective way to drive traffic to their door. Groupon introduced performance marketing to small businesses. In the past, merchants would spend money on yellow pages, radio ads, and television ads, and they had no idea if it ever worked. In this case, there is no risk and they only spend money if Groupon actually delivers real customers. That is what makes it so compelling and why so many merchants have started to adopt the service.

All of these factors combined result in a compelling, broad thesis in local commerce. The use case immediately resonated with me as a consumer and it also drives enormous value to the merchant. We were monitoring the early performance of their first market in Chicago, and it was just off the charts. I made five trips to Chicago and did everything I could to try to create an opportunity to work with the company. Luckily enough, they gave us that chance a little over a year ago.

Shah: Fantastic! Earlier you talked about three axes you look at: the market, timing, and the team. Tell us a little bit more about the team in reference to your investment in Groupon.

Lee: The Groupon team is spectacular. The founder/CEO, Andrew Mason, is fiercely intelligent. He is the visionary behind Groupon and he came up with the product idea. He was the one that really defined it, created the use cases, and he continues to innovate on it. The guy works like a Trojan. He is always online, doing whatever he can to build the company and promote the cause. He is passionate, and if you spend one minute with him, you will get a sense for his passion and excitement. For him, it has nothing to do with the money. Andrew loves the idea of providing discovery tools to consumers, impacting hundreds of millions of people around the world with his service, and then driving new business to merchants, and in many cases keeping local merchants—that otherwise may not survive—alive.

Andrew is also a magnet for incredible talent. He has assembled a world-class team around him, including a number of executives from senior roles at some of the best-known companies in the world.

We are extremely fortunate to have the chance to support Andrew and the team at Groupon. He has just done a great job defining the company and getting it off the ground.

You look at a lot of the great companies that have been built over the last decade, and they have been started by guys that share similar attributes with Andrew.

Shah: This is incredible indeed. Tell me more about several other key attributes that you look for, especially around age and experience.

Lee: What are the common traits of Mark Zuckerberg from Facebook, Andrew Mason from Groupon, Larry [Page] and Sergey [Brin] from Google, Jerry [Yang] from Yahoo!? These guys are all young, first-time entrepreneurs, and in most cases, this is their first real job. In many cases they were still in school, either in undergraduate or graduate programs, but all had the characteristics I talked about earlier. They are wildly intelligent. They are defining their product-market spaces. They are fiercely passionate about it. They work twenty-four hours a day on it. They are magnets for talent. These are all the characteristics that I have found drive the really nonlinear outcomes.

Shah: So there is a pattern that most billion-dollar successes in the consumer space were built by young, first-time entrepreneurs?

Lee: Yes, there is a pattern that the biggest consumer-facing businesses over the past decade have been started by passionate young guys. They have this vision for and are deeply knowledgeable about a product-market space and are able to execute against it. This does not mean there is an age bias when it comes to investing, though. At the end of the day, we are always going to look at the criteria I described before.

Shah: Our other book that we are working on, called *From Idea to Billion* [forthcoming], has looked into one hundred or so billion-dollar start-up successes of the recent decade in a great detail. We have put these start-ups into three sectors: mobile, consumer internet, and IT software/technology. The pattern we found resonates with exactly what you mentioned earlier. We found that most IT software/technology successes came from more experienced founders, but the consumer internet successes came from younger founders. It really boils down to who has put in their ten thousand hours to identify and solve large pain points in specific areas. For experienced people it tends to be the IT/enterprise technology area and for college students and the younger crowd it tends to be mobile apps and consumer internet.

Lee: I totally agree with that. The enterprise IT and more business-oriented innovations tend to come from more mature, more established entrepreneurs and operators. Consumer web ideas tend to come from the younger, almost product-manager type. They are building something that they frankly find useful for themselves and it turns out that tens of millions of people around the world find it useful too.

Shah: They have such an early exposure to those new technologies and new ways of doing things. The older you get, the more set in your ways you are and you cannot think of some of the things these young entrepreneurs can think of.

Lee: Agreed. Younger entrepreneurs have grown up when the internet was pervasive. The internet really became well known starting in 1994, when Mosaic came out. If you were eight to ten years old starting at that point, you effectively grew up with the internet. If you were twenty years old, you really did not. These companies have the benefit of being created by the guys who grew up with the internet and have been immersed in it from a young age. They are cutting-edge thinkers.

Shah: Any other exciting company in your portfolio that you would like to talk about in reference to the key success characteristics you mentioned above?

Lee: I will talk about the founder and CEO of TrialPay, Alex Rampell. When we first backed him, he was twenty-four or twenty-five, though he has been an entrepreneur since he was fourteen. He was a self-made millionaire by the time he was sixteen or seventeen. He paid his way through Harvard. TrialPay is probably his fourth company. He just fits all of the criteria that I described before. Alex is wicked smart. He defines the use case and the whole product domain of alternative payments. He is a magnet for incredibly competent people. He works ungodly amounts of hours. He is a prototypical entrepreneur, a guy we love to back.

Shah: When you look at the product like TrialPay and play around with it, does it tell you a story?

Lee: One of the benefits of investing in consumer products is, as a consumer, I can go play with it. If it is an enterprise product, it is a lot harder for me to judge if one storage array is better than another one. I don't get an intuitive sense about that. But when I go and use Groupon, and I talk to my wife and five of our friends about it and all five of them say it is really cool, that's an interesting set of data points for me to add to the decision-making process.

Even if a product is not useful to me, I can see why it might be useful to others. I will do as much as I can to get a read from people in the product's target market, to give me a perspective on whether or not they think it is valuable. That is definitely part of all of the work that we do.

Shah: Besides the virality and viral channels, what else stands out to you in a great product?

Lee: Engagement. Do I go back and use the product on a consistent basis? Is the experience such that I am getting value out of it consistently? It does not have to be every hour or every day, but is there something there that is new and insightful on at least a weekly basis that is going to bring me back in?

Angie's List is a great example of this. One of the things that we really like about Angie's List is that when you own a home, issues come up all the time. You need help in managing that home at least a few times a year. We were curious as to how frequently a typical homeowner goes to Angie's List. It turns out that the average person goes into the site eighteen times a year and buys services at least three times a year. Also, when they buy, they are buying services worth hundreds of dollars from plumbers, roofers, handymen, etc. There is a consistency and a long-term engagement in an economic relationship between the consumer and Angie's List that is really valuable. When they acquire a customer, they acquire them for a long time. They use the service for years. The average customer is on Angie's List for well over five years, and that number is growing every day. When you find companies like this, which have these long-term, deep, economic relationships with the consumers, it is a good place to be in as an investor.

It does not have to be Google, where you are going back every single day to run five to ten searches. There can be other use cases where getting this long-term engagement with the consumer can be really powerful in the economic sense.

Shah: Every great company that identifies great market opportunity or shows market traction will sooner or later attract a lot of competitors. My first investment I helped with at SoftBank was Insider Pages, which was in the same space with Angie's List and Yelp. Groupon also has tons of followers and clones. What is the key to maintaining an early competitive lead? How do you sustain that? What have you seen great companies do here?

Lee: It depends on the company. There are some companies that just by virtue of time have natural barriers to entry. I would argue that companies like OpenTable and Angie's List are natural marketplaces, which yield one or two winners. OpenTable has a natural marketplace for each of the cities it operates in. I am only going to want to go to one place, look at the restaurants that are available, and make reservations. I am not going to want to go to three or four different places. As a result, they drive the most traffic to that web site. As the restaurant, I want to be associated with OpenTable because it's getting the most traffic. I am not going to want to deal with three or four different vendors. There is a natural network effect that comes into play.

The same thing is true with Angie's List. There are other people who have ratings and reviews for all sorts of different product and service categories. However, there is a certain type of review, a certain quality of the review and a relationship that Angie's facilitates between the service provider and the consumer that nobody else has been able to really capture.

In order for someone to replicate either the marketplace dynamic of OpenTable or the marketplace dynamic at Angie's List, you would have to spend, I would argue, hundreds of millions of dollars to go acquire the millions of consumers and small businesses that use those services. In both of those cases, it took them a lot of time and a lot of patience to build the marketplace. They are both ten-year-old businesses, and they kind of grew up under the radar.

OpenTable got started in the last internet bubble. People ignored this space for a long time, and all of a sudden ten years later it is a multi-billion-dollar company. Angie's List is over ten years old. They built it slowly and gradually. They are headquartered out of Indianapolis and nobody really paid attention to them. I think they have the chance to be a multi-billion-dollar company. In both cases, it takes patience, perseverance, blocking and tackling, and really committing to a vision.

In the case of something like Groupon, there are significant competitive barriers. It is easy to get into this market, as the barriers to entry are quite low. However, the barriers to scale are extremely high. It is very hard to run this service in hundreds of cities, dealing with millions of consumers and thousands of merchants on a daily basis. Doing all of the recruiting, all of the merchandising, all of the payments, all of the returns, all of the customer service at that scale is very complicated. Execution and a lot of very good blocking and tackling become critical to the business being successful. What Groupon has also been able to do is build some great products on top of the execution that has allowed them to distance themselves from the pack.

Now, for most companies in the online space, there is not a lot of defensible IP and the winner really is just the one who can execute most effectively. One of your questions was about the importance of being first in the market. I do think that is helpful, but if you do not couple that with great execution, that lead will not last very long.

Let me give you an example. We were investors in Friendster. They were the first in the social media market and yet they lost out to Facebook, LinkedIn, Myspace, and many other players in that space. We had the right thesis, but the wrong horse. In the case of Groupon, they are first in market, but they also have the best execution. I think we have the right thesis and the right horse. Friendster lost due to one or two very simple product decisions, which were unfortunate in retrospect. The contrast with Groupon is stark. In both cases I think we had the right thesis, but in one case we had the wrong horse and in the other case I think we have the right horse.

Shah: This is very insightful. What are other key areas in execution that entrepreneurs should pay more attention to?

Lee: Great execution is a function of two things—cultural bias and being a magnet for talent. At most of the best companies today, you see a cultural element of having that rhythm or methodology I alluded to earlier, to everything they do. And then there's the magnet for great talent.

Now, the execution gets harder and harder as you scale. I look at the talent that Andrew Mason has assembled at Groupon and it is A+ across the board. It gives me great confidence that they are going to be able to continue scaling the business for a long time to come. Those two things together, the cultural bias and being a magnet for great people, are the things that I think are key to executing successfully.

Shah: Any particular cases where you have to have a business model figured out before you invest vs. other cases where you say let's figure out the product and adoption first and we can worry about the business model later?

Lee: We tend to want to know what the business model will be. We are not overly wedded to it. There are plenty of early-stage seed companies that we invest in where we do not know exactly what the business model is going to be when we get off the ground. Generally speaking, we have a thesis for what it will be. In the case of Groupon, it was very clear what the business model was. In other cases, it is a little murkier. What we really look for first is adoption and engagement of a product. If you have adoption and engagement, you will eventually find a business model.

If you do not have adoption or engagement, the business model does not really matter. The most important thing is getting the right product, the right adoption, the right engagement. When that stuff comes together, then you will be able to monetize it.

Facebook never worried about the business model early on because they had great adoption and great engagement. Twitter hasn't been focused on the business model, but it has great adoption and great engagement. Obviously Facebook has figured it out, and Twitter will eventually figure it out. Ultimately, both companies are going to be worth a lot of money because they are great products that consumers flock to and stick with for long periods of time.

Shah: As an investor and board member, I am certain you follow certain key metrics to make sure a company is on track. What gives you an early sign that a company is getting off track?

Lee: Adoption and engagement. That is what matters. If people start talking about the product less or they are using the product less over time, those are two big signs that there is a problem. Really great products continue to show linear growth in both adoption and engagement. And while there are a bunch of different ways to measure these data points, when you see declining curves, in either case, it is a real problem. Eventually monetization and conversion metrics enter the conversation, but in the early days, adoption and engagement are the priority.

Shah: In those cases of declining or poor adoption or engagement, you look at it and say, maybe we need to pivot. Or you may conclude that this is not recoverable and needs to be sold or shut down. What is that thought process for you?

Lee: I do not think there is one recipe. I think you have to look at each situation on a case-by-case basis. Typically, though, it's tied to tweaking the product and looking at the features, looking at the little things, the human factors, engineering, the screen flow, [the way web] pages are designed, stuff like that. One needs to look at the features that have been removed, added, and at data from A/B testing on everything, to see where things might be going wrong. Then you decide whether you want to go back to an old design or do something else. Those are the things we spend most of the initial time on. If we go through that whole process and it is clear that it is a structural issue or a systemic issue, then maybe it's time to pivot. Regardless, you want to rule out all of the product stuff first before you pivot to a different use case.

Shah: What qualifies for such poor structure or systematic issues?

Lee: You have exhausted all of the tweaks you could and after a few months of testing several different screen flows and designs, people are just not coming back. They are churning out quickly, and you are losing viral, organic traffic. It's usually after three to six months [that] if you are not able to right the ship, it is probably a good indication it is not working. And typically, the web is a pretty efficient marketplace. When there is a good product out there, people talk about it and traffic flows to it. If you cannot attract a meaningful audience and engage that audience, it is usually a sign that something is off.

Shah: And that defines the degree of pivot?

Lee: Exactly.

Shah: It is great when a company continues to do well. In these cases, how do you decide between whether to keep growing or to sell it? What is that decision process for you?

Lee: It totally depends on the market size. As an example, in the consumer internet space now, the market dynamic is such that the companies are going public at valuations we have not seen in a decade or longer. The online markets are so big given that there are two billion people online now. Last year they spent twenty trillion minutes online. Those numbers are growing double digits every year. You have a market that is absolutely enormous by any definition, and you have companies growing faster than companies have ever grown in the history of our civilization.

Three years ago, Zynga was the fastest-growing company ever. Last year, Groupon was the fastest-growing company ever. I am sure a year or two from now, someone will eclipse Groupon. You have billions of people online, growing 10 percent a year, spending twenty trillion minutes online. Such growth and scale account for a huge portion of our media consumption time, and an increasingly large chunk of our commercial behavior. The mechanics to acquire customers and monetize them are well understood today. This combination creates a tremendous growth potential for consumer internet start-ups.

Think about how an idea from a twenty-eight-year-old kid in Chicago [Andrew Mason] turned into a multi-billion-dollar business. That was not possible five or ten years ago. Opportunities like this are a possibility because the markets are so big. If you believe in the product, you believe in the use case, and you have the right team—you should ride the opportunity as long as you can. Returns in venture capital are driven by your big winners. If you have something that is playing in a big market and is a leader in that category, and it can run for a few years, you have to let it run. That, I think, is the right thing to do.

On the other hand, if you have a bounded market, where there is a limited audience, say something else may be going wrong with the company, it may be time to assess and sell. It might make sense to take advantage of the liquidity option available to you at that time.

Shah: Great insight. As an entrepreneur turned investor, what advice would you like to give to aspiring entrepreneurs?

Lee: First of all, building a company is hard. It is not for everybody. You have to be deeply passionate about it and really committed to making it work. Two, you will likely fail at some point along the way. That does not mean the company will fail. But you will make a decision, or have a bias or opinion, that will be wrong so you need to be intellectually honest and step back, admit that, pivot, and move on. Three, when you look back on it, you want to make sure it was the most rewarding experience that you ever had. I was an entrepreneur for ten years and the two companies that I started and played a big role in building—I still look at those as two of my most enjoyable professional experiences ever. It was really hard work and there were some painful, long nights, but I really, really enjoyed it.

I think it is important for the entrepreneur to be very present and make sure they take a step back and enjoy the success and the process. The end of the road, the liquidity event, the IPO, when you actually go through it, it ends up being pretty anticlimactic. The really rewarding experiences were the first customer that you closed, the product that you shipped, the great employee that you hired. Take real pride and joy in those events and enjoy that path and that journey. Because when you look back in the rear view mirror, that's the part that is the most rewarding and most special. It actually is not the exit event, not the liquidity event. That is merely one step along the way and maybe a final step in some cases.

The part that is really enjoyable and is a lot of fun is all of the blocking and tackling, all the late nights, all of the blood, sweat, and tears, all the scars—that is the part that you really have to embrace, be very present for, and enjoy. If you can do that, then the chances of you being successful are very high.

Back to my first point, it is hard work—very few people are intellectually and emotionally predisposed to it. You have to be really sure that this is something you are going to commit yourself to. If you ask any successful entrepreneur, they will tell you that it was not the destination. They oftentimes do not know what the destination is going to be ... but it was the journey that was so rewarding.

Ken Howery

Founders Fund: Paypal, Facebook, SpaceX, ZocDoc

Ken Howery *is a managing partner at Founders Fund. He was a co-founder of Paypal and served as the company's first CFO. While at Paypal, Ken helped raise over $200 million in private financing, worked on the company's public offerings, and assisted in the company's $1.5 billion sale to eBay.*

Before launching Founders Fund, Ken was a member of the research and trading teams at Clarium Capital Management. He was also a partner with Peter Thiel in his private venture investing, where he performed due diligence on deals, including the initial investment in Facebook. Ken is also a member of the selection committee for the World Economic Forum's Technology Pioneers program. Venture Capital Journal has named Ken one of the Top 10 Venture Capitalists Under 35.

Drawing from his incredible journey as an entrepreneur and investor, Ken provides invaluable insights into what attracted him to join the founding team at Paypal, the key characteristics that made Paypal so successful, what Ken saw in Mark Zuckerberg and his team to make that first venture investment in Facebook, the fundamental success drivers for consumer internet companies, and why entrepreneurs should go after ambitious and risky ideas.

I love Ken's opinions on building and investing in start-ups, which comes from his involvement in two of the most successful start-ups in history, Paypal and Facebook.

Tarang Shah: What are some of the key reasons start-ups fail?

Ken Howery: Most start-ups probably fail for a few common reasons. Team construction is one of the most important things in start-up success. Usually, if you have the wrong team, the company will most likely fail. This can result from the team not getting along or communicating or working well together. In fact, a lot of companies that fail are not killed by other competitors. They are killed from the inside out because the team is not functioning as it should.

Shah: Take us back in time when you decided to join PayPal. What attracted you to it?

Howery: It was actually the team. The thing that has been the most important factor in my experience has been trying to either work with or invest in the best people possible. PayPal was no exception. Peter Thiel was one of the smartest people I met during my four years on campus at Stanford. Even back then, he had a track record for starting things which had been successful.

He started the *Stanford Review* on the Stanford campus, which was still going strong ten years after he had started it. He had started his first fund, called Thiel Capital International, which had been growing since he started it back in 1996. His successful track record was extremely important in my decision.

Max Levchin, who was the chief technology officer and co-founder of PayPal, was one of the best programmers either Peter or I had ever met. He was just crazy smart and very impressive. The two of them also have complementary skills—Peter has a great business mind and Max has a great technical mind. The main thing I liked about PayPal was the impressive team.

Shah: What was PayPal like when you joined?

Howery: It was basically Max, Peter, and me. Then, around the same time, we brought on Luke Nosek, who I currently work with now at Founders Fund, and then two other engineers. When we started off, the company was called Field Link, which was doing Palm Pilot encryption. It obviously started doing something much different than what the company ended up doing, but it was a rallying point for us to raise enough money to get started and to bring a very talented group of people together to start working on building a company, which ultimately led to what PayPal is today.

Shah: What are some of the key lessons for the entrepreneurs from your co-founder experience at PayPal?

Howery: There were tons of lessons, but I will pick three key ones. First, we recruited for talent, not experience. The original executive team we hired consisted of almost nobody that had payment experience. And almost nobody had internet experience on the original team. We basically tried to recruit the smartest people in our network and assumed that they would be able to figure it out.

If you look at the average age of the executive team, it was around thirty. Having experience did not matter. We went through so many business models that had we recruited for experience, we would have recruited the wrong people.

What we ended up doing was nothing close to what we had started doing. People who had no experience were able to shift what they were doing as we shifted business models. One of the benefits of nobody having payment experience was that no one realized what "couldn't be done." People had no established ways of thinking.

Second, we launched quickly and iterated. We did not find a business model that worked until our sixth business model. It took us a while to launch our first product because it was important to get the encryption perfect, but even then, we easily could have optimized it more before launching that original product. Luckily we did not, because we were building the wrong product.

Our focus at the time was building a mobile payment solution, in particular enabling payments on Palm Pilots. We ended up launching our Internet product before the Palm Pilot product was released, and it was a good thing we did. We soon realized that nobody was using our mobile payment solution—it was a decade too early. The internet product took off and we later discontinued our Palm Pilot product.

I think the key lesson we learned is to launch fast and iterate. You should not try to get something perfect because you might be developing the wrong thing. Once we realized that the mobile payment product was way too early, it still took us a while to figure out the right business model using our online payment platform. Luckily, we eventually found a model that worked, which ended up being a way for small businesses to accept credit cards, and in particular, small businesses on eBay. It is hard to predict in advance what people want.

The third lesson is to not be greedy. We basically raised money whenever we had the opportunity. It felt like we were always fundraising. It resulted in much more dilution for everyone, but that is the only reason we were able to survive as a company. PayPal was started at the end of 1998, but by the time the dot-com bubble popped, we were burning $10 million a month. It is likely we would have gone bankrupt had we been greedy.

The other way in which "do not be greedy" works is in hiring. The company gave generous stock-option grants to employees so we could attract the very best people. Ultimately having a talented team was the difference between succeeding and failing.

Shah: Very insightful! Are these lessons still applicable when you are looking to invest in start-ups?

Howery: I think all of these are still applicable. Among the many lessons we learned, all three of these still apply today. These have nothing to do with technology or market, or anything.

Shah: These lessons are timeless, indeed.

Shah: What was Facebook like when you first encountered it for the initial investment, and what was your impression when you completed the due diligence?

Howery: This was the summer of 2004. We spent most of our time doing due diligence with Mark Zuckerberg and Sean Parker. The Facebook team was pretty small back then. We also spent time with another company co-founder, Dustin Moskowitz, and I met a few of the other people on the team.

There were a lot of things that we really liked. The company basically needed money to buy servers. I have found that any time a company needs money to buy servers, it is probably a great investment because it shows the company is growing quickly. It is usually a pretty good bet. It also looked like they would be successful at locking up the college market. They had somewhere around 500,000 users when we invested. It was obviously pretty early, but it looked like they would hit a million users before long on their then-current trajectory. They were successful at locking up colleges where they had rolled out their service.

The order in which they were rolling out their service was very strategic. If there was one college that had a competing product, Facebook would roll out at the colleges around that particular campus. The assumption was that enough students had friends from multiple colleges that if you got all the colleges around one particular campus to sign up, then eventually you could get the campus in the middle as well. The team was very methodical.

Sean Parker was obviously a market expert with his experience at Napster and Plaxo. We loved Mark's vision. We believed the company itself was a good bet. Another thing that was in our favor was that everyone thought that social networking sites were a fad. They saw that Friendster had taken off in 2003 and signed up millions of users. By mid 2004, Myspace had passed Friendster and everyone's assumption was that social networking sites were like clothing companies, a giant fad. One would go out of fashion one season and the next season there would be a new one. We knew though that it wasn't true. We had been involved in Friendster and knew the actual Friendster story and realized that Friendster failed for different reasons than people thought it did.

Shah: It was not so much about the market—it was more about the decisions around their technology.

Howery: Absolutely. It was actually the technology. It was one of those companies where the technology did not scale and it was taking people a full minute to log on or check a message. That was the reason people switched to Myspace. The crazy thing is, even though Friendster did not work for a very long time, it still took almost a year before Myspace passed Friendster. Basically, it meant that the network effects were so strong that people were willing to endure a very painful user experience since their friends were still on the site. That fact reinforced our belief that this "fad theory" really did not apply. Most people thought social networking was a fad because they did not understand the specifics of why users actually left Friendster.

The best investments are in companies that are fundamentally good, but that nobody thinks are good. This directly applied at Facebook, which is what allowed us to have the opportunity to invest, making the angel investment on Peter Thiel's behalf, at the $5 million valuation.[1] It was a combination of being a really good investment and the fact that nobody thought it was a good investment.

Shah: That prevents the competition from crowding the market and also driving up the valuation to some crazy numbers. Now, two key competitors, Myspace and Bebo ended up selling to big corporations and then losing their edge. But then Facebook kept on growing like crazy around the world. Very few companies get to this level of scale as a start-up. What underlies that success?

Howery: One particular thing in the Myspace and Bebo cases is that when these companies get acquired by big corporations, they usually stop innovating or they innovate a lot slower. Part of that is because the acquiring company often transitions out the start-up management, or the start-up culture gets screwed up, or the key employees are incented by stock in the corporate parent instead of the start-up, which changes the incentive structure. A company that has been acquired is almost always at a huge disadvantage at continuing innovation.

---

[1] In 2011, Facebook was rumored to be around $80 billion in valuation.

On a more general level though, another really important thing that allows companies to scale up as a start-up is having a really strong sense of mission, which has to be a lot bigger than just about making money. A company that has a bigger purpose to try to make the world a better place and improve people's lives—unifies a company and its employees. It allows the company to attract the very best engineers.

The very best engineers often get multiple offers and are recruited by the very hottest companies at the moment, whether it's Apple, Google, and/or Facebook, so they can go almost anywhere they want. They are usually not motivated by money, but rather by working on and solving very difficult engineering challenges. Also, a lot of them are motivated by doing things that matter. The very best employees like having a mission-driven company. It encourages people to work their hardest because working toward a bigger mission gets people out of bed in the morning more so than just getting up to make money. It is almost like you don't mind putting a lot of extra hours in the office, because a lot is riding on that.

For example, Palantir Technologies is currently our single biggest investment. They are a mission-drive company that is building analytical tools that help catch terrorists and detect bank fraud, among other uses. One group of engineers did not leave the office for a week straight because they had a deadline they were working against. They would program all day and sleep when necessary because they believed that if they missed this deadline, lives were at risk and people could die. With that kind of mission, normal things like going home and watching TV, or whatever people spend their time on, become less important. You would not see this type of dedication at another copycat company.

The other thing that you have with mission-driven companies is that it allows companies to have a very long-term focus. If a team is motivated by a mission, they are not going to sacrifice the long-term mission by working on short-term projects that distract from the vision or push for an IPO sooner than makes sense just to get some cash out—because the mission matters most. It allows you to have a very patient strategic plan.

Shah: So if the mission is to get someone to the moon, you are not going to sell your spacecraft halfway there.

Howery: We actually have a company making rockets! Elon Musk[2] plans on running SpaceX for the rest of his life. As a result, one of his long-term goals at the company is to get a man to Mars. He thinks it will take between ten

---

[2] The former CEO of PayPal and the founder of Tesla Motors and SpaceX.

and twenty years to accomplish that. It is a mission-driven company, so he is fine being very patient and making sure he is focused on long term vision for the company.

Shah: What is the key quality of individuals like Zuckerberg that allows them to attract very smart people, very early on in the company?

Howery: I think the mission does contribute to that, once again. In the Facebook case, the mission was allowing people to be more connected and open in a way they had not been possible before.

A high-quality team also attracts smart people. Smart people are able to get other smart people to respect them, which as a result enables them to recruit really good people.

Take Peter Thiel when he was CEO of PayPal. Almost everyone that meets him is impressed with his intelligence. As a result, he is able to get lots of other really smart people to want to work on whatever he is working on. Good people attract good people. The same thing applies with Larry Page and Sergey Brin. They are obviously very smart individuals, and as a result they have been able to recruit among the top computer scientists graduating every year.

Shah: What do you think is the ideal relationship between entrepreneur and investors?

Howery: Having seen this from both sides, my partners and I believe that an investor's role is to back the best people possible and then let them run the show. We do not believe in the concept of adult supervision or of second-guessing our team's decisions. We believe that there is a very high bar in order to achieve success at a start-up, so it means we can only back the best entrepreneurs. But once we do back those people, we are able to help any time we are asked.

If help is needed, or even just support or advice, we are completely behind them, but we believe that the entrepreneurs are the ones who are thinking about their companies when they wake up, in the shower, when they are at dinner with their friends, and when they go to sleep. There is no way we could ever hope to come close to thinking about the companies or spending as much time with the issues as they do. We do not believe we are able to make better decisions than they can.

Basically, entrepreneurs make all the decisions. We will draw on everything that we have seen in our experience and our perspectives, and if we think a founder is making a mistake, we share the reasons why we have an altered point of view. Ultimately though, we want to support our founders. Ultimately it is their company.

Shah: When you meet with entrepreneurs to review their business plans, how much weight do you give to the product vs. market vs. team?

Howery: The team is our most important consideration, especially as they will no doubt have to iterate on the product over time. In comparing product versus market, I believe having the right idea with the right timing is more important than having the product exactly right. Ideally you have both.

We do have product experience as a team, so we are able to evaluate consumer internet products. A good design and flow is important. But if you are thinking in terms of trade-offs, a product with long-term barriers to entry is more important than the product's exact UI [user interface].

For example, designing a product that has network effects is obviously very powerful and something we look for—and have in many of our companies. How the product overlaps with the business model is also very important. In terms of market, timing plays a very crucial role.

Shah: Tell me more about how you look at market timing.

Howery: Typically, if we see two companies pitch the same idea to us in one week, we will not invest in either. At that point it is too late. Too many people are focused on it already. It is going to be too hard to be the winner at that point, as another team probably has a good lead and it will be hard to compete against them. It is a much better strategy to invest in a company before it is clear what category the company belongs in. Once "social network" is considered a type of company, it is probably not the ideal time to start investing in social networking companies. At that point, whoever is going to be the winner in social networking is probably already established. It gets a little tricky because you could say there were already two social networking companies by the time Facebook got started, but Friendster could have easily won had the technology worked.

Shah: Friendster was pretty early in social networking and very few social networking companies were known then.

Howery: Most people did not yet think of social networking as a category. It was still pretty early. The social networking category got defined much after Friendster got started. So Friendster had great timing.

Shah: Do you end up with investments that are way too early?

Howery: It is always hard to know if it is too early. I don't have any easy rule for determining whether it is too early. I assume if you are the only company doing something and nobody is using it, eventually you might have to conclude that you are way too early. I think you have to rely on usage at a certain point.

PayPal mobile payments were too early. It required the smartphone to be invented before it became practical and hence was one decade too early. This goes back to iteration. You launch something and if nobody is using it, eventually you are not going to be able to raise another round of financing and the company goes out of business. If nobody is using the product you launched, it is too early, and you should iterate and find something else. That is what we did with PayPal.

Shah: Brilliant insight. What sort of team do you need to objectively recognize that something is not working? Is there a cultural thing that some teams are just better at iterating and failing fast than others who hang onto the stale ideas for too long?

Howery: I think it is a skill that certain teams have more than others. As an entrepreneur, you want to be somewhere in the middle of a continuum, which on one end is listening to every single person and being very flexible, and on the other end is being very dogmatic. Essentially you need to be somewhat dogmatic because if you listened to everyone, you might become skeptical that your company was going to work. So if you were not somewhat dogmatic, you probably would never start the company in the first place, you would just be afraid to do anything and would be convinced you would fail.

If you are super dogmatic, then when things are not working, you may never change direction and spend all your money on the wrong idea and go bankrupt. It is important to be somewhere on that continuum where you are dogmatic enough to start the company and you are flexible enough that once you see the data and recognize something is not working, you change direction as necessary.

Shah: If the next Zuckerberg were to come into your office and pitch his or her idea to you, what will stand out about him or her?

Howery: A lot of good entrepreneurs we back are not really sales guys. They are usually more techy. Someone who looks at problems, is very analytical, and likes solving problems. Mark fits that profile. He does not come off as sales-y at all. He seems very genuine, thoughtful, and responsive, and that is actually a profile that we like and think is a good profile of a founder/CEO.

Obviously certain types of companies will have more of an enterprise sales component, and you probably want a different profile of person running those types of companies, but it largely depends on the industry. I think one of the secrets of most consumer Internet companies is that most of their value is not driven by business development deals. The value is driven by product innovation. Those types of companies is where we have tradition-ally done all of our investing. The sales or business role is not as important.

As a result, you want a CEO who is going to be better at focusing on prod-uct and product development rather than doing deals. At best, doing deals might be a slight positive and at worst it might just be a huge distraction. It is probably the wrong profile to look for in backing consumer internet entrepreneur founders.

Shah: Agreed. To your earlier point, if you can build the network effect into the product, then you really do not need to sell; it will sell on its own. How do you know that a start-up you invested in is off track and there is no more Plan B?

Howery: Often, but not always, you can tell it is off track if the company is not able to raise their next round of financing. If they are not able to con-vince the "market" that this company is valuable, it is often a huge red flag. There can be exceptions, such as where they just switched business models, a big deal is just about to close, or market conditions change and nobody is investing. In general though, it is a pretty big indication that things are off course.

Shah: Even before someone gets to the fundraising, in the board meeting or from tracking company's progress, how do you know that something is not working out?

Howery: For most consumer Internet start-ups, our first indication would be that they are not able to get any users or usage is flat. And unless the company has some big ideas on how to fix that, it would obviously be a red flag. Another red flag would be if the company is having team issues. For example, I would become concerned if the founders are having huge prob-lems all the time, or one of the founders leaves. Also, another example would be a company whose product launch is perpetually delayed.

Shah: What is your thought process in deciding whether to shut down, sell, or keep funding your start-up?

Howery: In terms of selling a company, as long as the founder is still run-ning the company and still has more good ideas, it is probably not the right time to sell. That would be our advice to a founder. If he or she was com-pletely set on selling, we would be supportive because our goal is to sup-port our founders, not rule them. If someone wants to sell for liquidity reasons, we have developed stock called Series FF stock, which allows founders to sell some of their shares, to get some cash and take liquidity pressure off of themselves so they can continue building the company if that is the decision that makes most sense. We have that in place to discourage founders from selling just for liquidity reasons.

Shah: Is it really popular with entrepreneurs?

Howery: We try to do it in all of our deals. The number of companies that have it is in double digits. There have even been other law firms and VC firms that have copied it as well. In fact, there are more instances of FF stock outside of Founders Fund companies than there are in Founders Fund companies. Founders are not selling a huge percentage of their stock, maybe 5 to 7 percent in a financing round, just enough to pay back college loans, pay down a house mortgage, or just take some financial pressure off so they can spend more time focused on the company and not be stressed out with other obligations.

Shah: What attracted you to ZocDoc?

Howery: ZocDoc is one of our recent investments. The business model is to be "Open Table for doctors." Prior to starting the company, the CEO was on an airplane flight with a head cold and popped his eardrum. It took him three days to find a doctor in New York City, even though it is the city with the most doctors in the country, to take a look at it. Driven from this personal problem, he started this company to make it easier for people to find a doctor and book an appointment.

When you go to the site, you can search by specialty, location, and insurance carrier. The site will list doctors that fit the criteria you've selected. When you get your search results, you find one that you like, you then see their open appointment times, and you click to make an appointment. At this point, the company has launched in 11 cities across the country, and have signed up large numbers of doctors in cities including New York, Los Angeles, Silicon Valley, Chicago, and Houston, among others.

If I get sick today, I should be able to log-in to ZocDoc on my phone or computer and find a same-day appointment or at the worst case a next-day appointment. The company is growing and expanding like crazy. The business model works and the doctors pay for the service. The doctors love it because they can fill more of their appointments and get new patients.

We invested in the company for two reasons. First, it is a network-driven business. If am searching for a doctor, I want to go to the network that has the most doctors on it, which is ZocDoc. And if I am a doctor, I want to list my appointments on the web site that has the most patients who are looking for doctors. Basically both sides feed on each other, similar to eBay. Second, the team is very strong. Cyrus Massoumi and his co-founders, Oliver Kharraz and Nick Ganju, are extremely hardworking, very smart, and extremely long-term focused. It is a mission-driven business. They want to improve healthcare in this country. It was recently rated the number one place to work for in New York City. We are very excited about the company, its track record, and its potential to keep growing.

Shah: There is just a lot of inefficiency in the market and ZocDoc is a great example of how the internet is helping us solve it. I see mobile having similar potential in addressing some key inefficiencies in the market. What are the most common entrepreneurial blindsides you have seen? What advice would you give to budding entrepreneurs wanting to build billion-dollar companies?

Howery: I think many entrepreneurs, at least many first-time entrepreneurs, pick an idea that seems "manageable" or "less risky" than other ideas. In fact, these "safer" ideas may actually be riskier than bigger ideas. The problem is, an idea that does not seem risky to you probably doesn't seem risky to lot of other people. Given how risk-averse our society has become, it will actually invite more competitors, and so it is going to be much more difficult to win in that market than it first seems.

For example, if you are building the next iPhone app that tells you where the closest ice cream stores are, it may seem pretty low-risk, but there are not any real barriers to entry for that app and the bar to starting a competitor is low. The chances of that being a long-term business are pretty low. The bigger ideas are the ones that seem more ambitious, that seem riskier, that seem harder to do, and they are the ones actually worth doing.

It is not only that fewer people are trying to do those types of companies because they seem so hard, but it goes back to the mission-driven company point. If you are building something that is really exciting and hard, you can attract the best employees and the best engineers, they will work the hardest, and it will be more likely to work. I do not think you could convince a top MIT or Stanford computer science programmer to develop the ice cream iPhone app. So my best advice to entrepreneurs is to take big risks and be as ambitious as possible.

Shah: I cannot think of any other name than Elon Musk when it comes to having a big ambition or vision.

Howery: Elon is an incredible entrepreneur. Many people thought he lost his mind when he started SpaceX, that the company would never work. Even when we invested back in 2008, potential investors thought we were crazy to back this rocket company. We followed this company over a period of six years, had kept track of it, and so what we knew was that the company itself was very promising. By the time we invested, Elon had taken enough of the risk out of the company—because he had invested $100 million of his own capital, built an incredible team, and had successfully developed a lot of the core technology—that it made sense for us to get on board. Also, the fact that nobody else thought it was a good investment is what made it a really great investment because like Friendster, the category is not defined yet and it won't see much competition any time soon.

Alfred Lin

Sequoia Capital: Zappos

Alfred Lin is a partner at Sequoia Capital who works with consumer internet, consumer mobile, gaming, and SaaS companies. He is on the boards of Achievers, Humble Bundle, and Stella & Dot. Before joining Sequoia, he was chairman and COO/CFO of Zappos. Alfred has been VP of finance and business development at Tellme Networks, co-founder and general manager of Venture Frogs, and VP of finance at LinkExchange, and has invested in companies including Ask Jeeves, MongoMusic, MyAble, and OpenTable.

Alfred is a rare combination of start-up operator and venture investor. Here he shares insights drawn from his experience at LinkExchange, Tellme, and especially Zappos—which built an engine of operational excellence encompassing culture, hiring, innovation, and the challenges of growth.

Tarang Shah: What are some key reasons start-ups fail?

Alfred Lin: Start-ups fail when they're started for the wrong reason—when they're made to flip, as opposed to being a company built for the ages.

Think what you're uniquely good at, what you're most passionate about, what drives your economic engine. Some people just focus on the economic engine. That's a huge mistake. In good times, when money is easy to get, you see a lot more entrepreneurs coming into the system, like we saw in 1999. But most didn't stick it out. Those that stuck with it continue through good and bad times.

Shah: During that time, you were operating a VC fund, Venture Frogs.

Lin: Yes. The number of people who left investment banking or consulting in 1999 to come to Silicon Valley to start a company was very high. Nothing wrong with that, or with banking or consulting backgrounds, but suddenly they saw that the easier route was to start a company, and sell it for a few hundred million in a few years. If they owned 10 to 20 percent of the company, it would be a life-changing amount of money. That was why some of them came out here—not because they wanted to build a company that they were super-passionate about.

Shah: Today, when you sit down with an entrepreneur to discuss his or her idea, how do you understand and assess motivation for starting the business?

Lin: We ask a lot of questions, and we have a very well-tuned BS meter.

For example, we probe the inspiration for the problem an entrepreneur is solving. Why this particular problem? What happened that makes this their mission in life? Some people have very articulate reasons—they might have family members affected by a problem. While that could sound naive, it also shows true commitment—rather than an attitude of "this can make me rich and famous," or "this is an interesting enough problem until I find another more interesting problem."

Shah: This really focuses on authenticity and purity of motivation. Let's go back to when Tony Hsieh asked you to join LinkExchange, the company he founded with Sanjay Madan. What was your decision-making process? How did you validate their business idea and, more important, their passion and motivation?

Lin: LinkExchange was an interesting situation. Tony and Sanjay's original business was web site design. They built these wonderful web sites, but nobody was visiting them because no one knew they existed.

The question was, how do you promote and drive traffic to new web sites? Back then, 1996 or 1997, it was not easy to buy internet advertising and get listed on Yahoo!. Tony and Sanjay were trying to figure out how to promote the sites they designed. One idea they had was to connect all the sites through a banner advertising exchange. That wasn't the original idea for the business, but they became super-passionate about solving the problem of driving users to a new web site.

Shah: You were in business school when Tony reached out to you?

Lin: No, I was at Stanford in a PhD program in statistics, but I dropped out to join LinkExchange.

Shah: What convinced you to leave school and join Tony?

Lin: I came to Stanford a year before Tony and Sanjay, who were friends of mine. Originally, the call was, "We're coming out. What do you think about starting a Subway franchise?" I asked where we should put our first location. They thought any place on Stanford's campus. There was already one on University Avenue, so I didn't think it was going to work.

I told them they needed to come up with a different idea. Then they started building web sites, but it was more of a consulting service. They called me to help out there, too, but I didn't think it was interesting or scalable.

Then they started LinkExchange. So you see, it was a series of calls. I liked the idea of driving users to a new web site, and started working for them part time. Tony wanted someone who could help him with finance. I told him I didn't really know anything about finance, but I knew numbers. That was how it started. Once Sequoia got into business with LinkExchange, I decided to quit my PhD program and join the company full time.

Shah: You were friends with Tony for many years before joining Link-Exchange. What was the chemistry like between you? How did it develop?

Lin: Initial chemistry is useful, but sometimes it's not a good predictor. It's actually more important to develop a relationship over time. When you go to networking events, you notice that people are trying to project a positive affect because they believe first impressions are so important. They are—but the effort to make a good impression is still just a signal. In a relationship over a longer period of time, you really come to understand each other.

Tony tells the story of our meeting as a joke about why I was the COO/CFO of Zappos. At college, he was running his pizza business with Sanjay. I had a large rooming group and I wanted to get a good deal by pooling our buying power. I bought whole pizzas from Tony, took them upstairs, and sold them by the slice. Although he ended up making more money in total, I made more money per hour because all I did was negotiate, pick up the pizza, take it upstairs, and sell it by the slice.

I used to hang out in the pizzeria almost every day. We talked about a lot of things. We knew we had similar values, thought about the world in similar ways, and had similar backgrounds.

Both our parents wanted us to play musical instruments, and both of us hated it. Both of us were asked to get a PhD, and neither of us wanted to do that. We were ultimately much more interested in building businesses. We had different ways of looking at problems, we solved them from different angles, but we ultimately got to similar solutions, which was very interesting.

I was exposed to Tony's way of thinking and he was exposed to mine. That's how you develop a relationship.

Let me back up and clarify the pizza story, because there's more to it. The untold element is that I was not trying to make money—I was trying to do a service for my roommates. Let's say the price was $2.00 a slice downstairs. I would go downstairs and negotiate with them and it would total $1.25 a slice because I bought the whole pizza. The funny part is, though, I always got $2.00 per slice from my roommates. They'd much rather give me dollar bills than quarters. Quarters were a prized commodity in college. You needed them for washers, dryers, vending machines, arcade games. We didn't have a change machine in our dorm, so you had to go to the bank for change.

So a quarter was worth more than a quarter. I made money because people valued quarters at more than their face value. If lots of people value something differently than you do, and they're willing to pay more for it, you've got a business.

Shah: That's quite applicable to start-ups. For a start-up to be successful, the whole ecosystem or value chain needs to win, not just one or two components of that chain. If you're really squeezing juice out of someone to make your business model work, it's not likely to sustain itself for long.

Lin: One more thing: I don't think it's smart to create a co-founding team quickly. Sometimes people feel the need to start a company together because they're about to graduate, or because they suddenly click when talking about a problem they share. That may work, but think about the courting process in a marriage or partnership. It's normally a few years—OK, maybe two or three days in Vegas, but that's different. Now about half of marriages end in divorce. If that's the hit rate for something where the courting process is a few years, why do you think you'd have a better chance of finding a cofounding team by rushing the process?

We ask people on the co-founding teams how they got to know each other, how long they've known each other, and how they know they'll work well together. Those questions are pretty important.

Shah: Many people think, "You have a technical skill and I have a business skill, and we went to school together, so we're good to go as cofounders." In most start-ups, you end up spending more time with your co-founders than with your spouse. You go through a lot of aches and pain together. If you haven't built a strong relationship, it's going to show. Alfred, do you believe that a start-up needs multiple founders to succeed? Or can a sole founder make it happen?

Lin: It can be only one person, though it's very lonely to be a solo founder. It's easier to have a partner to bounce ideas off of, to be the yin to your yang. I don't think any one person is complete in their thinking, in their processing of information or ideas. Of course, partnership can be frustrating, but working through that frustration is the very thing that can help you avoid blind spots and missteps.

Shah: What attracted you to Zappos?

Lin: Tony and I started Venture Frogs in 1999. We had a $27 million fund, and we invested that in twenty-seven start-ups. In 1999, we thought it was a good idea to invest in internet start-ups—but by 2000, it was pretty clear to us that 1999 was probably one of the worst times to have invested in the internet, and in technology in general.

We had OpenTable and Ask Jeeves in our portfolio. They didn't need our help. Some companies I'm not sure we'd have been able to help, because they were in businesses we didn't understand. Tellme and Zappos were the only two companies that Tony and I thought we could help. Tony wanted to help Zappos first, and I wanted to help Tellme first. After helping Tellme get its financial health in order, I went on to help Zappos. It was always a fun company, and a really fun experience.

Shah: You saw Tony's incredible commitment to making Zappos work. He even sold his apartment and put all his remaining money in the company. Is this level of commitment rare, or is it typical of successful founders?

Lin: Successful entrepreneurs just keep at the problem, again and again, every single day. There were many times where Zappos looked like it could flame out. In the early stages a company is very fragile, and near-death experiences happen more often than one might think. Most successful start-ups have stories about how they weren't sure they were going to make the next payroll, or how they were going to run out of money if a deal didn't close soon, or they'd have had to declare bankruptcy if they hadn't closed on a financing round by a certain date. Sometimes you just have to keep going forward and believe you're going to survive.

When people are working on their true passions, this kind of thing doesn't cause them to quit. They're working on something they enjoy.

Shah: When a company starts gaining traction, the next milestone is scaling it to realize its full potential. What's the key to scaling beyond initial proof of concept?

Lin: I can point to a few tenets of scaling a business: know your market, know your business, know yourself. The corollary is to know what you're good at, and focus on it. Surround yourself with people who are good at things you're less good at.

The same is true with your business. Know what your company is good at, and focus on those things. Don't try to do things your company is not good at. Know your market. What competitive advantage does your company have in its market? How can it create value out of that market? After that high-level exercise, it's about the details. Scaling is about making small improvements every single day.

Shah: Zappos was taking on established players and a mature market. That's a monumental task, like Netflix taking on Blockbuster or Amazon taking on Circuit City. How did you define Zappos as a business, define its unique competitive strength in its market?

Lin: The road was not as straight as we might have liked. First, let's understand the market Zappos was going after. The shoe industry was more than a $40 billion market just in the US. At Zappos' founding, almost none of that was transacted online.

The main objection to the idea of selling shoes on the internet was that you have to physically try on shoes before you buy them. That was certainly the conventional wisdom. But people failed to go more than skin deep and ask why. Why do people have to try on shoes before they buy them? Wouldn't they prefer to try them on in the comfort of their homes? Would they be fine with returning items if we made it simple to do? What if we could solve that problem by offering free shipping both ways—would that help? Are there any parallels for consumers' propensity to try things on at home instead of in a physical store?

Our cofounder, Nick Swinmurn, had already done the research to understand our market and the market dynamics. The approximation in this case was mail order. Back in 1999, five percent of the $40 billion shoe market was sold via mail order. It wasn't rocket science to think that the internet would be bigger than mail order.

Part of our thinking was that if everybody believes that selling shoes on the internet is a crazy idea, and we figure out how to do it, we won't have competition for some period of time.

In terms of knowing our business, selling online was a good idea because of economies of scale. An online store could provide greater selection than any physical store. At a physical store, you're limited by display and storage space. But online display space is almost free. Shelf space for an internet business is also less problematic. You can put inventory in a centralized warehouse and distribute it to customers from there.

In terms of knowing ourselves, Nick, Tony, and I had no retail or shoe experience. We hired an incredible retail talent named Fred Mosler, who understood that industry better than anybody we knew.

Zappos' initial competitive advantage was providing a vast selection. This went back to the original problem that Nick was solving—he couldn't find a particular pair of shoes he wanted. He started Zappos to solve that frustration for many others like him.

Then we asked ourselves: when people start copying us, how are we going to differentiate ourselves? In 1999, most companies wanted to differentiate based on price. We couldn't effectively compete on price because we'd get killed by a competitor with a larger bank account, one willing to lose more money to win market share. So we took the opposite approach, which was to compete on service, to provide a great shopping experience.

Even a company like Zappos pivoted many times. It went from a selection company to selection and service. Our tagline was still "The Web's Largest Shoe Store." But we were slowly adding service elements—free shipping, free return shipping, wide selection, 24/7 call center, 24/7 distribution center, and so on. We eventually changed our tagline to "Powered by Service." We are a service company that just happens to sell shoes, handbags, clothing, and, one day, anything and everything. Customers said to us time and time again that Zappos is like "happiness in a box." Today, we've evolved to "Delivering Happiness."

Shah: How do you approach the scaling process?

Lin: Zappos has been very good at trying new ideas, killing bad ideas quickly, and iterating where refinements are needed. If we really like an idea, we try to achieve a balance between maintaining our broader vision and not being religious about how we implement the idea.

Shah: What aspects of your pivoting process can entrepreneurs learn from and implement at their own start-ups?

Lin: Innovation is an important part of Zappos culture, and of our core values. Two of our core values, "embrace and drive change" and "pursue growth and learning," helped us continue to refine our ideas.

Shah: When someone at Zappos comes up with an idea, how do you test the idea to determine if it's worth implementing?

Lin: There's no standard process. I think having one makes it too formulaic, and then people try to game the system. At new-hire orientation, we tell our employees that if you think you have a good idea for the business or the culture, you should run with it. If you're passionate about an idea, the company has about two thousand employees—you certainly can find ten, twenty, or thirty people who are just as passionate about it. Get them together and try to make something happen.

The first test is if you can get those ten or twenty or thirty people. If you can, there might be something to your idea. Let's say you do get a team together. People generally start saying, "Great, but how do we get something off the ground without any funding?"

My general response is that money solves only one problem, which is a lack of creativity. Try to do it without any money and see how far you can go. Build a prototype that doesn't cost very much. Fast prototyping leads to fast learning whether an idea is good or bad. Then launch the prototype and get feedback. Eventually the data will prove itself. If it's compelling, then of course we start putting more effort and resources behind it.

Shah: What key initiatives and operating metrics have you followed at Zappos?

Lin: It's more about the philosophy of metrics than the metrics themselves. While they're important, financial metrics are backwards looking. Most companies close their books and look at their metrics at the end of the month. At Zappos, we had daily sales reports by brand, not just for the total company. We had inventory reports by brand. We knew every single day how well we were doing. Then we made sales reports available every hour. Eventually, they came out every fifteen minutes. You can run reports in real time, but they still tell the story of what happened. Try to create metrics that are forward looking, that are leading indicators, and track those.

On the Zappos blog, we put a call to action for improving your core task by one percent every day. If you compound that each and every day, at the end of the year you'll be thirty-seven times better than you were. That's the kind of thing good operators get their teams to think about.

Another thing: there are a lot of people with CXO titles around the table. We should replace the X with an L for leverage. Every person in the company can be a CLO. Every single day, come in and think about the top few things we need to do to create the most leverage in the business.

Shah: Give me an example of how you created such leverage at Zappos.

Lin: Conventional wisdom teaches us to reward individuals' high perform-ance. It turns out that may not be the most leveraged thing to do. We have a large workforce at Zappos. There are routine tasks such as picking, where the task is to find items in our warehouse, pick them off the shelf, and put them on the conveyor belt for packing and shipping.

There is some variance in how quickly people are able to pick. The top folks might be able to pick 20 to 30 percent faster than the average. If we reward those folks, they're more than happy to take more money. The more lever-aged question, though, is how we get the top performer to teach the rest of the team to pick 10 or 15 percent faster. Build the performance metrics for those top people so they help increase the team average.

Shah: While most CFOs on Wall Street see their role as cutting costs and reducing risk, your operating philosophy is appropriate allocation of risk. Tell us more about this philosophy, and how start-ups can apply it.

Lin: Yes, I take a different view when it came to my role as CFO and COO. Don't just reduce risk and cut costs—make it everyone's job to maximize expected value while reducing risk. Also, a lot of people think in terms of tradeoffs, of either/or. But anybody can do the either/or calculation. The companies that win are thinking and.

Shah: What were some of the most pressing operational challenges you faced while building Zappos, and how did you go about solving them?

Lin: My biggest challenge came when I was asked to figure out how to run our fulfillment center in Louisville, Kentucky. I had no experience managing a 24/7 fulfillment center with the goal of fulfilling orders as quickly as possi-ble. I thought I'd better find someone who really knows something about it. So I hired Craig Adkins, who is now VP of fulfillment services at Zappos. Over time and with Craig's help, I listened and I learned.

The one advantage of having no experience is that you're not encumbered by how things should be done. I often found myself asking, "Why is it done this way?" If the answer—the core principle—makes sense, then it's usually a good thing. If the core principle doesn't make sense, it's probably an area where you can innovate and come up with a new way of doing something.

Shah: What was your process for identifying people like Craig to build this exceptional team at Zappos?

Lin: This might sound overly simplistic, but I think it has to do with trying to find the best and the brightest, people with a very positive disposition, with the attitude that we can solve any problem. We focused on hiring people who were both passionate about the Zappos culture and really good technically.

At Zappos, we had three main tenets for building the team. One, hire for both cultural fit and technical abilities. Two, hire slowly and fire quickly. Three, every hire we make should raise the average of the team.

It's hard to hire slowly when you feel overwhelmed and any warm body can help you immensely. But before you hire someone, step back and feel the weight that every new hire adds. It alters the DNA of your company. Feel the weight: hiring a "B" player will cause your team to accept mediocrity in a hire, and then mediocrity in the work they do.

On the flip side, when things are not going well, you want to let people go quickly. That's hard to do; we convince ourselves that we haven't given someone enough time to grow, or enough feedback to determine that they won't work out for the long run. But if a person isn't scaling today, and the company is growing really fast, faster than the person is able to scale, the gap just gets bigger and bigger. So as soon as you see that someone is not scaling, take corrective action to get them back on track, or it's never going to work.

In general, we don't have a problem with firing bad employees. It's harder letting people go who are good but not great—we can't have a great company if our people are not great. Again, step back and feel the weight of being a good but not great company. Also, don't forget that you can raise the team average both by adding great people and by subtracting those who are below average.

Shah: If the next Zappos were to pitch you their business plan, could you identify it as the next compelling thing? What would you look at and say, "Yeah, this could be another Zappos"?

Lin: I don't think we could have, early on, identified Zappos as the breakout in our portfolio. Obviously, when you go into business with a company, you think it is going to be great; then you go through many "mood swings" along the way. Our screen is simple. We look for entrepreneurs who are very passionate and often have a personal reason to care deeply about the problems they are solving. Entrepreneurs we want to work with as business partners. We look to see if a company's solution could be a unique product or service in a large and growing market, where market forces are favorable to the company. We look for a great team that will continue to innovate on the product or service, build defensibility around it. And a desire to win in that market.

Shah: Can you put Stella & Dot, one of the companies you recently went into business with, through that screen? What attracted you to the opportunity?

Lin: Jessica Herrin is a very special entrepreneur. She is passionate, not just about designing and creating great jewelry and building a great social selling platform, but also about creating opportunities for women. This is her higher cause: that she can do good for women by building her business. She gives women opportunities to make a decent living if they want to, or to make supplemental income while maintaining a flexible schedule.

Shah: As you mentioned earlier, start-ups often go through one or more near-death experiences. What are some early signs that a company is off track?

Lin: Jim Collins has a book on this topic, *How the Mighty Fall*.[1] The first sign is hubris. When arrogance develops, that's when things start going downhill. You may not see it until two, three, even five years later. But when people become arrogant, they stop listening to their customers. They stop listening to their partners. They believe that they've created a rocket ship, and it will continue to be a rocket ship.

The second sign is the undisciplined pursuit of more. It is growth at all costs rather than growth in core and adjacent markets. Even Zappos had this situation where we expanded from shoes to handbags, which made sense, and then apparel, which made sense. But we also expanded into electronics for some time, which really didn't fit. We justified ourselves into thinking that it might.

Shah: What common entrepreneurial blind spots have you seen?

Lin: The most important thing is that many entrepreneurs don't realize their own blind spots. Most people know their obvious weaknesses, but it's more difficult to find your blind spots, because by definition you don't see them. You have to surround yourself with people you can ask honestly, who will objectively help you identify your blind spots.

Shah: As a smart operator at LinkExchange and Zappos, and now as an investor at Sequoia, what are your thoughts on considerations for exiting a start-up?

Lin: In general, if you want to build a business for the long run, you don't exit. You ride things out and go all the way. Sometimes people get tired of it,

---

[1] Jim Collins, *How the Mighty Fall* (Jim Collins, 2009).

lose passion for the business, or maybe a large class of shareholders are looking for liquidity. If that's the case, a secondary transaction might help, but sometimes when you start exploring a secondary transaction or look for liquidity options, acquisition offers trickle in—and sometimes those offers are hard to pass up. But if you're looking to build a long-standing company, staying on the path is the right choice.

Kevin Hartz

Xoom, Eventbrite

Kevin Hartz is co-founder and CEO of Eventbrite, a company that is transforming event ticketing by enabling anyone to sell tickets to any event of any size and type. Kevin was previously co-founder and CEO of Xoom Corporation, an international money transfer company that services more than 30 countries worldwide. He began his career as a product manager and later co-founded Connect Group, a start-up providing high-speed internet access to the hotel industry. Connect Group was acquired by LodgeNet.

Kevin has been an active early-stage investor and advisor to start-ups such as PayPal, Pinterest, Lookout, Milo, TripIt, Flixster, Airbnb, Yammer, and Trulia. In his spare time, Kevin advises university students on entrepreneurship through Youniversity Ventures.

Using examples of well-known start-up successes like YouTube, Dropbox, and Facebook, as well as his own companies and investments—including Xoom, Eventbrite, PayPal, Friendster, and Airbnb—Kevin shares gems of learning. In our interview, he discusses the way he disrupted existing markets with Xoom and Eventbrite, how he picks start-ups founded by Stanford students, and the key traits that make a successful entrepreneur.

I first came to know Kevin when I reviewed Eventbrite for investment and was extremely impressed by him. He has a rare combination of skills in both entrepreneurship and early-stage venture investment. What I love about Kevin is his unparalleled reach in the Silicon Valley start-up ecosystem, his uncanny knack for picking great entrepreneurs and start-ups, and building them (not to mention his own ideas) into household brand-names.

Tarang Shah: Tell me more about your seed investment approach.

Kevin Hartz: Through Youniversity Ventures, I have been advising and coaching Stanford students and other students on entrepreneurship to coach them and help them get started as they build their businesses. We've seen some of the best companies come out of the universities, started by first-time entrepreneurs.

Shah: You have a very balanced perspective from both sides of the table as an investor in early-stage start-ups, as well as founder of Xoom and Eventbrite. When you started Xoom and Eventbrite, what was the process of coming up with the idea and launching it? Was it a personal problem you were trying to solve? Or did you look at different trends in the market to see where opportunities may be?

Hartz: It was a pretty collaborative process, for one. Xoom really came out of bouncing ideas off Roelof Botha[1] and Peter Thiel[2] when they were at PayPal. They are both very smart people and they were in this market that I was interested in: payments. So the first step for me was identifying a market that I was fundamentally excited about and looking for more opportunities within it.

The second part of it was this notion—and a very important one—of finding a specific trend, technology, or market trend that is emerging. At that point, PayPal was growing very fast and it was creating a new market upon which other payment services could be created. So the idea of Xoom was almost peripheral to PayPal, and then growing into its own. That's a consistent theme. The PC revolution began and Apple and Microsoft felt it would last and people built applications on top of that. More recently, the iPhone revolution and mobile devices have created a platform for people to build on top of that and create new opportunities. Same with the Facebook platform.

Shah: You can see Zynga's amazing growth by leveraging Facebook as a platform.

Hartz: Precisely. And that's entirely what Mark Pincus was thinking when he started Zynga. The platforms like PayPal, Facebook, iPhone, etc., have opened up and radically changed landscapes in some manner and enabled either distribution or a new technology or applications on top of these platforms.

---

[1] Botha is now a partner at Sequoia Capital and an investor in both of these companies (Xoom and Eventbrite).

[2] Thiel was an original investor in Facebook and now runs Founders Fund.

There's a good speech that [YouTube co-founder] Jawed Karim gave to University of Illinois research students about why and how YouTube grew. He was talking about how a number of different factors like broadband penetration, camcorder usage, etc., were catalysts to YouTube's phenomenal growth. But also there was a specific event. There was the tsunami on December 26, 2004, and people were sending around large files of personal video taken of that tragedy. So in addition to the adoption of enabling technologies like broadband and camcorders, consumer behavior like peer-to-peer sharing of video files was really taking off.

Then also Adobe Flash had become big business and had become a truly viable platform for video publishing and playback. And people were doing a lot of self-publishing, as shown by amazing growth of Wikipedia, Blogger, etc. All these different components played into the broad trend of what became YouTube. It allowed self-published videos without having to have a big streaming client on the computer, and broadband made it easy to instantaneously watch these videos on your PC. So there's always, in any phenomenon, a set of factors reaching a certain critical point—like Moore's Law—enabling these new market opportunities.

Shah: How does the idea of Xoom fit into this market opportunity thinking?

Hartz: In the case of Xoom it was great, smart advisors [Botha and Thiel] who were close to the problem and saw the opportunity. And then there was globalization. The world is globalizing more and more. There are ups and downs, and waves of immigration and anti-immigration sentiment, but in reality the world is opening up and becoming much more of a global place. That is driving more people to move overseas. And then they send money back home to their families. So if you are a subscriber to globalization, free markets and open economies, then global remittance has a play in that, and Xoom is the player doing exactly that.

Now if you look at the market dynamics, it's still a very fragmented market. The market leader, with the most global market share—but still has less than 30 percent—is Western Union. It offers a very traditional, inexpensive method to send money internationally. But then it still leaves open another 70 percent, which is quite fragmented and run on traditional methods and pre-internet technologies. All those factors create the right environment for start-ups in this area.

Shah: And how about Eventbrite?

Hartz: Ticketing online is fundamentally broken, on both sides of the market. The event holder, the host, the venues, and the ticket sellers on one side, and the ticket buyers on the other, are both dissatisfied from a number of different perspectives, and we think that the timing is right for disruption. And also there tends to be other tailwinds that you find to help your business along. In this case, it was the rise of social media.

In the case of Eventbrite and ticketing, all of a sudden social media has become an important driver in the sense that people are sharing the events that they plan to attend and this, through social media, drives more sales and attendance. It's really not known to many people that Facebook and now Twitter are some of the biggest sources of traffic for us. Facebook is the largest source of traffic to Eventbrite. People are reading about what their friends have bought tickets for in their newsfeed or on LinkedIn or Facebook, and what conferences they are attending. This drives lots of traffic for us.

Shah: That's a very good point. When you look at start-ups like Eventbrite, Xoom, or YouTube, each of them had a set of market and technology forces that came together at a particular point in time and thus created a perfect market window for launching these companies. A year or two earlier or later, and these companies probably wouldn't have seen such growth. Do these teams hit the right market timing purely by luck or is something more at work here?

Hartz: There's always an element of luck but I really attribute it to the teams. At YouTube, between the founders Chad Hurley, Steve Chan, and Jawed Karim, there was a massive amount of talent involved in what they did. I think a lot of people have described it as dumb luck, but so many people had tried before and after and failed. The intelligence of that team and the way that they experimented with the concept and features was exceptional.

Another great example is Facebook. You know, Facebook was not the first mover. Unfortunately, I was an investor in Friendster, which was the first mover. Facebook was the team that had the massive talent and right DNA, and was able to continue to build and scale the right team around it. Meanwhile, all the other competitors really didn't dedicate themselves completely and fell by the wayside, or sold out. And so, it's really clear to me that the team should always be ahead of market.

I can argue that Steve, Chad, and Jawed[3] would have been successful with YouTube had they started a year before, and likely a year after, because of the combination of the things that they did, and the same is true for Mark Zuckerberg or Bill Gates or Steve Jobs. Steve Jobs started Apple in the seventies and he built an incredible company. Then, when the company

---

[3] Chad Hurley, Steve Chen, and Jawed Karim.

was in trouble, he came back and reinvented it and built an even bigger company. It's really the adaptation and talent of the entrepreneurs themselves that are key to start-up success.

There are certainly cases where not-so-great entrepreneurs have been in the right marketplace at the right time and certainly benefited financially, but the best companies are built and run by exceptional entrepreneurs like the founders at YouTube, Apple, Facebook, etc. So, when you asked me where to focus on for identifying promising start-ups, I would definitely say it's always the function of team dynamics, the founding team, and the team built around the founding team as an extension of the core DNA. That's the most important factor in the determination of success.

Shah: Great insight.

Shah: When you look at a young group of entrepreneurs at Stanford, what stands out in the ones that have potential to create the next big thing? What are you looking for in the ones you back as a seed investor?

Hartz: One thing I like to think a lot about is the psychology of the person. In a first-time entrepreneur, generally under the age of twenty-five, there's this insane amount of enthusiasm and idealism that never wanes, and that's what you find in a teenage Steve Jobs, Bill Gates, or Mark Zuckerberg. So I generally look for a first-time entrepreneur under the age of twenty-five, who is extremely excited, has a certain hunger, and is first- [or] second-generation immigrant. There's a hunger to succeed in the first- and second-generation immigrants. Although Steve Jobs, Mark Zuckerberg, and Bill Gates weren't first/second generation immigrants, Larry and Sergey, Jawed, and Max Levchin[4] were.

Another important element I look at is their family background. I like to hear a lot about their family story, what struggles they overcame, and their achievements. I often see really good entrepreneurs with parents that were in academia and coming from a strong, really high-intellect caliber, as well as strong work ethic. For example, Max Levchin's mom is a physicist, and Jawed's father is a research scientist.

Shah: I believe Sergey's and Larry's parents were in academia/research as well. How do you contrast this to someone coming from a business family, with an entrepreneurial spirit in the blood and having seen big businesses built and run by the family?

---

[4] Levchin is the co-founder of PayPal.

Hartz: I think it's the hunger, the work ethic, an intellectual horsepower, and curiosity you seek. Children tend to rebel against their parents, and so if you come from an entrepreneurial family, you are probably not going to like the instability and the ups and downs of things, and you tend to be less entrepreneurial as compared to someone like Bill Gates, whose father was in a law firm or Mark Zuckerberg, whose father is a dentist. So perhaps ones coming from high brain power, but very stable, conservative families tend to be more entrepreneurial.

I've heard stories of people whose parents are entrepreneurs. When I hear somebody describe their parents as entrepreneurs, it usually is in a negative light of the ups and downs and instability. And so, if you survey and look at all the actual backgrounds of successful entrepreneurs, my feeling would be that a parental entrepreneurial case would almost work against you.

And then the other factor that works against you in the entrepreneurial side is that entrepreneurship is generally less prevalent in privileged families. I am not from a super-wealthy family, but I never had it hard growing up. On the other hand, a lot of kids from my town don't have that hunger to achieve. They came from the upper-middle class and they ended up going into banking or consulting. They are feeling more entitled and really don't have as much drive. When the entrepreneurial father or mother hits it really big, the kids do feel entitled and don't feel the need to make it big in the world and prove themselves.

Shah: That sounds counter-intuitive. Especially in India, it's the other way round. Most business owners' kids end up running family businesses or creating their own ventures. So you are really looking for "underdogs"?

Hartz: That's exactly right. The underdog is so much more important to me, but there are certainly examples to the contrary. Scribd, a Y Combinator company that's doing remarkably well, was founded by Trip Adler right out of Harvard. His father is a really famous entrepreneur who I believe has brought at least a couple of medical device companies public. You know, there's always exceptions to the "underdogs" theory. I went to school with Estée Lauder's granddaughter and she is one of the hardest workers I know. She's working at the family business and she's very talented, very smart, and a very hard worker, an exception vs. what generally tends to be the trust-fund kids that go off and blow the money.

You know there's a Greek saying that "the first generation makes it and the second generation spends it, and the third loses it." The money begets complacency. In the entrepreneurial family, the offspring tend to not be as entrepreneurial, as driven, as hungry.

Shah: So the profile I have so far of an entrepreneurial college student that you like is a first- or second-generation immigrant from a stable family, an underdog from a not-that-well-known family, and just hungry to make his or her mark in this world. What am I missing?

Hartz: Hypercompetitive.

Shah: Where does hypercompetitiveness show up when you meet them?

Hartz: I think of the "PayPal mafia"—they are just so competitive. In anything they do, like playing chess or building start-ups, they all want to outdo each other. They have this super-high degree of competitiveness.

Shah: So there is a tremendous pressure brought onto them by themselves given their extremely high intellect and hypercompetitiveness.

Hartz: Yes, they put a lot of pressure on themselves and they are never satisfied. Let me give you an example here of Roelof Botha, a PayPal mafia member himself and investor in YouTube, and my start-ups Xoom and Eventbrite. We had a Xoom board meeting the day they announced the YouTube acquisition. I would say the most distraught or upset I've ever seen Roelof was that day. I had never seen him so frustrated before. He really wanted to see YouTube go the whole way, become a stand-alone company. Here they have one of the highest IRR [internal rate of return] investments in the history of Sequoia Capital, an amazing rocket ship called YouTube, and he was upset that they didn't stay independent and that they were going to be a subsidiary of Google.

This is insane, super-high competitiveness. I don't know this for a fact as I haven't spoken to Max Levchin, another PayPal mafia, since the acquisition of his latest start-up, Slide, but I can tell you that he sold the company for $300 million, and I bet he's very distraught over it because it's not a multi-billion-dollar company and it's not beating its competitor, Zynga.

Shah: Amazing. Now I am a big fan of YouTube as a service and investment. Its growth trajectory is unmatched by even Facebook or Google, or any other companies we know. It's the unbeatable growth curve so far.

Hartz: You got it. And you have to concede, there is some luck but there was a lot of pent-up demand. You know, YouTube should have been founded or discovered earlier. When something grows that fast it means that there was a lot of pent-up demand that hadn't been satisfied in the market.

Shah: Agreed. Now we have a complete profile of a promising young entrepreneur—a hypercompetitive college student, first- or second-generation immigrant coming from a stable academic/research family, an underdog who is hungry to make his mark in the world. And he is not in the game to become rich or famous.

Hartz: Yeah, I feel all you need is that. They'll find the right markets. When I invested in PayPal, it was called Field Link, a security software company, and that was even before they started the next business model of transferring money over Palm devices. The product was quite before its time and didn't get much traction. But the team was so smart and hungry that they figured there was a huge opportunity in online payments. They quickly pivoted the business to what became the PayPal we know today.

Shah: Is this entrepreneurial profile only applicable to consumer internet and mobile app start-ups? Or is it equally applicable to enterprise-based software and technology start-ups, where the domain expertise does play a significant role besides the other factors you just described?

Hartz: Big enterprise start-ups like Trilogy Software started as an undergrad project and became a really big company, though it ran into some problems later on. However, if you look at Mark Benioff, founder of Salesforce, or David Sacks, founder and CEO of Yammer and former COO and head of product at PayPal—they all are more experienced. I agree with you that going into the enterprise market is a more challenging environment for first time entrepreneurs, as there is a challenging sales process that is more likely to trip up first timers. That may be changing, though. Sacks is an interesting case, for example, of where you see consumer acquisition principles applied to the enterprise.

I also believe you gravitate towards what you know or understand better. For college students, the consumer internet and mobile apps tend to be something they understand better than most of us. There's that old saying that you can go to a college campus and find out what's going to be happening tomorrow.

Ten or twelve years ago, if you went to a college campus, everyone was listening to music on their computers, which seemed like a crazy thing. Now nobody has a television at college campuses. They all watch shows or movies on their laptops. The students tend to be early adopters. There is a lot of consumer phenomenon like Napster and Facebook that started on college campuses. A lot of students become early adopters of technologies. They are close to those and then apply them around businesses.

I really like what Paul Graham is doing at Y Combinator because I subscribe to his philosophy. What is a good founding team for Paul? It's the first-time entrepreneurs right out of an academic setting, and usually there's an engineer as a co-founder, etc. The thirty-six companies that were in his latest class, pretty much all of them were consumer. So there is a pattern there that many successful consumer internet and mobile companies are started by the profile we discussed earlier.

Shah: In all these cases, whether enterprise software or consumer internet, being close to the pain point and experience/exposure in the same or adjacent space comes across as a consistent theme. Do you fund single founders or does it need to be multiple co-founders?

Hartz: I subscribe to the theory that it's really hard to pull it off as a single founder. As a sole founder, you just don't have somebody to bounce ideas off. You don't have somebody to pick you up when times are tough. You need that counterbalance. I've rarely done it and it hasn't worked out in my case when I've invested in single founders.

Shah: What specific challenges did you run into in those sole founders?

Hartz: Single founders don't have as dynamic an environment. Things don't change that fast without a business partner as a sounding board. There's not enough challenges and pressure. Investors or advisors can only challenge the entrepreneur so much. They must have a counterpart, at least one other counterpart in the organization, pushing them and giving them checks and balances. Otherwise, it's easy to look on the blue side of things or end up on the wrong track.

Shah: What are your key success criteria for a start-up, especially at the seed stage?

Hartz: There are some general characteristics like 1) going after a big market, 2) having a strong team and 3) a competitive advantage.

Xoom is a great example of a market with a very clear total addressable market [TAM]. There is this remittance market, immigrants sending money back to their families, and it is tracked by the central banks of almost every country in the world. Inflow is reported, along with the sources, and who the providers are. You have a very specific figure of what is the worldwide global remittance market. Those are always the easiest or best cases.

Amazon, originally as an online book seller, had a very good handle on the TAM for books. A lot of commerce plays have very clear TAMs.

The second attribute is strong team. There are a lot of theories stating that if the market is big enough and the team is not strong, you can backfill with a better team over time. But a strong team really is critical—a high performing, excellent team is always the last company standing.

Facebook I think is one of the best examples of that. They really did set out to build the best development team, the best network ops, the best infra-structure scaling team, the best user experience, and the best visual design team. They have this excellence in all different areas and they invested heav-ily in recruiting and building the team. We all know the caliber of Google engineers has always been the greatest. This emphasis on team excellence is an important ingredient for start-up success.

So big market, strong team, and now the third attribute is how you are different or better from the competitors. Great teams can typically solve that or create to that. In the internet space, you have fewer technology breakthroughs in play. You are not patenting a direct design like in the bio-tech space. You have to win on other competitive advantages, like having the network effect to acquire customers.

Shah: One can easily copy the Facebook page design the way it is right now, but that does not translate into big business for you, as it will be quite a challenge to get past their network effect at this stage.

What is unique about Mark Zuckerberg, Sergey Brin, Larry Page, Steve Jobs, Bill Gates and other game changing entrepreneurs that we know? What makes them so different?

Hartz: What comes to mind is something Peter Thiel once said, "Mark really wants to win." People who want to sell their company to Google don't fit that description. I don't know Mark Zuckerberg personally, but from an outside appearance, he fits that category of entrepreneur that wants to win, really wants to win and has an obsessive and "never say die" drive. It certainly has to be more than that.

You have to recognize that you can't scale individually, so you have to build the team around you to get there. To be a successful entrepreneur, you have to come at the problem from a very nontraditional contrarian stance. I talked to a Brazilian journalist recently and he could not believe why Face-book would ever be worth $50 billion. It has been that way all the way since the beginning. Even Airbnb is a great example of a company where people consider it such a strange thing that people would open their homes up for renting, but the company is growing so fast. eBay, in its day, was perceived as a strange, dirty, flea market online but now has become a global e-commerce player. I think there is also a contrarian element that you will find in these entrepreneurs. They seize upon ideas others would not believe in until far later, after it is really too late.

Shah: Like a crazy guy in the corner tinkering with some stuff that no one initially pays any attention to and well before you know it, he is on to something big.

Hartz: Most end up being crazy entrepreneurs, but a few end up being missionaries. That distinction is key. You see dysfunctional characteristics in certain entrepreneurs. They are either not willing to open up, not willing to be coachable or listen, or they cannot make their own decisions and need to talk to many people to come to a decision.

I think every great founder has a certain style that makes him successful. The best characteristics are common among them though. Good decision making skill, surrounding themselves with smart people, strong work ethic, and intelligence is at the core of what the Silicon Valley is all about.

Shah: If the next Zuckerberg were to run into you on the Stanford campus, would you be able to identify him?

Hartz: I hope I would be able to. I do not think there is any investor or anyone who has not passed on somebody. Everyone has their stories on how they passed on YouTube and passed on Google, Twitter, etc. There are various fundamental reasons behind it. Even with the formulated approach, there is still a high degree of failure, but you are producing mass amounts of start-ups.

Back to Paul Graham—he has a few thousand applicants to decide from, but the majority of those, if you look through where they have documented the hit rate, the majority do fail, but there are some really great companies in the making at the same time. The other side is that, I think what investors do is wait for things to prove out a bit. The way to increase the success probability is to wait. If you invest in Facebook at a $100 million valuation when it was on the high-growth trajectory, then it is not even a question of identifying Zuckerberg. You already know who the market leader and the winner is.

Shah: That is a good point. You have taken out a lot of risk at that stage but then your returns are not as good as early stage investors in Facebook. What is a key to building the successful team?

Hartz: Complementary expertise of the founders. We spoke before that it is hard to start a company by oneself and having somebody to keep you in check and have well-rounded expertise across several areas, whether it is engineering and marketing, or product and engineering. The success formula you see today is a good combination of product design and engineering.

I will point to Airbnb, where Brian Chesky is the all-around CEO, but he is also a graduate of Rhode Island School of Design. He is a visual designer. The second co-founder, Joe Gebbia, is a great visual designer. The third is Nathan Blecharczyk, a computer science graduate out of Harvard. There you have the great balance of expertise together. They have a very resolute passion. They are so rabid in terms of how much they believe in the cause.

The other one I would say is very, very similar to that in terms of rabid team mentality is Dropbox. Co-founder Drew Houston is a fantastic entrepreneur. Airbnb and Dropbox are out of the same Y Combinator class, one season off. They are very similar companies in terms of mentality, passion, drive, and talent.

Shah: Any other elements key to start-up success?

Hartz: I think network is very important. The PayPal mafia was successful because they collaborated and supported each other. You have a network to turn to for answers. That notion of how to get great advice and information is key. So many great companies have come out of Stanford because you bring great minds together and they congregate at the computer lab and exchange information. Maybe universities are not as commercially entrepreneurial focused, but they are still the biggest producer of the best companies.

Y Combinator is also creating a new environment to bring great minds together and collaborate and do great things all around entrepreneurs. I attribute the success of Y Combinator to their community. There is a network of talent to draw upon. Connecting people, providing references. Having those resources of people around you is invaluable.

Shah: Agreed. You can save many days and months of work by tapping into someone who has gone through similar experiences or faced similar challenges and learned from them.

What are some of the key metrics you follow on your seed portfolio to separate the ones that are showing great potential vs. the ones that are struggling?

Hartz: Typically it is very obvious. I am an investor in a company that I believe is going to be something great. It has just two founders. It's a great company, there are similar players in this space, but I believe the space is still very undefined, and customers are very much loving and enjoying the product. There seems to be some type of market forming. For me, that is fairly obvious criteria to know if something is succeeding.

At the very early stage, when they have not launched a product yet, you can try to bet on a team based on that criteria of intelligence, product sensibility, and so on. Then they launch the product and start getting users. The customers that use it rave about it. Then they start to see that hockey stick emerge, where you have people raving about the service and loving it and it's growing fast.

The next piece is, can it scale and can it build out the rest of the team? Can it move beyond just a founder phenomenon? Many companies flame out at this stage. When you look back, there are companies that get sold in an asset sale or get shut down. Everything seemed to be going their way and they were growing like crazy, but they were not able to get to the next step of building out a team and really scaling the business.

Back to being an investor at Friendster, it got that initial traction and started to see the momentous growth, but it did not make it to that next level. So ability to scale and build out the rest of the team becomes important metric beyond initial rapid traction.

Eric Hippeau

Lerer Ventures

SoftBank Capital: The Huffington Post, Yahoo!, Danger

Eric Hippeau is a partner at Lerer Ventures, a seed-stage venture capital fund in New York City. Eric's prior investment firm, SoftBank Capital (where he was managing partner and president of SoftBank International Ventures), was the first institutional investor in The Huffington Post, an alternative internet news site and blog founded by Arianna Huffington and Kenneth Lerer.

Eric served as CEO of The Huffington Post until 2011, when it was bought by AOL. Prior to joining SoftBank, he was chairman and CEO of Ziff-Davis, publisher of PC Magazine and other technology publications.

Eric now serves on the boards of several public and private companies, including Starwood Hotels and Resorts Worldwide, Buddy Media, and BuzzFeed. His prior board positions included Yahoo!, Yahoo! GeoCities, The Huffington Post, and CNET.

I had the fortune of working for and getting trained directly under Eric while at SoftBank Capital. He was also instrumental in SoftBank's first investment in Yahoo! in 1995.

What I love about Eric is his knack for identifying promising markets and entrepreneurs, while sorting through tremendous amounts of primary data from industry contacts and secondary data from publications. His sharp intuition and decision-making abilities that cut through the heart of the investment issues are second to none.

In this interview, Eric draws from his tremendous experience as an operator and investor and takes examples from investment successes like Danger and The Huffington Post to highlight how he goes about identifying promising markets and entrepreneurs, common pitfalls in building start-ups, what triggers early exits, why market timing is crucial, and the new real-time development environment that start-ups are competing in today.

Tarang Shah: The majority of start-ups fail. They shut down or fail to return more than what was invested in them. What are the main reasons why they fail?

Eric Hippeau: In no particular order, they are as follows: The marketplace did not develop the way it was expected. Every start-up makes assumptions about where the market is going, and in this case those assumptions were proven to be flawed or the marketplace is going in the other direction. Or the established, successful company you didn't expect to come into this marketplace moved in and sucked the air out of it. These are key marketplace reasons for failing start-ups.

Ultimately, you can put forward your best prediction, best thought and analysis, but you won't be able to entirely predict accurately how the market is going to develop. You are putting out your best judgment.

Things happen with the marketplace that you might not have predicted. Some of the things that can happen do not necessarily kill the start-up, but can even enhance the market opportunity. But some will kill your market opportunity and there is nothing much you can do about it. You can change course, move into adjacent areas and change your business thesis, but you've got to move quickly.

The second biggest reason why things don't work out is people. The people who you backed or trusted to do this are not capable of doing it for a variety of reasons. They don't recognize that they need to perhaps hire better people than themselves. There can be lots of problems with the top management itself. Many founders have proven not to know how to manage growth or opportunity, and they wait too long to replace themselves with adequate competence or a better CEO. Or the CEO hires the wrong people and takes too long to replace them. By the time they get to it, the marketplace has shifted.

Very rarely do you see successful companies fail for lack of financing. If they are successful at hitting the key metrics that they should be hitting, they will raise financing.

Shah: So the inability to raise adequate financing is more a function of not hitting the key success metrics, and in that respect getting financing is a result and not a cause of poor performance or failure.

Hippeau: Exactly. I know people who overextended themselves expecting the market to happen or happen quicker than it did and found themselves in big trouble. So one more important reason for start-ups failing is timing. You can have the best idea in the world and have figured out where the market is going, but if your timing is wrong, you can fail. Meaning if you are too early, you are going to exhaust yourselves and run out of steam and money. If you are too late, you are unlikely to end up in the number-one or number-two position.

Shah: Because the rules of the game and key leaders have been established.

Hippeau: Yes. You may not recognize who they are. So getting the timing right is critical. Arguably, all of the big successful companies that I have been involved with had the element of timing right. Sometimes you can say it was luck or whatever, but many may never realize they had it right, as it's easy to attribute success to what you did personally.

As an example, there were a bunch of video companies that got started in the late nineties that could have been YouTube, but they lost because there wasn't enough broadband penetration. That was a fundamental flaw in the market analysis as broadband took longer to deploy than they had originally estimated. On the other hand, if you were to start a company to compete with YouTube today, you would be an idiot.

Shah: So maturity and penetration of supporting infrastructure is key in ensuring the right market timing.

Hippeau: Yes. You can't fight timing. There is nothing much you can do if you are too late or too early. You can change strategy, you can do something else, but you can't fight time.

Shah: You can have all the money in the world and the best management to execute, but you can't create YouTube when YouTube already exists.

Hippeau: Yes. We as VCs recognize how important timing is through experience, but there is a lack of recognition in the entrepreneur community about how important the timing is. If someone comes to me with an idea, I know there are half a dozen people who have the same or similar idea. You see those companies that say they are in a stealth mode and they are the only one to do this, but it's rarely true. The moment you are thinking through something, there are half a dozen companies who are thinking the same thought. So you should try to figure out where his company stands in relation to others, who these other companies are, whether he is too late or too early compared to them, and so on and so forth.

Shah: From Ziff-Davis to ZDNet and from Yahoo! to Danger, Huffington Post, and Thumbplay, you have demonstrated remarkable ability to pick compelling new markets. What's your secret sauce?

Hippeau: Barring a small percentage of young people who can spot new trends, the people who can identify trends have many years of experience in the marketplaces that are changing quite a bit. Obviously the technology, internet, media, etc., sectors are changing a lot. The more things change, the more experience you get. You have to look at things that are happening from a variety of different angles. You've got to consume a lot of information and you have to understand why people are doing certain things and whether that will be successful.

Then you must look back and review the products and companies that became successful, especially when you thought they wouldn't, and ask, "What did I miss there?" Or maybe to the contrary—and actually often to the contrary—"I had a feeling that his product or company would be successful but it looks like it's failing. Why?" So you have to have checkpoints and look back and say, "Yeah, I was right or wrong," and make some adjustments based on why you think you were right or wrong.

You are not going to get everything right but you've got to get more things right than wrong. Otherwise you should go open a hamburger stand or something.

Shah: So you should develop a model by testing successes and failures in your area of interest?

Hippeau: Yes, and that is going to determine your personal instinct. I don't believe in pure instinct when it comes to investing. Yes, there is something like an instinct, but that instinct has to be formed. That instinct is going to help you act quickly on whether you are faced with an investment decision or judgment on something. This quickness of mind or decision coming from the instinct is more important than thinking, "this trend is important," and spending days on it. Because by that time that particular investment opportunity has already passed by. So you have to train yourself at making quick judgments and then looking back to figure out whether you were right or wrong.

Shah: To get to that quick judgment on a particular opportunity, you should have inserted yourself in the education process of that new trend much earlier, and hence when it's presented to you, you are ready with a quick judgment call.

Hippeau: That's right.

Shah: Compared to five years ago, has the venture investment model changed or is it the same?

Hippeau: Mobile is a different ecosystem, and hence there are different rules for investing there than before. On the technology side, the cost of technology is almost nothing right now. You've got cloud computing, cheap servers, open source, and easy-to-use tools, cheap bandwidth, etc. The actual cost of development is also really small. So what happens then is we are in a much more connected, collaborative environment where you use other people's tools.

For example, at Huffington Post we have an identity system like Facebook, Yahoo!, etc., but we want to use other companies' identity systems because they have much larger communities. So I don't have to worry about developing my own ID system—I can use Facebook Connect. I will leverage everyone who has a critical mass—I don't need to do everything by myself.

That exists in some other areas as well. So in other words, the building blocks, which you had to develop on your own five to ten years ago, are now easily available in this connected, collaborative ecosystem today. As a result, it's much cheaper and faster and you can get to prototyping, testing, etc., much faster and with less capital expended.

I am not sure that if this new model really favors Silicon Valley as a prime hub for start-up and technology innovation. In a world where engineers were scarce, and you had to have much more in-depth proprietary knowledge, it made sense for start-ups to be in Silicon Valley for cost reasons.

We are seeing great development happening in New York now for instance, with lots of start-ups, much more so than ten years ago. This is because the access to technology and the cost of technology is much more spread out. We like to do 24/7 development, and hence we have developers in all major time zones. For example, we have developers in Eastern Europe, Asia, South America, and the US. So when we come up with things that need to be done, we write a ticket during the day and the next morning when we come back, it's done.

Shah: So that's a real-time development.

Hippeau: Exactly, and you are leveraging this global, connected world of developers and that happens to be very affordable as well.

Shah: So these give you a relatively inexpensive development toolkit to hit the ground running and the ability to react rapidly to the market. However, the flip side is that you can't compete on technology anymore and the competitive edge has to come from somewhere else.

Hippeau: Again, the timing is important. The first one to come with the right product built the proper way is going to get first-mover advantage, which is huge. Your barrier to entry will become that you get to critical mass before anyone else does. To protect your position through technology is not a very good idea because that's not where the technology is going.

Think classic IT services companies like Oracle. Their business model is to come up with a very high-maintenance proprietary software at your premise at a very, very high cost. The software will be hard to use, hard to maintain, and will need training of hundreds of people their way. After all this, the customer starts benefitting from it. Contrast that with Salesforce.com, which is developed once, constantly updated, costs much less, and the benefit to the customer is instantaneous.

Shah: And in many cases it's crowd-sourced or open-sourced, where the company is getting "free" development from industry experts.

Hippeau: That's true. In our case at Huffington Post, we use our audience to provide us with information, cutting the cost of journalism, and that's a huge barrier to entry. We leveraged technology to build community and tools, and they trust that we are going to publish their content responsibly.

Shah: Eric, you have been part of many successful start-ups. What are the common characteristics behind their success?

Hippeau: What was common in all of them was that they recognized that the market was about to shift dramatically. In the case of Danger,[1] the company figured that the smartphones at that time were higher-end and very enterprise-focused. So they came up with the concept of consumer-focused smartphones that can be made cheaper, and with features that can be updated over the air. They were quite early, but they made it happen. The fact that you could buy Sidekick for around $200 with all the smartphone features and capabilities and software that could be updated over the air was huge.

In all of these cases you have to have a strong and brilliant management team. So putting the right management team was absolutely critical.

Shah: So besides strong and brilliant, the management team also needs to be humble, as you just showed.

---

[1] The maker of the Sidekick 4G smartphone, which was sold to Microsoft.

Hippeau: You have to be results-oriented. If your ego gets in the way, you are not going to get the results. In the case of Huffington Post, it was the recognition on part of the founders, Arianna Huffington and Ken Lerer, that blogging was going to become mainstream.

Blogging will become the way people get informed and engaged with the news. If you remember, when they started, the people were saying that this won't work as no one will care about others' opinions and views and it would be tough to get any distribution for little blogs and it would never be mainstream.

Today we have 20 million monthly uniques and 400 million monthly page views as per comScore. We are the largest online news company that is not affiliated with any legacy brands like CNN or CBS. If you look at any online newspaper, we are bigger than *New York Times, Washington Post, USA Today,* and everybody else.

And now people come to us for a complete news package. They get breaking news and opinions, and they are able to comment and engage. They are able to get a fuller experience about the current events than you would from most other sites, which are flat and static. But again, when it got started four years ago, it was Arianna's blog, and now we have a full-fledged news brand.

In the case of Thumbplay, there were two major trends. One was that the walled garden[2] as part of the carrier had a long history of failing. The telcos are not media companies.

Secondly, the consumption of music and ringtones on mobile was going to become mainstream. Additionally, we planned to offer an all-you-can-eat subscription model, which no one was offering and could be very effective for consumers. The carriers couldn't keep up with the demand, as they are not media companies and couldn't source enough content. They made it very difficult for people to find and download content. So that opened up a whole new market for Thumbplay.

And Thumbplay from the get-go was a true expert in direct marketing. Increasingly it displayed an online and then mobile-direct marketing expertise that almost no one has in the market. So it was the market opportunity and the knowledge that carriers will never be media companies, combined with

---

[2] Walled gardens occurred when carriers like Verizon, AT&T, and Sprint didn't allow open access to handsets, but controlled and charged for all applications and content consumed on the handsets in their networks.

the online direct-marketing expertise with subscription model, that made Thumbplay.

Shah: Though both the largest market and a great team are important in building huge start-up successes, do you put more weight on one vs. the other?

Hippeau: I don't know as a rule of thumb that you can say it's the market, but the fact is that if you can be confident that the market is going to be large, it's easier to build a business that, while it might not achieve the number-one position, might become successful in a large market rather than miss the market entirely. Because in a larger market, there is not one company that is not significant. A large market allows you a lot of leeway. There is much more flexibility than if you are building something in the market that is developing really large and fast.

Shah: A large market allows you to experiment with different business models. If one doesn't pan out, the other one is there.

Hippeau: And if the market doesn't develop, it doesn't matter how smart you are or whatever, you aren't going to do anything.

Shah: What are other things you look at that can tell whether something will be a $10 million market or a multi-billion dollar market?

Hippeau: Obviously this is where experience and good information and good intuition are going to come in. Take Google, for instance. It was relatively easy to predict that the online advertising market was going to be big because there was already Yahoo! and others, because that is where the audience was going to move to. It wasn't going to be able to predict that people would welcome paid inclusions or paid ads, because that was a brand-new concept that was to some degree contrary to the common thinking of the time—that the users or people are somewhat wary of advertising, and they are going to be very suspicious of people who pay more to be put in Amazon. But the first one, which is that the market space was going to be big, that was a relatively easy call to make.

Shah: In the case of Thumbplay, there was unresolved, large pain in offdeck content [outside carrier controlled]. In the case of Huffington Post, blogging was growing and was going to be mainstream.

Hippeau: Absolutely. In the case of Huffington Post, it wasn't just blogging, but it was also news and current events. People need to keep abreast of what is going on in the world. Will they do it online or will they want their news to be mixed with opinion? That was the call. You have to say, well, in a world where supposedly news is delivered to you in an objective fashion . . . people want the news and the facts, and they can form an opinion.

It turns out that what people want, really, is how they should be thinking about this news. So you could argue one way or the other. On the other hand, the news market has been established for centuries now as something that a large part of the population makes use of to keep up with what is going on in the world.

Shah: The way it is done, using blogging was a disruptive twist to the established daily news market.

Hippeau: Democracy exists. Democracy is large, and the market is going to be online. Will I be successful at disrupting it? That is the question.

Shah: What determines whether one can disrupt the existing market or not?

Hippeau: That is not obvious. If it was obvious, everybody would be disrupting. That's the part where you have to have some sort of a judgment. The new idea on how to organize the marketplace is that it is something you as an investor can really believe in and you as an entrepreneur can deliver on. It is just not good you had the idea. Can you actually execute a new idea? If you build it, will people come? As we know, there are a lot of misses and a lot of miscalculations, but that is why it's called venture capital.

Shah: At the same time for something to stick like it is sticking right now with Huffington Post—was it an unaddressed latent demand that you knowingly or unknowingly tapped into? Or was it a new behavior that you exposed people to and eventually became must-have?

Hippeau: I think in this case, it is a notion that technology is not kind to gatekeepers, and that the gatekeepers in this business were the journalists. So, therefore, you were conditioned to getting your news from people who made the decisions when to give it to you and how they verified it. Is it true? Can I prove it? I am only going to give it to you when I can do all these things. That is the classic gatekeeper. A class of professionals who you entrust to deliver, in this particular case, news.

What happened with blogs is that suddenly you were getting your news from people who were not the gatekeepers, who were people that, over time, you hopefully came to trust as well. People who because of their position in life and their title or their professional experience, whatever, are people that you implicitly trust. That was the big new thing. The professional journalist was not going to be necessarily the main person or the only person that you were going to get your news from.

Shah: So the latent demand was to get news and opinions from broader sources. But the way the industry was structured, it just wasn't possible to get that and this disruption tapped into that latent demand.

Hippeau: Also to some degree, the industry—like a lot of times when you disrupt an industry—has become fat and happy and complacent. In this particular case, what you had was a lazy-cycle kind of people, a lot of them with monopoly-type businesses—city newspapers, or the evening news. They became lazy and complacent in these slow, lazy, 24-hour cycles and didn't realize with technology, there is no reason to deliver the news on an every-24-hour basis. You can deliver the news on the second.

So that has completely changed the habits and the working cycles that the industry had become accustomed to, and as a result, it became a very disruptive force, because why would I wait until the next morning to read the news if I had something at the tip of my computer? The medium was not appropriate either. You are not going to publish a newspaper every second, so the medium had to change in this particular case, and, of course, that became online.

Shah: Eric, if you were to pick between an existing industry that you can disrupt, because the size is known and the players are known, vs. going into a new market you can't really size, and you don't know the parameters that may lead to making it a couple of billions-of-dollars market, which would you prefer? And what would be the criteria in deciding?

Hippeau: I think a lot of times we assume that existing markets are going to change faster than they really do. We have to be very careful not to get overly enthusiastic. People are set in their ways and there has to be a compelling reason to change. Take Amazon as an example. Even though Amazon was very successful at disrupting the book business, it is still not the dominant way for people to buy books. Other people who have tried to sell books online have not been successful.

On the other hand, where technology really changes people's habits dramatically, like advertising and like we just said, news, then you can say, Wow! It's even better if there is a demographic aspect to it. In other words, as in the case of online, young people become the dominant force and as a result as they get older, they develop brain habits along with them.

I have tried creating new markets. There's always a big question mark. Will the market develop? Will my timing work out for me? Again, for the people who tried to disrupt or to bring video to online in the late nineties, they all failed. Not that it wasn't a great idea, but the timing was wrong. Not because of the infrastructure, broadband, and other things, but because the speed of computers was just nonexistent. If they had waited another two to three years, they would have been YouTube.

Shah: How important is it to nail the business model early on?

Hippeau: It isn't so much that I think you don't need to nail it early on as much as I don't think you can. Or you need to believe that you can do it given everything you know about the company and the market. You have to have a business model at the beginning that is defensible, that all the assumptions ring true.

But having said that, you are going to have to be nimble in making major or minor changes. I go back to Google. It was only really late in the development of the company that they came up with a business model. And yet, investors smartly backed the team. It is not that it is not important. You have to have a business model at the beginning that you think is viable, but you also have to be realistic and realize that the business model is probably not going to make it.

Shah: There could be a couple experiments along the way to see what works.

Hippeau: Maybe the consumer or the client changes. We all react in a different way and you have to be quick on your feet and go the way they want to go.

Shah: In the process of building start-ups, most of them get off track. At what stage do you know the off-track start-up is irrecoverable?

Hippeau: I go back to the people. If you start losing confidence in the team, it's easy for you to convince yourself, hey now, I'm going to give them another chance or they will see how to correct this or they will listen to my advice. Most of the time or a lot of the time, that's not the case. Once you start having doubts about the team, you really have to pause and say, do I want to continue? Particularly if it is at an early stage, when it is more difficult to change.

If you have a founding team and it's their vision and you start losing confidence, it is not going to be that easy to replace them because it's their vision. Later on, when you have a bigger team and a product and you have some sort of a business going, it is a lot easier to change them—hire a CEO for instance.

Shah: What are the things that make you lose confidence?

Hippeau: Poor decisions, inability to react to change—the pace might not be the one they expected, or they don't have the ability to build a team. Kind of like, "I'm the visionary here and I know how things are working out. I am not going to listen to anybody."

David Lee

SV Angel: Twitter, Foursquare, Flipboard, Dropbox, AirBnB

David Lee *is a Founding Managing Partner of SV Angel, an angel investment firm co-founded by legendary investor Ron Conway. SV Angel is an investor in leading companies such as Twitter, Foursquare, Flipboard, Dropbox, and AirBnB.*

David focuses on investments within the consumer internet, mobile, video, and other IT industries. Prior to SV Angel, David was at Baseline Ventures, a leading seed-stage venture firm. He also held business development roles at StumbleUpon and Google, and he was a corporate attorney at leading technology law firms. David has an MS in electrical engineering from Stanford, where he was a National Science Foundation graduate fellow; a JD from NYU; and a BA from Johns Hopkins.

While at SoftBank Capital, I came to know David through our funds partnering on a number of investments. It's hard to find a start-up in Silicon Valley that hasn't talked to SV Angel. What I love about David is that he embodies Ron Conway's investment philosophy of backing best-of-breed entrepreneurs and leveraging SV Angel's tremendous expertise, network of contacts, and ecosystem to build the next billion-dollar start-ups.

Tarang Shah: What inspired you to pursue entrepreneurship? Can you take us from your early entrepreneurial dream all the way to how you met Baseline/Ron Conway?

David Lee: My dad was an entrepreneur. He invented the first fully auto-mated fortune cookie machine and built a business around it. He wanted to use that first product to build a larger line of products at scale. He was definitely the major influence in my life in this regard. Funny enough, his experiences influenced me to do what I'm doing now—serving as an adviser and agent, rather than the founder or principal. I saw every day how hard it was—being alone, getting rejected by customers, dealing with ruthless com-petitors, etc. He was very successful—he sent me and my sister to college, for example—but I saw how hard and grueling it could be. And I didn't think it then but probably knew deep down that my strengths and personality might be better suited to what I'm doing now.

I went to grad school in engineering mainly with the goal of becoming a professor. I liked teaching but hated research so ultimately decided to do something else. I went to law school with the ultimate goal of helping peo-ple like my dad—giving general business advice and help that would help them succeed. My random path ultimately led to Google. Ron was an angel investor in Google. I met him in early 2005. At the time, he was interested in online video. I was working on some stuff for Google Video and we seemed to click.

Around 2007, I wanted to do something more entrepreneurial and I reached out to Ron. He was an investor in StumbleUpon and introduced me to them. They were then acquired by eBay and I didn't want to stick around since I just came from a big company [Google] and wanted to pursue a career in start-ups. Ron and Steve Anderson reached out to me and I eventually joined them at Baseline Ventures.

Shah: What was immediately striking about Ron Conway when you first met him?

Lee: I remember thinking that he was unbelievably friendly and genuine for someone that accomplished. I observed how he interacted with other peo-ple, and he was the same way with anyone regardless of who you were. I liked that. He was also a really fun guy to be around—great storyteller.

Shah: What makes Ron one of the most successful angel investors and SV Angel one of the most successful angel funds of our times?

Lee: The main thing is that Ron genuinely loves what he does. Not many people can truly say that. His work is his life and vice-versa. I think Biz Stone [Twitter co-founder] once said that you never know when it is work or play with Ron. And I think that's it. A lot of people say they love their work, but not a lot *truly* love it like Ron does.

I also say that Ron has the highest EQ—or emotional intelligence—of anyone I've ever seen. In the high-tech industry, having an above-average IQ is almost a prerequisite because everyone is smart. But not many people generally have the high EQ. He is the best listener I've ever met. Anyone who has talked to him with his notebook open and pencil in his hand can attest to this. But this isn't some touchy-feely, Pollyanna-ish thing. He's a great communicator, he understands personal dynamics, and he isn't afraid. He's seen almost every situation and so his judgment is beyond comparison. Finally, Ron is among the best "pattern recognizers" out there.

Shah: What did you personally learn about entrepreneurship and angel investing by working closely with Ron? How does that translate into what entrepreneurs can expect and benefit from working with you, Ron, and the team?

Lee: I learned everything about this business from Ron. I also learned a ton from Steve Anderson at Baseline Ventures. They taught me the basics and fundamentals of venture and angel investing. But being around Ron and getting his daily advice on the things I mentioned above—how to handle situations for example—has been incredible.

Ron showed me that investing is a lot simpler and harder than people think. It's simple but not easy. The only thing that matters is your reputation. Everything else is a second-order effect. If you have a great reputation—especially among founders—then everything else will ultimately fall into place. Having a great reputation means adding true value to the founders. But doing that consistently and repeatedly requires a lot of hard work. Think about it—yes, Ron has been doing this longer than most—"80 percent of success is showing up" as Woody Allen says—but the other 20 percent is the hard part. If you ask founders like Marc Andreessen [Netscape, Opsware], Ben Horowitz [Opsware], Mark Zuckerburg [Facebook] and Jack Dorsey [Twitter] about whether Ron adds value, I'm pretty sure they would say resoundingly yes. That's a pretty amazing run. And not easy. So the main the thing I've learned is the importance of adding true value to the founders.

We work with a relatively large number companies and try to add value when they ask us to. Because of our portfolio size, we get involved at inflection points—financings, business development, key hires, and M&A. A big part of it is being a "human router." We don't take board seats. Also, because of our breadth of coverage, we see a lot of situations and try to use pattern recognition when we advise companies and when they ask. We don't give our opinion unless they ask.

Shah: What are some of the key reasons why start-ups fail?

Lee: A lot of this is correlation and not causation. For very early-stage companies—the three-to-five person companies just starting—one thing we've observed is that some founders don't or can't recognize when something isn't working. That is, maybe they are being a little too slow and emotionally wedded to their idea. It's impossible to say when is a good time to change direction—only the founder knows that. And the easiest thing to do in hindsight is to say that it was a brilliant move if it worked and they were "too slow" if it didn't. But it's impossible to say that *that* is the reason why it failed—there are a lot of "slow" founders who succeeded too.

Shah: What are some of the most common entrepreneurial blindsides?

Lee: One blindside we see in some consumer internet founders with awesome technology is that they treat customer adoption as a second priority. They think that their technology is so cool that ultimately users will adopt in droves. Yes, it's great to have differentiated IP or incredible engineering talent—it can take a company to the next level. Facebook is a great example of that. But that's not sufficient for early success. And if you don't get that initial wave of users, then you could be dead on arrival.

Shah: What needs to happen for creation of a billion-dollar start-up?

Lee: I believe it's impossible to say without a huge degree of hindsight. But if you look at a lot of the defining companies, they have defining founders. Ben Horowitz has a great blog post on this. That is, these founders define their product, business and culture. They talk about their company with a larger vision that attracts top talent to join them. And they're usually developers or have a deep appreciation for the importance of having great engineers. But such talent is incredibly hard to spot. It's easy to look at Mark Zuckerberg, Jeff Bezos, and Jack Dorsey now and see how special they are. But what were they like when they first started? What drove them? And I think that is where Ron's pattern recognition is a differentiator—he can spend 30 minutes with a founder and get a decent feel because he spent time in the early days with Larry Page and Sergey Brin, Shawn Fanning, Sean Parker, and Mark Zuckerberg. He's not a fortune-teller, obviously, but such incredible experience doesn't hurt either.

Shah: How does angel investing work? What's a process an entrepreneur planning to raise angel round can expect?

Lee: Angel investing was historically about individuals who gave founders their "first check" because they were too early for the larger guys. You'd go to them, make some progress, and then seek venture financing. It's pretty much the same process more or less but now there are more investors—

individuals, micro VCs, VCs who do seed and so forth. Generally, individual investors are faster process-wise because they're the decision makers.

Shah: You, Ron, and the SV Angel team have identified and invested in some of the great successes of our times including Twitter, Facebook, etc. What do you look for in the companies you back? What really stands out when you meet with these promising start-ups?

Lee: Our preference is for founders solving a problem for themselves. It's more of a bottoms-up approach than looking at a market and saying, "There's a big market." There's a lot of debate among investors whether markets or founders are more important. We look at founders first and hope that we back the ones that are only interested in solving interesting or hard problems. And those, in our experience, usually lead to big markets. Another advantage of a founder building a product or service to solve her own pain point is that she doesn't have to do market research or focus groups—she is the target market.

And so I think what stands out in the promising founders is this genuine authenticity. It's like the Supreme Court justice's definition of pornography—you know it when you see it but you can't define it. When a founder tells a life story about how they approached the problem, what it means to them and their vision for the future—that's what we're usually drawn to. It's not always sufficient for success. There are many founders we backed who built something for themselves and didn't succeed, but it could be sufficient to get an investment from us.

Shah: Which are some of the notable investments you will like to mention? What attracted you to those opportunities?

Lee: It's easy to point to the winners and say that those are the ones I am very proud of, but then I would definitely be giving myself way too much credit for their success. Some of the notable investments for me are 20x200 and Rupture.

Jen Bekman started 20x200. It's a site that caters to the "middle market" for art. After asking all the normal questions, I asked her how she would define success in 5 years. She didn't talk about users or money. She simply said, "I want everyone to have an art collection." I thought that was pretty cool.

Another memorable one for me was Shawn Fanning, who started Rupture because he was so into World of Warcraft (WoW). He played the WoW game so much that he gained something like 20 pounds. When you heard him talk about why this mattered to him, that was pretty cool. These companies may not be household names, even though Shawn is pretty famous.

But they're memorable because of their founders and their passion for solving problems they feel so compelled to solve for themselves and others like them.

Shah: What are the key characteristics common among the most successful entrepreneurs you have backed?

Lee: I will base the answer on my venture investing experience of only four to five years. But one common thread among all the successful founders is fearlessness. And I don't mean "fearless" as in they are risk-takers. I mean fearless as in not being afraid to fail. Funny enough, very few people have that quality. Very few people want to take the last shot. Not being afraid to fail makes you work harder—you see the upside with no downside. It's like that Michael Jordan quote, "I've missed more than 9000 shots in my career. I've lost almost 300 games. Twenty-six times, I've been trusted to take the game winning shot and missed. I've failed over and over and over again in my life. And that is why I succeed."

The one founder that comes to mind for me is Dave Friedberg of Weatherbill. He's an unbelievably smart guy but also has the guts of a cat burglar. I'd argue that a lot of people have the former but not many have the latter, and when someone has both, it's pretty awesome.

Shah: What stands out when you meet these promising entrepreneurs?

Lee: I believe promising entrepreneurs are magnets for talent. We are living in times where more and more start-ups are emerging than before. The major downside of that is, it's harder and harder to hire. So one question I ask when I meet a founder is, "would I work for him or her?" I'm 42 and nearly twice the age of some of them. That doesn't matter. Some people have different leadership qualities. It may be because they're insanely smart or oddly charismatic. But the real question is, will I work for them and I am sure many talented folks will be asking the same question. They will vote with their feet and career and to me that's a great filter.

Shah: As an avid sports fan, how do you go about applying some of the success principles of sports to angel investing?

Lee: I played a lot of sports as a kid and spent a lot of time with engineers in grad school. I use sports analogies all the time because I've always thought that great athletes and engineers have very similar mindsets. They're both judged by binary outcomes—win/lose, faster/slower, etc. There are no grey areas. And often what separates the likes of Michael Jordan from the others is their competitiveness and drive. Some of the *most* competitive people I've ever met are engineers. Another common characteristic is that the athlete and engineer/coder is doing exactly what they've always done since they were little—playing sports, playing with computers, tinkering, etc. The really great ones love it more than anything. For example, Tiger Woods plays at The Masters not because of the pot but because he's playing golf at the highest level against the best players in the world. Similarly, engineers like to be challenged—work on the hardest, virtually unsolvable problems. I'm sure there are a lot of holes in the comparisons, but it's an easy reference for me.

Shah: Fantastic! What's the ideal relationship between the entrepreneurs and seed/angel investors?

Lee: Ideally, there's some rapport. And that comes in a lot of flavors—shared domain interest, similar personalities, etc. I only want to work with people that I get along with. That's another thing I learned from Ron—that it's never fun to work with people you don't like no matter if they're going to make you a lot of money.

Shah: What separates exceptional teams from mediocre teams? What stands out in exceptional teams when you meet with them?

Lee: One thing we look for is chemistry between the founders. We like founders who know and trust each other deeply. We're not huge fans of founders who just met. Again, it's not categorical and we're definitely going to miss a lot of companies, but generally we are drawn to founders who have a history together, are on the same wavelength.

Shah: What are some of the key characteristics of the start-ups at the seed level that point to potentially a great company in making? How are these characteristics different from the ones at Series A?

Lee: In the consumer internet sector, most start-ups are pre-revenue and the good ones grow like crazy. We invest in that growth. We're not sure how that growth is going to morph into value, but that's our thesis.

As a distinction, at the Series A stage, there's still great growth but the revenue model or business prospects are a little more fleshed out. On the other hand, at the seed stage, you're really funding that growth—literally keeping lights on, maybe hiring one more developer. At Series A, it's more about company building.

Shah: What separates start-ups that make it from seed to Series A? What needs to happen during that period? What are some of the most common mistakes entrepreneurs and investors make during that period?

Lee: The start-ups that graduate to Series A have data that supports their story. I know that sounds vague but that data could be number of active users, revenue, etc. You have some data that supports why you think this could be a billion-dollar company. I think investors at this stage are not only looking for a large market but some momentum—growth—that shows that you're going to be one of the winners. Your second derivative should be increasing—you grew 10 percent in one month, 20 percent in the next month, etc. Founders who don't recognize this and rely solely on their technology—those are the ones who struggle. Another way of saying this is that you need to find product/market fit in order to get a Series A. Marc Andreessen wrote the best blog on this concept of product/market fit. I think he coined the concept.

Shah: At seed stage, to what extent do you factor in the market opportunity (size, potential, etc.)? What are some of the signs that point to potentially billion-dollar markets in making?

Lee: At SV Angel, we invest in megatrends such as real-time data, collaborative consumption, etc. But we don't emphasize particular market sizes—it's important to consider but not as important as evaluating founders. Again, we think great founders seek to solve hard problems, which usually lead to big markets.

We get the megatrends from talking to founders. Top-down market research is not as useful for emerging trends that we see at our stage. We like talking to founders and see what they think is cool and interesting. When a lot of founders are talking about the same thing, that's when we sense a trend.

Shah: How often do you end up with start-ups that are too early or too late?

Lee: All the time. It's the same as being wrong.

Shah: How do you deal with start-ups that are too early or too late?

Lee: We don't get involved. We let the founders try to navigate that.

Shah: What are some of the key characteristics of great products that really stand out when you first review them or run across them?

Lee: The main characteristic for me is someone who builds for themselves. This isn't a perfect heuristic. But it could also be a product that is clean, simple, and useful. My favorite example is SnapJoy. When I first heard their pitch—organizing your photos—I was very skeptical because there were a lot of similar apps. But I tried their product and loved it—very simple, clean, and useful. It's still early to tell whether they will become a household name, but I just remember using it and really liking it even though I thought I was fatigued from all the photo apps out there.

Shah: What are some of the key aspects of execution that lead to start-up success? What are the most common mistakes you have seen in execution?

Lee: I think the key aspects are making fast decisions. The most common mistake is trying to be perfect. A lot of people point to folks like Steve Jobs and say that all details need to be perfect in order to launch. But the exception doesn't make the rule—there is maybe one Steve Jobs every five life-times.

Another mistake at the earliest stage is trying to do too many things. Sometimes even trying to do two things can be too much. If you think about a lot of great services—Google, Facebook, Twitter, Dropbox, Foursquare—they all started doing one thing well or being defined by one gesture—tagging photos, checking in, simple storage. They used that initial gesture and grew from there.

Shah: In what case is it imperative to nail down the business model early on? Is it something you focus on at seed/angel investing stage?

Lee: At angel stage, growth is more important than business model. You hope that the growth translates into economic value eventually.

Shah: What are three things you as an investor wish every entrepreneur knew?

Lee: Firstly, at the early stage, optimize for value add and not dilution. Secondly, be very self-critical and thoughtful about what constitutes "value add" for your start-up. And thirdly, think about where you want to be in 18 months, which is usually the amount of time funded for a seed round, and your biggest risks are in getting there. Every investor you add to your team should help you with mitigating those risks. If an investor doesn't add value, don't let them invest.

Shah: What advice will you give to young entrepreneurs trying to build successful start-ups?

Lee: Growing up, my dad used to give me all this advice, and like a lot of kids, I resisted a lot of it. One thing he'd say over and over again is, "Don't follow money. Anybody can make money." And as I grow older, I have a greater appreciation for what he was trying to tell me. He was telling me to do what you love and don't take the easy way out.

Ted Alexander

Mission Ventures: MaxLinear, RockeTalk, Enevate

Ted Alexander *is a managing partner of Mission Ventures and has been with the firm since its founding. Prior to joining Mission Ventures, Ted worked closely with a successful Mission Ventures portfolio company investment, Sandpiper Networks. Ted's investment focus has been predominantly in the areas of communications and infrastructure, and he is currently serving as a director for Enevate, ID Analytics, LeisureLink, Ortiva Wireless, RockeTalk, and Verimatrix. His prior board positions include MaxLinear and Networks In Motion.*

Ted is also an ex-platoon commander in the US Navy SEALs and a former division officer aboard a US Navy destroyer.

I came to know Ted as fellow VC in Southern California when I was at SoftBank Capital. I have been big fan of Ted's portfolio companies and his investment philosophy. Over the years of interactions and deal sharing, I have learned a lot about venture investing from him. In this interview, Ted provides incisive insights into key aspects of start-up building, including characteristics of promising markets, compelling entrepreneurs, team building, creating products, and start-up execution and exit.

What I love about Ted is his clarity on start-up success criteria, the humility and mindfulness in his approach, and the way he identifies and builds great start-ups like MaxLinear, Enevate, and Networks In Motion.

Tarang Shah: What are the key reasons why start-ups fail?

Ted Alexander: I think to some degree it centers on the clarity of vision. Exactly what is the problem they are trying to solve? Why is [the solution] more beneficial than other methods that are out there? [How can they create] a team that is stroking hard and get it delivered more cost effectively than any other place that the enterprise or consumer could buy it?

My favorite team leadership book is called, *The Five Dysfunctions of a Team.*[1] It is kind of a leadership fable by a guy named Lencioni, and he talks about a start-up company where they bring in a woman that the chairman knows, who led a company in a different area to lead this new technology company. It goes through explaining how she gets this dysfunctional team finally stroking in the right direction.

Building a team that is based on trust and clarity of vision is key to success. I think forty people stroking together in any industry can take over the automotive industry. They can take over the mobile industry. You really can. It is amazing how difficult it is, how rarely one of those exceptionally talented teams all work together with a real clear vision of where they want to go. One of my portfolio companies, MaxLinear, is a great example of this. They were just able to have a really crisp, clear view of what they needed to accomplish and get a really high-quality team stroking together.

Shah: What are some of the key metrics you follow in your investments?

Alexander: Metric number one is to get the prototype out in five months. Then, once you hit that, the next metric is going from there to getting two customers. I think it also depends market by market, company by company.

Software companies you can get off a lot sooner than, say, a chip company. So a software company is actually funded through to meaningful revenue or even profitability. With a chip company, I might just be funding to a prototype and then actually putting more money in because it is so capital intensive. You have to do it that way. It really depends on the various markets that I am addressing.

I think the important point to make to entrepreneurs is that this whole business of funding start-up companies is milestone-based. The goal is that you are basically trying to cross a desert and get from oasis to oasis. If we lay out three key milestones that we are going to achieve in the next eighteen months, I want the next set of investors to come in at a 2.5x valuation to the round. I would rather they come in, in the next round. If we don't get to

---

[1] Patrick Lencioni, *The Five Dysfunctions of a Team* (San Francisco: Jossey-Bass, 2002).

2.5x or so valuation, then I probably took too much risk for my investors and obviously I either shouldn't have come in or should have come in the next round.

If you get the right venture investors, the right syndicate, you want to fund it from the starting point in the desert to that next oasis and achieve your milestones. Hit the market hard enough to get that next round of mark-up in valuation. It makes sense to me, but it is a lonely trek.

Shah: What is more important? Market? Management? Or differentiated technology?

Alexander: Maybe nine out of ten VCs will tell you it is the CEO or management. I am a believer that it is the market, in that if you are in a high-growth market you can attract the right management team. And ultimately, if you have the right product, you can really get ahead of the curve relative to competition, whether they are big companies or small companies.

You can even afford to make a couple of mistakes and still stay ahead. This is where venture opportunities are really built—in a high-growth market— because you suddenly establish yourself in a place that, ultimately, the likes of Google and other big players wake up and say, "Ah, I need to be in that space. Let me acquire the king."

The challenge for venture capitalists is in figuring out not where everybody is investing today, but where is everybody going to want to be in two to three years from now. I want to pick the right team. It's going to be on the crest of that wave when that time comes. We'll make some good calls and some bad calls.

In the case of MaxLinear, eight founders worked for about eighteen to twenty-four months on little to no salary. The team had a great experience building chip sets in markets that they were going to address when I invested. And based on their credibility and design of really great chip sets, we were able to bring along a couple of Tier 1 customers. The team was a very cohesive unit. It wasn't about egos. It was truly a meritocracy.

As the company continued to grow, the founding CEO was not wed to one of the other engineers being a VP of engineering. He ultimately brought in another VP of engineering to be the lead guy of all the other founding engineers. As I stated before, it was real clarity of vision around what they were going to do. They focused on the mobile TV market and started over in Japan and Korea. They have an "unfair" technical advantage. They are able to use old process technology, 0.13, when the Qualcomms and Broadcoms were using 0.065 animator design techniques, and they were still able to make their chipsets smaller and higher performance than the ones who were using the newer techniques.

Shah: And that was because of their technical know-how primarily?

Alexander: It was. They basically had a breakthrough in the PA [power amplifier], RF [radio frequency], and digital aspects of things. A combination of the three gave them a higher performance. They picked the right market and within that market, they obviously gave themselves unfair advantage in which to compete. It was a lot of smaller egos, a lot of humility, a lot of good basic leadership to set a strong vision and get everybody working together on it.

Shah: It has really grown rapidly.

Alexander: Yes, it has gone from single-digit millions to double-digit millions the next year. And they did $52 million in 2009 and $69 million in 2010, and have great gross margins of 68 percent.

Shah: What would you prefer to do: invest in a new market or disrupt an existing market?

Alexander: Honestly, it is both. I have RockeTalk, an example of mobile social networking, and I have Enevate, which is a next-generation cell phone battery. It is now running. Lots of people in the world want to work with them. It is really going after the existing cell phones and your battery, delivering 30 percent-plus increased energy density, so greater time between charges.

All things being equal, everybody in the world will take 30 percent-plus more charge power. It is a mature market and it is hard to break into that ecosystem, but if you have a big enough value proposition, you are there. Everybody wants to work with you and capture more margin based on the value you are bringing. You cannot disrupt existing market with 5 to 10 percent better. You have to wow the customers.

Shah: How do you identify multibillion-dollar high-growth markets?

Alexander: I spend most of my time having lunch and coffee with great technologists who have a good perspective on what is going on and the markets that they work in. Whether that is actually an ex-VP of production at Qualcomm or somebody that is running the Linux unit at Cisco that is involved with the business strategy for those companies.

It is hard to find people that have a good feel for things technically while at the same time really understand what's going to be happening with the business or enterprise or value proposition over the next two to three years. I am also asking people these questions. I also look at what is going on at *Fast*

Company and *Wired* magazine, and some of the online blogs, to truly try to educate myself about what people are excited about and what the trends are that matter in the world.

Shah: Is there a common pattern you see where something is on its way to becoming a household new behavior?

Alexander: I think at some point you can gauge the user uptake. The hard part is, before you have any of that uptake, trying to get a sense for [whether] this will take off or won't take off. I will give you couple examples from my portfolio. As mentioned, we made investment in a battery company called Enevate that has could increase battery life by 30 to 50 percent. When you think about all the applications that are showing up on cell phones, and the amount of bandwidth people are consuming, the batteries on iPhone and the Blackberry won't get you through the day. There will be more and more applications that need power, so I think power is an interesting place in that domain.

Another trend where we made an [investment] is in the "voice messaging" space, in a company called RockeTalk. In India, there is this crazy following with cricket. Communities are coming up and RockeTalk could [create] a great communications tool for communities like cricket lovers, etc.

Actually what's happening more than creating communities is just sort of one-on-one communications. Sometimes you don't necessarily want to call your wife, but you just want to say, "Hey honey, I'm at the supermarket. Call me and let me know if there is anything you need. I'm getting the milk and cereal." She can click and say, "Don't forget to get diapers." You know. You don't have to wait for it to ring. Sometimes you don't want to talk to your mom. Sometimes you just want to say, "Hey, mom, just letting you know I'm thinking about you and love you. Here is a video clip of the baby and me walking through the supermarket."

What is happening in India is there are a lot of people actually realizing that a data plan for unlimited data is cheaper if you can use voice messaging rather than buying a voice plan. Most of the phones that you see when you walk around in India have no minutes on them. They are a kind of a status symbol. People are working until they get their next five hundred rupees so they can spend fifty of them on another few minutes of cell coverage.

Now what is happening, people are paying for unlimited data plans and they are using this application. The carriers are saying, here is an application I can give to people that makes them use data. I couldn't sell data to Tarang's mother over there but here is a voice plan where you also get video and picture imaging, and you can share voice messages with your son back in the

States. She'll probably buy that all day. It's basically e-mail that comes through an e-mail server, and it is like voice recorded. It comes to my computer. It comes to my cell phone. It is growing very quickly.

We have gone from having next to nobody six months ago, to ten thousand a month to twenty thousand active users to one hundred thousand new downloads. Very recently RockeTalk overtook orkut and Facebook as the largest mobile social network in India.

Shah: Fantastic! So it is a synchronous communication using rich media?

Alexander: Nextel Lite with the cab drivers. "Hey we need somebody at Fourth and Elm," but every taxi cab driver hears that. That required a direct link. That's billions of dollars in infrastructure they actually deployed to have that type of service that is pulled now to an enterprise for $20 per caller vehicle, per month. We're using a data connection that already exists. And it's faster than e-mail in arriving.

Shah: Is there a common theme in your investments in how you identified the promising markets and companies?

Alexander: I am a big fan of Peter Lynch who ran Magellan—the greatest mutual fund, the eighties leader and maybe the early nineties. One of his books was about how he made investment decisions. "Folks, you want to know my secret? My secret is really simple. When I walk into a Starbucks and I see what they are rolling out, and I have this feeling that all the employees get it, and they somehow or other emanate what the priorities are: We're fast. We're efficient. We're high quality. Great experience every time. Very consistent. You know what you're going to get when you get that mocha or that hot chocolate. I can't quite define for you all the elements it, or why some businesses get there and some don't, but there is sort of a fundamental feel when a company is on to something. I don't blow off that intuition."

He was in a way looking at trends—what is going to grow and what's not. I think you try to develop within yourself that divining rod, that kind of magnetic compass. If you talk a lot to the right people, you develop your own sort of sense for what the trends are that make sense. Where are things going? I think LBS [location-based services] is going to take off on handsets. I talk a lot to smart people, but even then it's like you kind of have to follow that deeper instinct and develop your own. I like to read what everybody else is doing and follow the same trends of all these other smart people.

Shah: So really being a student of the industry and the market and then you start developing intuition about where it's going and what may stick. Ted, how important is market timing in building great start-ups?

Alexander: I'm a non-timer. I don't believe in timing. I think that it is there through product that needs to be built and if I can build it for Tarang for the fraction of the cost and it has performance that you can't get anywhere else, I am confident Tarang is going to buy it. If I have gross margin built into that product, I can build a business over time. If I am trying to time the market, the reality is if I build that company and there is gross margin in it, I can build a profitable company and survive and it will continue to grow, year in and year out, at a reasonable pace.

In reality, the markets are in our face. We can maybe not sell as many but we will still sell enough to be profitable. Or the markets are behind us and with us. The wind is at our back. We frankly can get a valuation that we are not even worthy of. People pay a lot more for us than it is worth, because people are already paying for shares in other companies that are more than they are worth. Again, to me it is not about market timing as much as it is about having a good vision and solving and executing it.

If the markets are with you or against you, you can still be successful. If you are just trying to quickly stage your company and get your IPO and get yourself out of it, then you are dead. You find yourself chasing trends that are imaginary ones based on people making money vs. people really selling products of deep value. I am chasing markets in the future that are growing and I am also trying to predict the timing of when the market is going to take off.

Shah: What is your definition of "A" players and how do you go about separating As from the Bs and Cs?

Alexander: I would say the "A" players have an insatiable appetite to win. They just love it and they love to compete. For me, I am less excited by strategic thinkers. I frankly like people that are very tactical and have three key priorities for that twelve months with the sub-priorities that fall underneath that, and who can make sure the entire team knows exactly what they are and hold themselves accountable towards each one of these goals.

And they measure individual performance based on the contribution to the larger team goals. I also find that the best leaders have a great deal of humility. I think confidence and humility are kind of hand-in-hand. That is how you really get the most from your people. And you have the best feel for how things are going and how your customers are feeling about things when you are a direct but open listener to what's going on.

I find arrogance really hurts the individual, hurts the team. You don't want the guy with the most "gifts" but frankly can't fit on any really great team and just misses why that is so detrimental to a team no matter how great his gifts are. There is no doubt that some of the A players oftentimes appeal to intellect, but a lot of that comes from a real passion for what they do. It's not because they are the valedictorian of Harvard, MIT, whatever. They just get really passionate about the LBS space or chip design or music, and they dive deep into something that resonates for them.

Shah: Do you fund teams of co-founders only or single founder as well?

Alexander: I would tell you that one lone passionate entrepreneur with a strong vision can really be enough for us to front. Perhaps that person is a long-term CEO or perhaps they are willing to attract that right CEO. They must have the right vision and we'll work with them. It doesn't all have to be laid out. It takes one strong high-quality individual with a good vision, and we're willing to invest and work with him. That's what we've been doing with RockeTalk.

Shah: Does age really matter in entrepreneurship?

Alexander: I would be disingenuous to tell you I don't have an age bias because innately many of the founders and technologists that I have met are exactly that. They are late twenties or thirties, and they just kind of think differently and say, "Hey look. Here is how I can approach this problem," and solve it more effectively than their elders. Frankly, a lot of older people become comfortable with the incomes, with having the executive assistants and having a lot around them.

The young, who we haven't really explored at some levels, have almost a naïve passionate belief that they can do things that the older aren't really tractable enough to undertake. They have almost learned too many lessons. There is a bias toward the younger, high-energy, twenty- to thirty-year-olds. I would like to believe that I am open enough that if there is a talented technical person who has a passion or vision for some new products, some new market, that I might buy it, even from somebody who is in their sixties or seventies. If they show me right thing, I would grab on to it. But most of my entrepreneurs and founders have been in those late twenties, early thirties.

Shah: A lot of investors want to invest in repeat entrepreneurs who have had prior success the second or third time around. Do serial entrepreneurs have the same success rate as the first-timers?

Alexander: Yes and no. The reality is it is hard to have a first success. Who knows, one in four or one in five, if you are venture backed. You can have a second one, sure. Maybe your odds are two in five. It is still very hard. The odds are always against you at some levels. What are you going to do when you back a bad venture? I guess I would rather bet on a success-ful one who has done it in the past than one who hasn't.

Shah: What are the key cultural differences between successful and medio-   ·
cre start-ups?

Alexander: For me, two points always stand out. First one: is this action-oriented energy that comes from high-quality start-ups as opposed to those who only want to sit and meet and strategize. It is like get together, make a plan, and start trialing, changing, and improving upon. It is more the mindset of the high-quality start-ups. It is really about we only have so much time and we have to move quickly to build and execute and do something because many other people have it. Again, high-quality, rapid execution is one point. The next thing I notice is that the culture is very team-oriented. It sounds easy, but really the best start-ups are typically stacked full with a half dozen high-quality, thoughtful leaders and in some circumstances each of them could potentially be a CEO or real leader of a company or division of a big company. They all are very goal-oriented and in sync together.

Shah: What are some of the key characteristics you look for in products you invest in? How do you look at value proposition within those products?

Alexander: The first is really incredible creativity and second is really understanding your customers. Surprising them by knowing their needs bet-ter than they do. My favorite product right now is RockeTalk. I think it is an incredibly creative application. They worked very closely with the consumer to build a product. I think it is a great company and still applying tremen-dous creativity and incredible wisdom. It is surprising the consumers with just what they need.

That is just like the part of Google making the internet really accessible and easy to use, or Facebook allowing me to connect to my friends and family in ways I could not before, or advertisers who want to leverage Facebook and suddenly I am receiving great content on six friends in my network that are driving the Prius. There is [the] latest information on Prius using the Face-book DNA. Now I have the latest information on Prius, more effectively personalizing it to me and something I want to hear.

Shah: What separates an exceptional execution from a mediocre or sloppy one?

Alexander: It is truly exceptional people compared to mediocre and sloppy people. A lot of these people are highly aggressive and know how to lay a great plan and really drive a team effectively together. With my best compa-nies, I can walk up to the front receptionists and say, "What are the key goals for the company?" and they will know. As a group, they know what kind of revenue they need to hit, and by the way, "the CEO is telling us that we are focused on profitability and getting one, large enterprise customer."

With some of my less-organized and less well-led companies, it is a little bit more glossy-eyed. It [all comes down to] a broad picture of what the goals and priorities are and everybody in the team understanding what they need to accomplish and all stroking together in that direction. The most difficult thing is often breaking down the most simple concepts into clear, measurable goals.

Shah: How do you build a sustainable competitive advantage?

Alexander: Some companies uniquely have an unfair advantage. For example, Facebook right now. They have a sustainable competitive advantage by the whole network effect and the whole community effect. Say competitors re-create that somewhere else. How are all these Facebook users going to pull out and move into something else?

I have another company called ID Analytics that is doing identity fraud and credit analysis for many of the large companies—Discover, Citigroup, Bank of America—and really to get our algorithm expertise, you have to give us a bunch of your data. It makes our data network even stronger for the next set of customers. If you and I wanted to build a company that competed with them, it would be hard because these large corporations are already giving them tons of data. It is very difficult for you and me to come in and prove we can be better than them. Their data just continues to get more powerful on a daily basis. Those are really exciting and hard to find, unique barriers in technology companies.

The other kind of barrier is continuous innovation, and it is hard to stay at it. We try to stay ahead of the curve. To some degree, I do not want to be having to play leapfrog the next time, but what I would do is point to some of the companies that I have not felt have been as great. ST Micro is one that has not been innovating, Texas Instruments has been asleep at the wheel.

I like to see companies that make strategic bets. When you look at Google going into mobile, if you asked half [of all] Americans, they would probably say there is no way Google will make it in mobile. And the other half would say, they may pull it off.

I look at the leadership and say, win or lose, there may be a call based on their judgment to grow shareholder value. The reality is, a lot of CEOs in those positions just try to hold on and grow slightly less than the market itself. Why take a risk when they can keep that job for the next five to ten years and grow the company 10 percent on basic momentum? The rest of the industry around them is growing at 20 to 30 percent ,and they look okay because they are growing 10 percent. I still prefer the guy that has the guts, puts it all on the line, and is betting big. They reach for the next big spot. As an investor, I make a decision to go with them or against them. I like people to be victorious and make great calls. I think that is what is exciting.

Shah: I agree. Most people forget that innovation is a hypothesis. You are bound to get some wrong and some right. In the same vein, the start-up is also a hypothesis. It is not like the outcome of the story or the game is known from day one.

Alexander: You have to be willing to take risks. It is so funny how stupid and simple a thesis is. I have studied one thousand of the best people and business people in the world. They have two fundamental traits that have made them successful. One, they are actually not very diversified. They make one big bet and they go along on it. The second point that I think is pretty consistent across many great people, is when they make that big bet, they are right. I thought Apple was going to own the world back in 1995. Then the Palm came out and you thought it was the next great thing. The Palm died as well. Now you have the iPhone.

Shah: Mike Maples is a big fan of the hedgehog vs. fox theory. It is an interesting theory. The fox knows so many ways to capture a hedgehog, but the hedgehog only knows one way to prevent getting captured by the fox. That is good enough for him because the moment he sees the fox, he knows how to roll up like a ball and point spikes outward so the fox cannot touch it. Translation for business is pretty good here. It classifies investors into two groups, hedgehog and fox. The fox knows a lot of things, lot of business models that can be successful vs. the hedgehog who only knows one big thing, only one model that is highly likely to be successful.

For Steve Jobs, it could be just creating an unbelievable consumer experience and then take it all the way. To your point about being more focused than diversified, it really makes a lot of sense. Know one thing so well and be able to take big risks or bet on that one.

Moving on, is the first-mover advantage overrated or does it make a huge difference in the success of the start-up?

Alexander: When somebody says they want to be the first mover, I am usually skeptical. If they want me to fund it and they are going to be the first one, I would say it is more about momentum. Once you have it, it does build on itself. I am never going to fund a company when you are telling me you will get the first-mover advantage.

If I see something that has momentum, like a social network that is growing, that is almost a first-mover advantage that I want to ride on top of. That is how I look at it. It is like a rapidly growing social network that is moving out ahead of everybody. That is great, but I am not going to invest because somebody is giving me a story about how they are going to end up that way.

A lot of business plans come to us, talking about how they are going to have first-mover advantage. It is not something to fund a business upon if it is not already there and you are watching the momentum growing. My job is not to bet on anything. It is really to take money and give it back at a higher return while eliminating all the risk I can. If we can do this, we think we will be first mover. There may already be somebody else who has spent the last year building the product and is ready to launch it the day I am coming in. Hopefully on top of it, we will have first-mover advantage.

Shah: Funny thing is, Facebook was not the first one. There was Myspace and then came Facebook. And Google was probably the ninety-ninth search engine to launch.

Alexander: That is a good point. It connects to your point earlier about how important it is to really know the customer. You get that from talking to your early customers and really understanding what they are looking for and having that continual dialog. Clearly, with all the other social networks up there, the guys at Facebook understood more deeply what people wanted in terms of community and connection, and what is going on in their lives that the other players did not get.

Shah: Who has better probability of winning: a great product with mediocre go-to-market strategy or great go-to-market strategy with mediocre product?

Alexander: In all my companies, there is a love/hate relationship between the sales guys and the engineers. The engineers feel they do not need sales guys because the products are so good. The sales guys look at the "piece of shit" they get, and they say if it wasn't for them, this thing would not move out of this office building. If I had to pick between the two, I will pick an amazing product. I have seen incredible engineers who have a breakthrough product and you show it to a larger corporation, they say "holy cow." They have to have it. The performance of it just stands out so much that you don't necessary have to have a sales force at the onset. Great products sort of rise above the crowd and eventually you can find the right sales people.

Shah: It is incredibly difficult to make products that customers love. It's a tall hurdle. When the start-ups get off the track, at what point do you know they are beyond recovery?

Alexander: It really depends on the opportunity. I have had one semi-conductor company where we invested and understood that the company was at certain points of technological innovation. But as we brought a couple of newer, deeper technical people in, we realized that they weren't getting the kind of breakthrough performance that they thought they were. So we brought due diligence in. We weren't able to ascertain the performance before we invested. Once we recognized that they are not hitting key performance metrics, we just let the founders know, "Look, we know we have probably lost a million dollars at this point, but let's shut it down, and we'll take the other $3 million we have in the company back."

More typically though, you are focused on the milestones that you need to hit. And you know, after the first round, every month you are showing up and you get a sense that you are going to achieve them or you are not. Not often. Once in a while the company is going to hit the milestones, but the market has changed so much or the competition is hitting milestones that are bigger and more meaningful, that it is also not worthy of participating, not worthy of continuing forward.

It's all about looking where you think they are going to get to, whether they get there or not, how far off they are, and if you believe they will actually get there with a little more cash or not. Ideally, we hit these milestones and they have brought on a CEO or are going to get the company into meaningful revenue, call that $5 million-plus, and we are going to have a road to profitability. So we need $3 million more in cash to get it to break even, and so we do a $5 million round with one other investor, and we think we can get $15 million the next round. I'll take that bet for a little more cash to get them there and see if we can get that valuation uptick.

Oftentimes in tech companies where it is not working out, you can feel it in the energy of the general employees as you are walking through and saying hello to people and seeing which companies are excited about the customer interaction and who is wearing their [company] shirts in the office. All the subtleties of the energy in the office and how everybody is enthused or lack thereof communicates to you whether a company is well led and on to something, or is in disarray.

Shah: Do you keep funding the start-up or do you sell it? When you are evaluating that decision, what is going through your mind?

Alexander: If people realize it or not, this is one of the biggest issues for VCs to try to decide—which companies you fund going forward and which ones you do not. There can be a lot of tension because two very small individuals in a VC group may have different opinions about which remaining companies deserve what amount of money. At the end of the day, the decision point has to do not with how much money has gone into the company. Instead, it rather needs to be a forward-looking opportunity based on where it is and that obviously takes into account how well they have executed in the past.

Also, it's about which of the remaining companies is going to have the biggest ROI impact on your portfolio moving forward. It is always nice if you have adequate reserves across the portfolio and everything is executed to plan and there is an equal amount of capital that is left for all of your companies.

But the reality is, you have to work as a team within your partnership, because usually the resources become limited over time and you have to define where those dollars are going to have the most impact for your investors over the years ahead. Our job is not to make every single company successful. Our job is to take one dollar and turn it into ten.

Shah: That does require making a call on which one to let go or stop funding vs. which one to double-down on—put more dollars to work given potential for higher and relatively low-risk return.

Alexander: Some die because they try to keep everything alive. That is where the most tension comes up between the partners in the VC fund.

Shah: Because everybody loves his or her baby.

Alexander: It becomes kind of personal. That is where as VCs we have to kind of drop our egos and really not worry about whether it is my deal or not. We get to support two of these four companies and not worry about whose are whose.

Shah: Within the ones you decide are the winning ones, at some point you will have acquisition offers on the table. How do you decide between keep funding towards IPO vs. taking an acquisition offer now?

Alexander: That is exactly right. What is the best time is to maximize that opportunity? I am familiar with companies in the past that had $200 million offers to be bought, who waved it off and felt there was an half-billion opportunity twelve to eighteen months ahead, only to find that their window passed and the most they can make from it is $50 million or less. You have to be wise as you go through these things.

Shah: What's the role of a VC in building great start-ups?

Alexander: I think building companies is really an art. I feel I have been fortunate to have been mentored by two, high-character, very good venture capitalists with a great deal of humility. They explained to me and taught me the craft of building companies. I view my role as a venture capitalist not as the expert, not as the player who has won four Super Bowls, or who is actually the quarterback on a team, but kind of a coach who is there on the sidelines.

I think sometimes VCs see themselves as players on the field and try to take ownership of the strategy and certain elements of the company that frankly have to be fully owned by the management team and led by the CEO. In fact, VCs are great coaches in building companies and can apply that particular skill set, make better progress to a variety of industries, but the experts and brightest people around any table in any industry are the management team and not the board members or advisors.

Shah: What advice would you give to entrepreneurs who are aspiring to build billion-dollar companies?

Alexander: You have to get more fundamental about the kind of advice you give your kid as he gets older. What are you passionate about? What are the pains in the world that you can solve more effectively? Ideally, that it is a big addressable market, but if your particular passions aren't addressed towards a billion-dollar market, that doesn't mean you can't make yourself a very wealthy man.

I find that the guys at MaxLinear, people at Networks In Motion—they were passionate about building services and products. They saw that ultimately Verizon, Intel, and some of these carriers needed their expertise and technology and said, hey, we can solve that for you. Did they approach it from an aspect of I want to build a billion-dollar company, or I want to have $20 million or $50 million in the bank?

I think when you are focused on making the money, you sometimes miss the gaps in between that really allow you to maximize your skill sets and the areas that you are really passionate about and then apply them more effectively.

All the students that are going to business school say, how do I get rich and become a partner somewhere real quickly? That is not really the question. The question is, what am I good at and how do I take those talents that I have and apply them really tangibly into some team to openly yield some reward for me and my family?

If it happens to be a billion-dollar company, cool. If it happens to be in a small start-up that might grow into something that is worth $50 or $100 million, awesome. But I am going to feel more richly rewarded when I have applied my greatest skill sets to the company that can maximize them the most.

Robert Kibble

Mission Ventures: Greenplum, Shopzilla, Sandpiper Networks

Robert Kibble *is a co-founder and managing partner of Mission Ventures, a Southern California venture capital firm investing regionally in technology companies since 1997.*

Robert worked for twenty-one years as a founding general partner of Paragon Venture Partners, a successful Silicon Valley venture capital firm, investing primarily in early-stage information technology companies. His early career included investment banking on Wall Street, and he was an investment professional at Citicorp Venture Capital. He serves on the boards of directors of Eveo, Nexiant, SodaHead, and Mochila. He is a past board member of the National Venture Capital Association (NVCA).

As a venture professional based in Southern California, I have seen Mission Ventures identify and back some of the region's best entrepreneurs and start-ups, many under Robert's leadership. In this interview, Robert draws from his thirty years in venture investment, discussing some of his most successful investments, such as Sandpiper Networks, Greenplum, and Shopzilla, and providing an end-to-end view on what it takes to build successful start-ups.

Robert delivers balanced insights on market size and timing, entrepreneurs and teams, and business models and products, highlighting not only what he did right, but also things he could have done differently to extract even better value out of investments. His humility and objective view of the start-up building process is especially inspirational.

Tarang Shah: What are the key reasons start-ups fail?

Robert Kibble: Well, there are obviously lots of reasons. Does it fail or is it not as successful as you had hoped? I would say the market is not what it was initially perceived to be. It was different. It was either too small or it's a question of timing—too early or too late. To me, that's probably the biggest single reason.

Shah: Turning the question around, what needs to happen ideally to build a billion-dollar start-up?

Kibble: I think that first, it comes back to market. It has to be a very fast emerging market that takes everybody by surprise, as being as large as it turns out to be, and very fast growing. I think again the market size and the market dynamics are critical.

Second, I think you have to have some significant advantage over competitors who are there already. Or let's assume that it's a market that most people haven't recognized yet. Then it has to be something that makes a company defensible over potential new competition. If it's a deep technology, obviously that helps, because it can give you time to market and a competitive edge. If it's not particularly technology that is a barrier to entry, then I think execution, market momentum, and keeping ahead of the competition makes it so difficult for other folks to follow.

We've got many examples of that. Take the iPhone as an example and think of all the other companies that are trying now to catch up with Apple. It's kind of too late, or maybe a better example is iTunes. The technology for iTunes can't be that difficult. The market timing was absolutely right and they got such momentum right out of the gate that it is really extremely difficult to catch them.

I think all those things: market timing, size of market and momentum, and the ability to erect barriers to entry—technology but not necessarily technology—can set walls. Then execution and great market momentum so that people have a really hard time catching up. We had the good fortune to invest in that type of a content delivery networking company, Sandpiper Networks, but frankly, our initial technology, although it did catch up, was not as good as Akamai, and Akamai really stole the show. We never caught up to Akamai and we sold the company to Digital Island. But Akamai was really the lead and they executed extraordinarily well. They really beat us to market and we just couldn't catch up.

Shah: What are your investment criteria?

Kibble: Well, herein lies the magic of the venture capitalist and the art form of venture capital. You listen to these entrepreneurs, but VCs are not experts in [a particular] technology. VCs are not experts in markets. Even if you find a VC who has a great technical background or comes from Cisco and knows everything about the direction Cisco is heading, you are still not necessarily up to date on the new idea or technology.

For most of us, we are technology voyeurs. We have a sense of what might be an interesting market. But I would say that more likely we have a good sense of what is not an interesting market, and there are plenty of places we would avoid. But in terms of new market opportunities, products and services, it has to be something that really isn't being written about by Forrester or any of these big research firms. It's generally something before it is recognized. And it is tough to get your arms around the market opportunity other than having almost a sixth sense that it stands a good chance of being compelling in a short time frame.

The people who work in that field, the entrepreneurs, often have a passionate belief that their thing is actually going to take off, and there are lots of start-up companies that have that passionate belief. The only way in which we can try to figure out if they are on to something is to listen to their logic, listen to their presentation, read the business plan, and do some—hopefully intelligent—due diligence relating to whether they are right about their intuition, that their thing is really here and now, and that we aren't going to have to wait two to three years for it.

I personally tried to get into two companies that were trying to be YouTube. One was too early and one was too late. The one that was too late was only six months too late. The one that was too early was four years too early. Each company we moved and changed into something else, and they were quite successful but of course they are not YouTube in terms of scale and market impact. They are just real businesses with real revenue and profits.

I think it probably has to do with intuition—listening to the entrepreneurs, their logic of what they say, and doing due diligence, and checking it out. I was fortunate enough to be in a partnership many years ago that was the lead investor in SynOptics Communications, which eventually became Bay Networks and was acquired by Nortel. It was competing with the likes of 3Com, but eventually it was competing with the likes of Cisco. A lot of people at that time turned the deal down because they felt the market was too small. It turned out they were wrong by an order of magnitude.

Frankly, I would have a hard time proving that we were right in pressing on with it. It was just one of those things—an intrinsic sense that if you could indeed put ten megabytes of data on a twisted wire that was already in a building in the telephone cabling, you could form a network that would be immensely useful to people at a very attractive cost. People did want to network their computers together, and the speed limitation was significant. It was a much better technology than using the token ring networking technology.

A lot of people can look at the same facts and do a fair amount of due diligence and reach different conclusions about whether that market is going to take off and whether it is going to be really big. If you look at some of the star performers in venture capital, some people have a better understanding and sense of that than others.

Shah: Tell me about Shopzilla, which turned out to be a big success as well.

Kibble: I think in the case of that company, in a way, the key thought was that e-commerce, new to the internet, was in fact going to evolve on its own and was going to be very big. The reason why we invested in that company initially was that they had gotten what appeared to be an interesting edge, at least at that point in time.

They had a very simple survey that was presented to people upon checkout. They had already signed up one or two fairly large merchants. From checkout the consumer was asked to fill out a very simple survey and its information was aggregated with lots of other data on checkout and was sold back to these merchants as research.

We thought that was a very good toehold to get into the e-commerce stage. It wasn't necessarily a big product-market opportunity by itself, but it could evolve with some very smart people, working right on the leading edge in internet technology at that time. It appeared to be a great opportunity to transition in some way ultimately into a service for serving consumers on the internet with an e-commerce offering.

We did not know exactly how it would be. We had an idea that at one time it would simply be a marketplace we would develop for selling—not really like eBay but somehow being an intermediary with all this information being able to facilitate a marketplace. We didn't really have the vision at the beginning that we could provide a comparison shopping engine. That really happened down the road.

A remarkably talented group of entrepreneurs were at the leading edge in terms of internet technology, and they passionately believed that they could move something forward very rapidly. They had an initial product, which was research of consumer buying habits on the internet. We could transition it somehow or another into providing additional services. That is really what the idea was and what we expected. I think they executed very well, and it could easily have been a disaster because in some ways we were a little too early.

We probably spent more money than we should have. If we hadn't raised $50 million in the last private round, I think the company could have been sold for very little. We had a little bit of luck and the $50 million went down to $3 million and then it started going up and by the time we sold the company, the cash was now up to $26 million. It was a cash machine. If we had only raised $20 million and not $50 million, I think the company would have been sold for very little.

Shah: That touches on market timing and raising enough money to get to the next milestone.

Kibble: The competitor, PriceGrabber, was sold for $400 million or $500 million, slightly less than Shopzilla, but relative to the capital invested in the company, it was actually a much better investment. I say that because it is relevant to your point about timing. Shopzilla really only found its real positive niche with the comparison shopping engine after spending an enormous amount of money, incurring losses, and PriceGrabber founders ended up far more richer than the founders of Shopzilla. In fact, I think the PriceGrabber founders are probably worth a hundred million each. They entered at the right time. Great market timing.

Shah: What are the signs of being too early or too late?

Kibble: You know you're too early if people don't buy your product. You should analyze rapidly customer reactions, and what lies behind them. That's one way of knowing. Too late … there is just competition. People are there ahead of you. I think those are two simple ways. I have had situations where the company recognized it was too early, and we have managed to trim back expenses and buy time and maybe break even, and the market has finally caught up with that, and the company has done quite well since. It has made seriously good strides.

We have a company now where I think that's the case, where we were probably a little too early to begin with. The initial investors had a hard time with the company, and we did the recapitalization.[1] The company went through two CEOs and now it's going great. It's a company called Greenplum.

---

[1] Changed the ownership structure to reflect the current state of the business, which usually means valuing company a lot less than the valuation of the last financing round.

It's in the data warehousing space. It's a software image solution competing with Netezza and Teradata, but it is software only. It runs on HP and IBM hardware.

I would say the timing was too early initially but now it has caught up and the capital investment looks like it was a pretty good bet even though we had to put up with the early difficulties of a slow-moving train. We did move our projections. A lot of entrepreneurs have operating losses. We had more capital in the company than was ideal. We just were frankly too early, and a lot of that capital went to fund losses. But you have to look and see whether the market is still there and what the competition is and what your early-adopter customers are saying.

Later, DATAllegro in Orange County was a competitor but DATAllegro had far fewer customers even at the time it was sold to Microsoft. It really only had two customers. Microsoft bought it because of its technology, which was pretty good. We looked at both companies at the same time actually, which was interesting.

Greenplum really took off about the time Microsoft bought DATAllegro. I don't know what Microsoft has done with it since, so I can't really comment on that, but I know that at the time, we had many more customers and much more revenue than DATAllegro. The market was just beginning to really boom and now the company is doing extraordinarily well and was acquired by EMC in July 2010 for twenty times revenues.

Shah: But the market was still too early?

Kibble: It was still too early, and we had problems with the technology. It took longer to really get it working well. Everything worked out in the end.

Shah: What characteristics do you look for in entrepreneurs you back?

Kibble: There is a difference when you are talking about an entrepreneur and a CEO. Sometimes they are the same person, as you know, but many times they are not the same person. I think that CEOs in management teams are able to thrive and do well in small, high-risk, start-up companies, but they are not the people with the original passion and vision and energy who put everything on the line. You know, mortgage the house, start the thing with your credit card, or what have you. That's the entrepreneur. That's the passionate, visionary entrepreneur. Nothing will stop him or her from trying to achieve their goal.

The best type of entrepreneurs in this case, I believe, are the ones who want to change the world. They have a real passion. They want to do something that really matters. It's not the money that matters to them. They would like to make some money, but that's not the real motivation. The motivation is that they have this passion to do something to change significantly some service or industry because of what they are offering to the market. Those are the type of entrepreneurs I prefer most of all.

Then there are the more mercenary entrepreneurs who may still be very successful, but they are really in it because they want to make a lot of money. They may still do very well, but I prefer the first type if you can find them. I think those are the players that can really make, at the end of the day, a huge difference. Look back on the history of some well known names, and I think Bill Gates, Steve Jobs, and Jeff Bezos are examples. Those are passionate entrepreneurs that want to change the world, and they happened to make a lot of money in doing so, but first and foremost they weren't in it just to make a quick buck.

It would be great if you could find the entrepreneur who could grow into the company's great CEO and take the company through various stages. There clearly are some, but they are few. Bill Gates is one who you would have to say was that person. Michael Dell was that person. There are others closer to home. I guess Irwin Jacobs[2] was that person.

Of course, we all know there aren't that many that can quite do that. They are great entrepreneurs and they transition to founder or chief technology officer. I think Farhad Mohit at Shopzilla is something like that. He transitioned into founder and strategic visionary, and I don't know what he was called—chief technology officer or something. Still an incredibly valuable, brilliant guy, but not really the right guy to build it into a sizable, enduring business.

Professional management is somewhat different. Entrepreneurial CEOs, I don't look at them as entrepreneurs but people who are very good at operating in a small company environment. They can motivate change. They may be on the team right from day one, but they are not the visionary entrepreneurs typically. They are emergency CEOs—someone hired to bring in some order out of the chaos and put some processes in place. He can latch on and articulate the vision of the founder very successfully and be a great spokesman for the company, but he is not the person who came up with the original idea. He is a professional entrepreneurial manager, and those types of people are very valuable.

I think Bill Cook, who is the CEO of Greenplum, was brought in as the fourth CEO. He is doing a terrific job at Greenplum but what was he before?

---

[2] The founder of Qualcomm.

He was VP of domestic sales for Sun Microsystems. He has never been an entrepreneur per se. At Greenplum, he is in an entrepreneurial environment. He is a good CEO for this environment, but he is not the passionate visionary who came up with the data warehousing concept and idea. These are people who are all good at what they do. They can be really valuable.

It is very unusual as we said earlier to find the Bill Gates of this world who can be the entrepreneur and CEO through various phases in the company's growth. There are, I suppose, one or two in every portfolio who will take it to fifty million or one-hundred million or even take it to a billion dollars.

There is one in our portfolio that I like to think is that guy, by the way. We have a company that went public, called MaxLinear.[3] The founder, Kishore [Seendripu], has clearly got the smarts. He has the passion. He has the drive. He was the original visionary. He has a unique ability. He has an MBA as well as a PhD. He has all the basic qualifications and he is sharp enough and adept enough that when he talks about that company he can talk in great depth on every phase of the business, whether it be marketing, sales, operations, technology, or even finance.

The guy is a truly remarkable individual to be running a company, as complex a business as it is, as an international business from day one. I think he is a remarkable individual. He does fit the entrepreneur/CEO mold. Maybe he will reach out for a CEO to replace himself, but I would bet on Kishore to be capable of taking that company to many hundreds of millions and still be successful.

Shah: This is your definition of an A player, right?

Kibble: I think passion is always very important. I think it's good to have a passionate team. I am not sure when you talk about an A player. If you have a good CEO, does the CEO have to be passionate to be an A player? I don't think so. He must be really confident. He needs a high level of confidence in any functional area he is in, and I think we all can recognize it. It's somewhat like tasting good cabernet sauvignon. Most of the time, most of us, will get the better wines right [in a blind tasting]. There will be variations of that and I think the same with management.

If you worked with ten CEOs over a course of a few weeks, most of us would rank them probably more or less the same ranking. This guy is the top one. This one is a B. This one is a C. We would probably have more or

---

[3] A provider of radio-frequency analog and mixed signal semiconductor solutions for broadband communication applications.

less the same answers, and we would have the same reasons they are an A player. It would be related specifically to the function and job that they have in this company, this industry, this time.

The big mistake that venture capitalists make is you sometimes grab someone to be a CEO of a company, and because they have been very good at one thing, you think they can do it in another industry and another segment or other. Many times they can't. There are a few management people that you can almost put anywhere. They will be pretty darned good and successful because they are sharp enough about business and they understand the dynamics of any business and what is really important to that business, and they know how to lead. There are a few people that can transition across every sector and be like an executive athlete of A-capability almost no matter where you put them.

There are other folks who are successful in an area because they grew up in the early-stage business, and they know how the early-stage business works. Put them into a consumer-oriented distribution company where they may have had no prior experience, and they make terrible mistakes. All they do is carry their past prejudices and experience history with them, and they don't adapt it to what is a completely different business environment with different levels of importance. Many people can be an A player in one set of circumstances, but not necessarily in a different set. If you took all the A player CEOs, 20 percent of them only would be transferable A players across almost any industry in any company.

Shah: When we talk about execution, it means many things, but to you, what are two or three things that you sum up as great execution?

Kibble: I suppose first of all they make a good business plan. They are able to adjust quickly to changing circumstances, and they are extremely adept, I think, at driving the company's key operating matrix to success. They really identify what is absolutely key, assuming they get the strategy right to begin with, and they really identify what the most important things are in the company to get right, and they hire the right people, and then motivate people with great leadership.

Great leadership to me is motivating a whole team of people to work flawlessly. And by flawlessly, I mean without a lot of friction. You want people that can finish each other's sentences, who understand the philosophy, the way in which you conduct business, and what's important. They are all working in the same direction and not at cross purposes but very much in harmony. There is a consistency of vision that has been articulated to the company and in a way that really drives results. Very goal oriented. Results,

results, results. There are no shortfalls or failures. That will lead to flawless execution, but it is not easy to do, and it requires very good communication in the company, a sense of good ethics and a real culture. It's consistent with all that.

Shah: What's the key to landing a successful business model?

Kibble: I think at the end of the day, you do have to develop a scalable business model if you are going to build something of real value, of tremendous value. Many of these business models that we look at, and sometimes invest in, unfortunately turn out not to be scalable. I think it is a characteristic of success. You need operating leverage, scalability, replicable processes for serving customers. It has to be scalable.

It is very often the case that you have to zigzag a little bit with the original offering. I think very successful companies have really changed from what they originally intended to be or do. They effect a change because they did indeed find it wasn't scalable on what they were originally doing, although they thought it was, and they needed to adapt, do something that is somewhat different.

Shah: What are the key metrics or milestones that start-ups should strive for?

Kibble: They are different for every company. I think the initial product has to be developed, engineered, and out within a certain time, and within a certain cost. And we've got to plan the initial customers, key customers that will give the company and the product credibility.

Shah: What have you seen the successful companies do to sustain the initial competitive lead?

Kibble: I think these companies are the ones that just come up quickly and are paranoid. You have to continually look over your shoulder and be aware of what is happening in the marketplace, and adapt to what is happening. You must make intelligent decisions to keep your lead and competitive advantage, whether it be developing the next product, which will give you additional performance, or making a key acquisition in order to serve your customers better with a better product line or offering.

I just think it is being very much in touch with a changing market and a changing need for your customers and being ready to serve them with the best possible solution at the best possible price before anyone else can get to them. You can't relax.

Shah: At what point do you know an off-track start-up is beyond recovery?

Kibble: One would be to see that your company is out-marketed, out-performed by competition. Another would be that the company just consistently doesn't seem to be able to make its revenue projections. They have either chosen the wrong market, the wrong pricing, or the wrong business model. They are consuming too much capital relative to what would make it a decent investment. That's where it becomes very difficult.

What do you do? If you try to sell the company now, you'll get almost nothing for it. Do you put a little more in hoping that you can get it to break even? Now you think it will be a more attractive acquisition. It may not be a great exit for you, but at least you'll get your capital back and maybe a little more. It's a real trade-off. That decision is really, really difficult. You know pretty soon if it's going to be okay. They may have a reasonable return at two to one, possibly even three to one if you get lucky on the exit. Then you can identify those that you still believe could really be big winners. As time goes by, it gradually becomes clearer and clearer into what bucket these companies fall into.

Shah: Are entrepreneurs in their twenties and thirties better in coming up with and building billion-dollar start-ups than the older entrepreneurs?

Kibble: Yes, in general.

Shah: Do second-time entrepreneurs have the same probability of success as first-time entrepreneurs?

Kibble: Do I think they definitely have a higher probability of success? Without a doubt. They can't fail. I mean, they do sometimes, but they have a higher probability of success. They have been through the whole thing.

Shah: Do you prefer to invest in new markets or disrupt existing markets?

Kibble: Take Greenplum. It is really disruptive in the existing market. The warehousing market has been around a long while. NCR was the first one to address it back in the eighties, I think. Governments and businesses are absolutely overwhelmed by unbelievable amounts of data. The acceleration in the amount of data that is being produced is just skyrocketing, and that provides an opportunity to disrupt a market with respect to analyzing that information in a much more efficient way. Previously it was impossible.

I think there are some great businesses in which you disrupt an existing market. I would go with the broad generalization, however, that you will make more money probably if you are first in what turns out to be a completely new market.

Shah: Between two competitors, does one with better go-to-market strategy win over one with the better product?

Kibble: Yes, the market strategy over the better product.

27

Rajiv Laroia

Flarion Technologies

Dr. Rajiv Laroia was the founder and CTO of Flarion Technologies, a mobile technology company that was sold to Qualcomm for $805 million in 2006.

Dr. Laroia became head of Lucent's Bell Labs Digital Communications Research Department in 1997, landing what seemed a dream assignment—invent a way to put broadband internet over a wireless connection. While there, he and his team created a technology called FLASH-ODFM, a unique system for carrying the internet over wireless. Believing in the viability of this invention, Dr. Laroia started Flarion Technologies to further develop and market it. The start-up quickly received attention from big-name companies in the industry.

In this interview, Dr. Laroia shares his fascinating journey of taking on giant, established players to become one of the very few wireless start-ups to win the game against the big "gorillas." Starting with how he came up with the idea for a new wireless technology, Dr. Laroia recounts why and how he spun it out of Bell Labs, how he built a world-class team and culture of success, and how he handled a few mistakes made along the way.

Tarang Shah: How did you come up with the idea of Flarion and how did you launch the start-up?

Rajiv Laroia: I would basically describe it as an accident. We were sitting in the lab and we looked at the existing wireless international standard. It was 3G wireless at that time. We concluded that the 3G standard to provide wireless data was designed by people who understood voice communication but did not understand data. These standards really were not suitable for where the world was headed. Being at Bell Laboratories, it was our charter to guide the future of the company and if we did not like where the world was going, it was our job to figure out where it should be going.

So I started this project to design the next generation of wireless data system from scratch. Our only objective was to design the best wireless data system that was not constrained in any way because of what already existed. We started the project inside Lucent Technologies and developed what we thought was a really good system. We did not get any traction inside of Lucent. Nobody was interested. In fact, Lucent felt that our technology was of no value.

We absolutely believed in what we had done, and so I had to find a way to commercialize the technology. I approached the Lucent New Venture Group, whose charter was to spin off technology that came from Bell Labs but was not core to Lucent's business. I told them that Lucent does not want to do anything with this technology, so maybe you should spin it off. They said, "This is great, but it is not our charter. Our charter is to spin off technology that is *not* core to Lucent's business. What you are doing *is* core to Lucent's business."

Of course, I said, "If it's that core, why isn't it getting any traction inside?" So then I went to VCs and raised the funding and we spun the company out of Lucent. Very quickly, Lucent regretted spinning it off, because not only was the technology viable, but it was much better than what existed. Right from the start, we started competing with them and winning against them and that is when they realized they made a mistake.

Shah: Didn't it feel like a risky proposition to let go of a stable job and spin-off as a start-up?

Laroia: It's different for different people. Personally, I thought there was no risk in the whole undertaking. We firmly believed in the technology that we had developed and we knew that it was the right solution. We had so much confidence in our own abilities that there was no perception of any risk. We had confidence in our ability to innovate and solve system problems. Also, seeing how hard it was to do anything inside a big company, we just did not think there was any risk in going on our own. Maybe naively and foolishly at that point, I must admit, because there were risks. We just did not see them.

Shah: How did you validate the concept?

Laroia: The world was setting international standards for wireless data and billions of dollars were being spent in an effort to get technology to the market. It was clear that there was a market. We looked at the standards and concluded that they were inadequate and fell way short of the claims. It was 1999 and they did not even mention the word "internet" even once in those standards. There was no mention of IP [internet protocol] or of how IP would be carried over wireless.

The then-current standards were set by a committee that only understood how to design circuit switched wireless voice systems. They had no understanding of how Internet Protocols would work over wireless links.

When we looked at it, we knew this would never work. The market had been established. It was already there. But there was no technology to fill the void. It was clear to us that the entire world, all the international standards, were headed in the wrong direction. The prevailing thinking was that if you spend enough money you can fix the technology.

There are two ways to design a system to carry data over wireless. One was to build wireless links and then redesign the internet to sit on top of these wireless links. But the internet was far bigger than the wireless piece. The internet already existed and worked fine. The protocol worked fine. So the only other option was to redesign the wireless links so they can carry the same wired Internet Protocols over the air. That seemed like the right way to do things.

There was very little understanding of all of that in the wireless community. So they were just doing what they always did. They were designing circuit switched links over the air. We knew that it's not going to work very well with data traffic.

Shah: I can relate to that. At that time I was marketing CDMA[1] technology and the concept of real-time data wasn't there. The killer app for data was e-mails and other asynchronous communications.

Laroia: For real-time broadband data to function well over wireless, the link has to have a very small delay or it does not work well. If you have a 10 Mbps link but the delay on the link is large, you may not be able to get more than 100 Kbps over this link. The Internet Protocols are flow-controlled and simply do not ramp up to the full rate of the link if the delay [jitter] is large. Without making delay the focus, you cannot get Internet Protocols to work well.

People were designing to the wrong metrics. They did not understand the implications of link delay and were focused on the physical layer capacity.

---

[1] Code Division Multiple Access, a wireless technology commercialized by Qualcomm.

We understood this very well. So we said, "let's design a system with small link delays," and that is exactly what we did.

We knew that all the hype around 3G was not going to make it work. 3G was supposed to be deployed in 1999 and it did not even show up in the market until 2007.

Shah: Would web browsing work well over 3G?

Laroia: Even that didn't work very well. Even if you had a fast, 10 Mbps link, but with a one second round trip delay, a typical web page may require sixty to eighty roundtrips to download. This means that it would take a minimum of sixty seconds to download the page even if it was a 10 Mbps connection.

Shah: How did Flarion compare with other wireless start-ups at that time?

Laroia: There were a lot of wireless start-ups at the time we started, but they were all addressing vertical markets. Nobody was prepared to take on all the big boys of the industry. It appeared to be a very daunting task to take on the entire wireless industry. We believed in our technology so much, and we believed in this area so much, that we were not afraid to take on the entire wireless industry.

Shah: How much actual testing had to be done to see if your technology would really work well to carry internet over wireless?

Laroia: To do the testing, you first have to build. Building requires a lot of money and resources. We did a lot of testing and it worked flawlessly, but it had to be done after we started the company and built the technology. We did not do any testing before we built it because we did not have anything to test.

Shah: So it was only an idea when you started the company?

Laroia: It was only an idea.

Shah: When you spun it off with venture capital funding in 1999, I believe the venture money was not very difficult to land. Tell us a little bit about the venture funding process—how long it took and how easy or difficult it was then.

Laroia: When we were looking for money, it was late 1999 and when it got funded it was early 2000. Back in those days, anything was getting funded. Our job was to make sure that we took the money from the right people. Getting money was not a problem or the issue. I think we did very well on that account. We got money from the right people who added a lot of value to what we were doing. Our VCs were very helpful to us. The only thing we knew was how much money it would take to make it a reality, and that was upwards of $100 million. At that point, it did not scare anybody.

Shah: Did you take a team from Lucent to go with you to spin-off? How did you build the initial team?

Laroia: I was a new department head at Lucent. I had nobody reporting to me when I became a department head. I hired four to five people. I hired them fresh out of graduate school because that is how I wanted it to be. They were fresh guys who did not know much about any of the existing wireless systems. I did not want anybody with a colored opinion of how the wireless system should be. I had four people working with me, all fresh out of school. Nobody, including me, had ever used a wireless system before.

When we started designing the system, I had not used a cell phone. While we were designing this technology at Lucent, all department heads had to carry cell phones, so I got one. I used to lend the phone to the team members by rotation over the weekends. I wanted them to use it and have the opportunity to learn what a wireless system was. We had no preconceived notions as to how a wireless system should work. We just started from scratch.

Shah: And with no experience whatsoever in building wireless products?

Laroia: No experience in building in any products, period. Five of us in that department spun off to the new company. There was one person who used to work at Lucent Ventures on the business development front, who also joined us. So there were six people that spun out of Lucent and started the company—me and four technical guys and one guy on the business development front.

Shah: Tell us more about the how you built the "A" team.

Laroia: The first thing we said was [that] we need a CEO. I was not going to do that job. I had no interest in doing it. Even if I try another company at some point, I know that I do not want to be the CEO. That is a different job. That is not my skill set. If I do that job, I am definitely doing something that somebody else can do better than me and the job that I can do better than anybody else is not being done.

I was very clear that we needed somebody that could focus full-time on running things while I focused on technology and innovation. It worked out beautifully. Ray Dolan joined as the CEO in the first week of May, three months after we spun out in February 2000. We hired a bunch of really good people. We hired somebody really good and experienced from US Robotics who I had known before. Every time I visited companies while at Lucent and met somebody who I thought was really good, I would note that down. I said some day if I ever do a start-up I would call these guys, and I did. They all joined. We had a really, really exceptional team on all fronts—technology, business, and sales. In the end, it was all about the team. If you have the right guys, you can do almost anything. If you do not have the right guys, the obvious mission that seems to be within reach just slips away.

Not to say that we did not make mistakes. We made one or two hiring mistakes in the beginning and it took us longer than it should have to rectify those mistakes. But we did rectify them and then we got good at correcting our mistakes. If we made another mistake, we would be very quick at fixing it. The first time around it cost us a lot and it took us a long time, but that whole process forced us to sit down as a team to figure things out.

In the beginning, everybody was new to everybody. My relationship with the CEO had to mature over time. After we got on the same page, it was easier to identify mistakes immediately. We were really good at making sure that if somebody was not working out as part of the team, we corrected [that] immediately. In a start-up, nobody can hide, so if somebody is not working out, it is not good for them either. They are under tremendous stress and pressure as well. Actually getting rid of the wrong people is a relief to everybody, including the people fired. In a big company, you can do nothing for five years and it would be five years before somebody would discover that you have not done anything. But in a start-up, you are visible the moment you join. Everybody has a piece and if one piece is missing, the whole system isn't coming together. There are no excuses.

Shah: Any mistakes that you can talk about that fellow entrepreneurs can learn from?

Laroia: We made a couple of senior-level mistakes. I do not want to go into details because I do not want to identify anyone. We eventually recovered from those. A senior-level mistake always compounds itself. If you hire the wrong guy, they in turn hire the wrong people, so such a mistakes can be really expensive to recover from and sometimes kill the company. But we did manage to recover from those and learned to not repeat them and correct them before a lot of the damage is done.

Shah: What are some of the dos and don'ts of start-up hiring?

Laroia: If somebody had spent a long time at a big company, then we would scrutinize that hire very carefully because a big-company culture was the exact opposite of what we wanted to create. I remember once we were interviewing someone who spent a long time at [a big company]. He had been working on a small project that was not successful and was shut down. I asked how many people his project had. He said 170. Then he told me that the project was not successful because the company was never committed to it and did not fully staff it. He was talking to a company with 45 people and a very ambitious goal and was telling us that 170 people was not enough to do a much smaller project. I realized this was not the kind of person we needed to bring into the company. He would require ten times the people to do anything.

We developed somewhat of a bias to hire people fresh out of graduate school. They are motivated and enthusiastic, really eager to learn, and their opinions had not been colored by any existing system. We had very few experienced people. There were only two experienced people in the whole engineering team who had ever built anything. One was the guy from US Robotics and other was from a cable modem company.

Shah: This is key. If you are going for something huge and disruptive, less color and more enthusiasm is the combination to go for.

Laroia: But you need some experience too, so we made sure that we had the right guys with the experience. But really, there were only two of those. The rest of the team was just raw. We did hire a very accomplished coding theorist from Bell Labs that really helped.

Shah: Every great start-up has built a great culture. Tell us more about how you built the culture at Flarion?

Laroia: The right culture is very important for a start-up's success. I believe that even if you change all the people in the company, you cannot change the culture of the company except if you change them all at the same time. You can keep replacing people, but you're not replacing the culture. In my experience, companies like Lucent that had a monopoly culture were lost and had no vision. It is specially hard to change the monopoly culture.

Monopolies promote employees for the wrong reasons. You promote people who don't take risks, who like the status quo, who do not have a vision. As a result, it is very difficult for such companies to do well in a competitive environment. I was very painfully aware of this. In contrast, at Flarion, the core team was great because they were all fresh and were willing to learn and design a new system, and in the process they were getting experience that they would normally not get in a big company in twenty years. They were incredibly excited about what they were doing.

Now when you set up a culture, everybody that comes in fits into the culture or they do not survive. The culture propagates and that was very important. The same thing happened at Flarion. The technical team had a very high standard and this set the bar very high for everyone else. Good people want to work where they see other good people. So we ended up with a great business team as well.

Shah: What were some of the key characteristics of that culture? It differs from start-up to start-up, but what was core to your culture?

Laroia: It was a culture of innovation and excellence. Some overhead for processes had to be there but we never had processes for the sake of processes.

We also tolerated people with personality issues and quirks. We tolerated them because we hired them for their talent, not their personality. All bright people have egos and many have other quirks. We decided as long as we could make it work, it was fine and we would put up with their egos. We had a team where we had prima donnas with strong beliefs and opinions. And when people are good, they often have those characteristics. But we decided we should try to live with that. That is what makes these people valuable. We never tried to make ego a big issue and say "this guy said this to me, I am going to fire him." That was never the case. We appreciated people for the value they brought and tried to manage the baggage they brought, but we did not get rid of anybody because of the baggage.

Eventually, everybody saw that and everybody understood that. We put people in the right roles. Obviously, people with a lot of baggage were not put in managerial positions where people skills were the most important thing. They were in technical roles. There were other folks with better people skills that were doing the managerial roles. So the whole thing worked well.

If you have to maintain a culture of excellence and innovation, you have to remember that it is different than running an average day-to-day company. Very bright people have personalities that you have to learn to put up with. It came as no surprise to me. We just had a culture that put up with things.

Now at the end of the day, you realize it is not the engineers that can make that much difference if the company does not have a vision. It takes very few people to take a mediocre team and have them perform like an excellent team. On the other hand, a few wrong people at the top can take an excellent team and make them perform mediocre. You need just one person, like Steve Jobs, who has a vision, and it can make so much difference to a company. The guy with the vision makes so much difference. Vision and leadership. They are both very, very important.

Ray played an excellent role here. The most important thing for the company was my relationship with Ray. We had a great relationship and there was good communication and chemistry between us. We understood each other's strengths and weaknesses and covered for each other's weaknesses and let people play to their strengths. He left all the technology decisions to me and I left most of the running of the company to him. It was an excellent partnership.

Shah: How long did it take for your relationship to jive? Was it six months or more?

Laroia: It was six months to a year. It takes some time for trust to develop in any relationship.

Shah: How did you establish yourself as someone who matters in the market dominated by eight hundred-pound gorillas like Qualcomm, Lucent, Ericsson, etc.?

Laroia: We started trying to compete with all the established players. Everybody saw wireless as the biggest market ever. So the market was established, but since we were a small start-up in the middle of giants, our credibility was questionable. We realized that even though we were good, nobody else knew that. We needed to be very, very credible and visible. It is not good enough to be good, but in that situation, we needed other people to know that we were good.

One key thing that we did early on was to put together a phenomenal technical advisory board. Our technical advisory was the best out there. Then, we got Andrew Viterbi[2] to join our board. That changed how everybody viewed the company and it opened all the doors for us. That was a game-changing move for the company.

Shah: And Andrew could play that role while still at Qualcomm?

Laroia: He quit Qualcomm and joined our board. He also invested in our company. I still remember the first time we approached Nextel. We got a meeting with the Nextel CTO Barry West in no time! We were essentially a no-name company at that time claiming to have the best technology—but then, every start-up claims to have the best technology. We met with Barry and his technology team in Virginia. Barry introduced us to his technology team by telling them that even though we were a small start-up, Andrew Viterbi was on our board so we must know something.

Shah: Because when a guy like Andrew joins your board, that implies that he has done his diligence.

---

[2] Co-founder of Qualcomm.

Laroia: We were competing against CDMA. Our technology was based on OFDMA, which at the time was widely believed to be a non-viable technology with lots of issues. When Andrew, the co-inventor of CDMA, joined our board, people questioned those issues far less than they would otherwise.

Shah: That was a very smart move on your part.

Laroia: All of a sudden we went from being one of fifty wireless start-ups to being "the" wireless start-up.

Shah: What were the key metrics that you were able to show a year later?

Laroia: Working prototypes ahead of schedule. In March 2001, a year after we started, we had working prototypes at the CTIA wireless show and no other company in the world had working prototypes, maybe except Qualcomm. I am not sure about that though. But no one else showed up.

Getting to prototype had to happen like clockwork. In a start-up, there are no second chances. If you put out a schedule and your products do not work, your investors lose confidence. And if you have to go through a second round of funding a year after, it can be very difficult. A second round would have been very difficult to raise if we had missed anything. If the technology did not work or did not work as we said or was late, we would not have been able to do a second round in the middle of that kind of market.

Shah: How did you make sure there were handsets available that can work with your system? Why would someone like Nokia or Motorola make handsets for an unproven system like yours?

Laroia: We built our own handsets. They were prototype handsets. We were also working with Motorola [Nextel's supplier] to incorporate our technology in their handsets. In addition, we built PC cards in seven different RF bands. Since we were non-standard technology and nobody knew which wireless spectrum we would be deployed in, we had to build products in every possible band.

Shah: At Ericsson, I was responsible for a wireless product called CDMA450, which required downbanding 3G systems to the 450 MHz band. We were successful in lining up handset vendors, but it was a tough endeavor to convince them about the market opportunity of this new system.

Laroia: We produced our products in seven different frequency bands including the 450 MHz band. We did different trials in different parts of the world in different bands. We had to make sure we had products in every different band. And we did all this with less than a hundred engineers.

Shah: It's amazing the size of the problem you guys took on. It takes incredible guts to go against the big guys like Ericsson, Lucent, etc.

Laroia: I think we were foolish—we just did not know. But our strength was our motivated and nimble team. I remember that we had to deal with Siemens. T-Mobile was deploying in Europe but they did not want to buy from a small start-up company, they wanted to buy from Siemens. So we were selling to Siemens, who was reselling to T-Mobile.

As part of the diligence, [Siemens] sent a team to New Jersey. I gave the team a tour of our labs. I showed them our base stations, phones, and PC cards and mini-PC cards. After I went through the whole thing, the first question I got was, "how many people did you say you have in the company?" [I answered and] the guy's jaw dropped.

Everybody that was a part of Flarion claims that that was the highlight of their career and the most fun they ever had working. Everybody worked very, very hard, but it did not feel like work.

We were an incredibly motivated team. I will give you an example. Nextel was doing some testing on our equipment. There were two camps in Nextel—one wanted to deploy our technology and the other was in favor of deploying CDMA. There were people inside Nextel that were making our life hard. As they were doing testing, they had physically locked the base station equipment so we couldn't do an important software upgrade that was key for showing our performance.

We upgraded the base station software over the wireless link using our mobiles and restarted the base station. When people have the motivation to do something, incredible things happen. Nextel did not know that we upgraded. They thought they could prevent us by locking the equipment.

Shah: I have seen this time and time again in start-ups that succeed. Their teams do not seem to be hindered by what we call traditional problems. They make thing happen against all odds.

Laroia: We would design something, come up with an idea, and a week later, it would be in the product. In big companies, all the people are just trying to find ways why not to do something. With us, we really had to be looking for ways to do something. If somebody said it could not be done, that was never good enough. We always found a way to do it.

Shah: Any war stories you can share, especially how you took on the big guys?

Laroia: The key thing was, all our competitors, and they were big competitors, did not want to see us succeed. Everybody, all the wireless companies were trying to kill us. Every single one of them. We have plenty of stories. We did a trial with Vodafone in Japan. We had told them that it would take us only six months to build equipment in their band. They said they wanted to not just do a trial, they wanted to compare us to Ericsson's 3G system. We shipped them our system ahead of schedule. Then they delayed the trial a few months because Ericsson's equipment did not show up. After another few months, they just tested our equipment as the competition never showed up. The reason the equipment did not show up was that Ericsson did not want a "Coke and Pepsi" test because they were afraid of the outcome.

Shah: After the merger of Sprint and Nextel, you had a setback.

Laroia: Yes, because Nextel wouldn't be able to buy the commercial system from us anymore, and that was a setback. However, Nextel did an eighteen-month commercial trial on our system in a 1700-square-mile area covering Raleigh, North Carolina. All the big operators and vendors from around the world came to Raleigh to test the system. By the way, Nextel told us that the first four modems sold during the trial were bought by Qualcomm.

Shah: And it eventually led to them buying you guys, which is not a bad thing.

Laroia: They must have liked what they saw. Because during the Nextel market trial, every European operator and vendor sent their team to Raleigh to test the technology. We got so much mileage out of it because everybody could see the performance. We got so much traction with T-Mobile that they started deploying our systems.

Shah: Tell us more about your thinking process when you received an acquisition offer from Qualcomm for a hefty sum. What goes on inside the mind of an entrepreneur when such an offer comes along? How do you decide if you want to sell it now or keep building it towards big IPO?

Laroia: As a founder, I wanted the company to be independent. That was the most fun thing to do. However, most people are only looking for financial return. They do not have any emotional connection to the company, and they should not. Emotionally speaking, I would want to run an independent company and be successful at it and see the technology change the world. However, the key investors are only interested in the financial return. I realized that my objective at that point would be different from everybody else's. If your interest is only financial return, you may decide one way. If there were some additional emotional factors, you may decide another way.

The good thing is, most people's interests are almost completely aligned. We did get interest in buying the company, but one thing I can tell you for sure is, one should never run the company assuming you are going to sell it. You should always make all decisions assuming that you want to run the business. If an interesting offer comes along the way, consider it. At the end of the day, you have to do what is right for everybody involved.

Shah: Any final message for entrepreneurs aspiring to build successful start-ups?

Laroia: Dream big and follow your dream!

Jim Boettcher and Kevin Mcquillan

Focus Ventures: PCH International, Starent, Pure Digital, PA Semi, Aruba Networks, Financial Engines, Centrality, DATAllegro

Jim Boettcher is a co-founding partner of Focus Ventures. He has led the firm's investments in CoSine Communications, Netscaler, PA Semi, Pure Digital, Starent Networks, Telera, and Teknovus. He is more recently responsible for investments in 3VR, Cyan Optics, Infoblox, Marin Software, MuDynamics, PCH International, Pivot3, and Stoke.

Jim initiated customer and partner relationships in Asia for numerous Focus portfolio companies, including Netscaler and Pure Digital. Outside of his work at Focus, Jim has successful investments in companies such as Prism Radio Partners, Deep Tech, Hello Direct, US Filter, and USA Waste. Jim was recently highlighted on the AlwaysOn VC 100 List and Forbes magazine's "Midas List."

Kevin McQuillan *is co-founder and general partner at Focus Ventures. Kevin focuses on investments in the software, internet, and communication markets and has led the firm's investments in Active Software, Agile Software, Alteon Web-Systems, Aruba Networks, Commerce One, Com 21, Copper Mountain, Financial Engines, Pixelworks, Vina Technologies, and Virtusa, all of which became public companies. His more recent investments include BookRenter, Brand.net, Data Robotics, Delivery Agent, LogLogic, Panasas, Reputation.com, Ruckus Wireless, and Sepaton.*

Prior to co-founding Focus Ventures, Kevin was a managing director at Comdisco Ventures and a general partner at Dominion Ventures. He has been listed on Forbes magazine's "Midas List" as a top technology investor and was also high-lighted on the AlwaysOn VC 100 List.

Among the top later-stage venture investors, Jim and Kevin have witnessed start-ups that could execute well and scale to billions as well as start-ups that struggled to scale beyond initial traction. Drawing from their portfolio of successful billion-dollar start-ups, Jim and Kevin provide invaluable insights into why start-ups fail at the growth/scaling stage and the key to execution and pivoting. The duo also dis-cuss how scaling in Asia first can be beneficial for some start-ups; what separates extraordinary entrepreneurs, teams, and investors from others; and how one should exit for maximum value creation.

What I love about Jim and Kevin is their depth and breadth of experience in identifying promising start-ups and scaling them successfully towards the billion-dollar exits.

Tarang Shah: What are some of the key reasons why start-ups fail?

Jim Boettcher: I think number one is poor management. Poor management could be all the way from the board doing a lousy job hiring to the CEO not having the quality people. Two, I would say a part of a lot of start-ups issues is that the market never comes—they're way ahead of the market. They get a product out there and they can't sell it because the market hasn't really developed yet.

It kind of goes with poor management. They have bad judgment. They could be scientists or university professors who just fall in love with their tech-nology, and they think it's great. Rather than doing market research, they just assume that the market is going to be there because they're so clever and they're such geniuses. And they convince some people to raise some money, and they build the product, and they find out nobody wants it. Two years or three years ahead of its time.

Then there are a lot of companies with great ideas, and they should make a lot of money and do well, but they just execute poorly. They don't hire the right people, they don't do the right budgets, they don't set the right priorities, and they don't know how to do sales and marketing. It's just execution. It could be a great idea, a great market opportunity, a great product, but they just aren't good managers.

Shah: What are some of the most common entrepreneurial blind sides you have seen?

Boettcher: Not really taking the time to understand what the market is and what the customers want, and being enamored with their technology. Also sometimes you see people who micromanage. They know how to do it themselves and they hire people who are a little weaker than they are so they can boss them around and micromanage and call all the shots. In fact, successful companies have to build teams, and they hire people who are better than they are, so they can actually accomplish more as a team. But I've seen a lot of cases where you get an egotistical micromanager who wants to make every decision and that just doesn't scale.

Kevin McQuillan: The other issue, too, is most CEOs who fail are too optimistic. They don't seem to have their head in reality about what the market is telling them. They also don't hire quality subordinates. Net-net, they are really not being honest with themselves about what reality is.

Boettcher: At the end of the day, venture capital is a tiny, tiny business compared to all the other corporations out there. They're not that many good managers that can run and scale a start-up to be a successful company.

Shah: What stands out when you run into those good operators? What sets them apart?

Boettcher: I will give you an example of the company we invested in about three to four years ago. It's called PCH International and the entrepreneur is Liam Casey. He named the company after a highway in California, Pacific Coast Highway, also called PCH. He is Irish but he doesn't drink, doesn't smoke, and he has lived in a hotel room in Shenzen, China, for fifteen years building the company from zero to $600 million.

If you meet him, you'll see that he is bristling with energy, bristling with ideas. He's got intense passion, he is all about work, he works 24/7. He travels economy and he has lived in a hotel room for fifteen years running his company. He's got the fire in his belly. When you meet someone like that and you say, "Okay he's got a few flaws, he's got a few weaknesses, but he is a rock-star entrepreneur overall."

I met him five years ago and it was probably two years before we invested. He just had so many rough edges where he was not investable, but we got an ERP system done and we hired a CFO. Finally, after a lot of work, he was presentable enough to take to other venture funds for funding, but you could tell he was a winner. He had that fire in his belly, he had that vision, he had that understanding of the customers and market. He was off to a good start, he was doing a lot of things right, but he just was too rough around the edges.

The board did a great job of helping him hire high-quality people and build the right team around him. Recently, James Fallows wrote about him in a book[1] and called him "Mr. China." He's also done interviews on CNN, etc.

Shah: When you meet with an "A" team or an exceptional team, what stands out about them in the very first meeting?

Kevin McQuillan: I would say the number one thing we look for is whether they really have a passion for the business or whether they are what I would call a hired gun or more professional manager who doesn't care whether he is making widgets or erasers. You want somebody who is really passionate about the business, fairly well connected in the industry, and really wants to succeed. When you hire these professional managers, you can tell they're in it for a job basically, rather than really wanting the company to be successful.

Shah: Does that show up in the very first meeting?

McQuillan: Sometimes it does. Sometimes it doesn't. It depends. I can tell pretty quickly if the person has been a hired gun, or if they booted the founder out, they've got some guy from, say, HP—I don't mean to pick on HP—kind of a middle-level manager who now is CEO of this company. He really doesn't have any passion.

Shah: Versus if the whole team is stroking together with passion, it comes through in the meeting.

Boettcher: Exactly. The dynamics in a meeting are often very telling. If you have a CEO who comes in and brings a CFO and the VP/sales and VP/marketing, but he dominates and doesn't get his team involved in the discussion and presentation, and they just are a bunch of vegetables sitting around the table and he's the dictator, that's usually not a good sign. If a guy interacts with his team and there is a sense of humor and a sense of respect, you can tell and pick up on that. That's what you want to see.

---

[1] James Fallows, *Postcards from Tomorrow Square: Reports from China* (New York: Vintage Books, 2009).

Shah: Jim, in your paper about the China Paradigm Factor, you separate companies into two categories: revenue growth start-ups vs. venture stage start-ups and then explain how you value them differently. Can you tell us more about it?

Boettcher: Well you know it's kind of like today's discussion about whether there is an internet bubble or all these social networking companies are really worth what they are. You've got two ways to evaluate a company. If it's revenue stage, like a lot of our companies, the value of the company comes down to revenue growth plus profitability. It can be baby diapers or internet social networking sites. At some point in its history or life, it's going to come down to revenue growth and profitability. So if it's an established company, it's fairly easy to analyze and do comparables and things like that.

But if it's a start-up and it doesn't have any revenue, then the value equals $P \times S \times E$, where the P is the magnitude of the problem that the company is going to solve. If it's a cure for cancer, that's huge. If it is a better improvement on a baby diaper, that's not so exciting. Big P is what captures venture capitalists' imaginations. If it is the next-generation, solid-state battery that is going to have longer life and many more duty cycles, then P is very high.

S stands for the solution, the elegance of the solution. How unique is the intellectual property, how high are the barriers to entry, how hard is it to execute, how many patents do they have? And so forth.

E is for the entrepreneurial team. A lot of biopharmaceutical companies get high valuations because of the quality of their team. When the company is just an idea, then you have to decide what the pre-money should be for a seed round or a Series A round, and you can use a formula like that. Even those companies eventually, someday, are going to be valued at revenue growth and profitability, but along the way you've got a lot of hype, a lot of psychology, a lot of marketing, and a lot of sizzle to sell. That can change the value of a company dramatically.

Shah: This is wonderful. Kevin, what attracted you to Aruba Networks?

McQuillan: Aruba came to us through a co-investor, Sequoia Capital. We invested with Dominic Orr in a company called Alteon earlier in his career. It was very successful. It was sold to Nortel for five to six billion dollars. Dominic is just one of those passionate guys. He is a great manager. Now he came from HP so he goes against what I said earlier. His view of the world was that all these corporations had to find ways to help their mobile workers get access in corporate databases. And hence the need for the wireless infrastructure for the campuses for these corporations.

We got excited about Dominic because we had invested with him before and made a lot of money on Alteon, we thought it was a great market opportunity, and they were leaders in their space at that time. We also looked at another company previously, before we did Aruba, called Airspace. We came very close to investing, but unfortunately, they turned our offer down and took the cash from Cisco. So we basically invested in Aruba. We did a [ton] of work in this market. We do that a lot—we will go look at a market that we're excited about, we'll look at all the private companies, and we'll try to pick the number-one company in that space. So that's how we got involved with Aruba and why we got excited about it.

Shah: Tell me more about Pure Digital. It's been through several interesting turns before hitting success.

Boettcher: Pure Digital is a very wild story. They were doing something different when we first invested in them. They had started out as a single-use digital camera and video film/camera company and had a distribution deal with a bunch of drug stores like Walgreens, Rite-Aid, etc. The thing that got us in the deal is that the CEO had sold his previous company to a company in Japan and he really wanted our help in Asia to scale the business.

One of the things we did, for example, is hook him up with our portfolio company, PCH International. In three months, PCH designed a complete line of accessories for Pure Digital, and Pure Digital was able to start selling them directly online. All the packaging and the manufacturing was done in China and shipped directly to customers from China, so Pure Digital didn't have to do anything. Pure Digital did about $400 million of revenue last year and the cameras have about a 40 percent gross margin. The accessories did about $150 million in revenue with about a 70 percent gross margin. So the accessories contributed almost as much net profit as the cameras. Now that's the value add and synergies one can create between the portfolio companies.

Shah: Amazing story. What excited you about Starent?

Boettcher: We have a very rigorous process for tracking deals and we sort them out by the top early-stage investors. When they do a funding round, it is usually followed by another funding round ten to twelve months later. Starent was one of those companies that was on our radar. We were in Boston cold-calling on companies and so we said, "Let's check on Starent." We got in there and it turns out that, the day before, the board had decided to do a Series C, and so our timing was very good. Then, we started talking about what was important to Starent and they said, "We can't sell to the tier-one telcos in the US—Verizon, AT&T, T-Mobile and Sprint. They just will not buy from start-ups."

So we told them that we have very good connections in Asia and we can work with you and help you get some customer traction in Asia. Then, once you get that, you can come back to the US and maybe get some success with these big telcos.

We helped them get into KDDI in Japan and helped them with China Unicom. We have a very close relationship with Samsung. Samsung invested in them and actually helped them to secure SK Telecom in Korea. So, when they added China Unicom, SK Telecom, and KDDI, three of the most innovative, progressive mobile carriers in the world, they came back to the US and went to Verizon and said, "Mr. CTO, we're working with three of the most advanced mobile companies in the world. You at least have to give us a trial."

And the guy said, "Wow, I guess you're right." So, he gave them a trial and Verizon said, this is the best system out there. They told Nortel, "we're not buying anymore of your boxes and if you want to sell to us, you should source it from Starent." Then Starent ended up getting Sprint and went to Europe and got Vodafone, and that enabled the IPO.

But all their success started out of Asia. We are doing that with some of our other companies now. We help them get traction in Asia first. The Asians, and even the Japanese, if they see a company that has the best technology, they'll buy it. We have been doing this for over ten years. It's been very helpful, not only to help the portfolio companies, but also it allows us to get into a deal we normally would not have been able to get into.

Shah: There is a very distinct advantage and Asia is not an easy ecosystem to develop but once you have access to it, it's amazing. I know the story way too well. I was lead product manager at Ericsson for their 3G systems and by the time we had the system ready, Verizon, Sprint, and the rest were already buying from Lucent, Nortel, and Motorola. Our first breakthrough was with Tata in India followed by China Unicom. So Asia is a great place to gain initial rapid traction. What's the key to scaling the companies beyond initial proof of concept and early traction?

Boettcher: I think it goes back to management. You must have the right guy that can execute when there is an opportunity. Look at Pure Digital. The management basically read the market and said the single-use camera business is tough, it doesn't scale, it's a much more lower margin than we thought. But some of our customers are showing interest in a reusable video camera, which would be a new consumer product category. They had the vision and courage to go and make that happen, and it became a new category and was a huge success. In the Starent case, the guy knew that it was the only successful telecom infrastructure box company in the last ten years. So he had a very good product, but he had the vision to understand he needed to improve it in Asia before he could come back and make it successful here in the US.

Now there is another company that failed, and we wrote it off, called Clear-Cube. It was a cool product, a blade PC, and it solved space and security functions and manageability. We invested because they had a great initial revenue traction, like zero to $40 million in three years. But they didn't have very good investors. The board got full of themselves, and they raised money and they spent a lot on sales and marketing. It turns out that the addressable market wasn't as big as they thought at those price points.

The early revenue ramp was because of the fact that government, national security, and financial institutions paid a premium for the security and the manageability. But once that was saturated, the prices were too high for the educational, and call centers, and all of the main market. Failing to understand this, the board made a big mistake and they pushed the company to accelerate sales and marketing. They burned through all this money before they realized that and it was just too bad.

But those are three examples where the first two really executed very well. The third executed poorly and that was the board's fault as much as it was the management's fault.

Shah: What are the key metrics you track to make sure your start-ups don't get off track or get ahead of themselves.

McQuillan: We put a plan in place usually in January or December and we go to the board meetings, usually meeting six to seven times a year. You're tracking what the plan was and what adjustments you have to make and making sure they're not spending too far ahead of what the market is telling them.

Boettcher: The good CEOs will know if they will hit the plan or not. I had one company who had a plan of $80 million in revenue this year and they raised a big round and they are going to spend accordingly. Now it looks like it's going to be more like $60 million and so the CEO said, "Okay, we're going to cut back on our spending dramatically in line with our revenues, because we don't want to burn up all our cash before we have proven some next-stage proof points so we can raise money at a higher evaluation." So, it's a dynamic thing. Once you produce your revenue forecast for the year, you have to reduce your cost for the year. That's just good management. Not everybody does that, though.

Shah: Is there a behavior you see in the board meeting that is indicative of the quality management and a well-run start-up?

McQuillan: Yeah, I have a theory. I don't know if Jim agrees with me or not. The better the quality of the board and the investors, the better the quality of the management team. They kind of go hand-in-hand. Now there are always exceptions, but in general, that's what you usually see.

Boettcher: I agree.

Shah: Tell me more.

McQuillan: Just look at the numbers in the venture business. There are four hundred to five hundred active venture funds. There are basically twenty-five that make any money. The vast majority of them have 80 percent of the profits in the industry. Part of the reason for that is because they have access to better-quality companies, and they have access to better-quality managers.

Shah: Does the quality of the current investor show up before you invest or does it unfold post-investment?

McQuillan: I would say both. It's like anything else in life. People want to hang out with successful people, right? Nobody wants to hang out with the duds. The better entrepreneurs want to go with the people who have been successful in the past and who have added value to their previous companies. They need to do due diligence on the venture capitalists just like the venture capitalists do due diligence on the companies and management teams. At the end of the day, it's the management teams that matter, and sometimes investors forget that. They are there to help and give advice, but not run these companies. So in the dysfunctional investor group or board, usually you get one large investor who wants to dictate what the direction of the company should be and a lot of times they're wrong.

Shah: So instead of being a coach, they just want to be a quarterback.

McQuillan: Exactly. If you look at the way that Benchmark Capital is run, they give all the credit to the management teams. They take very little credit themselves. Most of the pictures are not individuals—they take pictures of the group. It's something that they founded the firm on from day one.

Shah: Do you run into cases where you are too late to market as a start-up? It's relatively easy to recognize before you invest, but much harder once you are in the one that turns out to be too late to market.

McQuillan: Yeah. I'm just trying to remember one off the top of my head. We thought it was a great market, we were just too late and weren't the leading company in that space.

Boettcher: Miradia was a Worldview investment and so it actually had good investors. They were developing a competitive video image display chip to TI's MEMS[2] product and their development was delayed. They had technical problems getting the yield up, and by the time they were getting close to getting the yield right, basically the prices had come down and other technologies had cut off and the market just sort of evaporated.

And so even though we were close to getting the product finished, the board just looked around and said, you know guys, we just missed it and so let's just sell the intellectual property and distribute whatever cash is left. That was actually the right thing to do. Because they were a year and a half late, the market just passed them up. The same thing happened at one of our other portfolio companies. They just hit technical problems, we couldn't get the product right, we couldn't get the price points down, and we just basically were too late to the market. The competitor out of England just blew the doors off it.

Shah: What are some of the big market opportunities developing in front of us right now?

McQuillan: I see that cloud computing is going to be a massive opportunity and lots of very successful companies are taking different aspects of that marketplace.

Shah: What do you analyze to build the hypothesis about emerging, promising markets?

Boettcher: Well I think part of it is just intuition. I analyze this using what I call an IT opportunity stack. It's like the seven-layer OSI[3] model. Each layer contributes and interacts with the layer above and below it and if you go up to the top layer, it's application and at the bottom layer it's physical transport. There is a similar thing in the whole IT sector where at the top layer again are applications that interface with human beings—and that's the social networking sites like Facebook, YouTube, and so forth. But as you go down one layer, you come to devices like Pure Digital, and then the layer below, you've got the screens and the touchpads, and then you go down further to the semiconductors, and then you go down to the materials, and so forth.

As you see trends, like mobile computing or social networking, or video on the internet and then cloud computing, you can look down that stack and you can see what the key enablers are going to be. The technology keeps

---

[2] Texas Instruments microelectronic mirrors.

[3] Open System Interconnection.

progressing in all of these areas and is enabling exciting new applications and experiences for consumers. At the end of the day, people have to buy some device to get access to those applications and experiences. Underneath these devices, there is this rich IT technology stack where innovation is occurring and those innovations enable these exciting human experiences.

At the end of the day that's how we work, entertain, educate, and communicate, and that drives every investment in the venture community.

Shah: That's an excellent way to look at innovation. I can just put that together in my head by looking at something like Dropbox as a consumer-facing application. But there is this huge data infrastructure underneath that needs to support that kind of service. And every new consumer-facing application needs the enabling infrastructure that trickles down to various layers in your IT opportunity stack.

Boettcher: The iPad wouldn't be what it is unless Steve Jobs had the vision to acquire PA Semi, which enabled very hot, powerful, but energy-efficient processors. That gave the iPad a ten-hour battery life with high performance. Most people don't care and they don't realize that Steve Jobs had the vision three years before the iPad came out to say, "I want to acquire this company because I want to have high performance, low-power semiconductors in my next generation of products and a whole new category of products."

He thought through what he wanted to do and he just needed to find the right components to put it together. He paid $300 million for eighty-five engineers when he acquired PA Semi. We call it the highest executive recruiting fee paid in the history of venture capital.

Shah: But for such amazing solution to the real problem, he got a steal deal.

Boettcher: Yes. The company had a lot of good backlog and that was a big issue. They had a very good order book and a backlog of design wins. But when Apple bought it, they shut them all down.

Shah: Who wants the competition? That's amazing. What did you guys look at when you invested in PA Semi? It was quite forward-looking as your investment was far ahead of anyone knowing about Steve Jobs' vision of iPad. What attracted you to this opportunity?

Boettcher: That really comes back to execution. PA Semi had one of the best semiconductor design teams on the face of the planet, and that's eventually what Steve Jobs saw. But we saw that early on and said look, this is a great team, and you want to back great teams like this. They're coming up with some very innovative products. We talked to a number of analysts and their customers, especially in the military and aerospace, who said, "These guys have the best products hands down—highest performance, lowest power consumption of anybody out there."

There were a couple of larger competitors, but these guys were getting design wins one after the other, so it was just clear that these guys were winners in their space. Now it takes a lot of money to do what they were doing as an independent company, but it was clear to us that these were the kind of guys you want to back.

Shah: And then your investment hypothesis turned out to be right on spot. When you put together and monitor the operating plan for a start-up, what are the early signs you look for that tell you the company is deviating and getting off track?

McQuillan: You start looking at the pipeline. If the pipeline starts to dry up, and people aren't closing the deals they had promised they would be closing, you know you have a problem. Sometimes the problem is that management teams are pretty optimistic in general and they really don't want to cut the burn rate. They don't want to slow down the spending because they think, we just had a bad quarter or bad month or whatever. A better board would say, "You guys, before you go hiring these additional five to ten sales people, let's really wait another quarter and see if these bookings come along or not." That's where I think a lot of quality boards will step up and basically put some governance on the business. Just wait and see a little bit before you ramp up hiring and spend.

Shah: This is where the quality board stands out from the average board.

McQuillan: If you don't have a strong board, a lot of times they will basically run the company off the cliff. The last thing you want to do is raise money in down quarters.

Shah: That's the worst thing from a valuation and morale perspective.

McQuillan: If you are running a start-up company and you've been telling your family and your wife, "Hey, we're going to make a lot of money here some day. We're just going to raise another round, and it's going to be a little bit higher than the last one." Everybody is excited. It's when you start seeing your equity stake get diluted substantially, all of a sudden all those hours you're working need to be justified, and your wife says, "What are you doing? Go get a real job."

Shah: That's so true. Taking this a little bit further, when you see that the pipeline is drying out, at what point do you know that this is heading into a negative spiral where there may not be a Plan B?

McQuillan: When the market isn't growing, or we're the fourth player in the market and we lost ground in market share. Then you have to start thinking about how can we salvage this, maybe try to sell it. A lot of times what will happen is, like with Pure Digital, we invested in one business but ended up putting a bunch of money on a different business that was somewhat related. Usually if you have really good, smart people in there, somebody is working on a kind of new technology in the background. Sometimes you get lucky and the new technology is pretty intriguing, and you leapfrog a bunch of your competitors. Other times you come to the conclusion, "Guys, we're better off selling this now and getting what we can for it."

Shah: This is a key point.

McQuillan: I'll give you another example. We're in a company with Menlo Ventures called Centrality. What they built were chips for GPS. We ended up selling the company, but we did very well. I will give credit to its CTO for being objective and proactive. We had a board meeting in Asia. The company was doing well, the pipeline was building, revenues were building, and everyone was excited. The CTO took us aside—the board and the CEO—and said, "Guys, we need to sell this now." I looked at him like, why? He said, "Look, you don't understand. The market is going to change drastically in the next twelve months and we're not going to win. The value of this company is going to deteriorate if we wait." The reason was the iPhone and all these other mobile devices incorporating GPS into their platforms.

Shah: The same thing is faced by all the standalone GPS terminals in the car.

McQuillan: Exactly. I give the CTO a lot of credit. He knew what was going to happen and he acted on it. We had the company sold in ninety days. We made a lot of money on it.

Shah: Yeah, and if you had denied the market reality and just waited six more months?

McQuillan: We would have barely gotten our money back.

Shah: That leads into the exit decision. That is one of the key things. How are we getting out?

McQuillan: The best way you make money isn't by selling companies. It is for somebody to come and buy your company. That is where you make your most money. If you are trying to sell a company, you're not going to make very much money. Again, it's all about creating value and making a valuable asset that lot of people want because, like anything else, the more competitors that want to buy your assets, the higher your price is going to be.

EqualLogic is a perfect example. We were about to start the road show, take the company public, and we had EMC and Dell competing for it. Finally that weekend, before we started the road show on Monday at 8 a.m. in New York City, we told Dell if you want to do this it's now or never. Michael Dell told us on that Sunday night that okay, this is a done deal. He knew if he waited until the company went public, it was going to cost a lot more. A great acquisition by Dell because it made them substantial multiples of what they paid us for it.

Shah: If the public market had priced it, they might have had to cough up probably $3 to $4 billion dollars instead of the $1.7 billion they paid to acquire pre-IPO.

McQuillan: Dell had distribution, so it was an easy thing for them to put EqualLogic products through their distribution channels.

Shah: Any other key considerations when it comes to exit decisions?

McQuillan: What entrepreneurs have to remember is that VCs are in the portfolio business. In a single venture fund, we invest in lots of different companies over a fund where an entrepreneur has basically all his marbles tied up in one company. So, if the management really wants to sell, there's not a whole lot the investors can do. Management is usually pretty good about deciding when it's time to take their marbles and go home vs. let's go put some more cash and get another card turned over.

Mike Hodges

ATA Ventures: Tellium, Zoosk, Biometric Imaging

Mike Hodges is a managing director at ATA Ventures. He has built a reputation as an operational wizard, successful CEO and interim CEO, and is credited with several successful turnaround efforts, including Tellium, a telecom networking company that began as a technology spin-off from Bellcore in 1997 (Tellium completed a public offering of $1.5 billion in 2001).

Mike currently serves as a director on the boards of PixSense, Billeo, Clustrix, uCIRRUS, Trilibis Mobile, KreditFly, Medagate, and Zoosk. Prior to his start-up success, he was a division president at Spectra-Physics, during which time it grew to become a $300 million company on the New York Stock Exchange.

Telephony magazine named him as "The Best CEO You've Never Heard Of" and said of him, "Mike is money. He's the first guy you should turn to when the game is on the line and the last guy you should ever bet against."

Drawing from his turnaround successes like Tellium and recent investments such as Zoosk, Mike provides incredible insights on the operational reasons start-ups succeed or fail. He also shares the way he uses key metrics like gross margin to make investment, operational, and strategic decisions.

Tarang Shah: What are some of the key reasons why start-ups fail?

Mike Hodges: The simple answer is that they run out of money before they are able to build a sufficiently profitable business. The companies that fail are the ones that don't execute their plan—the ones that initially claim they can get to cash breakeven on $6 million, but after spending triple that amount are still not there yet.

Investors rarely shut down companies that are "on plan." Assuming that is it not just a lame idea, it's due to execution, and often because the product is late. But in general, the start-ups fail for the following key reasons: 1) poor product specifications, 2) poor project management, 3) a product no one wants—and hence poor gross margins, and 4) general chaos caused by an undisciplined CEO.

Overlaying all of this is what I would call "smoking too much dope." Every-one just being oblivious to reality. This always seems to get worse the higher you go in the organization. If you really want to know what is going on, ask the folks doing the work at the bottom of the pyramid. I like the idea of walking around late in the day, which might mean 10 p.m., and asking engi-neers how they are doing in regard to their schedule. People are more honest at 10 p.m. "What is the chance we are going to make this schedule?"

As information travels up the chain of command, it tends to get more opti-mistic at every upward transition. Often a CEO can be the last to know what is really going on. There is a fine line as a leader in setting a bold vision and being able to lead people where maybe they don't want to go, and mer-rily leading them off the cliff while being oblivious.

Often individually, everyone knows they are not going to make the goal, but the company ethic is that it would be disloyal to state out loud that "we can't possibly hit our revenue number" or "we can't possibly meet our schedule." This is a fine line when you are trying to achieve a very tough goal, but the organization must differentiate "hard" from "ridiculous." Recognizing prob-lems early on and fixing them works. Obliviously ignoring them does not.

I'll tell you a story from when I was a young engineer. I was responsible for the digital section of a system that mated up with an analog section designed by someone else. I would not be able to even test my part until the analog part was completed since my input was his output. My boss came by once and asked me if I was on schedule. I replied, "Sure." Actually, I wasn't but I knew the analog guy was way behind such that I would be done ahead of him. So, to me, I was on schedule. It is like the old story, you know, if a bear is chasing you, it does not matter whether or not you are faster than the bear. What is important is that you are faster than any other guy.

So, the companies fail because "they are on drugs." I am not saying real drugs, of course. I just mean that they are not tuned into reality. They specify things that are really unrealistic to begin with. Then, as things are falling apart, they get more oblivious. This causes them to be late and causes them to lose more money and things continue to spin downward out of control.

Shah: Why do so many projects come in late?

Hodges: Two reasons. Number one is the product specification. It is either not clear, not up to date, or may not even exist. The usual case is that it existed once, but went through continual change that was not managed.

And by a good product spec, I don't mean something that has to be fifty pages long. On two pages of tiny print, you can get all the core specs clearly defined. Two pages that are on the wall of every engineer's cubical, and every single time that there is any change, it gets reflected in this spec. Another really simple concept.

Go into most project teams and ask if they have a spec. The answer will typically be, "Of course we do." Ask to see it and the answer will be, "Well, it's here somewhere. Let me go hunt for it." When you find it and ask if it is current, the answer will be, "Well, almost." When you dig into it, you find it is way out-of-date. The process degrades into hallway conversations and e-mails of someone asking an engineer, "Can you make the bus run a 2 GHz rather than 1 GHz?"

"Okay, I'll try."

Rather, what needs to happen is a disciplined approach where nothing is changed without writing it down and every change is negotiated. You just can't keep adding features and expect a project to still finish on the same date. Either the original schedule was a complete sandbag, which is really rare, or every added feature must result in either another feature deleted or a schedule slip. No one ever wants to believe this reality.

A variation on this topic is that the product is over specified. The best product spec is based on the starting premise of, "What is the minimal feature set that will motivate a customer to buy this product?" Add features on the next spin, but get something out there first.

The number two reason that projects are late is that something key that was assumed would work, didn't work. This is solved by pushing the test of every critical unknown up as early as possible in the schedule. The first task of a project is, how do we test out any core piece of technology that we don't know will work or not. What often happens is that the tough stuff is left for the latter part of the project while the easier stuff is done first. It's human nature to knock off the easy problems first, but it is really bad project management.

This degenerates into the hysteria curve. This is a project where day by day the general level of hysteria rises up to the culminating point of midnight before the product ships, when hysteria peaks. The solution is to invert this curve and force as much hysteria as possible as early as possible such that on the day before the products ships, everyone goes home early. To do this, you must force the organization starting on day one to think of every possible thing that could go wrong, prioritize the list, and make sure you attack the biggest items first.

The first obvious category is to ask, "Does this project require us to do something no one else has ever done before?" The next category is "Does this project require us to do something that no one *here* has ever done before?" These are the first things to jump on and develop tension over. Leave to last the things that you know you can do, since you have done them before. Create sufficient tension early to prevent hysteria later. The above comments were directed at engineering projects, but of course, the same can be applied to sales targets, production targets, and all projects. Create tension early to prevent late-stage hysteria. Plus, you will live longer.

Shah: What is the role of the start-up CEO? What is the one thing that you wished every start-up CEO knew about his or her role?

Hodges: It is really a lot about saying no. In every successful company, there is someone who is strong enough to say no. I briefly met Jeff Hawkins, creator of the Palm Pilot, at the very beginning of his company. He was well known for saying no to a lot of features that were suggested for the product. When the Palm Pilot came out, you just picked this thing up and without the manual or anything it did exactly what you thought it would do. It was very simple. It was everything that you really wanted. Part of why it was great was because it was not cluttered.

If you look at the iPhone or the iPod, I think Steve Jobs is likewise notorious for being hard to please, and I think part of that also is saying no to things that he perceives as crappy. I think if you look at any of the Apple products, they are often faulted for not having some of the necessary features. The iPad does not support Flash—a hell of a thing to say no to. The point is, it is very easy to say yes to all these things that are coming at you. Most people don't like being the bad guy. I would argue that the above two products were great because the respective CEOs said no to a lot of features that were suggested.

When I arrived at Tellium, I found a situation where the management team had said yes to everything. Whatever the customer had asked for was answered with, "yes, we are very smart, we can do it all." If you say yes to everything, it is like saying no to everything because you cannot do everything.

Shah: Start-ups are working with very limited resources. Eventually, you are going to have your back against the wall and you can't afford to lose focus.

Hodges: Yes. Pretty much everyone's job in the company is to say yes. If you are an engineer, your job is to come up with ideas. Your job is not to say, "no, that is a bad idea and I should not think about that." Your job is to come up with ideas. If you are in marketing, your job is to come up with concepts. If you are in sales, your job is to find new customers and maybe markets. All through the organization, people are charged with creating things. Oddly enough, you would think that the CEO would be the superset of the creator of things. But rather, the CEO must have discipline and know when and how to say no. Otherwise, you just end up with a company that isn't productive and can't get the necessary things done.

It isn't that you say no to everything and it isn't that you say yes to nothing, but you have to be willing to make a lot of unpopular decisions, ones that maybe a lot of people will not like. But, nobody else is paid to say no.

Shah: Where do you see the effect of an undisciplined CEO in the start-up?

Hodges: It's in the vision and the purpose of the company, in its clarity, and how well it's communicated and understood at all levels. An interesting exercise is to walk into a company and ask three people what is the purpose of the company. If you get the same answer from all three, it tells you that the CEO is doing their job. One clear statement, not a bunch of nonsense like, "We try to make great products." That does not tell anybody anything. The criterion of a clearly stated purpose is whether people within the organization can use it as a basis to make decisions. A good purpose statement is, "We want to put a computer on every desktop." This tells a lot: the customer, the size, the cost, maybe even the shape, etc. It's very clean and provides guidance.

Shah: Like Steve Jobs said for the iPod, "a thousand songs in your pocket."

Hodges: Yes, that's a great one. Very simple and very clear. Everybody already knows all this stuff, but something goes wrong before we get to the bank. It is like being overweight or out of shape. Everybody knows the answer. But most everyone does not do it. You could stand up in front of a group and say, "You know what, there has been a scientific study that says if you are in good shape you will live longer." Nobody will say, "I don't believe that!" They will all say, "Oh yeah, we know that, but ..." and then the excuses. So it comes down to discipline. Management discipline. And it starts at the top. If the CEO is late to meetings, never documents conversations, changes his or her mind every day in hallway conversations, and never follows up—then this behavior will just be endemic through the whole organization.

Shah: What are the key characteristics of the successful start-ups?

Hodges: When I was much younger, I would have bet on a great team going after a mediocre market over a bunch of mediocre players going after a terrific market. Now I see it differently. I see more than anything else, being in the right place at the right time is unbelievably important. New and booming markets are much more forgiving when it comes to execution. They can cover up a lot of sins. And perhaps the most telling test of a team is how they perform when business stops booming. Often you find out that the market was carrying the team more than you thought. The first order effect is really being in the right place at the right time.

The visionaries that build great companies see something the rest of us don't see. I can remember an early Apple ad showing an Apple II in a kitchen. This was before the first spreadsheet program [VisiCalc], which is really what made the Apple II take off. So at this point, it was just a computer without much software sitting in the kitchen. I thought, "Why would I want that?" It was a product looking for the market at that time.

But then the spreadsheet came out and all of a sudden it took off. The other piece of the magic, besides being lucky and being at the right place at the right time, is whether or not you can come up with a vision of how you can capitalize on that market. The market is one of them, but you have to have somebody who has and can articulate a vision. If you look at great companies, it's a combination of being in the right place at the right time, second, having a vision, and third, being able to capitalize on that vision.

Oracle and relational databases is another example. Relational databases were a subject of interest when I was in college in the seventies. I thought it was interesting, but never thought it would be an exciting market. Larry Ellison saw the same thing I saw, but he saw something a lot more and had a vision of how he was going to build the company on that concept.

The answer to your question is I think, while many people will talk about teams and stuff, to me the highest order of things is the market. Is it a new, booming market that perhaps does not exist yet? Second, you have to have somebody in the company that has a vision of how to penetrate that market.

I will give you one more example. Look at the computer market. Mainframes from IBM dominated in the late sixties. They missed the move to mini-computers and that market ended up being dominated by DEC in the late seventies. Then DEC missed the jump to personal computers. So a big part of it is seeing a market that others miss.

The third thing after market and vision is passion. A passionate guy with a good market vision is unstoppable. Maybe much more likely to succeed than someone with a lot more experience and knowledge. Sometimes it isn't the smartest guy that wins, it is the guy with the best vision in a newly emerging market and somebody who has the passion to work twenty-four hours a day, seven days a week at little or no pay to make this thing work.

Shah: What signs point to the development of a huge market?

Hodges: I guess the first way I would look at it would be to just look at technologies. Recognize that technologies all have lifetimes, typically five decades. The easier picking is in the first and second decade. By the later decades, you are following lots of other folks who have already spent a lot of time digging in the same gold mine. It is very different to enter the personal computer market in the third decade [2000s] vs. the first decade [1980s]. Effectively the market has matured and is different. Think of all the different technologies: computers, personal computers, phones, mobile phones, routers, semiconductors, internet, social networks. All of these are on different timelines. Some of these technologies get reinvented and therefore get to start a new, five-decade lifetime, like phones to mobile phones or computers to personal computers.

Within these lifecycles, the first two decades are the target for VCs. Imagine a gold field with a fifty-year lifetime. Different folks are successful in the first twenty years vs. the last twenty years. Typically, the longer you wait, the more money it takes to establish a new position. Consider the relative cost of funding a semiconductor company today that can compete with Intel and Qualcomm as compared to 1970. All markets tend to commoditize with age and this is not a great place for a lean start-up. Also, the longer that a lot of smart people solve problems within a technology, the fewer openings there are for new entrants. Many times after hearing of a business pitch, I want to say, "Wow, that would be a great idea if this were 1990."

So, timing is an integral part of the market. And if you are starting development on a product, you can't compare yourself with what is in the market today, but what will be in the market in two or three years in the future. The folks at Microsoft, Dell, Apple, etc., are not sleeping. They have a lot of money and they are rolling forward.

Shah: How does one know that the trend that is brewing better be caught now and it's not way too early or too late?

Hodges: Well, that's the tough one. Being too early is the same as being wrong. Being too late is also the same as being wrong. Goldilocks. You have to hit the window. The HP 35 calculator in 1973, the Apple II in 1979, the Palm Pilot in 1996, the iPod in 2001, the iPad in 2010. All great products hit the right market-timing window. Any of them five to ten years earlier or later would have been a different story. It's really tough, so answer how to spot these. We just talk about them after they happen and try to make intelligent comments.

Shah: What attracted you to Zoosk?

Hodges: The guys at Zoosk were one of the first to jump on writing Facebook apps when the APIs were opened up 2007. One of their apps morphed into the product Zoosk is today. What was key was the Facebook connection and bringing a Social Network aspect to on-line dating.

The online dating market is a large and established market. Zoosk went after a whole new segment and they went after it in a different way. They went after the Facebook generation. Rather than filling out a long questionnaire at Match.com or eHarmony, there were no questions. Just put your picture and a short profile up and have fun with it. They went after a big market, but with a new and unique vision. Alex Mehr and Shayan Zadeh are tremendous co-CEOs. I have worked with a lot of CEOs and here are two guys who have little management experience and I would put them in the top 10 percent of all CEOs I have ever worked with. Part of it is being really smart.

The other is having no fear about trying stuff. The environment today allows and rewards experimentation. An example would be the experiments in monetization they went through, from free to an advertising-based model to charging $7, then $19, then $30 a month. Lots of big decisions. If I were in a company twenty years ago and we decided to make such a decision, you would send somebody off to think about it for a couple months, you would have some meetings, you might hire somebody from McKinsey to come in and talk to you. You would try to think your way through the problem.

Shah: And you would do it also in a binary form as to whether you are going to move your entire customer base into subscription-based model from a free, ad-supported model, rather than doing what Alex and Shayan did, which is, let's try this on a very small percentage of my customer base and see what happens. And then move a large part of it to a new model, but still keep some on the old model to see how they are performing against each other.

Hodges: Yes, that's it. I remember, three of us—Alex, Shayan and I—were discussing it on a Friday night at my house and Alex said, "We will try charging $7 per month in Australia starting tomorrow morning and I will call you on Sunday and tell you what happened." That was it. Since they maintained really good user metrics on their subscribers, they were able to analyze the change and quickly draw a conclusion. Within the week they converted their entire user base, which at the time was about five countries, to the new pricing.

Shah: What struck me the most about Alex is how he has recognized that this is an experiment business and you would never know what would work beforehand. You need to know the range of motion and experiment within that range of motion and see what resonates and sticks with your customer base.

Hodges: Since the cost of experimenting is very low, you just keep trying stuff.

Shah: So in these experiments, there is an underlying behavior that you are uncovering that you may not be aware of.

Hodges: It's just that. You don't know and, with an internet-based product, it is easy to experiment. Perform A/B testing maybe multiple times a day where you try small changes and measure their effect. Rather than rely on your intellect to figure out the best method for converting users to paying customers, you take a stab at and then experiment like crazy. If you have twenty million users, you have a lot of data to play with. It's experimentation rather than thinking your way through the problem. It's getting daily feedback rather than feedback from a twice-a-year software release schedule. Very powerful.

Shah: I was reading an article about Edison. It's quite fascinating how he invented quite a few things that have changed our lives, including the light bulb. He in fact pioneered the concept of "dogged trial and error." He was probably the first entrepreneur or inventor you can point to who was extremely good at the "fast fail/iterate" method.

Hodges: You are exactly right. Also, he did not try to think what was going to work, he just tried lots of different filament materials for the light bulb. I think he went through hundreds of experiments of different materials. Let's just try stuff.

Shah: He also had specific metrics to measure whether he was succeeding or not.

Hodges: It is measurement that Zoosk does very well. It is not just trying stuff randomly, as it could easily degrade into just stupidness. It is trying things once you set up a structure, so when you get a result, you know exactly what that result means. And a key aspect of Edison's success was that he was very structured. He took very good notes and he compared all the different filaments against one another so that once he collected a lot of data, he could then turn that data into useful decisions.

Shah: I was a product manager for two major wireless systems at Ericsson and we did product/software releases every six to twelve months. Now we are in the new era of "real-time crowd sourced" product management.

Hodges: That is a great way to put it.

Shah: Having practiced old-school product management, I am fascinated by this new technique. It's the future. Do you think this is very specific to mobile or consumer internet businesses only, where you can experiment fast and cheap? You come up with a feature over the weekend, experiment during the day or within a matter of few days or weeks, and then say, execute this vs. that. I am not sure if you can do that with something like iPhone or iPad. You just have to know that it is going to work when you launch in the market.

Hodges: The deeper you go into hardware, the tougher it is, but the principle still holds. The faster you can iterate and the faster you can get a minimum-featured product into the marketplace, the better off you will be. An extreme example is the three- to five-year design cycle in automobiles. Still you see some manufacturers who innovate incrementally rather than be caught in a very long design cycle.

Shah: Toyota did that beautifully. It took them couple days to change an assembly line to stamp out new cars as opposed to traditional weeks or months.

Hodges: Even if you are in that kind of industry and the examples do not map over exactly in the same way, I still think the basic idea that quickly iterating and launching new products or features is always better if you can. The idea of "crowd sourced" product management can be applied to lots of areas.

Shah: Let's talk about one of your turnaround successes, Tellium. When you were brought into the company to fix it, there were some sixteen to nineteen different projects and only seventy people. You knew right away that this is a crime for the start-up. This could not be done by any measures. How did you narrow it down to few projects that you thought would really make the difference for the company?

What intrigues me is that as investors, why we do want entrepreneurs to go after big markets, but when they are looking at the big markets before inflection point or before the market is clearly defined, it's not very clear what narrow slice of the market will turn into a multi-billion-dollar segment. Those things are not known yet and the market is still in its infancy. At that stage, how do you pick the specific slice of the market and know it could be a huge market segment rather than just cast a broad net and see where it catches some fish?

Hodges: I think it is an easier answer than you might think. It is one of the advantages of coming in as an outsider. It is often a lot easier to see the answer because you are not encumbered with the politics or attachment to the products because they are "your products."

In multiple cases, I came in as a new person and just looked at stuff. My primary tool is gross margin. The price you get in the marketplace for your product is the market telling you information. If people love your product, they will pay you a decent price. If they don't like it so much, they will nickel-and-dime you about the price and you will be forced to cut your price and in turn will be reflected as a crappy gross margin in your P&L. This seems so obvious that it seems stupid to say. But it is just amazing how companies hang onto selling products that are not the ones that customers love, and hence pay a good price for. Companies rationalize and continue to sell low-profit products for all sorts of reasons. The biggest offender is that it is generating a big, top line [revenue]. My view is that for a high-tech start-up company, this makes zero sense.

In the Tellium case, they had three product lines with respective gross margins of 70 percent, 0 percent, and -200 percent. I mean, how smart do you have to be to figure this one out? The 0 percent product had a $20 million PO [purchase order] from Quest, which was impressive for a company with no revenue, but in a market where the price was continuing to fall like a rock. The -200 percent product was technically very cool and we had a lot of IP that really locked up the area, but the reality was no one wanted it for anywhere close to the cost.

I came in as an outsider and said let's kill the 0 percent and -200 percent product lines. We cancelled the $20 million PO. That got a lot of people, including the board, pretty excited—as in, "Are you crazy?" But then we put all of the wood behind one arrow and put all sixty engineers on the 70 percent gross margin product, which was a Layer 2 optical switch. With everyone focused on just one product, it took us six months to get a prototype and another six months to get into production. Lucky for me the product shipped $50 million in revenue in the first year of production, and $100 million in the second.

The compounding problem was that we had across these three product lines twenty-seven different projects. It is often difficult to get the right answer when you ask how many projects are underway in a company. My approach was to get every engineer in the company in one room and start with the first guy and ask him what projects he is working on. Write it in on a big piece of paper and stick on the wall. One project per page with a list of who is on the project. Then go to the next guy. We ended up with twenty-seven projects on the wall. Every person was on three to five projects.

I was an engineer once and I have been to this movie. It is very hard to say no when you are an engineer. You want to work on new projects. Whatever project you have been working on is, by definition, starting to get boring and old. As an engineer, you will always say, "Sure, I will pick that up." But in fact, it is very hard to do multiple things at a time. Especially if you have a software bug or if you have an architecture decision to make. It might take seven to eight hours of just constant focus to work through it. If you are interrupted constantly with multiple meetings and multiple objectives, it is very, very tough. Engineers can do one thing at a time well. Maybe they can do two tasks, but once you get past two, I think it becomes very unproductive.

So, being an unbiased outsider helps. Also, asking the obvious stupid questions is effective. Getting everyone together and asking really stupid questions works surprisingly well. Trying to be the really smart guy in the room usually fails. They end up trying to redesign the -200 percent gross margin product. How's that? Stupid is better than smart.

Let me give you another example. This particular company was doing about $30 million a year with twenty products that had lost money for many years. I was sent in to run it and fix it. It turns out I had a really big advantage because I knew absolutely nothing about the business, which was analytical chemistry instrumentation. I went in and basically made a list of all twenty products and I went with that list to seven different groups.

I went to the controller and asked him which of the products he liked the best—rank them. I went to the manufacturing engineering group and QA group. I went to two salesmen and had them rank the list. I got two friendly customers and had them rank this list. I had them tell me which ones they liked. I had seven lists when I got done, and what was amazing was that they were almost all exactly the same ordered list.

When I thought through it, here is what I realized: if you have a product that the customers really like, the sales guys like it too because the customers like it and hence they can sell it at a decent price. They don't have to discount it in order to sell it. Therefore, the finance guys like it because it is on the high gross margin end of the spectrum. If you go to the manufacturing or QA group, the products they hate are the ones that don't work. The customers figure out which ones don't work and then refuse to pay the price and the sales guys discount it, etc.

In summary, it was really a gross margin list. It seems too obvious to me when you look back on this. It is pretty straightforward. Part of it is bringing no baggage to the conversation. Just walking in and finding what makes money and what does not. The lists are always the same. In this case, we killed half the products and two years later the business was profitable.

In a start-up, if people come to me with an idea where for the first few years the gross margins are going to be 25 percent, I push back. The reply is always that later the costs will come down and that they will raise the price later. Very often they don't, or they do, but very slowly. My gut reaction is, if this is a great product, why won't customers pay a decent price right out of the blocks?

Many times I have had people say their product is unbelievable. It is ten times better than every other competitor. They have everything and the competition has nothing. But then say they want to price it at 10 percent below the competition. Why would they do that? If the features are as good as you are saying they are, you should be able to sell it for double. It's really a test of how good is this product. Lots of folks fool themselves into thinking their product is a lot better than it really is. The best tool to cut through the noise is gross margin. The bottom line is that the price is a message from the marketplace. Listen to it and believe it.

Shah: Assuming the gross margin is very good, how do you make sure that you are going after a huge market opportunity?

Hodges: The harder problem is when you have one product with an 80 percent gross margin, but a very small market, and another product which has 20 percent gross margin, but a huge market. If I were inside a big company, I would answer this question differently, but as a start-up in Silicon Valley, I would say I do not have the luxury to compete in a 20 percent gross margin business because a bunch of other people all of whom may have more money than me will be in there also. If all I can get is 20 percent gross margin, the market is telling me that I really do not have much of a differentiation over the other guys out there.

Shah: I think what you are highlighting here is an interesting concept that I am studying as part of this research. When you look at a start-up, even one that is doing very well, at one point you have to make an exit decision. I have seen that many times. The exit decision is forced closer to the early signs of the market getting commoditized. If you find that your product is already doing 20 percent gross margin, you are probably already into commoditization, which is not going to fetch much value for your start-up.

Hodges: Agreed. If you are struggling to build up a business with 20 percent gross margin, it means that early on your expenses are going to be way more than what 20 percent of gross margin can bring, and so you will be losing money for a bunch of years. This means you are going to be raising a lot of money and selling off a lot of equity in the company. If you cannot sell the company for a lot of money, nobody is going to make money on this deal. This is bad.

The different scenarios are number one, good gross margin, big market. This is one that we all like. Number two is poor margin, small market. No one wants this one. Number three is good gross margin, small market, and number four is poor gross margin, big market.

I would argue number three is a possibility if the funding is managed correctly. This might mean you don't fund it through VCs and organically grow the business with the entrepreneurs retaining ownership of the company. Raising a lot of equity money into this situation may result in no one making any money as the exit price only covers the VC liquidation preferences.[1] Number four is a dangerous area for a start-up and I would stay away from it.

Shah: Wonderful way to categorize start-ups! This is very important for entrepreneurs and investors to understand. Now let's look at the businesses that do not have business models figured out early on. If you look at the early days of Facebook or Twitter, the business model wasn't there for several years in the company's growth. And, arguably, Twitter is yet to nail down the business model. YouTube never had a business model per se, even when they got sold for the hefty sum of $1.65 billion to Google. How do you get market information through pricing and gross margin, when there is none?

Hodges: This becomes a harder problem and potentially a very deep hole to fall into. My answer would be that it must really have a skyrocketing user acceptance. Going back to Zoosk, we funded them in 2007 before there was

---

[1] Typically, venture capitalists get liquidation preferences. A liquidation preference means if the VC had invested $5 million in the company, the first $5 million from the sale of the company will go to the VC first and the rest will be divided among all other investors and the VC, depending on the ownership and other terms.

a business model, but they had already gotten one hundred and fifty thousand users in August, four weeks after launch on August first. By the time the funding closed six weeks later, they had five hundred thousand users. The feeling was if there is this much excitement over a free product, there has to be a market for a paying users within this group. You know right away that something is going on here.

Shah: So the key metric here is that users are eating it up on an exponential curve?

Hodges: It really has to be huge. Google, YouTube, Twitter, and Facebook. All of which had arguably tough monetization strategies at the beginning, but all had huge user acceptance. But it has to be an exploding demand. Ten thousand users downloading something for free doesn't cut it.

Shah: You know that you are hitting the nerve of the market, either when somebody is paying you 80 percent gross margin for your box, or when you are signing up a multiple of one hundred thousand users a month.

Hodges: I have had entrepreneurs come into see me at ATA Ventures and say they have this web idea. This is a true story. I ask them how they will make money. They say that they have no idea, but if we will give them $5 million, they will hire a marketing department so they can figure out what the market is and how to monetize this. My reaction is, "Are you crazy?" Go find one hundred people or a thousand that want to be customers and see how much money they will give you. Start with your mother and your girlfriend, but get some paying customers. Guess what, if they won't buy it, that's a really strong message. Once you have a thousand customers paying you money, then you have some real knowledge of your marketplace. Then you talk to VCs about raising serious money.

Shah: What advice would you give to entrepreneurs aspiring to build wildly successful start-ups?

Hodges: Understand your market. Its needs, pricing, and its window within its own life cycle. Be realistic about pricing information. Be clear on how your product stacks up against others in the market. Does the pricing information from the market jive with your own assessment of your product? Make sure you have good data in regard to the decisions you are making. Be disciplined in your management approach. Be realistic about schedules. Manage with a combination of top-down directed conversation and vision mixed with strong listening.

Shah: We all know that building start-ups is a very hard endeavor. We will not be on schedule. We are not going to ship on time and we are not going to meet our sales numbers. What does a good CEO do at that point? Does he lower the expectations? What is the actionable thing for a good CEO here?

Hodges: If you catch problems early enough and you have a strong and smart team, I think you can brainstorm your way to a solution. Meeting a schedule with the right product should be the expectation. Time is the biggest enemy. This is why you must flush out problems early. As a CEO, you have to be ahead of the problem. You must have backup plans and ways to get early indications of problems. In direct answer to your question, you must be honest. Honest with your investors and board, honest with your employees, and honest with yourself as to the real situation.

If the company severely misses, i.e., crashes, the question the board will ask in regard to the CEO is, was it an issue of honesty, competence, or just bad luck? If it is the first, you won't get another chance. If it is the second, the question is did you learn from it and change? If it is the last, you get to go another fifteen rounds.

Alan Patricof

Greycroft Partners: Apple, AOL, Office Depot, Audible, *The Huffington Post*

Alan Patricof is the founder and managing director of Greycroft Partners LLC. A longtime innovator and advocate for venture capital, Alan entered the industry in its formative days with the creation of Patricof & Co. Ventures Inc.—a predecessor to Apax Partners—and today, one of the world's leading private equity firms with $35 billion under management.

Over the course of his forty-year career in private equity, Alan has been instrumental in growing the venture capital field from a base of high net-worth individuals to its position today of having broad institutional backing. He also played a key role in the essential legislative initiatives that have guided the evolution of venture capital.

Alan helped build and foster the growth of numerous, major global companies, including AOL, Office Depot, Cadence Design Systems, Cellular Communications, Apple, FORE Systems, IntraLinks, Audible, and the Huffington Post. Alan was also an owner/investor in New York Magazine, which later acquired the Village Voice and New West magazine. In 2007, he was appointed to the board of the Millennium Challenge Corporation by President George W. Bush. In 2011 he was reappointed for a second term by President Barack Obama.

Leveraging his forty years of experience as a private equity and venture capital investor and by using examples from some of the best start-ups of the last four decades, Alan provides wonderful insight into what he looks for in the entrepreneurs that he backs; how he identifies promising markets, including online social media;

the importance of company culture; and when and how to exit for maximum value creation.

Tarang Shah: What were the key success elements in the start-ups you were associated with as an investor, including AOL, Apple, and the *Huffington Post?*

Alan Patricof: I would say that in all cases it's always the individual or team that really is the pervasive element that gets one enthusiastic, and secondarily, the idea or the product. In the case of Apple, it was the team and the idea—and the timing was also right. We were not the initial investors but came in a year or so after they had already started to gain significant traction in the market. They did something like $7 million in revenue in the first year of business, virtually. And so the idea had taken hold very quickly. It was a very early trend, called the personal computer, and the idea seemed right for the time. But most importantly, it was the founding team—Steve Jobs, Steve Wozniak, and Mike Markkula.

In the case of AOL, we were coming into a company that had just gone through a Chapter 11 proceeding. Jim Kimsey, who was the CEO, backed by Steve Case, who was the marketing guy, seemed to have a clear vision of how they wanted to use the original AOL platform to go beyond the field of playing chess or checkers or simple games between people, but rather use it as a communications tool. The idea was good, and the people behind it seemed to have a vision of what they wanted to do.

Take the deals we are doing today. It's almost always the people that we're backing first and foremost. Then secondly, understanding whether they have a sound idea and whether they are able to assemble a team. It doesn't relate specifically to those deals, but over the years I found that one of the highest indicators of probability for success is when you find a leader who wants to do something and it's similar to what he did before and he or she is able to attract the people with whom they worked with before. I think that is, to me, the highest indicator of success.

We have a couple of companies that quickly come to mind. You wouldn't have heard of it yet, but one of the companies is called uSamp. It's a sampling business based in California. Another one is a company called Extreme Reach, which is in Needham, Massachusetts. In both cases, these are teams of people who worked [together] before in another company and had a similar background. When the leader had a vision for something new, he wanted to start up, people—I wouldn't say they rushed out the door—but they certainly confirmed the validity of the concept and their confidence in the leadership by joining on. To me, they were voting with their feet—maybe not with their money—but they were voting with their careers. I keep looking for that. I find that is a very strong indicator of success, and I will continue to look for those kind of companies.

So the leadership is critical. Having the charisma, the experience, the team leadership, all of those qualities are very significant.

Shah: This is quite fascinating. So you would give a lot more weight to the guy who has attracted a couple of other individuals who have worked with him in the past over someone who walks in with a business plan without a team of people who have worked with him before.

Patricof: Exactly.

Shah: Is there a better probability of younger entrepreneurs building billion-dollar start-ups compared to their older counterparts?

Patricof: No, I don't think so.

Shah: Do serial entrepreneurs have a higher probability of success than the first-time entrepreneurs?

Patricof: I would think so, because they have been there before.

Shah: What role does the market play in the success of start-ups?

Patricof: Well, today, particularly in the consumer area, we are working on a viral [social graph] basis and I think it's very hard to predict. I mean, no one could have predicted Foursquare. They probably couldn't have predicted Twitter, and yet they have taken off beyond people's expectations. So, I think that we are living in an environment right now where some of the successes have to do with whether the idea just catches on to a public need or a pain point, or to create a new demand.

But, obviously you are trying to identify those big markets. We have a company called Joyent, which is in the cloud computing area, and we believe that that market is about to explode. It is already exploding and it's going to be a giant market, and so we are participating in that marketplace. In that case, we have identified a market.

So there are a limited number of those types of markets you can find, but we keep looking. Another such market is advertising tools. People are trying to find ways to advertise more efficiently. Measurement tools and companies that can do advertising more efficiently by utilizing the social graph, and therefore make better and more effective ads that are more directed, are attractive. I think that is a big trend.

Also, the whole area of local marketing is right now a big market. We have so much more information about consumers now that everybody wants to identify specific types of individuals and not waste coverage and thus make your ads more efficient. That's a very big market opportunity and we certainly are trying to participate in that area. So finding markets is just being alert to what's going on in the marketplace. That's really what it takes.

Shah: Would you prefer to invest in new markets rather than disrupt existing markets?

Patricof: I would rather disrupt existing markets.

Shah: Why so? Is that because the market is known and proven?

Patricof: Well, because in an existing market, companies tend to get lazy and they get complacent and they are committed to the way they have been doing things in the past. Someone who comes along and helps them put a whole new concept of how to do it I think can have a very significant impact quickly.

Shah: And it is hard to move the old dinosaurs, right?

Patricof: Yes. That's an advantage to the new guy. That's why Apple was able to pick off the personal computer market from IBM.

Shah: Is there something particular you look for that tells you that this is the beginning of a big trend?

Patricof: I think it's a question of going to enough conferences and enough meetings and meeting enough companies and getting the sense that there's something happening in a particular area that is getting a lot of attention. Some of it is also luck to get the right instincts at the right time. Today we have thirty-four active companies in our portfolio, and I can't tell you which one is at the start of a dramatic new trend. The only one that gets close with that would be Joyent, which I think is right at the heart of the cloud-computing area.

But in terms of big trends, I think the biggest trend today is the social graph, social marketing, and no one knows what's really going to take off. It's just a question of what catches on. For example, a start-up called Formspring had twenty-five million unique visitors in a matter of months. Is it going to continue to add twenty-five million a month? No one really knows. You have to make some bets and you hope you're going to hit some right ones. When we started *Huffington Post*, I don't think anyone had any concept that it would be this big or this fast. We will have six hundred million page views for last month and forty million unique visitors! Now that's phenomenal.

Shah: Yes, that is phenomenal. Building a media company in such a compressed time frame. Huff Post was the investment from the recent fund I was part of at SoftBank Capital.

Patricof: Exactly.

Shah: What was your investment hypothesis for Huff Post?

Patricof: The founder, Arianna Huffington, had a lot of personality, a lot of style, a lot of good contacts, and I thought she had identified an opportunity which was to become the newspaper of the web. And that's really what's happened.

Shah: Did you look at the blogging market at that time to realize the potential of such blogs?

Patricof: We had been an investor at paidContent, a financial blog, so we had seen the promise of blogs. But that had not escalated to the point that *Huffington Post* did. Tina Brown's got The Daily Beast. It's doing very well, but it hasn't exploded yet like Huff Post. Tina Brown is also very talented.

Shah: And so if you had to separate the personalities or leaders in those and assuming that both are equally good, what separated one site from taking off compared with the other?

Patricof: Well, obviously it's the management team that was attracted to the company. Arianna also hit a nerve in the social environment that would fill the gap in aggregating the online news.

Shah: Existing media companies like CBS and CNN had a huge online presence, but still Arianna was able to walk into the well-established media industry and create something big, right under their nose. Did she disrupt the existing market or create a new one?

Patricof: I think she did both. She showed old media companies a new approach to presenting news in a more attractive manner and she also built the new audience who wasn't there before. She recognized that the web was going to be the source of news. And there have been many other news sources that have come on since then and none of them have reached or achieved the heights that she has.

It has to do with the team she brought in. She also applied a segmented approach to building the company. She started one way, for example just in politics, and then broke into lots of other areas including business news, entertainment news, sports news, health news, etc.

Shah: The traditional model of media was really focused on journalists who publish news on a daily basis in a pretty standard format. Arianna invented the "crowd-sourcing news model" to get news and opinions on current news/issues from qualified subject matter experts and opinion leaders. It is fascinating how she has built it. It is something that existing companies would not have thought of.

Patricof: Yes.

Shah: Alan, you talk a lot about the importance of team. Beyond the initial team of founders, how does one take the core DNA and build it out as they expand the team, like Huff Post has done?

Patricof: I think that to a great extent the CEO creates a culture, creates an environment around their own personality. And I know there are exceptions to the rule, but I really think that at the end of the day, people want to follow someone they believe in whose personality is there and they have comfort that they can pull it off.

The great example of that is Steve Jobs. I think that's critical. The reason I say this is because I have had debates with people who say you can have lots of people who lead companies and have no personality and they seem to do pretty well, so that defies what I've said. On the other hand, I really do believe that a person who has got charisma and can lead and inspire people is very important, but I can't prove it to you.

Shah: Agreed. Compared to established public companies, here you are really creating something so new, and traveling in uncharted territory, that you have to lead with charisma rather than $10 billion of balance sheet behind you.

Patricof: Yes, and you have got to get people willing to go through sacrifice. You have got to get people who are willing to endure hardship. There are times when business is lousy, you've got to cut back salaries, you've got to do all those kind of things, and those are times that you've really got to believe in the person who is the leader. It's like going into battle. Do you have confidence this guy's going to get you out? You wouldn't want to land on the shores of Iwo Jima with someone who you thought couldn't get off the beach.

Shah: That's so true.

Patricof: That's my personal belief. Now other people will then point you to leaders who they say had no charisma and they just pulled it off.

Shah: But that will be the exception to the rule [rather than] than the norm.

Patricof: I believe that being a charismatic person, and having a lot of energy, and instilling confidence in people helps you succeed. Because no matter what the company is, there are always patches of rough periods during a start-up's lifecycle. There is always a struggle at some point to make ends meet and you want to have someone who can make it happen and you want to believe in them.

Shah: Agreed. As you say, there are many rough patches in the start-up's journey from seed funding to exit. Some companies are able to surpass those rough patches and come out okay with a new plan, while others falter and perish. When do you know that the start-up is beyond recovery? What is happening for an investor to conclude that this is beyond recovery or beyond Plan B and needs to be sold or shut down?

Patricof: The easiest way is to consider three critical elements. I always say: it's the people, the market, and the product. You know it's time to not continue funding [when] A—you don't think the people are as good as you originally thought they were. B—the product is continuously late. And, C—the market is just always a step out of reach. That's the no-brainer decision. If you have two of the three, it's a little more difficult decision. But probably it's worthwhile giving a little more support to the company. On the other hand, if all three ingredients are positive, I would suggest supporting the company.

Shah: Some founders continue to be CEO through different stages of the start-ups, whereas others get replaced at some point. I don't think it's done by design, but it happens that way. Do you prefer that the founder retains a continuous role as a CEO or would you say that just invariably there will come a point where I think they just cannot fill the role.

Patricof: Oh yes, very often. The hard thing is changing management. Someone will come in with a great business plan and say that they are going to change the CEO. Well to me that's something I wouldn't even consider initially as an investment.

Remember, the founder has got the energy and the dedication that goes way beyond what someone who is a hired gun has, especially in the early stage of the company. So, I'm not big on getting rid of founders until there's just no other choice because it's hard to replace that passion. Now, you know, Eric Schmidt came into Google but kept two founders in the critical roles and assisted them in achieving their goals. At an early stage that founder is very critical to success.

Shah: Can you shed some light on what triggers the exit? As discussed earlier, it's easy when the company is not doing well. When the company's doing well, what is the thinking process in deciding whether this is the right time to sell or keep funding and growing?

Patricof: First of all, I believe always in getting in line behind the CEO. So if the CEO has said, "I want to sell," I don't ever argue with them. I am not one to force a sale of a company where the CEO still believes the company's got more upside potential. I don't try to second guess the CEO.

On the other hand, if we are in a marketplace where there are excessive valuations around and there's an opportunity which seems to me to be way out of proportion to reality, I certainly at that point would make very strong suggestions to the management to say we are in a period of euphoria and even though we all believe in this, the potential valuations are so out of line to reality that I think we should take advantage of it. But only in that kind of exceptional case. If the company is building and growing, I have a lot of patience. I am not in the school of venture capital that just wants to turn over my portfolio every week or every month or every year. I'm willing to stick with it.

Shah: That makes lot of sense.

Patricof: Somehow everybody knows when the time is right. That's early or late. I think we have had a couple of sales in my new fund that happened in the first eighteen months that we never dreamed of. Someone came along before we even knew our revenues and wanted to pay a price that seemed, in terms of our time frame, that if we held it two or three years more we couldn't get a higher price. That seemed to be something we ought to talk about.

On the other hand, in my first fund years ago, I remember that we held one of the investments past the ten-year cycle of the venture fund. We held it for fourteen years until the time was right and then it returned more than the whole fund.

Shah: So it's a function of extracting the maximum value.

Patricof: The only thing that influences my putting any kind of pressure would be if the market is overheated and excessively valuing something. That's the only time I would interfere.

Shah: Between two competitors, who has a better probably of success—one with better product or one with better go-to-market strategy?

Patricof: I think one with the better go-to-market strategy.

Shah: Is the first-mover advantage overrated?

Patricof: No, I think first-mover advantage is important. I think that first-mover identifies the market. It's hard to move them out of it if they've gotten the share of mind. Like with a very effective market strategy. It's the first mover with a good market strategy.

Ben Elowitz

Blue Nile, Wetpaint

Ben Elowitz is co-founder and CEO of Wetpaint, a next-generation media company that is reinventing the media model on the social web. The company has more than nine million unique visitors monthly on all its web properties combined.

Prior to Wetpaint, Ben co-founded Blue Nile, the largest online retailer of certified diamonds and fine jewelry. He was an early employee at Fatbrain.com, an e-commerce company that went public in 1998 and was sold to Barnes & Noble in 1999. He is also an angel investor in a number of media and e-commerce companies, including Cheezburger Networks, which publishes the ICanHas-Cheezburger blog.

Ben is the author of Digital Quarters, a blog about the future of digital media. In addition, he writes Media Success, a newsletter for digital media thought-leaders. His work has been featured on CNNMoney, TechCrunch, All Things D, the Huffington Post, Forbes, Fortune, TIME, paidContent, and CNBC.com, among others.

Recounting from his successful entrepreneurial journey across several start-ups, including Blue Nile, Ben discusses how co-founding teams are formed, how the start-up idea is borne and initially tested, and how entrepreneurs convert the initial proof of concept into a highly differentiated company that makes it all the way to IPO.

Ben Elowitz: In your start-up success research, what did you find more important—creativity or analytical capabilities?

Tarang Shah: I think something as dramatic as start-up cannot be built with logic alone. There is a unique combination of passion and creativity that gives rise to brilliant ideas that prevail. In very few cases, like Amazon, it started out as a pure financial business plan. In the majority of cases, you really stumble upon the idea based on your past experience and your predisposition to an existing or emerging pain point, where you are applying some new technology to solve that pain point. Somehow that technology is "magically" ready when you show up with your ten thousand hours of dealing with that personal pain point. So there is an element of luck here, being in the right place at the right time.

And in most cases the founders have put themselves in the path of emerging technologies so they know when it's ready for prime time and how best to apply it to their way-too-familiar pain point. In the case of Hotmail, the founders couldn't e-mail each other across LANs and experimented with an emerging, web-based, e-mail concept to solve the problem for themselves, and in the process created a huge company.

The Cisco founders were working on two different networks and they wanted to exchange love notes to each other. So they figured a way to "network the networks" to communicate across islands of networks, and thus figured routers. The Dropbox founders were frustrated [with] carrying files on USB drives between dorm and campus. They leveraged emerging cloud storage technology to solve that personal pain point and built a billion-dollar company out of it.

But to create something like this, which is really a solution for the broader market need disguised as a personal pain point, I think you need to be very creative. How would you come up with an idea like "network of networks?" I think to come up with a start-up idea, one needs to be super-creative while taking that personal pain point way too seriously and feeling that compulsion to solve it. You cannot get there through logic. Most people will just shrug it off as a minor inconvenience and move on with their lives.

Now, on to you. Tell me more about what drove you to entrepreneurship. Is this something you were naturally inclined to from school days?

Elowitz: It is hard to say exactly, but I did several entrepreneurial projects while I was in college, too. Working for myself and starting little projects seemed like a lot of fun. It has never been about money or business. I did not know about money or business then. It was just about the idea of doing something that nobody else was doing, which I loved. I went to junior high in the San Fernando Valley. I lived on the west side of LA. So there were these really long bus rides and it gets so hot in the valley. I just started freezing a couple cans of Coke every morning and then realizing other people wanted them. I love that sense of seeing opportunity. It is not so much the financial side, it is just seeing something nobody else is doing and filling the need.

Shah: So nobody in your family was an entrepreneur?

Elowitz: Not really. My dad was a systems engineer at an aerospace company. He was an entrepreneur on the side, in that he would do real estate investing, but it never seemed like real business for him. Roots wise, my family situation growing up had lots of turmoil. From that, it made me look for something meaningful outside of home. I felt proud to identify myself with work and to create my own success. It is very deep for me; work and entrepreneurship gave me a way to take responsibility for myself and create my own success. For me, it was not anything my parents taught me or pushed me into. Our family was just turbulent. It was hard to get a sense of personal success. I found these other things that I could make important to me that were ownable.

Shah: So that led to you to tinker around with self-employment projects?

Elowitz: I think so. I grew up in a very strongly-identified Jewish home. There is something about Jewish culture that I identified with. In Jewish culture, we are given lots of freedom to explore things and are encouraged to ask questions until we truly understand things. I know that has been important for Larry Page and Sergey Brin,[1] who had that same sense of go explore, ask why, and look for the interesting opportunities. That part for me was strong in terms of values.

Shah: It's fascinating how simple principles like that can be such huge boost to creativity and exploration.

Elowitz: I did not know how unique that was until I met a lot of people as I got older. There's more besides nurture. I enjoy personality studies. On the Myers-Briggs [Scale], I am an NT or, as they call it, a "rational." Those are people who [want to] understand how the world works and why, come up with theories about things, and be able to put abstracts into theories to make sense of the world. So there is nature too.

Shah: Gus Tai[2] and I have had a lot of discussions about that. Both of us think that way when it comes to looking at emerging trends, products, etc.

---

[1] Co-founders of Google.

[2] General partner at Trinity Ventures.

Elowitz: I've heard that "NTs" are only 30 percent of the population, but they are a vast majority of entrepreneurs and a vast majority of tech entrepreneurs.

Shah: Quite intriguing. Tell us more about what transpired you to join your first venture, Fatbrain?

Elowitz: I was the third person hired after the founders started it. Gus Tai introduced me to the founders in 1996. The company went public in 1998, and then it was sold to Barnes & Noble subsequently. [That] was when I left Fatbrain to start Blue Nile, which we co-founded in 1999, and that company also went public. My current start-up, Wetpaint, we started in 2005. In between Blue Nile and Wetpaint, I worked in the dark days of the post dot-com bubble. It did not feel like the right time to start something to me so I went to work for a company called Precor that makes workout equipment, which was a lot of fun. I got what I consider marketing credentials there. Fitness has always been a huge hobby for me.

Shah: Precor makes the best elliptical trainer you can get. Expensive, but I loved them. Let's dial into Blue Nile as a case study. Tell me the story behind the idea and how it came about.

Elowitz: Back in late 1998, Mark Vadon, who was about to create what would become Blue Nile, said he wanted to get together with me and talk about this new idea. I said I was really busy and it took us a bunch of tries before I finally said yes to breakfast.

Shah: How did you two know each other? Was there chemistry between you and Mark when this meeting happened? Had you two built a good relationship leading to this breakfast meeting?

Elowitz: Mark and I had worked together at Bain & Company, which was my first job out of college. Going to Bain was kind of a surprise for me. I was "supposed to" go to Microsoft. I had eight job offers for Microsoft out of college, after I had interned there (and loved it!) during school. A friend of mine said I should look at Bain. I looked at the level of impact I could get and the level of learning I could get, but at Microsoft I would be in my home field. I figured I'd learn more at Bain. Neither Mark nor I were typical for Bain—he had studied Native American Studies, rather than business or economics—but we both ended up there at a white-shoe management consulting firm.

We never worked on a project together, but we were in the same office. He was one year ahead of me. We were both similar in many ways, not consultant clones for sure. We were both more unique individuals. We had been good friends. We saw each other as friends frequently. We had a lot of fun together. I left Bain in 1996 and Mark went to Stanford business school. We spent time together while he was in business school, too. And then we reconnected at the end of 1998. He knew I had gone to Fatbrain and what he saw in me was this person who was pretty far down the curve of building a great consumer internet experience.

Shah: So what happened at the breakfast meeting?

Elowitz: So we got together for breakfast and he said he went shopping for a diamond to propose to his girlfriend, Christine. I said that's great. He said that was not the point. He had been shopping for a diamond and in the process his friend, Jim Bloom, had told him to go online and do some searching there. Jim had suggested a couple sites and Mark had started to narrow in on a diamond he found on one of them.

One day he picked up the phone to call the seller to buy that diamond. He said to the diamond vendor, "Let me ask you something. This diamond is priced at $7,000. That must be a pretty big sale for you to do over the internet and over the phone." [The diamond broker] said it was about average. Mark said, "It must not happen very often, right?" [The broker] said it happens every day. Mark starts the gears turning. He begins to do the math. It was a terrible web site. It was not professional. It had a giant spinning diamond on the cover with a Pink Floyd *Dark Side of the Moon* black background and rainbow prisms coming out of it. Mark says that this [web site] is doing millions of dollars a year in revenue. He is telling me this story [and] I thought, "this is getting interesting." I had been selling computer books, professional books, technical books online, but diamonds? Huh?

He tells me the research he has done. He had market research on how big the jewelry market was and what portion of that is diamonds and what portion is loose diamonds, etc. It was obvious this was a great product for e-commerce. You can afford to ship it, unlike a lot of things that were so difficult, like heavy pet food.

Mark started telling me about the supply chain and the research he had already done to understand how a diamond goes from the mines and makes it to a jeweler. We knew there was a powerful opportunity to restructure the supply chain with scale. For example, we could centralize one inventory instead of having to invest in stocking up a whole bunch of retail storefronts, each of which has to have its own inventory.

As for me, I knew how to make a great consumer experience. I was a young kid, so I have to add a caveat, though: I did not know all that much. We were first generation. We were the right age at the right time. We were in a good spot to say we could totally turn this into something. He asked me to come with him to a fundraising meeting. I was still employed at Fatbrain, but I went to the fundraising meeting with a big VC firm in San Francisco. I showed up and I knew I could not back out now. I remember telling one of my close friends at the time that I thought it had a 30 percent chance of being successful. That seemed like pretty outstanding odds—and ones worth taking.

Mark bought that company, called Williams and Sons, where he bought his $7,000 diamond. He bought the web site, the diamond inventory, and had raised the venture money to complete that deal.

Shah: So, Mark wanted you to join him because you were part of the team that built Fatbrain and you understood how to build a compelling consumer experience on the internet.

Elowitz: The things he knew I would be good at were all the technology. I had studied computer science at Berkeley. I was one of the more technical people at Bain. He knew I would be a good starting person for all the technology and consumer experience aspects.

Shah: How would you describe the similarities and differences in personality traits between you and Mark? In our research we found that co-founders usually have complementary skills. One is more technical and the other is more business-minded. In Apple, Steve Jobs was a business mind and Steve Wozniak was a tech wizard. In Yahoo!, Jerry Yang was a business mind while David Filo was technically very savvy, etc.

Elowitz: I definitely brought the tech and engineering expertise to the mix. Mark is an incredible financial engineer. He is very shrewd. He is a super-smart business decision-maker. We both are analytical. The creative inspiration is often the most valuable part of start-up success and yet I am super analytical. Ironically, I had been pretty creative earlier in my career—until I went to work for Bain. The consulting system does not encourage creativity, so I felt like my creativity was dampened, replaced by things that are valuable, but muting, like professionalism and couth. Though we are both super-analytical, I would guess I was the more creative of the two founders. He was much more business savvy. And also he became a great operator.

Shah: The idea of selling diamonds over the internet would not occur to most logical, analytical people. How did you get comfortable with the idea?

Elowitz: At that time we started seeing people buying things online. There was enough proof that things could be bought online, but, seriously, diamonds? That was still an open question. That was a bet that most people could not get over. Most investors could not get over it either. As far as investors, it does not do you any good if you are too early. Was the time right? That was the other question most investors couldn't get comfortable with.

The great news was that we had a company that was already selling diamonds online. The question was, would transactions get completed online? Our diamond seller was already merchandising products online. He just could not take the transaction without a phone call. We thought: "Just imagine if we made the web site good." Will people actually buy it in a shopping cart?

When our shopping cart went live, we hoped somebody would use it. At the beginning, just like at Amazon in 1996, a lot of people would pick up the phone to call in their credit card numbers. About 50 percent of people wanted to call in with their credit card number, but the other 50 percent were ready to buy online.

Shah: Why diamonds? Because he ran into that? Why not gold jewelry?

Elowitz: It was where we started. There were a few things that made it super attractive. One is, he found this opportunity in a real situation of need; and that gave us an edge by knowing the consumer need well.

And that was where we went deeper. We gained some unique insights about the purchase process, like most customers of diamonds are men and when men are buying anything, there is a more analytical research process. A man wants to buy this diamond for his significant other. He is thinking, I have to buy this and it is so expensive I need to research it like crazy so I know what I am getting. Guys want to know the technical specifications of anything they are buying, whether it is a car, refrigerator, diamond, whatever. So we thought we can help guys with the tech specs on diamonds. We did that. We knew that tech specs had far more of a value-add when you purchase something like diamonds online.

Now these diamonds are certified by the GIA [Gemological Institute of America], so you actually don't have to see it to know exactly what it is. Each one comes with a technical illustration of its unique characteristics, and there is a guarantee when they are certified. Additionally, we can do things online that you cannot do in the jewelry store, like have tons of products and inventory. No physical jewelry store can hold tens of thousands of diamonds. It is too expensive. So the combination of tech spec, huge inventory, and GIA certification became appealing. Once we got up and running and people asked what was key to our brand, we said the product and purchase process has to be designed for men, but loved by women.

Shah: It is not like when man is buying a car for himself. You have to weigh in the other aspect of the purchasing process, who the diamond is for, a woman.

Elowitz: Exactly—we needed to appeal to both, even though their interests are so different. That made it twice as hard! So we looked for examples in brands that had a dual presentation. We looked at Lexus, which was quality and value, so the appeal was with the luxury of a European sedan, but a value price. Breakfast cereal Kix is "Kid-Tested, Mother-Approved." It has to be fun for the kids, because they are the ones who put it in the cart, but ultimately the purchase decision is made by mom, and mom wants to both feed this to her kids as a nutritional component and have them enjoy it. So we studied lots of dual brands like that.

Shah: Is this where your super-analytical brains came to work?

Elowitz: The brand side of it was not Mark and myself. Rather, it was our head of marketing, Carter Cast, who is just brilliant. He ended up being my greatest mentor. He was just brilliant on the brand side. He had not only the analytical discipline to deeply and quantitatively know the customer, but he also had an incredible creative sensibility. He created the brand in his mind and then on a blank sheet of paper. Then he got help from agencies to breathe life into it with design. I would say he taught Mark and myself everything we both know about building brands that are meaningful to consumers. And he built an incredible legacy with his impact on that company. Every employee, I'm told even long after I left, treated the brand standards as holy. Carter's great strength was art, not just science.

Shah: Amazing! What led to the company going IPO vs. its predecessor just running more like a lifestyle business? What had to change to get to that venture-return scale?

Elowitz: One interesting way to look at it is that we restructured an industry that was incredibly fragmented. The number-one player had 3 percent market share. The reason this industry has been so highly fragmented is because it is so capital intensive. To open up a jewelry store, you have to put a lot of money just into inventory. Credit terms in the industry are pretty loose, which created some opportunity. For example, it was not unusual for a corner jeweler to say, "Send me that diamond, and if I sell it, I will pay you, and if not, I will send it back in six months." A six-month loan on inventory. Can you imagine?

What we did, in a way, we professionalized the industry as a whole and that had not been done before. We acted like pros and ran it like a real business. My prior company, Fatbrain, in a lot of ways was run without a real strong professional discipline. I knew I did not want to do that again. We created a brand that was meaningful for consumers and we did that with a branded consumer experience. There are a million executional details underneath that. There are a million things on the supply chain side in terms of being able to have reliable supply in an industry where every SKU is unique like a snowflake.

Shah: That lack of professionalism in the market, lack of standards, always creates opportunity for someone like you to come in and do things differently. Why cannot Amazon add this as one more product? What did you guys do that your competition could not do?

Elowitz: I think there are two things. One is that executionally it is distinct and hard enough that Amazon would have to put huge resources in and would have to do it right. To sell certified diamonds, Amazon would have to enter one hundred thousand SKUs into its system. There would have been no way for the consumers to really figure out how to get what they wanted. The Amazon buying tools are not made for merchandizing it. They are not set up for that. That is the executional side.

The second one is more about understanding the customer. We were obsessively focused on the customer in a way that nobody else nailed. The customer is not just a particular person. Amazon is focused on the customer, but you have to be obsessively focused on their mindset, what appeals to them, the value they are looking for in this considered purchase.

A purchase at Blue Nile took place over a thirty-day period on average. It is like a car. You test drive it, see what you like and don't like about it. Diamonds are the same way, a very considered purchase. There were competitors that treated it like any SKU, they sold fashion jewelry, which is a lot harder to buy and has a lower price point and is harder to maintain stock on. They did not know who the customer was, man or woman. On the supply side, they did not understand the importance of selection and being able to get exactly what you want. One of them grew out of a family business in jewelry and the family business is not set up to offer the consumer what they need, which is the exact right diamond for the most important occasion in your life.

Vish Mishra

Clearstone Venture Partners: PayPal, Overture, Cetas, Mimosa, Ankeena, Kazeon

Vish Mishra has been a venture capitalist with Clearstone Venture Partners since 2002. Clearstone is an early-stage technology fund with more than $650 million in committed capital. The firm has offices in Santa Monica and Palo Alto, California, and Mumbai, India. Clearstone's notable investments are PayPal, Overture, Kazeon, Integrien, BillDesk, the Rubicon Project, United Online, and Vast.

A Silicon Valley veteran, Vish has over thirty years of leadership and management experience in the technology industry, covering computers, internet, communications, and software. He has served as a founder of Telera (sold to Alcatel) and co-founder of Excelan (sold to Novell), generating more than $1 billion in revenues. Vish has also served as a CEO and director of several start-up companies.

Vish is very involved with Clearstone's India strategy and investments. He has spoken at numerous industry and academic gatherings on topics about entrepreneurship, investing, and business-building. Through Clearstone's two-dozen investments with global operations, Vish brings direct knowledge about global investing and business trends.

Vish is also president of The Indus Entrepreneurs (TiE), Silicon Valley, and a trustee of its global board. He serves as an advisor to the Silicon Valley Center for Entrepreneurship at the San Jose State University College of Business. He is also a founding board member of San Francisco-Bangalore Sister City Program.

Vish looks for people who bring smarts, passion, commitment, and integrity to their new venture, along with market knowledge and technology expertise. Vish's

*personal philosophy, "investing in good people is the best way to assure success,"
comes alive in this interview.*

Tarang Shah: What are the key reasons for start-up failure?

Vish Mishra: The number one reason that businesses fail is because of people. "I ran into a marketing problem. I had a sales problem or I had an engineering problem. I had a capital problem." It's all about people. People do business with people. People buy from people. People sell to people. People engineer things. People repair things. I see the common pattern that they blame things on everyone else and the lamppost, but they never accept the responsibility that, hey, we failed because we had a people problem and we did not fix it.

Shah: What is specifically going on in the team that is failing?

Mishra: Teams are failing because they never had a real passion. The thing is that everyone says, "I have really assessed the need. I have really pointed out who I am up against. I know what it takes." It is okay to do all that stuff, but then, instead of succeeding, they end up where something is not going right. They are just not honest with themselves or maybe they are wishful thinkers. The signs are all there, but they failed to acknowledge they are there. "Oh, it couldn't be happening to me. I just found five more leads so let me go and make the sale."

The reality is that they are the first ones to know when something is not going right, so rather than fighting it and hiding it, they should come clean. They should tell the board and investors, "These are the things we have been working on and these are the things that are not working."

We both know how many times the venture has not gone anywhere after being there two to three years and the VC says, "Let's shut this company down," and they stop funding that venture. You put money in the venture, you hire the team, and in your heart you say, "Oh gosh, I was a sucker to fund this guy." And you never shut them down early enough. It just boils down to the people not being open, not being honest, and not taking guidance. The last thing the VC wants to do is to throw out the management. They give you signals, and warnings after warnings. After all that, it doesn't go anywhere and we say we have to remove the management. They knew it was coming.

Shah: What is a key to starting the company?

Mishra: I mentor a lot of entrepreneurs and I am constantly getting them to think in a very logical way about building a business or starting a company.

You start out by identifying a pressing need that exists in the marketplace. Nobody switches products or services or suppliers just for some minor inconvenience or minor cause. People will say, "Gosh if only somebody could solve this problem, I am prepared to do anything."

If you do a poor job at identifying the pressing need, you clearly don't understand the need at all. A guy who is working as a software engineer or maybe a supervisor would say to me, "I have been fighting this problem within my company for three years, but no one pays any attention to me." I tell him that maybe it is a problem for you. You were first in your little domain to run into this problem. But this may not be a pressing need for the masses and you can't build a big company on it. Understanding pressing need is the key.

Immediately after that, one should ask, "Okay, who else is satisfying this need and how well or how poorly?" If currently available solutions are not satisfying the need, somebody else has an opportunity to address it. Whenever opportunity comes along and no one is doing it well, I say, well that means you are going to see the daylight.

Shah: Poor understanding and identification of the pressing need is a common problem among many first-time entrepreneurs.

Mishra: Yes, and I look for entrepreneurs who have really understood the pressing need. They might still not have the technology but know a lot about need.

Shah: How does someone go about validating that pressing need?

Mishra: If you want to start a company, you really have to go to people who will talk to you. Entrepreneurs have to go out to get objective feedback on their ideas. It is one of the most important lessons I have learned. If you say, "I just quit my job and I am starting this company and if I build this product, would you buy?" Most people are really nice and kind, and they will say, "Oh sure, you know I'll buy." That is bogus market research.

My advice to entrepreneurs is to remove themselves from the assessment. Instead, say that a friend of yours is thinking of starting a business on this idea. Ask, "What do you think of this idea?" And people will be more likely to tell you the truth about the situation. Removing yourself from the assessment allows you to get the objective feedback.

The second thing is, if there is a pressing need, it is quite likely that someone else is trying to satisfy it. They may be doing a poor job of it. How else is that being done? I like to really assess how else the need is being satisfied and how well or how poorly they are doing.

The third thing is, what does it take to build a business around this need? What is your approach to it? Your approach has to be substantially superior to the approaches that you have evaluated. It has to be significantly better. Define your approach to solving the problem. Then address what it takes to build the business.

Be honest with yourself. I am really good in architecture. I am really good in engineering. I am not good at all in sales. I am not good at all in marketing. I have no clue about the finances. Be honest. You should identify that it will take these, these, and these kinds of people to build the company, rather than going to the VC and telling him, "Give me the money and I will get everything in place."

Since you are trying to fulfill a need that already exists and there are probably others already addressing that need, you have to be very clear on how you are going to compete with these people. If you don't understand the competitive landscape, just say, "I have no clue." Be honest. Because VCs like you and me who are fronting these guys, we know that nobody is perfect. Any business plan we fund is a plan for the future and it will change as the company builds. But I am looking for the honesty in the entrepreneur—that he is totally in touch with himself. Good entrepreneurs tell you, "I need help here, here, and here. Now it is quite obvious that I don't have all the answers, but then give me the money and I will learn the answers."

Shah: What separates "A" players from "B" players?

Mishra: A players are very secure. If an A player is an engineer, he is very good as an engineer. He may know nothing about sales. He may know nothing about legal matters. He knows that it is perfectly fine to have the best sales guy and the best lawyer to help him out. These players are very self-assured. They know who they are. They are impressed with themselves and they are secure.

B players have to have C and D players around them to say how fantastic they are, how good they are. The B players show up every day to say, "I'm the boss."

An A player will say, "I'm terrific as a technologist. You are a lawyer. I want you to be the topnotch lawyer. I cannot judge you but I will have others judge you."

One common mistake I have seen with start-ups is that the engineers have the tendency to want to know it all. They hire sales people and want them to teach sales to engineers. It is not the university that these guys have joined. This is not what these guys signed on for. They are not going to educate you about sales. If you want to go into sales, then go learn about sales. Don't distract the sales team with your insecurities; you hired them to produce results, not to teach you selling techniques.

I tell people, come to grips with yourself. I'm good here. I'm not good here. We are all alike because nobody is perfect. That's why it takes a team. If you really believe that your knowledge is supreme and you are really good at that, you should feel secure. You should not be threatened by anybody else, just because you don't know sales. Then you can hire the best people to round up the other areas you are not good at. That's what it takes.

Since Larry Ellison founded Oracle, he told everybody, "I can't have anybody else around my engineering. I run it." He is so good. He wants to have his hand on all of his products and technology. Look at how many people work at Apple. But Steve Jobs doesn't want other people to show Apple products or demos. He just says, "That's my gig." These are the people who have succeeded. They know what they are good at and they focus on that and hire best people to surround them in other areas.

On the other hand, Scott McNealy,[1] a hard-driving, super-generous and highly witty and opinionated executive had one big flaw. In my view he never really understood what functional aspect of the business he was really good at. Hence he was not able to make the greatest contribution. He could not be an effective leader toward the end after being at the helm of the company for twenty-six years. For a terrific individual who generated nearly a quarter trillion dollars of cumulative revenue for Sun, we saw him trying to run everything. Competition closed in and Oracle ended up acquiring Sun. Not a great ending for such an iconic, innovative company.

A good company that succeeds, whether it is a start-up or large company, has a good board where there is a good mix of people who bring a lot of experience on the board. I start bringing in guys who are more knowledgeable. I think it is all about having the right talent so the board is very, very informed, but also making sure that you are constantly looking at your team and saying, "Okay, who is really developing, or who is not developing? Who do I replace and who do I keep?" The VCs are constantly challenged. Team is a big component. You need a combination of both the team and VC, especially when you are building the company.

You also have to be looking ahead. What is your next territory, or region, or the market that you are going to conquer? Companies have failed in that

---

[1] Founder of Sun Microsystems.

respect. Money is coming in. Everyone is busy, but you forgot you have to keep your product fresh and the team evolving.

Shah: How do you go about picking entrepreneurs and building start-ups?

Mishra: We have a unique way to help build companies. We look for brilliant entrepreneurs with deep insights in a market or in user behavior and then co-create companies with them. This has led to the creation of over a dozen companies in the enterprise and consumer markets. As I mentioned earlier, concept validation and building a product that customers need are key to start-up success. We expose these entrepreneurs to our network and connections of potential customers and industry experts to help the company shape and validate their products and services. It also helps founders attract the best talent to grow their companies. Let me illustrate this through the following story of strong relationships with driven entrepreneurs that resulted in the creation of four important companies.

Enter T. M. Ravi, with a PhD in Computer Science from UCLA. I knew him as a personal friend who had achieved remarkable success as an entrepreneur and top executive. He was ready to quit entrepreneurship after his last venture. He credits me for literally talking him out of it. I said, "You are too young to retire. Why don't you meet my partner Sumant Mandal and explore some ideas?" Ravi went on to start Mimosa Systems. He named it after the street, Mimosa Way that he lives on in Portola Valley in the Silicon Valley. Mimosa was incubated at Clearstone and offered a novel way for the archiving, discovery, and compliance of email for businesses. It was successfully sold to Iron Mountain in 2009, where Ravi became Chief Marketing Officer.

Brilliant entrepreneurs typically associate with other brilliant entrepreneurs, and that is how we met Sudhakar Muddu, a friend of Ravi and also a PhD from UCLA. Muddu co-founded Sanera, a cutting-edge storage company that was acquired by McData. Muddu also was exploring his next venture and he became an Entrepreneur-in-Residence (EIR) at Clearstone and incubated Kazeon with Sumant Mandal's involvement. Kazeon revolutionized the way online information can be classified, managed, and retrieved. Clearstone helped Kazeon in many ways, from helping find co-investors, customers, employees and even a board member. Kazeon was acquired by EMC and Muddu moved to EMC to fulfill his obligations.

When Muddu was ready for his next big challenge, he partnered again with Clearstone and as a result, Cetas was conceived in Clearstone's Palo Alto offices. Cetas provides "big data" analytics as a cloud service. Clearstone provided seed capital and provided working space in its offices for nine top engineers. Many of these engineers were known to Muddu through his prior companies. Ravi left Iron Mountain and joined his friend Muddu as Executive Chairman of Cetas and also became a venture partner at Clearstone.

As Mimosa and Kazeon were becoming mature companies, we started engaging with Prabakar Sunderrajan and Rajan Raghavan, serial entrepreneurs with major successes—and friends of Ravi, Sumant and me. Clearstone helped start their company, Ankeena, in the burgeoning video space. Clearstone seed-funded Ankeena and assigned one of our associates to join their team. Ankeena provided a purpose-built, online, high-performance scalable video switch and was acquired by Juniper Networks.

Shah: That's amazing how working with Ravi led to four successful start-ups.

Mishra: Absolutely. The common thread here is that we try to find the A entrepreneurs and help them incubate their ideas, and they in turn attract other A players to build businesses with us. That is the fun of venture capital—finding and funding A players and building great companies with them.

Rich Wong

Accel Partners: Angry Birds, Atlassian, AdMob, 3LM

Richard Wong is partner at the venture capital firm Accel Partners. His investment focus is software, mobile, and internet services. Rich led Accel's investment in Angry Birds (Rovio) and serves on the boards of Atlassian, SunRun, MoPub, Qwilt, GetJar, and Parature. Rich previously led Accel's investment and served on the board of AdMob (acquired by Google), as well as 3LM (acquired by Motorola Mobility).

Prior to Accel, Rich was a senior vice president at Openwave, and an executive vice president at Covad Communications.

Rich is a key thought leader in rapidly emerging open-mobile ecosystems driven by Apple's iOS and Google's Android. Drawing from his expertise in the mobile sector, Rich provides incredible insight into two aspects key to start-up success: the authenticity of the entrepreneur and the ability to rapidly test and iterate.

Given our common focus on mobile sector, I had the good fortune of spending a little time with Rich. What I love about Rich is his depth and breadth of knowledge in the mobile sector and how he combines that with his sharp business acumen to identify and build some of the biggest players in the mobile sector.

Tarang Shah: What are the key reasons for start-up failure?

Richard Wong: I spend a lot of time thinking about a phrase, "the authenticity of the entrepreneur." What is the problem and opportunity that they are trying to solve? Very often, it takes on average five to seven years for something to play out to its ultimate success. In five years, it will definitely have changed several times in that period. The competition, the customer base—there are so many dynamic changes in the environment.

If you are an entrepreneur looking for a momentum play, maybe you read something or hear that certain sectors are "hot," you may not be in the right game. Even smart people that might try to learn quickly—sometimes they can get it right and sometimes get lucky enough to hit the momentum and winds at the right time. But more often than not, it takes longer than you think and it changes in the meantime.

If you are not an authentic entrepreneur, if you are not someone that really lives the space and has built the product for yourself, oftentimes you can miss a turn on the route. That authenticity of the entrepreneur is one of the most important things I think you have to look for.

One of the best examples are the two co-founders of Atlassian Software, Mike Cannon-Brookes and Scott Farquhar, who were both software developers graduating from the University of NSW in Sydney Australia. They built a software development platform—JIRA—"for themselves," solving the needs they felt weren't being addressed as software developers. In a short seven years, initially funded by only $10,000 from credit cards, they have been able to grow their business to over $100 million. What's unique about this is that they did it with *zero* salespeople—a great example of two authentic entrepreneurs, creating a spot-on product that was able to "sell itself."

Shah: That is great insight. Tell me more about it in reference to your investment, AdMob.

Wong: This is not the founder Omar Hamoui's first start-up. This might be his sixth or seventh start-up—few have heard of most of the earlier start-ups. I believe his last start-up was a company called fotochatter. It was basically some photo-sharing mobile site. He was essentially an independent mobile developer trying to figure out how to make money and then acquire traffic for his mobile photo-sharing web site. In that sense, he is a highly authentic entrepreneur who really knew what it meant to be a mobile developer.

In the first few years of AdMob's growth, it was not initially large advertisers who provided all the advertising. It was the other mobile sites that advertised to drive traffic. These sites were built by mobile developers like Omar himself. So Omar understood the issues and challenges faced by these developers in gaining mindshare and driving traffic. This authenticity allowed him to really build a product that catered to the key pain-point of the rapidly emerging mobile developer community. No one predicted the launch of something like iPhone, but the introduction of the iPhone and the mobile development community around it put his company into altogether a different orbit. That led to AdMob's success, and ultimately an acquisition by Google.

There is a company that is not as well known right now. It is a company called GetJar. They are an alternative to the app store. We just have to make sure that it becomes a real market segment and not an irrelevant segment. It is double-digit millions in revenue. There was this unknown guy in Lithuania, named Ilja Laurs. A lot of people said, "You are crazy. Not only is this not in London or the Bay Area, you cannot do VC investing in Lithuania."

Laurs was a Java games developer for years before he started GetJar. GetJar was really a side project for a long period of time. Just like how some people run open-source communities on the side, even though their day job is working at Oracle or PeopleSoft or whatever.

This is a great example of someone who is a really authentic mobile applications guy. Long before everybody else heard about the iPhone and iTunes store or the App Store, he was working on mobile applications.

Ilja understood the key aspects of developing mobile apps on a widely available yet difficult platform like Nokia. I have been around mobile now for ten years, and he comes up with subtleties that I would never had known. He is deeply authentic about the space he comes from. He can figure out stuff faster than you.

It was a complex and somewhat inconvenient investment. It takes two flights to get there from San Francisco. If he disappeared to Russia the next day, how would you ever get your money back? There was a lot of risk to it, but what really attracted me is he really knew what he was talking about in this particular category.

Shah: Agreed. If you are in the mobile content space, you know GetJar. When you are evaluating a company like AdMob or GetJar, who have authentic entrepreneurs, how much attention do you give to market size and market timing to decide if this is not only the right guy, but the right time and right market?

Wong: We almost always guess wrong on the timing. I think the reality is that you have to convince yourself that there is enough of a secular trend that this will become big enough in a strategic space at some point. You are never going to know for sure. Sometimes you just have to believe in the entrepreneur, and you really believe in his authenticity, so you just do it, even if not everything can check out in those last two dimensions.

Shah: Was GetJar very early in investment stage when you got in?

Wong: It was a Series A.

Shah: I look at start-ups in three stages—seed stage, early-growth stage, and scaling stage. The ones that make it all the way are doing something right at every stage. They are starting it right, they are doing initial experimentation and growing right, and then they are scaling it right. Have you seen specific characteristics that are consistent across all three stages?

Wong: I think a characteristic that actually relates to all three stages is a really fast test and iteration cycle. Some people can just build at a higher RPM than others. What other people think is a six-month project may be a two-month project. They learn how to push themselves and teams faster.

In engineering school back in college, we talked a lot about the concept of fighter jets' turning radius. If an F-16 turning radius was tighter than it could be for a MIG-28, the competitive game is over. You turn inside your enemy. You still have to turn the right way, but if your speed of iteration is so much faster, you are in a position to win every time, as long as you do not make big mistakes like turning the wrong way.

I think the speed of iteration metaphor is the most important across all three stages—it is just different topics that you are iterating. In the later stage, you are iterating international expansion, OEM, etc. In the early stages, you are just checking out the concepts.

Shah: Fascinating analogy using fighter jets. As you go from early stage to later stage, what changes as a measure of whether the company has a potential to become a billion-dollar company or not?

Wong: You become a little bit more financially driven and quantitative in later stages. You really tend to think about your cost disciplines a lot more because there is more to get wrong.

Expanding internationally in six locations and getting five of them wrong and, say, getting a bad GM of Japan hire who blows a bunch of money. If you have one of those, it is not fatal, but if you have three of them simultaneously blowing up—major distraction.

There is just a business scaling discipline that becomes more important for the people that really break out to the larger scale. It is a tough market.

Shah: At what point do you know that the start-up has crossed the chasm and it is really getting into the flywheel mode and taking on a life of its own?

Wong: When you really see and feel you are separating from your competitors, that is the moment that you start to feel better.

Shah: What led to AdMob success?

Wong: It was Omar. This is completely to his credit and that of his team. We also had a great board, with Jim Goetz who led the investment from Sequoia Capital, and Maynard Webb, the former COO of eBay. We worked together quite well. I think one of the healthy dynamics between the CEO and the board is maintaining the proper healthy level of paranoia. It will drive entrepreneurs crazy if you as board or investors are constantly bringing up issues, but the right level of paranoia keeps the pace of innovation very high.

Shah: What are the characteristics of an "A" team?

Wong: I think what matters most is team culture and unit cohesion. I almost in some ways recruit the personality type as much as functional skill. I have a triangle in my head—functional skill, raw intelligence, personal turning radius. Smart, hard-working, and paranoid together kind of radiates raw horse power. I stick with team and culture. You can almost always check the functional skill box pretty easily because it is pretty obvious. I think where people screw it up is sometimes you recruit people that nail that dimension, but on the other parts of the triangle they are not as good. They are great sales people but, truth be told, they are kind of lazy and the last success they had was partially because the product was so good.

This triangle is what you have to get right to build an "A" team. It sounds obvious that you want to build complementary team members and such, but a lot of people do not think about those other two dimensions. I would rather pick someone who has had years of experience as the VP of marketing, if they are hungry and will be up at 2:00 a.m. making sure the Twitter posts are going right, and on top of that, they know how to work well and complement the other guys and gals on the team.

Shah: What advice would you give someone trying to build a successful start-up?

Wong: If you are going to dedicate five to seven years of your life in a company, don't do it based on some tech article you read. Do your homework and strive to understand the space you are going into and try to understand the real drivers and issues behind it. Also, get the right advice and advisors around you. If you do your homework, it should be incredibly natural.

Randy Komisar

Kleiner Perkins Caufield & Byers: LucasArts, WebTV, TiVO, Pinger, Transphorm

Randy Komisar is a partner at Kleiner Perkins Caufield & Byers (KPCB). He was a co-founder of Claris Corporation, a founding director of TiVo, and he served as CEO for LucasArts Entertainment. Earlier in his career, Randy served as CFO of GO Corporation and senior counsel for Apple.

Randy is a lecturer on entrepreneurship at Stanford University and author of the best-selling book The Monk and the Riddle *(Harvard Business Press, 2001), as well as several articles on leadership and entrepreneurship. He is also the co-author[1] of* Getting to Plan B *(Harvard Business Press, 2009), a book on managing innovation.*

In this fascinating interview, Randy brings together his many years of experience as an operator and investor and applies key concepts from his two leading books. Starting with whether entrepreneurship is really the right career choice, he takes us through the process of building a billion-dollar start-up by analyzing the key characteristics of successful entrepreneurs; building A teams and a culture of success; executing against clear metrics; the reason not all founders make it to run public companies; and finally, how to determine if there is a Plan B and when to exit for maximum value creation.

---

[1] Co-authored by John Mullins.

Tarang Shah: In your book, *The Monk and the Riddle,* I really love your thinking about how people do "differed life plans" and how some people are just doing stuff for making money. They don't realize what it takes to succeed and then they are on a miserable path to just make money or do things other people value more than they do themselves.

I want readers to leverage incredible insights from your book and go beyond learning how to build billion-dollar start-ups, but I also want them to ask themselves if this is something they should be doing in the first place. The fundamental question is, "Who should pursue entrepreneurship and why?" In other words, is this a good fit for you, something that will innately motivate you? Is it what you really want out of life? Because entrepreneurship is going to take a lot of work to succeed, and there will be lots of ups and downs.

Randy Komisar: Great question. I wish more people would ask themselves that. In the late nineties, everybody thought they were an entrepreneur, everybody. They read the papers, they saw the young billionaires on the cover of *Fortune* and *Forbes* and *Businessweek,* and everybody believed that they should be part of that. I called those people the "carpetbaggers." They came in without a strong understanding of what entrepreneurship even was and while the going was easy, they were happy to speculate.

But when the going got tough, most of them disappeared. They disappeared because their businesses were not real, they disappeared because they didn't have the skill set to persevere, or they disappeared because they weren't tenacious enough. They didn't have the will to succeed. I am beginning to see that creep back into the culture again. The internet looks pretty easy, particularly to young people, and so they don't ask themselves the question you just asked, which I think is a really important one.

Shah: So what advice would you give them?

Komisar: It goes to this notion that John Mullins and I talk about in *Getting to Plan B,* which is if you assume that whatever plan you start off with is wrong, do you have the perseverance and dedication to get it right? Because that is the journey of entrepreneurship. The journey of entrepreneurship is not one of simply executing against a great idea. That happens very, very seldom. What we really find more often, of course, is the notion that it's a winding road, and you're going to have to have the commitment to get yourself from point A to an undetermined point B.

If you ask me empirically to tell you what it is in people who are more likely to succeed in that sort of environment, it is their commitment to a mission, a purpose. If they can articulate to me the underlying purpose for what they're doing in a crisp and distinct way, if they can do that with visceral engagement, then I have higher confidence that they will persevere as the tactics shift and as the facts come back mixed, some negative and some positive.

If what they are articulating to me is less a purpose and more of a plan, and the plan is largely driven by the financial results vs. the impact, then I have less confidence that when the going gets tough, they're going to keep going.

There are a lot of entrepreneurs who sort of howl at the moon and never actually are able to get to their final destination, in large part because—to be frank—they think they know what the destination is before they have even entered the market. And if you think you know what the destination is when you start and you later find out that that destination is either wrong or not proximate, then you test your commitment as an entrepreneur.

Shah: Kind of like that monk in your book who just enjoyed a ride on the motorcycle rather than thinking about the destination.

Komisar: That's right. Like all the rest of life, the wink-wink-nod-nod secret is that life's value is the journey. It's not about what you accomplish, it's not about whether you succeed, it's not about whether you achieve your goals. Ultimately those things are contextual. What really ultimately matters is, are you engaged with life? Are you breathing it in, are you enjoying the adventure that you have the privilege of waking up to every day? That metaphor is very much the entrepreneurial metaphor.

Shah: Let's switch gears now and talk about you as an investor. When you look at someone coming in, do most of them come in with a passion to solve something? As John Doerr always says, which is quoted in your book, big companies are built by solving big problems, right? So I'm sure a lot of business plans that you see say, "This is a big problem that I'm passionate to solve." How do you identify the person who is truly passionate about solving a big problem? What do you look at to say, "Hey, this guy can do it"?

Komisar: Everybody in the investment business says that they invest in people. It's almost cliché, but what does that mean? To be frank, I had been relatively intuitive about it and have become more objective about it since writing *Getting to Plan B*, because *Getting to Plan B* focused me on the qualities that make for that enduring, tenacious entrepreneur.

What I need is a recipe that includes a significant amount of passion for the purpose. What I need is a problem that is big enough that it's worth failing at. What I need is a team that is committed to the purpose, but curious and flexible as to the actual means, and willing to iterate and experiment and learn as quickly as possible while comfortable with the surrounding ambiguity. Because in a lot of cases, even with people committed like that to the purpose, they are still absolutely hell-bent on going directly from where they are today to the execution of a preconceived plan, whatever that is.

The problem with that is that it is a 1 in 100 chance that that is exactly the right process. So are they going to be flexible enough, are they going to be open enough, are they going to let their curiosity drive them more than their desire to quickly get to an imagined endpoint? If that's the case, they have the qualities necessary.

I see a lot of people come in with a strong sense of purpose who are inflexible. And as much as I may really resonate with those people and their passion, I am leery about entering into this journey with them. I am concerned that they won't have the flexibility that is going to allow them to discover the best plan.

Shah: Within the very short window that we, as investors, get to evaluate people, what's the best way to see if someone is inflexible or flexible?

Komisar: Today, for instance, I had two very impressive entrepreneurs in for my second meeting. I did a two-hour open riff with them. I brought one of my very creative and engaging partners in with me, so there were two of us with two of them. We just talked and I observed them. I watched how they responded to ideas out of left field. I watched how they responded to questions about the legitimacy of their hypothesis and where their center was, and whether they kept coming back to the center.

By no means is that foolproof, but by engaging them in sessions where you both roll up your sleeves, you get to see how they think. You get to see where their comfort level is. You get to see how open they are with each other and with you, and that is very helpful.

Shah: Because it goes to the heart of the message in *Getting to Plan B*, right? Those are the kind of engagements you have on a very routine basis in the process of building a billion-dollar company

Komisar: Exactly. It's a building process. Even when I was an angel and a virtual CEO, I would trust my gut enough to have a second meeting, but not to commit indefinitely. If I believed that the right ingredients were there, I would roll up my sleeves and offer my services for free. The goal was that if we worked together well, I would hope that there would be a basis for continuing the relationship with me as a valued member of the team. But I would not ask for that and I would not entertain that until such time as we had actually been through a number of sessions and I could confirm my intuition. Because the last thing I wanted to do was get locked into a long-term commitment with the wrong team, the wrong problem, or the wrong process.

Shah: Continuing that line of thinking, Randy, does that summarize your definition of "A" players, or are there other ingredients that we can add?

Komisar: I think there are many other ingredients. It goes without saying that you have to be smart. We don't even talk about that anymore, because that filter is understood. It goes without saying that I think you have to have some ability to lead.

Now, that leadership can take many forms. That leadership could take the form of the classic, outgoing, inspiring leader, or it could be a thought leader, a quiet thought leader, or it could be somebody who is more of an inside-people person. But it must be someone who can manifest an ability to lead the team and gather the other constituencies that are needed to win.

You are going to need investors, you are going to need employees, you are going to need partners, you are going to need customers. There are many different styles of how to do that, but there has to be some leadership in the mix.

I also think that it is very helpful to see a partnering gene in the person. Either they walked in with a good partner, somebody they worked with before, or they have a track record of working well with others. Partners tend to help with the first problem you raised as well, which is when the going gets tough, if you're having a really bad day, if the deal you thought was going to save the company didn't come through, your partner is there to help you emotionally get through it and vice versa. That creates a keel on this boat. So, that partnering gene is an important one as well.

Shah: Back when I was doing quite a bit of research on founders, there was a consistent pattern—that many successful companies had more than one founder. I think maybe that's the reason for it.

Komisar: I think that's right. I also think it is interesting, because many times when you break up the band—maybe there is a buyout or they've done it for ten years and have accomplished everything they can—the individuals are not capable of separately doing what they did together. There is a magic to the chemistry that can occur in a moment in time around people who may complement each other, may have a deep understanding of each other's motivations and moods and emotions, and can for whatever reason create a bigger whole than any single one of them can independently. There is a magic to that when it happens, and it's powerful.

Shah: So that definitely comes as not a gating factor—a requirement—but at least something you look at.

Komisar: It's a plus in my mind, particularly when you see people who have worked together before. When I see people walk in who have worked together before, you know that they have a rhythm, they're not going to have to go through the process of building a rhythm, seeing if the chemistry really works, and potentially having the relationship fall apart. Instead, you have people who say, "Yeah, I know how this guy works and I want to work with him again anyway."

Shah: That's a pretty strong statement. Someone they know kind of gives you the check mark. "I like this guy, I want to work with him, I want to risk my career, money, whatever it is, with this guy."

Komisar: Exactly.

Shah: On the subject of when you go from being a one-person or two-person team to building a company, the moment you add one more person you start building the culture. Many of them fail to show a consistent or a standout culture that is a reflection of the founders and their vision and their philosophy. First off, your thoughts on that and any advice you can give to entrepreneurs in building a culture of success, an extension of the original vision and plan?

Komisar: When I started out in the business some twenty-plus years ago, there was this notion that the way you started a company was that you got a couple of core people around you, got your investors on board, built-up a mission statement, and created a value statement. Then the value statement essentially became your line in the sand around your definition of culture. I have actually changed my view of that.

My sense is that the problem with that process of culture-building is that it's too abstract. Just like the "Plan A" problem that I talk about in *Getting to Plan B*. Trying to define a culture before you have actually done something, before you've actually worked together, particularly on the hard stuff, I find is unrealistic, to be frank.

I think what I generally like my teams to do now, rather than go through that hollow process, is to define their purpose crisply and distinctly, and then to actually work toward it. Let the culture evolve.

Now, good things and bad things will evolve in that culture. And as they evolve, you need to pay attention. I have actually brought in people to coach and work with teams to help mold cultures as they develop. Pay attention, solve the problems as they emerge, and reinforce the strongest characteristics. At some point in time, a year or two down the road let's say, you will be able to articulate strong mission and value statements that are aspirational, but also empirical.

Shah: Randy, what is the message in hiring? There are a lot of mistakes done in hiring. And every mistake can cost a small company a lot.

Komisar: Hiring is really, really hard. I think the best process I see is when you bring in a core team that has worked together before, say two to three co-founders. They then go to their network, to known entities. The technical lead goes to the technical community, the market lead goes to the marketing community, the CEO pulls together the right staff group.

So the first thing you try to do is hire known entities. Assuming that the core team is A-plus, their network is probably also top-notch. Then you go to the process of hiring new blood. This is where it gets tricky. But if you have brought in really great players and they keep the bar high, then you will end up with each one of them being able to hire more talent like themselves. You know the adage, A players hire A players but B players hire C players. I find that to be very, very true. So, hiring is critical.

I also find there is a concept I think about in hiring, which is to build complementary teams. There are some people who believe that the right answer is that every single person you hire is sort of prototypically perfect. They have no flaws, they have no limitations, they are complete, and I guess if you were to carry that notion one step further, you would assume that they could play any position on the field except where their domain experience limits them. But, I don't find that to be true.

What I find is everybody comes with their biases. Everybody comes with their weaknesses and their strengths. Combining weaknesses and strengths into the right teams can highlight the positive and diminish the negative. That allows you to get even more value from diversity than you can out of a more prototypical hire, assuming there is such a thing.

Shah: That makes sense. If you hire only pitchers in a baseball team, then all you have is nine pitchers.

Komisar: Exactly right. If I have a great person in charge of marketing who is very customer-focused, then I may want to make sure that the first couple of people that she hires are product-focused. If I hire a great person on the technical side who is really strong at building and leading teams, I may want to make sure they hire a few individual performers who are going to be great at actually developing the architecture, getting their hands dirty, and vice versa. I may find that I actually have roles reversed. That doesn't mean I get rid of the person—it means I think about their whole team and function holistically.

Shah: So you're thinking about what it takes to get this product out or understand the customer fully so we can build the right product in the right way? And what are the ingredients needed to make that soup?

Komisar: Yep.

Shah: Thanks, that's fantastic. Now, another interesting thing I'm finding is in some cases—like Bill Gates, and Steve Jobs, and Larry Page and Sergey Brin—is that they have been able to start from one- or two-man teams to take it all the way to running a billion-dollar company. Then, in other cases you see the guy takes it all the way to prototype, Series A—and boom— he's out doing something else and the company is not able to keep growing to become a public company. What, in your experience and knowledge, is happening here?

Komisar: First of all, it's important to realize that Steve Jobs failed when he was a young man and then later succeeded. It is also important to realize that Sergey and Larry probably couldn't have built Google without Eric Schmidt.

Shah: And then Bill Gates had to bring in Steve Ballmer right?

Komisar: Yes. In fact, I think the thing that is most defining about whether or not an entrepreneur can go the distance, whatever that means, is how much momentum the company and original idea have. If things are really going well, for example, look at Facebook under Zuckerberg. He is clearly not a deeply experienced CEO yet.

If your company is growing from ten million unique users to fifty million uniques to one hundred million uniques to three hundred million uniques, you get to keep the job. You get to learn on the job. A smart board will sur- round a young visionary riding a rocket ship with experienced operators— like Sheryl Sandberg at Facebook. But if you run into trouble scaling at ten million uniques, you may be out. So, the opportunity to learn and grow is to some extent based upon the independent momentum of the business.

Now, the other side of this is that some people have a natural desire and proclivity to improve all aspects of leadership, management, and operations. Some people don't have that. I think it's important early on to figure out where you lie. I think the problem is if you ask that question of yourself and you come up short, it's generally considered to be a negative determination, by you or by others. I think that's wrong.

I think we need to understand that, for instance, if you have an entrepreneur, somebody who is capable of launching great ideas, of bringing the other constituencies to the table and then handing those ideas to good operators to actually build into real businesses, that is the most precious resource/talent. To tell that person that, no, no, no they shouldn't go start another company, they should become a great operating CEO, does that person a disservice.

Shah: Yes, because he's good at seeding them, taking them to series A or prototype or whatever and then go off figuring out what is another need in the market.

Komisar: Yeah, so he may stay on as a board member, and he may stay on as an advisor. I always encourage him to do that, to continue to learn and be a part of the platform that he set in motion. But that being said, leading it, operating it, and managing it, may not be the best thing for that person. I've seen CEOs who have failed numerous times as leaders—who have bad reputations as CEOs, leaders, and managers—but then they land on a great idea that grows like wildfire and the exact same person is lauded by the market.

Shah: You made a very interesting point that you have an opportunity to go all the way, but then the key business metrics will show you and the board, and the public at large, whether you are truly grabbing that opportunity or not.

Komisar: The metrics to some extent actually could be a distortion. I mean the metrics around the CEO, the founder who ends up on a rocket ship by accident could very well turn out to be a false-positive in their ability to operate and run a business. So having a team around who can look through the data to really understand the pluses and minuses of the person's leadership and management skills is really important. That is what a good board does. It is awfully hard. A lot of people believe their own metrics. If your business is taking off, it is hard not to take credit for that.

Shah: And it's very hard for investors to replace someone who is bringing in those kind of numbers.

Komisar: Absolutely. That's why building complementary teams, shoring it up, putting succession in place is key. Your point though about the metrics is really important from another standpoint as well, which is that a lot of boards are very bad about communicating with their CEOs. One day they walk into a meeting and say, "You know what, we think it's best if you leave." I actually find that if you have a great dialogue, if you have them build metrics that you concur with, and if you hold them accountable before you need to tell them to leave, they will tell you they are failing.

Shah: Does this dialogue differ if it's a founder and not a hired CEO?

Komisar: Yes. If it's the founder, you treat that person as a peer investor, and you say, "This is our business, this is our company, this is what we created. What's the best thing to do for us?" And you separate that from their notion of what their role is. Don't make it judgmental. It's like, "Hey, it's not working." As a bunch of owners of this company, you include Ms. Founder in the decision. "What should we be doing?" That gives her permission to have that conversation with you without feeling like it is personal failure.

Shah: That's a very good point. How do you make that transition given they are still such a great asset to the company and they are very much part and parcel of the success that has been built so far?

Komisar: Clearly there are times when I'm very disappointed that I end up with somebody who is just not capable of getting it. They are sort of deluded and delusion is the worst of all maladies because fundamentally it means you can't change. If you can't see it, you can't change.

Shah: If you can't objectively face the facts, then you just don't have a new course that you can set on.

Komisar: Exactly.

Shah: This is such an important topic for success for any start-up. It is fantastic insight. Let's switch gears to the market.

Komisar: Good, let's do that.

Shah: Randy, you and I know that it doesn't matter how well you execute and how much ownership you have of a given market—if you own 100 percent of a niche market, you aren't going to create a billion-dollar company, right? So it all goes back to something you and John Doerr talk about a lot, which is that you have to solve a big problem to create a big company. When you look at an opportunity, how do you identify the markets you want to go after? And you know there is a very good likelihood that "Plan A" is not going to work, so how do you put those two together?

Komisar: Well, I do it from a deductive perspective. Rather than talk about markets, I start by talking about problems. Whose problems are they? The people with the problem should be my target customers.

The next question is, how are these customers characterized? This is an important question for numerous reasons. How many of them are there? How accessible are they? How are they defined, what channels do they currently use to solve this problem, or do they not solve this problem at all today? When I start answering all those questions, I begin to define a market.

I define a market by need, I define a market by demographics, I define a market by channel.

Shah: And of course size comes into the picture.

Komisar: When you put that all together, that's going to tell you whether the problem you're solving is a big problem. A big problem for one person is not a big market.

Shah: Many times entrepreneurs think the problem they are facing is the problem for the general market.

Komisar: Exactly.

Shah: Then there is a lot of hype and noise in the market that this is going to the next big thing, and you have to figure out a way to separate that from the one that is really going to stick.

Komisar: Yes. And that's very tricky. Now you're talking about execution. To be frank, a lot of foot races get lost even by great runners. So, we had this issue when we invested in Friendster. We understood—John Doerr in particular understood—social networks way before there was a Facebook. But we backed the wrong runner.

Shah: So that's the execution. You can't get the billion-dollar success without a big market or the right market, but once you have that, all gears shift to execution. Because someone will out-execute you, which happened in the case of Friendster.

Komisar: Exactly. I can go through the analysis you and I just went through. I can find the right problem, I can find the right market, I can find the right team, but you know what, I'm still in a race.

Shah: Because you cannot be the only guy in the market; there are a half dozen already thinking something similar or the same. And Myspace itself got out-executed by Facebook eventually.

Komisar: Exactly. And part of that was the slight deviation in vision between those competitors was crucial in defining what the market was for each of those three. They actually addressed three very different markets. Ultimately, they were differentiated by their own conceptions of how a social network would be organized and presented. Facebook identified the biggest one. They created the largest market by far.

Shah: They started with the colleges and then they got all the professionals in there.

Komisar: That's right, and Myspace basically built a media-centric social gathering. But what they didn't understand was how much of this was really about people first. They were defined by media. People were the grease on the gears. But at Friendster, it was even a smaller notion. It was an almost mechanical idea of understanding who you were connected to. That was the smallest of the markets.

Shah: Because one was focused on context, and the other was on the content, and then the third was based on relationships.

Komisar: Exactly. You said it perfectly.

Shah: Your talk recently on constructive failure is quite fascinating. You pointed to how one is still creating an asset though a start-up is failing. Not many people in venture business like to talk about failures, though it can't be separated from what we do.

Komisar: Absolutely. So let's start with the first one, which is constructive value. I think it is better to succeed than to fail. Don't go out and fail intentionally. Let's get that out of the way. Now the reality is in my business— the business of innovation—you are by definition going to fail more often than you are going to succeed. The business is a laboratory for new ideas. It is not incremental. I don't have a role in incrementalism in Silicon Valley. My focus is on creative destruction.

Our business depends basically on disenfranchising an incumbent. Even when we're creating something brand new like the internet, we are disenfranchising an incumbent, whether it's in commerce, in communications, or in the media. The reality is that we have to create sufficient schisms in the market for innovation to take hold. That being the case, I've got to reach very, very far to find them, and I will fail more often than I will succeed in achieving my goal.

Now, how do I turn that into something that is sustainable? How do you create an innovation flywheel in an environment where you're asking somebody to risk their careers, risk their income, and risk all the things associated with their income for innovation? Well, a lot of business cultures have failed at doing that. And that is why you don't find a lot of entrepreneurship clusters like Silicon Valley. Even in places like Western Europe. Certainly in other places in the world there is a dearth of breakthrough innovation in large part because the personal costs are too high.

Shah: As you say, the equation, the absolute number, is the probability of your failure times the cost of failure?

Komisar: That's right. To be frank, I can't change and it's not my objective to change the number of failures I have because it would mean that I'm not trying hard enough. If I actually lowered that number, I'd be getting conservative.

What I have to do is lower the cost. And Silicon Valley has been ingenious in developing such a culture incrementally over many years, but I don't believe anybody had the big idea to do it this way. I think it's simply the culture that has been reinforced now for over seventy years here. We will not personalize failure. We will re-engage experience in new enterprises. That means that we have effectively lowered the cost of failure for great talent. They become educated through the process of entrepreneurship, through what they have learned from their successes and from their failures.

There is a corollary to this, and it is the thing I also find missing in places where there is an emergent, but not yet florid, entrepreneurial ecosystem— the reinvestment of generational experience back into new innovators. And I don't mean just in dollars. I mean in time, counseling, mentoring, coaching, etc. Because what you see in a place like Silicon Valley is a constant reinvestment of successful people through angel investing, through sitting on boards, through coaching of the next generation of talent. And they are not doing that to get rich, to be frank. They are doing it because they are passionate about the next new thing.

Shah: Like Ron Conway and John Doerr.

Komisar: They are great examples. If you're a billionaire, you're not likely to make another billion sitting around with two scruffy kids trying to figure out how to make social networking pay for itself. But then, against all odds, someone does.

Shah: It's such an innate passion to pass it on to the next generation.

Komisar: Exactly. So those two corollaries go together there.

Shah: And I think the same model you take inside the corporation then, you know the cost of failure at a personal level is way too high and this is why people are so risk-averse within big corporations.

Komisar: And I have been speaking, for instance, with Intuit lately about the *Getting to Plan B* methodology. Intuit is very forward-thinking in trying to figure out how to create more acceptance of managed, methodical risk-taking. Not recklessness, but managed, methodical risk-taking against clear metrics in a *Getting to Plan B* way. But it's interesting when you go to large companies. A lot of companies always want to hear about the Silicon Valley model and innovation and how it works and how they can be more innovative. The first question I always ask them is, "Can you afford to fail more often than you succeed?" They look at you like, what are you talking about?

Shah: I have built investment cases in big corporations and in most cases there isn't much room for failure or experiments.

Komisar: Yep. I said, until you can afford to fail more than succeed, then your job is going to be to buy great ideas because you're not going to generate them inside.

Shah: Coming up with capital itself is such a big deal, and then if you fail, the cost of failure is just so high in the corporate environment.

Komisar: Hugely high, right? You're never going to see the capital again.

Shah: Exactly, you're just branded failure. That's it, period.

Komisar: I will tell you that I am more dubious about serial, successful entrepreneurs than I am about entrepreneurs that have experienced some failure.

Shah: That is interesting because I am testing the hypothesis that the serial entrepreneurs have the same probability of success as first-time entrepreneurs. But I have seen fewer big hits by serial entrepreneurs, and I have seen more big hits by the first-timers.

Komisar: There is some Harvard research that looks similar to that. If it's the Harvard research that was done, I actually think it is flawed in its methodology.

Shah: Nope. I built my own hypothesis and am currently testing it. Are entrepreneurs in their twenties and thirties better at coming up with and building billion-dollar start-ups than their older counterparts?

Komisar: Unfortunately, when people think about innovation and start-ups today, they immediately think about the consumer web. That's what the media focuses on. But that's only a small part of things. We have older CEOs and experienced founders doing quite well in life sciences and energy and enterprise, so I think that is a statement that is overly broad.

Shah: Yes, it's industry-specific. You can't see that kind of innovation coming in telco or enterprise software by entrepreneurs in their twenties and thirties. I totally agree with you.

In your book and study about "Plan B," you mentioned that some of the companies went to such a far length as "Plan F" before they succeeded, but in other cases they were sold or shut down right into "Plan A." What's key to this decision making?

Komisar: It's a very hard decision, and these are decisions that create a lot of anxiety. I look at it a couple of ways. First of all, this goes back to the *Plan*

B metrics. I need to have a good dashboard, so as early as possible I can identify where problems are occurring that challenge my assumptions.

And then I need to understand what the response is, the credible response, to those new metrics. Basically, the simple answer is as long as I have people reacting in a diligent way to a very well-measured set of assumptions, as long as I have people course-correcting, as long as I have people conserving resources by focusing on those leaps of faith and those alone, and as long as I've got resources remaining in the company allowing me to course-correct, I stay in business.

Shah: But if one hits the dead end and can't think of a way out of that, that's the end of the story.

Komisar: And then it's over. You must be very disciplined about such things.

Shah: Randy, what are your most favorite examples of exceptional products?

Komisar: Well, obviously all the Apple products are terrific. I think that the Amazon service is an outstanding service. I think that the Google service is an outstanding service. I think of the services and products here as being interchangeable. I think that if you take a look at what is going on in certain areas like science, where we're seeing incredible products for genomic health and customized, personalized medicine—that's all fascinating stuff.

You take a look at where I think the opportunities that we have seen exposed so far in things like Skype and Pinger and what's going to happen in VoIP and these sort of threats to the telcos. I think TiVo is an amazing product. I think it has transformed the broadcast media business in ways that TiVo unfortunately has never really been able to fully monetize, but fundamentally the media business will never be the same. It's a non-linear business going forward.

I think all these things are amazing products and I judge the value of the products in a couple of ways. Obviously, do they deliver great consumer value? Is there a loyalty to the product? Do they have impact? Do they generate constructive change? Is something better because of them, something significant? That is also important. Do we see a change of direction out of what we see happening online around social networking, for instance, or that we saw around search? These are big deals and so those are compelling, very, very compelling, products.

Shah: What is key to building such exceptional products?

Komisar: Well, you know there is a magic to it, but I think you can distill the magic into exactly what we started to talk about earlier. Was there a sense of purpose around solving a big problem? Did they bring together the talent that would allow them to iterate and improve as they attacked that problem? And did we find engagement by the customers in a way that allowed these people to quickly get to a scale where they could make a difference?

Shah: I see. And then it's a harbinger of change. Value-add and loyalty represents that.

Komisar: I think those are the right metrics for it.

Shah: Fascinating. Now in recent years we have seen rise of flywheel start-ups. What's driving these new genre of flywheels?

Komisar: Well, it really depends. What I normally find in a flywheel-driven start-up—meaning a Facebook, a Twitter, Groupon, or Myspace in its day—if you think about those sorts of models, what's really happening is they are riding the bronco, the wild horse of the consumer. It's not as if they are driving consumer as much as the consumer is driving them.

Shah: Very interesting.

Komisar: At some point the company has to create its own momentum, and it no longer can simply rely on the current in the river that it has found itself in. Then you get to really prove what kind of business and organization you've created. Once the current has died down and you have to bring out the paddles, now you get to see what you're made of.

Shah: I agree with you. So it's not a generic phenomenon, but kind of a sector-specific phenomenon.

Komisar: Exactly. The thing to be careful of is everybody talks about start-ups today, particularly in Silicon Valley—they're all talking about these consumer web phenomena. It is a very small part of the overall innovation taking place.

Peter Wagner

Accel Partners: Fusion-io, Opower, ArrowPoint Communications, Riverbed Technology, Redback Networks

As a partner at Accel Partners for 15 years, and now as an independent investor and company-builder, **Peter Wagner** focuses on the information technology sector, investing in start-up ventures as well as growth-stage companies. Peter has led investments in dozens of early-stage companies, many of which have gone on to complete IPOs or successful acquisitions.

Peter is responsible for Accel's investments in current portfolio companies Blue Jeans Network, Broadsoft, Complex Media, Fusion-io, Nimble Storage, Opower, and Qwilt. His prior investments include Acopia, Tellium, Riverbed Technology, Redback Networks, ArrowPoint Communications, Peribit Net-works, Altor Networks, Wichorus, Omneon, Northpoint Communications, Topspin Communications, Timetra Networks, and Infinera.

In addition to his US-focused investment activity, Peter led Accel's original initiatives in India, culminating in the formation of Accel India in 2008. Prior to joining Accel, Peter was a line manager at Silicon Graphics and management consultant at McKinsey & Company. Peter began his career as a physicist working in aerospace and nuclear fusion research.

Peter now works independently from the firm he helped build into an industry leader, but he is still dedicated to engaging deeply with talented founders to develop leading companies of lasting value in IT's most explosive markets.

Drawing from his highly successful portfolio of investments and citing examples from Riverbed, Redback, and ArrowPoint, Peter provides an amazing insight into why start-ups fail—including some of the most common entrepreneurial blind spots and mistakes, the characteristics of great founders and teams, the way that he identifies promising markets, and the keys to pivot and exit decisions.

What I love about Peter is his deep understanding of the IT landscape and the way that he identifies and builds the next-generation of start-up success stories. His ability to apply a consistent model of market, team, and execution across various IT verticals to identify and build great companies is remarkable.

Tarang Shah: What are some of the key reasons why start-ups fail?

Peter Wagner: I think there are obviously many, but there are two that I would highlight. The first has to do with team issues, and often this is traceable to the founder. One of the things that you are looking for in a founder is the ability to pull together a team uniquely suited to the opportunity. That has to do in many cases with the founder's ability to articulate a vision and get people excited about it and then bring people together to work on it.

When the team falls apart, either through disagreements or an inability to assemble anything other than a "B" team, that is often traceable to a misreading of the founder and his capabilities in team-building and the inspiration of others.

The second thing that I would highlight would be that start-ups sometimes fail because of a fundamental misjudgment in product-market fit. It's a break in the logic of the value proposition. Some sort of disconnect whereby what was thought to be the customer's need, and the solution to that need, end up being misjudged in some key fashion.

Shah: Where does the product-market misfit show up in the company you are looking at to invest?

Wagner: If it's an investment that you haven't already made and you are just learning about, it would most reliably show up in your conversations with customers or prospects. As you listen to them talk about their needs in their own words, that would be the ideal point—and the most common point—at which you might realize there is a disconnect in the value proposition.

Shah: So, in the reference calls you make?

Wagner: Yes, and if you are an experienced investor and you are working consistently in the same sector, you might actually already have some good appreciation of what the customer's requirements are even before you meet the company, just because you have been working in related fields.

Or, for example, it might be an area you've already had the opportunity to speak to customers in, based on adjacent markets that you have been scoping out. Or perhaps it is through a portfolio company that is doing something related, but not identical, where you have been able to learn a bit about the market in that fashion. That is one of the benefits of focus for an investor going deep in a few areas. You can walk into the investment conversation fully prepared.

If you do happen to invest in a company, and you're learning about this post-investment, it usually shows up in the company's first couple quarters of sales. You will see sales cycles elongating, deals not closing predictably, and the sales team consistently incorrect about when a particular deal will close. This tells you that we have not only probably misjudged the timing of the sales cycle, but misjudged whether it is going to close at all. The directness with which you are addressing the customer's problem is questionable.

Shah: If both indicators are present simultaneously, the flawed team and poor product-market fit, does that mean the company is destined to fail? Or do a lot of companies run into that by nature of the start-up building process, and some pull it off successfully while others falter?

Wagner: There are always examples of companies that turn it around, but it's not an easy thing to do. If I take the first set of failure modes where your early team is flawed, it is very hard to turn that around. The early team sets the culture, sets the tone for everyone that is hired later, determines the type of person and the quality of person that is hired later, and so if you get the founding team wrong and then the first ten hires wrong, it is very hard to recover from that. If your value proposition is wrong, if you have misjudged product-market fit, that can be tweaked. If you're off course by thirty degrees, then you can possibly fix that, and that often happens.

Shah: So it's a reasonable degree of pivoting.

Wagner: There is a question of degree in terms of pivots, right? A full-on restart where you are scrapping what you've done and you're now chasing something quite different—the odds are not good that will work. It's not uncommon for some corrections to have to be made after the initial market entry. In fact, that is to be expected. What you don't know is the degree. So that's why you try and keep your "go-to-market" investments, like the size of your sales force and your marketing expenditure, very constrained until you know that you have a value proposition that is working and a sales recipe that is consistent.

Shah: What is the trigger for you to tell that you have now the right product-market fit and you are hitting the inflection point? Where does it show up in your review?

Wagner: It shows up as deals that are closing rapidly. It shows up as a sales pipeline that is growing rapidly and in great sales force productivity. You have sales teams that are exceeding their targets and becoming very productive, meaning that your dollars per sales team are very high relative to what your expectations are for your particular line of business. It could be a different number depending upon what business you're in.

Let's say it's an enterprise infrastructure-systems company and you have sales teams that are selling very early on at an annual run rate per sales rep that exceeds $3 million. They are selling high hundreds of thousands of dollars per quarter per salesperson. If that is happening fairly early in the life cycle of the company, then you know you have a value proposition and a product-market fit that is working and it's time to scale that. If the sales teams are struggling to sell a couple hundred thousand dollars each per quarter, then you probably still have some work to do. That's what I mean by sales team productivity—the revenue attainment per quarter per sales team. Different types of business are going to have somewhat different metrics, but in general there is a sales-and-marketing productivity metric that is a key thing to watch. A lot has been written about the most relevant metrics for SaaS and "freemium" businesses. They have different input variables, different formulas, but the same basic idea.

Shah: When the current product-market fit is not working and pivot is inevitable, what separates the teams that are able to successfully pivot vs. other teams that fail to pivot successfully?

Wagner: The ones that course-correct generally are much better listeners and are very interested in listening. They have a desire to do so. They are more curious. They would really like to figure things out. A team that has a hard time course-correcting is very focused on scaling. They will prematurely pour investments into incremental features or expanded go-to-market resources, before they even know if their core value proposition is holding water. They are presuming success in advance of the customer actually demonstrating that the product is needed.

Shah: So the original hypothesis of the dog needing this particular dog food hasn't been proven yet and they're furiously putting the dog food up on as many shelves as they can get.

Wagner: A very common mistake. You can usually find enough positive comments out there in your interactions. Then, if you are that kind of entrepreneur, you will have some things to point to: "See? We have some evidence that this is being well received, so we should accelerate what we are doing." But the art lies in not being fooled and digging deeply and understanding really where you are on the playing field.

Shah: That's very helpful. What is your ideal start-up?

Wagner: An ideal start-up has a gifted founder. What does it mean to be a gifted founder? Well, they are coming from a unique situation that allows them to perceive an opportunity in a way that is different from other people. They can turn that perception into a vision of what they are trying to build. They can communicate that vision to others and then get other people excited about it. That is really the essence of the founder. Another aspect of the ideal start-up is that it defines its own market. It's not an entry into a market that has already been defined by others, but it actually creates a category, creates a market.

Shah: Even while disrupting the existing market?

Wagner: Maybe not disrupting a market per se. There may be markets to the left and to the right that are affected, but really I think more value is created when the company ends up becoming synonymous with its market. It defines the category in such a way that it's not just a better implementation of something that has been done before, but in fact is something completely new. Often, this means new vocabulary has to be created. There is an educational aspect to the sales process, but if you get that right, there is a lot of lasting value and defensibility.

Shah: That's a great point.

Wagner: Financially speaking, the ideal start-up is very capital efficient, does not require a lot of money to get into the market, doesn't require a lot of capital to scale, and has a financial model that enables this. Usually it has high-gross margins, fast sales cycles, low cost of customer acquisition, and fairly rapid time to initial deployment.

Shah: What attracted you to invest in ArrowPoint when you first looked at it?

Wagner: ArrowPoint went public and then it was acquired by Cisco as a public company. It was one of the original content networking companies back when load balancers were new. The thing I loved about ArrowPoint was it had that special founder, a gifted entrepreneur named Cheng Wu, who had all those characteristics I described before—exceptional vision, tremendous character and integrity, an ability to get people excited about the vision, and a great strategic mind. He was able to build a great team around him, which included a guy named Christopher Lynch. Lynch was a perfect complement to Cheng, a tremendous sales-and-marketing executive who was able to take Cheng's vision and bring it to the customers and the market in a way that could be sold very rapidly and efficiently.

ArrowPoint defined its market—the market of content networking and load balancers, what we call application delivery now—and did it in a capital-efficient way that did not require a ton of cash to get that product in the market and to get feedback on it. Ultimately, it had a very high gross margin, high-velocity sales cycle, and a financial model that turned out to be very valuable. I ended up doing another company with Cheng and Chris called Acopia, which came later. It was in the storage area, network file virtualization, and was also just a tremendous thing.

Another one I love is Riverbed Technology. Riverbed is also a networking company, and also a category definer, in this case in the WAN-optimization and application-acceleration space. Riverbed also had that perfect founder, and in this case, founding team: Steve McCanne, who really had the perception of the product-market side of it, the intersection of the technology and what the customers were looking for. And then Jerry Kennelly, who is a tremendous businessman, a guy with more of a financial background and a great leader. Jerry was CEO and Steve was CTO. So, we had this fabulous founding team and we had again a category-creation opportunity. It was a case, which is often true in the very best ventures, where you have a new technology enabling a solution to some acute customer pain in a way that wasn't possible before. Just the technology by itself would not have been interesting if it weren't also for the way Steve put it together with an acute customer pain point that hadn't been solved before.

Shah: That's the key.

Wagner: And it had a very capital-efficient business model. Riverbed did not require a lot of capital to get product in the market and get validation that we had a strong value proposition. Redback Networks would be another example, and again you're going to hear some similar themes. A great founding team with the ability to articulate a vision and recruit. In particular the principal founder, Gaurav Garg, who is one of the best recruiters I've ever seen. Gaurav could get people very excited about what was going on at Redback and was able to build a small-but-elite team that had unbelievable talent. A lot of this was a function of the quality of the idea, but also of Gaurav's ability to communicate it.

Shah: Yes, very exciting company. One of my ex-colleagues at Qualcomm ended up joining Redback and worked directly for Gaurav.

Wagner: Redback got their product into the market on a very small amount of capital with a small number of employees, so it had that capital-efficient, high-gross margin business model that I have talked about before. It's a consistent theme.

And also another consistent theme—they invented their category. This idea of a "Subscriber Management System"—a BRAS [Broadband Remote Access Server], as it would become known later—was a new idea. No one even perceived that it was necessary. It was closely linked to one of the major trends of the time, the deployment of broadband access with DSL, and it was a required piece of infrastructure that Redback had to invent and teach the world about. And in doing so, it became synonymous with the category. It had a very strong market position as a result.

If you define the category, then you teach the customer what it is and what the requirements are. You have a lot of credibility and a lot of loyalty from that customer base. You're not just the temporary price/performance leader, you are in fact the strategic thought leader for the market. That can allow you to have a much longer run of success.

Shah: Once you create that category and once its potential is recognized by a broader market, you're definitely going to attract competition. That usually drives the market towards commoditization. What is the key to sustain your lead as the market catches up and builds competitive products?

Wagner: This is why it is important to define the market and to invent the market. If instead you are a company that does a good job of utilizing new technology to create a better version of an existing category of product, you may have a moment in the sun. You're the hot product in town, but it will be temporary and someone else will do the same thing to you twelve to eighteen months later. So, sustainability and defensibility really comes from being the first to define a category. I think you develop a lot more "brand" that way, and with brand the customer associates more value and attributes more credibility to that particular vendor.

Shah: When you meet with these great founding teams you talked about, how much time does it take for you to recognize that this is really the team you are looking for? What really stands out about them in the very first meeting?

Wagner: When you have one of those great founders or founding teams, that is visible very quickly. It stands out in the first meeting. It's clear that you're dealing with a special group. What comes through is the clarity of vision, and the ability to communicate it and get other people excited about it. That is a large part of what being an exceptional founder is, and that comes out in the first meeting.

Shah: Does it really matter if it's a single founder or multiple co-founders?

Wagner: It's more common that there's multiple founders. I don't think it's necessarily a coincidence. Great founders typically are trying to move things along in their own mind to validate their own thinking, and that usually requires other people. It's hard to do that in a vacuum. You do sometimes find someone working independently, but it's unusual. It's not unusual to have maybe a principal founder and then some junior co-founders. In that case, there is a lot of focus on one of the individuals more than others.

Shah: How do you go about identifying the next big market?

Wagner: It's a combination of factors. There is the proactive strategic view, which comes from working consistently and in a very comprehensive way in a defined sector—so that you are highly up to speed and perhaps even a bit of a thought leader in that area. That puts you in a better position to recognize the next big innovation in that general space.

Let me give you an example of a new market that I really liked very early on, the virtualization market. I'd worked in IT infrastructure my whole career, and a big part of that in computing even before I was in venture capital. The next generation of flexible computing models and system architectures were something that we were always trying to push the envelope on when I worked at SGI [Silicon Graphics]. The precursors to virtualization came out of fields like grid computing and other branches of high-performance computing. By being very active in those predecessor phases, it puts one in a better position to intersect with and understand the next wave.

That's one aspect that you might say is sort of proactive or strategic, but you can't ever neglect the bottoms-up aspect of it. That's where an entrepreneur will come forward with an idea that you never would have thought of. Your job is to recognize this. Not to think of it, but to recognize it. That's the key difference between the investor and the entrepreneur. And so, if you can harness those together, the proactive and reactive, that's when you're doing your best work.

Your proactive or your strategic exploration of a sector allows you to understand the current state of the art. But then you've also got to be very open-minded, curious, and hold a no-biases ability to listen to an unexpected idea. That's where you're going to really have the opportunity to see a next-generation approach. And if you can integrate that unexpected idea into the world view that you have been able to build through your proactive work, now you have the best of both worlds. You have the ideal context within which to place the unexpected idea, and you have the ability to recognize the unexpected idea and its implications. And that's what you are striving for, that combination.

Shah: So you're not educating yourself on the market potential when something comes to you, but it's already known to you. Regarding market timing, too late is probably easily recognizable, but it's sometimes hard to recognize whether you are too early or way too early.

Wagner: It's very easy to be too early. It's one of the most common mistakes.

Shah: What are some of the signs that you are way too early?

Wagner: The key sign is when you're spending all your time educating the market and the market never seems to be much readier. There is always an education phase when you're doing a market-creation type of project. But if that education is never drawing to a close and you're in constant education, then you know that the market isn't ready.

There are ways to deal with this, which is fortunate because it is so common to be early. If you have a capital-efficient business model, you can survive being early, at least some amount of being too early, because you'll recognize it. If you're not burning tons of capital, you have some flexibility. You can wait for that market to catch up. You can find a niche where maybe you can get some adoption going, even if it is in a small market segment, but you can live there while the rest of the market catches up. That's in some ways what happened with virtualization.

Some of the earliest concepts had to live in the world of high-performance computing. Then when VMware itself was bringing virtualization as we know it today to market, they had to achieve profitability first on the desktop, and then in the test-and-development market. It was only later that the large market, the production enterprise market, caught up with them, and that's only in the last several years.

Because VMware was able to become self-sustaining on the desktop and in the test-and-development market, they insulated themselves from some of the risks of being early. If you don't have too capital-intensive a business model, then you have the flexibility to do those things. If you have a company that's burning $2 million a month, you don't have that choice.

Shah: Then you just have a ticking time bomb.

Wagner: Yeah, you've painted yourself into a corner. You have no flexibility in time.

Shah: What are three things that you wished as an investor that every entrepreneur knew?

Wagner: Focus is essential. Recruiting is the main job, and listening is one of the core skills. And I don't mean listening to venture capitalists. I mean listening to the market.

Shah: What are the most common blind spots you see in the entrepreneurs?

Wagner: The most common blind spot will be some insecurity that prevents them from recruiting the best of the best. Another blind spot would be a confirmation bias, which means that they pay attention to the data points that support their existing point of view. They sweep under the rug the ones that point out a disconnect.

Shah: So you want them to be blatantly objective and honest to themselves as to what they are seeing in the market.

Wagner: Yes. That is listening. The key thing is "sophisticated listening," especially if you are defining something new. The market doesn't have a frame of reference, so how you interpret the signals you get from the market is key. That is the essence of the great product-oriented entrepreneur. If Mark Zuckerberg had gone out amongst his Harvard classmates and asked, "What would you like in a social network? How about in a social utility?" No one would have known how to react to that. That would have been ridiculous.

Shah: Yes, because the focus group interviews in those market-defining cases are just useless.

Wagner: The entrepreneur needs to have a proactive vision that they are driving ahead with. In some cases, this requires certain amount of stubbornness. Coupled with it, though, is an ability to interpret feedback from users and from the market to modify that vision. It's a delicate dance. You can't be too malleable. Like you said, you can't just have focus groups and write down what people said and then do that. Listening here means the very thoughtful distillation of what matters from particularly credible sources of feedback, and then fusing that with the proactive, internally sourced vision. The best ones do that right. It's hard.

Shah: What are some of the signs that tell you that the company is off track?

Wagner: Dissidence within the team. This might not be overt arguments, but it might be that you can tell the team is not being completely open with each other, that there is some fear of bringing bad news. Other warning signs are sliding sale cycles and deals that don't close in a predictable fashion. And then a third warning sign is when there is never any new data. Month after month there isn't any sign of increasing understanding of market requirements or any uncovering of gaps in the product. The gaps are there, you just know about them or you don't. So if you don't see new data and new information, either about product market fit or about market readiness, then it just means that the problems are still waiting to be discovered.

Shah: How do you determine if the off-track start-up is beyond recovery and there is no Plan B?

Wagner: I think part of that has to do with the team. If you feel like you have a good foundation in the team, then many things can be fixed. But if you have a flawed team, a flawed culture, then it's hard to fix anything. That would be one judgment you'd have to make.

I think another judgment has to do with the broad market you're operating in—is there a rising tide? Is it generally becoming more important? Are customers generally becoming more interested in the space? Is there accelerating adoption of similar products or related solutions? If that's happening, then that means you have a more forgiving environment. You can make some adjustments and you'll benefit from those tailwinds.

So, if you're in a situation like that and you have the right team, then it's probably a good idea to try and make the corrections. But if you have the reverse, if you have a flawed team, if you have a weak foundation and things are getting harder, not easier, in the general marketplace, then it might be wise to find some way to dock the boat, as we say.

Shah: What are some of the key considerations in deciding between whether to keep funding or sell?

Wagner: I think you're trying to make the determination about whether you're in an expanding universe or a contracting universe. If you feel like the fundamental market and strategic trends are such that things are coming your way, you're being presented with more opportunities among customers and more partnering opportunities among the major players, and your strategic options as a company are multiplying—then that is an expanding-universe scenario. Then it's probably good to continue to build the company.

The inverse would be if you felt like the walls were closing in. You had fewer good options every day. Your flexibility was being reduced, perhaps because of competition, perhaps because of market maturation, perhaps because of a growing realization that you have a capped market. You just don't have the scale of opportunity that you thought you did. The analogy I sometimes use is a "box canyon." If you feel like you're walking along and those walls are getting closer on the left and the right, it might be time to sell—before it's totally obvious to the entire planet that you're stuck. Once it's obvious to everyone, you don't have a lot of good options!

Index

I

Lightning Source UK Ltd.
Milton Keynes UK
UKHW040043071218
333583UK00001B/166/P